INDIAN NUCLEAR STRATEGY
Confronting the Potential Threat from both China and Pakistan

D1783644

Sanjay Badri-Maharaj

Routledge
Taylor & Francis Group

LONDON AND NEW YORK

KNOWLEDGE WORLD

KW Publishers Pvt Ltd
New Delhi

First published 2020
by Routledge
4 Park Square, Milton Park, Abingdon, Oxon OX14 4RN

and by Routledge
605 Third Avenue, New York, NY 10017

First issued in paperback 2023

Routledge is an imprint of the Taylor & Francis Group, an informa business

Publisher's Note
The publisher has gone to great lengths to ensure the quality of this reprint but points out that some imperfections in the original copies may be apparent.

British Library Cataloguing-in-Publication Data
A catalogue record for this book is available from the British Library

Library of Congress Cataloging-in-Publication Data
A catalog record for this book has been requested

ISBN 13: 978-1-03-265439-3 (pbk)
ISBN 13: 978-0-367-43684-1 (hbk)
ISBN 13: 978-1-003-00505-6 (ebk)

DOI: 10.4324/9781003005056

Typeset in Adobe Caslon pro, Rhomus
by KW Publishers

KNOWLEDGE WORLD

INDIAN NUCLEAR STRATEGY
Confronting the Potential Threat from both China and Pakistan

This book examines India's nuclear strategy as it confronts the potential threat from both China and Pakistan. The potential threats - traditional as well as non-traditional CBRN threats - will be examined as will India's approach to dealing with them. India's nuclear arsenal, its dual purpose civil-military space program and its nascent BMD capability will be explored with a view to informing the reader as to the steps taken by India to confront its nuclear challenges.

In addition, the Indian nuclear doctrine and the strategy evolved therefrom is examined to demonstrate the flexibility inherent in the Indian nuclear doctrine while also highlighting certain areas that require attention.

By adopting an excessively secretive approach, India has failed to articulate its approach to nuclear strategy. It is perhaps time that India reconsiders this approach and facilitates a more public and forthright discussion of its nuclear strategy in light of evolving nuclear threats while simultaneously continuing to develop its capabilities so as to deter any potential conflict.

Dr. Sanjay Badri-Maharaj is an independent defence analyst and attorney-at-law based in Trinidad and Tobago. He has served as a consultant to the Trinidad and Tobago Ministry of National Security and its Ministry of the Attorney-General. He also served as an instructor to Coast Guard Officer Cadets. He was a visiting international fellow at the IDSA in 2016.

Contents

Introduction   vii

1.   Potential Threat: The Chinese and Pakistani Nuclear Arsenals   1

2.   India's Nuclear Arsenal—Current and Future Deterrent   31

3.   Tactical Nuclear Weapons: Options for India?   99

4.   Ballistic Missile Defences for India: An Essential Asset   155

5.   India's Military Space Efforts:
   An Important Yet Underappreciated Asset   197

6.   Responding to a Nontraditional CBRN Attack   209

7.   The Indian Doctrine: Credibility and Capability = Strategy   241

8   The Path Ahead: Shaping India's Nuclear Strategy
   in the Years to Come   279

Bibliography   287

Index   303

Introduction

——— ❖ ———

It has been two decades since India declared itself a nuclear weapons state. Facing the possibility of threats from both Pakistan and China, India's nuclear strategy has received less than adequate analysis with speculation and some alarmist reporting holding sway. In part, this has been caused by the opacity of India's officialdom on the issue of India's nuclear strategy. The deafening silence emanating from Indian officials has left an information vacuum that has made a discourse on India's nuclear strategy difficult. Since the 1998 nuclear tests and the publication of India's Nuclear Doctrine, India has continued to face endemic security challenges from both China and Pakistan. The latter, through the apparent induction of tactical nuclear weapons (TNWs) into the equation and a rapid expansion of its fissile material production capacity, has introduced an additional complication into the Indian security calculations while China has become increasingly assertive and intransigent in its conduct towards its neighbours, India included. In this sense, India's options and response to these challenges have been inadequately discussed.

India's nuclear strategy, facing a changing landscape, has shown some degree of flexibility though this has not been adequately articulated. Furthermore, discussion of India's nuclear strategy, such that it is, has been somewhat one-dimensional with an excessive and, it is argued, unnecessary debate over the stated Indian policy of no-first-use (NFU).

Completely absent from the discourse is preparing the Indian armed forces to face the dual nuclear challenge from two very different adversaries, while the size, composition and command and control structures for the Indian nuclear arsenal remain overly ambiguous. In the light of an evolving challenge, India's nuclear strategy, predicated on a credible minimum deterrence threshold, needs to be looked at in light of the prospect of lowered nuclear thresholds in the case of Pakistan as well as potential coercive nuclear posturing from China. In neither case can a nuclear strategy be divorced from conventional military strategy as any operation—offensive or defensive—will now have to be carried out with the potential of a nuclear escalation in mind.

This book attempts to contextualise and evaluate India's nuclear strategy as it deals with the dual challenge of its nuclear-armed neighbours. To this end, it has the following research objectives:

- To assess the nature of the current threat and future challenges that India's nuclear strategy must contend with.
- Re-examine India's nuclear doctrine in light of the said challenges and to suggest modifications to the doctrine where necessary.
- To evaluate India's current deterrent posture as it exists at present (within the scope of open source information) and its current evolutionary path. The speculated shape, size and composition of India's current deterrent will be examined and suggestions made for the modifications that may need to be considered in the future.
- Identify shortcomings, limitations—self-imposed as well as compelled—in India's deterrent posture and examine what has been done to mitigate against such shortcomings and suggest additional measures that may need to be considered. The impact and potential efficacy of ballistic missile defences, as well as the practicality of enhanced preparedness against decapitating or paralysing electromagnetic pulse (EMP) strikes, will be considered.
- Assess how India's nuclear doctrine integrates into its overall military (conventional) strategy and doctrines, evaluate what changes have been made to date and to determine whether further modifications to the latter need to be made in light of the lowered nuclear threshold versus Pakistan and the heightened assertiveness of China.
- Considering the impact and threat of an unconventional nuclear threat such as a dirty bomb or a low-yield nuclear detonation and whether a separate doctrine needs to be considered in the event of such an occurrence. The credibility of the existing doctrine and the response stipulated therein will be assessed and where necessary, modifications suggested.
- Examine India's existing nuclear strategy with a view to fleshing out the current approach and inmaking recommendations to improve India's strategy as it faces the dual challenge of dealing with both Pakistan and China.

To achieve these objectives, the book is organised into chapters, a conscious effort being made not to rehash the historical details of India's nuclear journey. The first chapter will address China's growing nuclear arsenal, its disruptive ballistic missile threat and its revised nuclear strategy as it pertains to any possible confrontation with India. This chapter will also examine Pakistan with its increasing fissile material production, the introduction of TNWs and the attendant lowering of nuclear thresholds.

Chapter 2 details India's nuclear deterrent, inclusive of the probable present force levels, future evolutions and requisite modifications within self-imposed constraints. Chapter 3 deals with the synergy of conventional and nuclear strategy, discussing possible options for conventional operations under a nuclear backdrop without crossing nuclear redlines, preparedness to minimise the effect of Pakistani TNWs if redlines are crossed. It will also explore the possible Indian requirement for TNWs and the arguments for and against such weapons. An examination of the chemical, biological, radiological and nuclear preparations as well as the enhanced air defences against short-range missiles will also be undertaken.

Chapter 4 will analyse the need for ballistic missile defence systems for India and the progress made to date in developing such systems in the context of improving India's air defences. Chapter 5 will deal with the neglected area of space technology and examine whether India's efforts in this sphere are adequate.

Chapter 6 deals with the unconventional nuclear threats such as the possibility of the use of a suitcase nuclear weapon, dirty bomb terror attacks or EMP strikes. The requirement for a calibrated Indian response to such strikes will be discussed. These are principally centred on preparing for such an eventuality and also for taking such steps as are needed to ensure post-attack recovery in the event of such situations.

The seventh chapter explores the viability and credibility of India's stated nuclear doctrine in the current and projected threat environment. This chapter will examine India's nuclear doctrine as married to its nuclear capability to give a glimpse into India's emerging nuclear strategy. It will seek to make recommendations for future developments and the need for additional enhancements with respect to the capability and organisation.

The concluding eighth chapter will seek to summarise the potential threat, the existing capabilities and the existing strategy and doctrine. It will thereafter explore and discuss some of the shortcomings observed in India's existing approach to nuclear strategy. Furthermore, recommendations will be made with respect to the reorientation of certain aspects of India's capabilities so as to achieve its security objectives against its adversaries.

Nuclear issues always attract headlines and this inevitably produces a flurry of alarmist conclusions extrapolated from limited information. This approach does no justice to the serious nature of the topic. Moreover, the unfortunate agenda-driven writings of some commentators lend themselves to producing little that is useful by way of information and a lot that this misleading. It is hoped that this book is a step towards addressing some of the more neglected aspects of India's nuclear strategy as well as examining some of the assumptions that are made.

It is to be noted that Indian analysis of nuclear issues has often embellished the Chinese and Pakistani capability while somewhat downplaying India's own prowess. This has the unfortunate result of skewing analysis into a somewhat alarmist or excessively negative framework. What this book seeks to do is examine the capability that India has as far as sources and documents allow. This would show that India's capabilities, while not yet matching China's are considerably greater than usually stated in open source documents. Even without recourse to classified or confidential documents, a selective approach to data interpretation results in a somewhat erroneous picture emerging as whole categories of systems is often excluded from calculations.

Its fissile material stockpile, for example, is potentially much larger should any or all of India's unsafeguarded nuclear reactors be included in the totals. Similarly, while there has been an obsessive degree of secrecy in respect of the production of the Agni missiles and the quantities in service, it is submitted that the few figures that have been discussed in the public domain may be based on incorrect assumptions and that the deployed strength of India's nuclear forces may be somewhat larger numerically than is normally assumed.

This is not to say, however, that India's nuclear forces are altogether adequate or entirely satisfactory in respect of quality and quantity. As will be shown, India's nuclear arsenal is dynamic and evolving with and has followed an incremental approach towards weapons development, especially in respect of its ballistic missile arsenal. Less clear is India's approach to the development of nuclear weapons, where concerns over the success of the country's thermonuclear capability have led to some doubts as to the efficacy of the Indian arsenal in respect of both the yields of the deployed weapon and in respect of their reliability. While both these issues, as will be seen, are somewhat overstated, there are legitimate questions that require cogent answers that have not been forthcoming from the official sources.

It should be noted, however, that nuclear weapons are not like conventional weapons where requirements to match force levels of opponents are often overriding factors in the enhancement of existing forces. India's nuclear arsenal need not match the numbers or the types of its potential rivals. Rather, India has to define what its targeting requirements are, examine the survivability of its weapons following a possible first-strike, and then examine the numbers and types of weapons that would need to survive a first-strike to inflict the required levels of damage on the attacking power with a view to such damage being of an unacceptable level so as to deter a first-strike.

India's nuclear strategy has not been adequately spelt out, although its nuclear doctrine, which would necessarily inform nuclear strategy, has been spelled out quite clearly. However, there is still some ambiguity in its wording which can at times lead to confusing interpretations as to the intent of the original text. The nuclear strategy that India adopts will inevitably be constrained by the doctrine thus laid down but will be given effect by a combination of a suitable arsenal combined with a clear approach to how nuclear weapons are to be employed in the event of hostilities and in the aftermath of a nuclear first-strike.

Nuclear Strategy: What is It and How Did It Evolve?
The renowned lecturer on strategy, Professor Lawrence Freedman, once defined nuclear strategy as:[1]

---

1. Lawrence Freedman, "Nuclear Strategy," *Britannica*. https://www.britannica.com/topic/nuclear-strategy, accessed on February 7, 2018.

…the formation of tenets and strategies for producing and using nuclear weapons.

Among the nuclear powers, the evolution of nuclear strategy has been most pronounced and articulated by the three largest nuclear powers—the United States, Russia and China. With respect to the United States, the evolution of nuclear strategic thought went through several phases:

Massive Retaliation

In the aftermath of the Korean War, when a conventional stalemate was the outcome of a three-year conflict, the administration of US President Eisenhower began to reconsider the American approach to nuclear weapons. Reflecting on the conventional war fought in Korea, Eisenhower was worried about the economic burden of conventional rearmament to enable a decisive conventional superiority against an enemy. To this end, with nuclear weapons becoming increasingly potent and available in larger numbers, the Eisenhower administration assigned a greater priority to nuclear weapons.

The 'massive retaliation' strategy that emerged therefrom was outlined in a speech made by US Secretary of State John Foster Dulles, in January 1954. In this speech, he declared that in the future a US response to aggression would be "at places and with means of our own choosing." This doctrine was interpreted as being a threat to retaliate with nuclear weapons in response to Soviet or Chinese conventional aggression anywhere in the world.

Needless to say, this policy came under severe criticism. The Strategic Air Command received a disproportionate budgetary allocation at the expense of the army and the navy. The corollary to this was that, as Soviet nuclear strength grew, the credibility of the massive retaliation doctrine would be in serious doubt. Furthermore, the neglect of conventional forces could have meant that a military challenge mounted by either the Soviet Union or China or acting in concert, especially around their periphery, could place the United States in an untenable military situation where a nuclear response to a conventional attack would be virtually suicidal.

First and Second Strikes

The Soviet Union tested the world's first intercontinental ballistic missile

(ICBM)—the SS-6—followed shortly thereafter by the launch of the world's first artificial satellite-Sputnik-1. The development of such missile capability offered the spectre of the Strategic Air Command's force of bombers being extremely vulnerable on the ground. Freedman notes that:[2]

> A devastating surprise attack was considered possible because, with improved guidance systems, nuclear weapons were becoming more precise. Therefore, it was not inevitable that they would be used solely in countervalue strikes against easily targeted political and economic centres. Instead, it was just as likely that they would be used in counterforce strikes against military targets. A successful counterforce attack that rendered retaliation impossible—known as a 'first strike'—would be strategically decisive. If, however, the attacked nation possessed sufficient forces to survive an attempted first strike with retaliatory weapons intact, then it would have what became known as a 'second-strike' capability.

Thomas Schelling, a prominent strategist, whose theories still hold validity, was wary of the first-strike concept and warned that if both sides sought a first-strike capability, in a period of tension, with uncertainty and distrust prevailing, misunderstandings could result in a first-strike being launched in the apprehension that an enemy first-strike was imminent. However, he further suggested that if there was confidence in their second-strike capabilities, then there would be considerable stability. Indirectly, this second-strike concept led to the prospect of viable arms control, whereby the two superpowers were able to appreciate that appropriate and adequate force levels would suffice to deter each other rather than an unending arms race. Yet, underpinning nuclear deterrence was a very basic concept predicated on the fact that nuclear weapons were unlike any other weapons hitherto deployed and which had destructive capabilities far in excess of any conventional weapon.

Mutual Assured Destruction

The second-strike concept ultimately morphed into the doctrine of mutually assured destruction (MAD). As ICBMs were placed in hardened silos and submarine-launched ballistic missiles came into their own, both

2. Ibid.

superpowers and even smaller nuclear states such as China, France and the United Kingdom, were able to field survivable nuclear arsenals, ensuring that at least a proportion of their nuclear forces would survive a first-strike and be able, through a second-strike, to inflict unacceptable levels of destruction on an adversary. While there have been attempts to circumvent or otherwise develop alternatives to this concept of MAD, the ability to effectively destroy an adversary after absorbing a first-strike, remains at the cornerstone of nuclear strategy.

In a sense, the destructive power of nuclear weapons also enabled an evolution of this strategy into one which permitted the deliberate targeting of civilian targets that would deter an adversary from an attempt at a first-strike. So-called countervalue targeting was the lynchpin of the MAD doctrine with not even the largest nuclear powers being willing to risk cities being destroyed by weapons that survived an attempted first-strike. It is perhaps this fear of a retaliatory strike on cities that allowed the uneasy peace between the superpowers of the Cold War era to exist.

Alternatives to Mutual Assured Destruction

There was evidence that the nuclear strategy of the Soviet Union envisaged using nuclear weapons to obtain a decisive military advantage in a conflict or in the alternative to reduce the damage that an enemy might do to Soviet territory. The development of an increasingly sophisticated Soviet ICBM force, with multiple warheads, raised the prospect of US nuclear forces being decimated and with the remaining US forces lacking a similar degree of accuracy, the United States being forced to resort to attacking Soviet cities, prompting surviving Soviet forces to do the same to American cities. As unrealistic as this scenario was, it did give pause for thought and began a shift away from the MAD strategy and its massive attack concept.

In 1974, United States Secretary of Defense James Schlesinger broke with the previously endorsed nuclear strategy and announced that future US nuclear targeting would be geared to selective strikes. This resulted in the development of a range of targeting options to convince the Soviet Union that it could not hope to gain a nuclear advantage in the event of hostilities. This became the central tenant of the 'countervailing' strategy first espoused in 1980.

Flexible Response

In the 1950s and 1960s, the North Atlantic Treaty Organization (NATO) was faced with the prospect of having to confront numerically superior Soviet conventional forces. One approach was to consider the use of nuclear weapons at a relatively early stage in the event of a conventional attack. This appealed to the Western European members of NATO as it freed them from the requirement of maintaining large conventional military forces while feeling secure in the belief that the Soviet Union had no interest in invading Western Europe that would be worth even the modicum of a risk of a nuclear war.

This viewpoint found less favour with the United States, however. Fearing the prospect of a nuclear escalation, the doctrine of 'flexible response' was developed as a compromise under which Europeans recognised the American desire for an extended conventional stage of warfare, thus preventing the first shots of a NATO-Warsaw Pact conflict automatically escalating into a nuclear conflagration. At the same time, the United States accepted the need for a clear link between a land war in Europe and the possibility of having to use its own strategic nuclear arsenal.

Limited Nuclear War

The concept of a Limited Nuclear War is one which gained currency in the 1950s and appeared sporadically as a potentially attractive doctrine up until the end of the Cold War. While the 'flexible response' doctrine did not compel NATO into adopting a particular course of action, the prospect of NATO being the first to employ nuclear weapons was always a possibility. Initially, as part of an escalatory use of nuclear arms, these would be short-range TNWs. Beginning with the Honest John short-range ballistic missile and including such patently absurd weapons as the Davy Crockett jeep-mounted tactical nuclear recoilless weapon, it was envisaged that the use of TNWs would have a 'force-multiplier' effect, boosting conventionally inferior NATO forces.

However, once Warsaw Pact forces obtained comparable capabilities with such weapons as the SS-1 short-range missile which could carry nuclear warheads and weapons of the Free Rocket Over Ground family which were also nuclear capable, any putative Western advantage was effectively neutralised. In practical terms, a defending force would either be compelled to use nuclear weapons almost immediately or face the prospect of using them over their own territory. Furthermore, there was little by way of escalation control. Should TNWs cause sufficient losses to an attacking force, it was always possible that the attacking force could escalate to the use of strategic weapons or at least theatre-level nuclear weapons in a very short period of time. Therefore, while theoretically attractive, the concept of a limited nuclear war would appear to be a contradiction in terms.

After the Cold War

In the post-Cold War period, the United States and Russia signed a series of agreements which led to a significant reduction in their nuclear arsenals. US strategic nuclear forces consist of some 500 Minuteman III ICBMs, 14 Trident submarines equipped with 24 ballistic missiles and about 200 bombers. The Russian force had more than 300 ICBMs, 11 ballistic missile submarines with some 800 nuclear warheads, and fewer than 80 aircraft bombers in its strategic nuclear arsenal. In both instances, these totals represent a massive reduction in the deployed nuclear forces when compared to the Cold War era.

While some countries, especially those less likely to get involved in major military conflicts demonstrated a readiness to renounce their nuclear capabilities, with South Africa destroying its small arsenal—reportedly some six fission free-fall bombs—that had been produced during the apartheid era. Ukraine, Belarus and Kazakhstan also gave up the nuclear weapons left to them, following the disintegration of the Soviet Union. In Latin America, Argentina and Brazil which had toyed with the idea of nuclear weapons in the 1970s and 1980s, moved away from that position to the extent that the region is free from such weapons.

In contrast, however, North Korea has conducted a series of nuclear tests, most recently of a large thermonuclear device, which when combined with its already impressive ballistic missile capability has caused much concern in the Far East. The United States having failed to contain the North Korean program through sanctions, incentives or the threat of force, now faces the prospect of a nuclear-armed North Korea posing a threat to its interest and allies in the region and is undeterred by either the conventional military or nuclear asymmetry that currently exists. The

North Korean nuclear conundrum reflects the limits of nuclear strategies and doctrines that evolved during the Cold War and will inevitably cause a rethinking of the American nuclear strategy in respect of the so-called rogue states armed with weapons of mass destruction. Previous experience gained in Iraq and, to a lesser extent, Syria suggests that strategies that dealt with chemical weapons are not applicable to nuclear weapons, especially if a state has deployed such weapons and has the means to deliver such weapons against targets important to a major power.

Israel, long suspected of being a nuclear power, finds itself embroiled in a seemingly unending confrontation with hostile neighbours in a region which has seen the toppling of a moderate dictatorship in Egypt and the rise of a much more Islamist-oriented government in Turkey. The latter two countries were previously favourably disposed towards Israel but may now be far more inclined to assume anti-Israeli positions. Israel also potentially faces the threat from an Iranian nuclear program that is clouded in ambiguity with a multinational deal to cap the aforesaid program being thrown into doubt in large part due to the hostile attitude of the Trump administration towards Iran. Yet, with turmoil in Syria, the decline of Iraq as a military power and a tenuous peace being maintained with Egypt and Turkey, Israel may be at less of an existential threat than at almost any time during its history as no single regional power or combination of regional powers currently has the means to pose such an existential threat.

The India–Pakistan–China nuclear triangle is one which has perhaps produced some of the most alarmist literature, almost all of which tries to portray the India–Pakistan conflict as the one most likely to start a nuclear war. While it would undoubtedly be foolish not to accept that the territorial dispute, stoked by aggressive and unchecked Pakistani support to terrorist groups operating against India, has the potential to escalate, India has been very circumspect about the use of force and the threat of use of force. Even before the nuclear threshold was formally crossed, and when India's forces were at least theoretically possessed of a greater margin of superiority over Pakistan, neither Pakistan's support to Khalistani terrorists in the 1980s nor its support to Kashmiri terrorists in the early to mid-1990s provoked India towards a military response. Even the 1999 Kargil War only resulted from a flagrant act of territorial aggression against India which had the potential to disrupt Indian supply lines, provoking a carefully calculated Indian response. The threat of war, much less a nuclear war, is therefore somewhat exaggerated at times.

Nuclear strategy is something that has to be constantly examined and revised as threats, capabilities and contingencies arise. One may sense that India has chosen to eschew the nuances of the flexible response and has rejected the notion of a limited nuclear war in its context in favour of a combination of a NFU policy along with massive retaliation. This, it is submitted, is decidedly a logical approach to take. The problem, however, has arisen with the introduction of TNWs into the Pakistani arsenal and the threat of their use in the event of an Indian military response. This has raised concerns as to the credibility of the massive retaliation concept, though some have argued that there is a sufficient doctrinal flexibility to cater for a calibrated response to such a threat.

As this book explores India's capabilities, its doctrine and the potential threats faced by India in devising its nuclear strategy, it is worth remembering that India has deliberately chosen to avoid the pitfalls of a nuclear arms race with either of its nuclear-armed neighbours. However, by adopting an excessively secretive approach to nuclear strategy, India has failed to articulate its approach to nuclear weapons or its response to new threats beyond a very skeletal publicly released nuclear doctrine. It is perhaps time that India reconsiders this approach and facilitates a more public and forthright discussion of its nuclear strategy in light of the evolving nuclear threats while simultaneously continuing to develop its capabilities so as to deter any potential conflict.

1

Potential Threat: The Chinese and Pakistani Nuclear Arsenals

When examining the potential threats posed to India by the Chinese and Pakistani nuclear arsenals, it is imperative to recognise that a potential threat needs to be differentiated from an imminent threat. While it may not be in vogue to admit the inherent sensibility of possible adversaries, despite a somewhat confrontational and difficult political and military history between India and its nuclear-armed neighbours, neither China nor Pakistan, despite the occasional bouts of bluster, sabre-rattling, excessive rhetoric and ludicrous threats that may emanate from time to time—formerly largely from Pakistan's political and military establishment but increasingly and more obnoxiously from China's state-run media—a rhetorical Rubicon has scrupulously been avoided being crossed though there have been occasions when rantings have come perilously close. In examining the potential threats, care should be taken to remember that nuclear weapons are unlike their conventional counterparts and do not require parity in numbers.

The nuclear strategy of China expounded at length in a seminal publication based on translations of Chinese official texts and statements on the subject by the Union of Concerned Scientists—and which is extensively cited later in this chapter—states that:[1]

> According to the PLA text, China's nuclear arsenal is not intended to win a war, eliminate an enemy's capacity to make war, destroy an enemy economy, decapitate an enemy government, or enact vengeance on an

---

1. Gregory Kulacki. "The Chinese Military Updates China's Nuclear Strategy," *Union of Concerned Scientists*, March 2015.

enemy population or its leaders. As a result, China does not need weapons designed to fulfill those missions. Instead, the size and capabilities of China's nuclear force are calibrated to assure Chinese decision makers have enough nuclear weapons to survive a first strike, engage in limited retaliation, and preserve future deterrence.

In the case of Pakistan, however, its nuclear strategy and doctrines remain vaguer that that of its bosom ally, with contradictory messages being voiced by both political and military leaders which at times make no sense. While the details will be discussed later in this chapter, Pakistan's nuclear strategy and doctrine would appear to serve a clearer political, much more than a practical military purpose. The political classes use the Pakistani nuclear deterrent as a rhetorical and political weapon to reassure a population in an otherwise failing state that the fear, greatly exaggerated, if not completely fallacious, of an Indian desire to extinguish the country's existence is kept at bay by Pakistan's nuclear weapons. For the Pakistani military, ever anxious to preserve its own position of dominance in a weak state, nuclear weapons offer both a practical demonstration of the ability to strategically match India while its custodianship of such weapons dramatically strengthens its internal position within Pakistan's domestic political hierarchy.

Given the current geopolitical balance in the Indian sub-continent, India's nuclear deterrent must be aimed at deterring potential threats from its two nuclear-armed neighbours. This does not mean that either China or Pakistan is about to launch a nuclear attack on India. However, the potential for such an attack presents an ominous challenge to India's security. Moreover, the ostensibly close collaboration between China, Pakistan and North Korea poses the additional challenge of an exchange of knowledge and expertise with respect to missiles and warhead design which offers the nightmarish possibility of Pakistan obtaining more advanced Chinese nuclear weapons designs as well as assistance in developing its missiles to higher degrees of sophistication.

However, care must be taken to not exaggerate the potential capabilities of either China or Pakistan. While the former is undoubtedly a most formidable nuclear power, its arsenal is as yet relatively modest and, as noted in the chapter relating to India's capabilities, within India's potential to match numerically, should India choose to accelerate the production of fissile material and delivery system. Pakistan's nuclear arsenal, on the other hand, has been the subject of much speculation and some alarmist discourse on its purported size and rapidity of growth based on a generous evaluation of the efficacy of their production facilities.

China's Nuclear Arsenal and Doctrine

It is estimated that China has approximately 260 nuclear warheads in its stockpile for delivery by approximately 160 land-based ballistic missiles as well as aircraft and has pushed towards deploying a ballistic submarine fleet.[2] The Chinese arsenal is expanding at a rate of at least ten nuclear warheads per year and this may increase exponentially. At present, each missile in the Chinese arsenal is equipped to carry a single warhead, with the notable exception of a small number of silo-based missiles that have been equipped to carry multiple warheads. As the number of missiles capable of taking multiple warheads increases, China's warhead stockpile would inevitably grow. Of particular interest is the fact that as Western analysts note, like India, China's nuclear warheads are not mated with missiles under normal circumstances and are instead kept separate in central storage facilities.

As only one of the five original nuclear weapon states that are quantitatively increasing the size of its nuclear arsenal, China's capabilities are also increasing as older missiles are replaced with more capable successors. It is pertinent to note that while China has undoubtedly allocated a proportion of its missile force for possible use against India and possibly even Russia, the country is increasing assigning a growing portion of its warheads to intercontinental range ballistic missiles with the likely potential target being the United States. This could be indicative of China's desire to possess an effective deterrent against the possible American hostility, but could also be seen as an indication of intent—China seeing itself as being comparable to the United States in the economic and military power. At present, the Chinese have only a limited number of warheads capable of reaching the United States. However, the US intelligence community predicts that by the mid-2020s China could more than double its number of warheads on missiles that are capable of threatening the United States to well over 100. At present, out of China's approximately existing

2.   Hans M. Kristensen and Robert S. Norris, "Chinese nuclear forces," *Bulletin of the Atomic Scientists* vol. 72, no. 4, 2016, pp. 205–211 at 205.

inventory of some 60 long-range missiles that can reach the United States, only 45 can strike the continental United States with the others being able to hit Hawaii.[3]

Table 1.1

Type North Atlantic Treaty Organization (NATO) designation	Number of launchers	Year deployed	Range (km)	Warhead × yield (kt)	Number of warheads
Land-based ballistic missiles DF-4 CSS-3	~10	1980	5500+	1 × 3300	~10
DF-5A CSS-4 Mod 2	~10	1981	13,000+	1 × 4000–5000	~10
DF-5B CSS-4 Mod 3	~10	2015	~12,000	3 × 200–300	~30
DF-15 CSS-6	?	1990	600	1 × ?	?a
DF-21 CSS-5 Mods 1, 2, 6	~80	1991, 2000, 2016	2150	1 × 200–300	~80[b]
DF-26 ?	?	(2017)	4000+	1 × 200–300	?
DF-31 CSS-10 Mod 1	~8	2006	7000+	1 × 200–300	~8
DF-31A CSS-10 Mod 2	~25	2007	11,000+	1 × 200–300	~25
DF-41 CSS-X-20	n.a.	?	?	n.a.	n.a.
Subtotal:	~143				~163[c]
Submarine-launched ballistic missiles[d] JL-1 CSS-NX-3	n.a.	1986	1000+	1 × 200–300	n.a.
JL-2 CSS-X-14	(48)	(2015)	7000+	1 × 200–300	(48)
Subtotal:	(48)				(48)
Aircraft H-6[e] B-6	~20	1965	3100+	1 × bomb	~20
Fighters[f] ?	?	?	n.a	1 × bomb	?
Cruise Missiles[g] DH-10 CJ-10	~250	2006?	1500?	1 × ?	?
DH-20? CJ-20?	?	?	?	1 × ?	?
Total					~183 (260[h]

3.   Ibid., p. 206.

a. The Central Intelligence Agency concluded in 1993 that China 'almost certainly' had developed a warhead for the DF-15, although it is unclear if the capability was fielded.
b. This table only counts nuclear versions DF-21 (CSS-5 Mod 1) and DF-21A (CSS-5 Mod 2), each of which has fewer than 50 launchers deployed. The conventional DF-21C and DF-21D are not counted.
c. The missile and warhead inventory may be larger than the number of launchers, some of which can be reused to fire additional missiles.
d. The JL-1 is no longer thought to be operational and the JL-2 may be close to becoming fully operational. Warheads for the JL-1 may have been retired by now and warheads for the JL-2 have been produced.
e. Bombers were used to conduct at least 12 of China's nuclear test explosions between 1965 and 1979. We believe that a small number of China's H-6 bombers may have a secondary nuclear mission. The aircraft range is equivalent to combat radius, which for some H-6 bombers can be extended with air refuelling.
f. A fighter-bomber was used in a nuclear test in 1972, but it is unknown whether a tactical bomb capability has been fielded.
g. US Air Force intelligence lists the ground-launched DH-10 land-attack cruise missile as 'conventional or nuclear'. US Air Force Global Strike Command also lists the air-launched cruise missile CJ-20 as nuclear-capable, but it is unclear whether that finding comes from a coordinated intelligence assessment.
h. The number in parentheses includes the 48 warheads produced for the four existing nuclear-powered ballistic missile submarines as well as about 30 additional warheads (including warheads for the DF-26, those awaiting dismantlement and a small inventory of spares), for a total stockpile of approximately 260 warheads.

Land-Based Missiles

In 2015, the Chinese Second Artillery—which controls its land-based missile force—took an important step towards the modernisation of its land-based ballistic missile force when it began equipping a proportion of the country's silo-based intercontinental ballistic missile (ICBMs) with multiple independently targetable re-entry vehicles (MIRVs). The upgradation of the silo-based missiles is part of a broader modernisation of China's land-based ballistic missile force, whereby it is replacing older, transportable, liquid-fuel missiles which are time consuming to fuel and launch, with longer-ranged, road-mobile, solid-fuel missiles which can be rapidly launched and based at new or upgraded Second Artillery garrisons. As a result of this effort, a greater portion of China's future land-based missile force will have greater survivability as well as being capable of being kept in a state of readiness. In addition, China is concurrently investing in improved communication capabilities for its nuclear forces to ensure the integrity of command and control arrangements for this larger and more dispersed mobile missile force.[4]

At present, the Second Artillery has approximately 160 nuclear-capable land-based missiles of seven types, half of which are short-range and medium-range with the number of long-range missiles increasing slowly.[5]

China continues to maintain one brigade of the DF4 (CSS-3) ICBM. This two-stage, liquid-fuelled missile was first deployed in 1980 and can deliver a 3.3-Mton warhead more than 5500 km away, a sufficient range to target India, part of Russia and Guam. The brigade has approximately 10 transportable launchers and these are in turn based in caves with a roll-out-to-launch capability. Each launcher probably has one or two reloads of additional missiles but the DF-4 will be replaced by the DF-31 in the future.

The DF-5A (CSS-4 Mod 2)—a liquid-fuelled, two-stage, silo-based ICBM—with a range of 13,000 km is China's principal ICBM and is aimed at deterring the United States and Russia. In service since the 1980s, the DF-5A is an upgraded version of the original DF-5 (CSS-4 Mod 1), which was first deployed in 1981. More recently, some of the DF-5As have been upgraded to carry MIRVs—this version is known as the DF-5B (CSS-4 Mod 3). China's ability to deploy multiple warheads has been the subject of speculation for some time but it might be suggested that it was spurred by US efforts to deploy a viable ballistic missile defence system. It is estimated that China has a total of some 20 DF-5s of both versions, of which perhaps half equipped with MIRVs.[6]

The backbone of China's ICBM force is the DF-31 (CSS-10 Mod 1) and its longer-range variant designated the DF-31A (CSS10 Mod 2). The DF-31, which first entered service in 2006, was terminated prematurely with fewer than road-mobile launchers being built. The 7000-km-range missile has taken over many of the regional targeting roles previously performed by the DF-4. Its longer-ranged variant, DF-31A (CSS-10 Mod 2), is a solid-fuelled, three-stage, road-mobile ICBM which is designed to reach targets in most of the continental United States. It has been estimated that China deploys some 25 DF-31A ICBMs in four brigades.

---

4. Ibid., pp. 206–207.
5. Ibid.
6. Ibid., pp. 207–209.

China's latest ICBM has been widely reported as being in development for more than two decades. The new, road-mobile ICBM is known as the DF-41 and, after a prolonged delay, the program has gathered pace in recent years with several flight tests being undertaken with some of them including tests of a MIRVed version.

India's immediate concern is China's potent force of regional nuclear-armed missiles. The backbone of the force is the two-stage, solid-fuel, road-mobile DF-21 (CSS-5), medium-range ballistic missile. The e DF-21 has two nuclear-armed versions: the DF-21 (CSS-5 Mod 1) and the newer DF-21A (CSS-5 Mod 2). The Mod 1 version has a range of at least 1750 km, with the newer version having a longer range of about 2150 km.

A third nuclear-armed version, known as the CSS-5 Mod 6 has been reported as having entered service. It is estimated that China has some 80 launchers for the nuclear DF-21. In addition to its nuclear-armed DF-21s, China has also deployed two conventional versions of the DF-21: the DF-21C (CSS-4 Mod 4) land-attack missile and the DF-21D (CSS-5 Mod 5) antiship missile which has been the cause of much concern.[7]

In 2015, China publicly displayed its new DF-26 intermediate-range road-mobile missile during a military parade in Beijing in September. During the said parade, no fewer than 16 DF-26 launchers were observed. With a range of 4000 km, the DF-26 poses a clear danger to India with most of the Indian landmass being within its range. With the potential of being armed with conventional as well as nuclear warheads, the DF-26 is a very flexible system available to China.[8]

Land-Based Short-Range Ballistic Missiles (SRBMs)

China's large force of SRBMs is, for the most part, fitted with conventional warheads. The notable exception is the nuclear-capable DF-15 (CSS-6) which may have been earmarked for a warhead tested on August 16, 1990. However, it is as yet unclear whether China ever fielded nuclear-armed DF-15s and while the capability exists, it is contended that most, if not all, DF-15s remain conventionally armed, augmenting

---

7. Ibid.
8   Ibid.

the country's arsenal of SRBMs. This, of course, poses the additional challenge for India as determining whether a missile is nuclear-armed or not could impact a timely response. Furthermore, the plethora of SRBMs available to China gives them the option of attempting to saturate or suppress any air activity undertaken in response to a Chinese incursion.[9]

Submarines and Sea-Based Ballistic Missiles

China currently operates a fleet of four Jin-class (Type 094) nuclear-powered ballistic missile submarines (SSBNs). All are based at the Longposan naval base near Yulin on Hainan Island. A fifth vessel is reportedly being built and it is as yet uncertain as to how many SSBNs China intends to build. However, the Jin-class is a somewhat noisy design as compared to its Western and Russian counterparts although it is a vast improvement over the one of Xia-class (Type 092) SSBN which, between 1987 and 2006, was China's sole ballistic missile submarine.[10]

The Jin SSBNs are designed to each carry 12 of the new JL-2 (CSS-NX-14) submarine-launched ballistic missile (SLBM), which has a range of over 7000 km, though it has never been tested to that range. The JL-2 is a vast improvement over the earlier JL-1 with a 1770 km range, which armed the Xia-class. It is of interest to note that despite a long history of making both advanced ballistic missiles and nuclear submarines, China took a long time to develop and deploy viable SSBNs, reflecting the inherent difficulty in building and operating such vessels and their associated SLBMs. It also shows China's commitment to adopting an evolutionary approach to weapons development—an indisputably sensible approach.

China's deployment of a force of SSBNs would appear to require a fundamental shift in its policy of nuclear warhead deployment. As has been mentioned before, China's policy has been one where warheads and delivery systems were kept separate and under strict and centralised control. For effective deterrent patrols to be mounted, it would be counterintuitive for the warheads to be kept separate, requiring the vessels to come into ports to have warheads fitted on their onboard missiles.

---

9.   Ibid., p. 208.
10.   Ibid., p. 208–209.

It is as yet unclear as to how China intends to resolve this shift in policy but it is of interest that SSBN construction has gathered pace in China, perhaps indicating a greater emphasis on this arm of the fleet. Once all five SSBNs are commissioned, China would have a total of 60 JL-2 SLBMs in service, as against some 150-160 land-based intermediate and intercontinental range ballistic missiles. With a large land mass, China might consider the enhanced survivability of SSBNs to be not significantly greater than that of mobile, land-based long-range missiles which might be easier to control effectively.

Bombers

Like all other nuclear powers, China's nuclear deterrent was at one time principally air-delivered. To this end, aircraft were used to deliver the nuclear weapons in at least 12 of China's nuclear test explosions conducted between 1965 and 1979. China continues to maintain a force of nearly 150 H-6 bombers, based on the old Tu-16 'Badger' from the erstwhile Soviet Union. In its new H-6K configuration, first seen in 2007, the aircraft can carry between six and eight land attack CJ-10K cruise missiles, each with a range of 1500 km. The older versions of the aircraft still continue to be in service with upgraded electronic warfare suites and some versions have the ability to carry antiship and land-attack cruise missiles as well. This makes the H-6 bomber force a potent addition to the Chinese nuclear forces.[11]

Nonetheless, the H-6 force is ageing—despite the new H-6K version—and while it provides a potent nuclear deterrent force for possible use against India through its land-attack cruise missiles, the vulnerability of the bombers to interception is relatively high. What this force of strategic bombers does, however, is give Chinese air power unmatched power-projection capability outside of the United States and Russia. This is combined with the undoubtedly formidable power of its long-range nuclear-armed, air-launched cruise missiles.

Cruise Missiles

China's extensive variety of cruise missiles also provides for a potential source of air, land and sea-launched nuclear weapons. While China's

11. Ibid., p. 209–210.

cruise missile capability will invariably be principally for the delivery of conventional warheads, China's extensive nuclear tests almost certainly involved research into cruise missile warheads and the delivery of such payloads by China's existing cruise missile inventory is not merely possible, but probable.

One of the probable nuclear-capable Chinese cruise missiles is the CJ-10 land-attack cruise missile, with a range of some 1500 km. Like the US Tomahawk and the Russian Kh-55, this missile is likely to be a dual-capable weapon—with either nuclear or conventional warheads being possible. The land-based version of the CK-10 is launched from a four-axle triple box launcher which is highly mobile. While the number of launchers and missiles deployed is somewhat uncertain, by 2011, it was estimated that at least 40 launchers and 200 missiles had been deployed. These figures would have undoubtedly increased. Furthermore, the CJ-20K, the air-delivered version of this missile, has been adapted for carriage by China's force of H-6 bombers, most notably, but not exclusively, the H-6K variant. A submarine-launched version, carried by the Type 093G class of nuclear-powered attack submarines (SSNs), is also likely to be in service as is a ship-launched version, embarked aboard the Type 055 class of destroyers. This widespread deployment suggests that the principal payload of the CJ-10 and its variants will be a conventional warhead.[12]

Enhanced Survivability Efforts

The debate over the size of China's nuclear arsenal must perforce cater to the extensive network of underground tunnels and facilities which have been created since the 1950s. While it is certain that not all of these are dedicated to the nuclear forces, they are undoubtedly geared towards protecting key military assets and concealing those assets from hostile reconnaissance efforts.

Some sources suggest that the total length of China's network of underground tunnels could stretch for over 5000 km, making the concealment and protection of a significantly larger force of mobile missiles and nuclear warheads possible, as noted by experts such as Philip Karber.[13]

---

12. Ibid., p. 210–211.
13. Philip A. Karber, "Strategic Implications of China's Underground Great Wall," *Georgetown University Asian Arms Control Project*, September 11, 2011

China's ability to conceal and protect its nuclear arsenal and perhaps disguise its extent presents a challenge to Indian planning only so far as it relates to the ability of China to facilitate a follow-up to an Indian retaliatory strike.

Chinese Nuclear Doctrine

China's nuclear forces are comparable in size and capability to those of Britain and France, although much more flexible. China may be operating under its own concept of minimal deterrence as might be indicated from a report by the Union of Concerned Scientists issued in 2015. This report analysed the 2013 edition of China's *The Science of Military Strategy* regarding the country's guidance on the limited role of nuclear weapons in its military strategy and stated that:[14]

Their sole purpose is to deter other nuclear-armed states from using or threatening to use nuclear weapons against China. In the words of the authors [of *The Science of Military Strategy*]:

As it has been for a long time, the objective of China's development and utilization of nuclear weapons is concentrated on preventing enemy nations from using or threatening to use nuclear weapons against us.

The report by the Union of Concerned Scientists goes to some lengths to outline the core principles of China's nuclear doctrine which might be summarised as:[15]

- China will not use nuclear weapons to attack or threaten non-nuclear states;
- China will not use nuclear weapons to respond to conventional attacks and
- China will use nuclear weapons only after it has confirmed an incoming nuclear attack.

---

14. Kulacki, n. 1.
15. M. Taylor Fravel and Evan S. Medeiros, "China's Search for Assured Retaliation: The Evolution of Chinese Nuclear Strategy and Force Structure," *International Security* vol. 35, no. 2, 2010, p. 79.

Three interesting aspects of Chinese nuclear deterrence policy are noted by the Union of Concerned Scientists, citing *The Science of Military Strategy*:[16]

- **The directed nature of the target of deterrence.** From the first day China possessed nuclear weapons, it openly declared and committed not to use nuclear weapons, or threaten to use nuclear weapons, against non-nuclear weapons states or regions. This restricted the use of our country's nuclear weapons, and the target of nuclear deterrence, to nuclear-armed states. China's nuclear deterrent is only directed at nuclear weapons states; it is only in effect against nuclear-armed states.

- **The limited objective of deterrence.** China's nuclear deterrent will not be used to deter non-nuclear hostile military activity and its effect in other non-nuclear military also is not evident. Strictly limiting the scope of the effect of nuclear deterrence to the hostile nuclear activities of nuclear-armed states makes the objective and the scope of the effect of China's nuclear deterrent progressively more focused

- **The defensive nature of the method of deterrence.** China upholds a policy of no-first-use of nuclear weapons, only using nuclear weapons in self-defence after an enemy country uses nuclear weapons against us. Chinese nuclear deterrence is built on the foundation of effective retaliation, and through the actual strength as well as the possibility of creating for the enemy unbearable nuclear destruction, accomplishes the objective of preventing an enemy nuclear attack. This is defensive nuclear deterrence.

Of particular interest—and strikingly similar to India's own nuclear doctrine—are the concepts 'assured retaliation' and 'uncertainty'. By uncertainty, China means that an enemy would not be confident in its ability to "significantly damage or destroy China's nuclear arsenal." China fosters this by not disclosing the size of its nuclear arsenal, investing in mobile, survivable land and sea-based missiles as well as its extensive hardening of silo-based systems and its network of tunnels. This uncertainty thus contributes to the concept of 'assured retaliation'. On the issue of uncertainty, the Union of Concerned Scientists states:

---

16. Ibid., n. 13.

On the question of nuclear deterrence, maintaining an appropriate degree of ambiguity, allowing opponents to guess about China's nuclear capability, the scale and timing of a Chinese nuclear retaliatory attack, etc. increases the degree of difficulty for the opponent's policy, helping raise the effective deterrent function of China's limited nuclear force.

This infers that China intends to be certain that a proportion of its nuclear forces—probably a significant portion—would survive a nuclear first strike in order to launch a second-strike which would inflict a degree of unacceptable damage upon the enemy. Therefore, in three respects—no-first-use, assured retaliation and deliberate uncertainty—China's nuclear strategy is very similar to India's. Indeed, at least in theory, one might suggest that India's nuclear strategy and the manner in which it has constructed its deterrence and fostered a deliberate level of uncertainty while espousing both the concepts of no-first-use and assured destruction, is very much modelled on China's approach although China has progressed much further along the path in respect of both creating a much more powerful arsenal than India's as well as articulating a much clearer doctrine.

The Union of Concerned Scientists report also notes that China has given some considerable thought to limiting retaliation, should deterrence fail. The report notes that *The Science of Military Strategy* provides the following guidelines regarding its limited retaliatory nuclear attack:[17]

- A Chinese retaliatory nuclear attack will be limited. An unstated number of China's surviving nuclear capabilities must be held in reserve for additional acts of retaliation.
- A Chinese retaliatory nuclear attack will target enemy cities, not enemy military capabilities.
- The objective of a Chinese retaliatory nuclear attack is to cause the enemy to cease future nuclear attacks against China.

China's counter-value targeting strategy—very much along the lines of India's—simplifies the requirements for effective targeting and retaliation

---

17. Ibid—see original Chinese text at "The Science of Military Strategy 2013," *The Federation of American Scientists*, https://fas.org/nuke/guide/china/sms-2013.pdf, accessed on January 26, 2018.

which would be necessary should a counterforce strategy be adopted. This is particularly important as China may not be confident that it could neutralise an adversary's capability to retaliate, especially true against larger nuclear powers such as the United States and Russia but would be equally applicable to smaller nuclear powers with mobile missile systems, such as India. China's strategy appears to be predicated upon the belief that a counter-value approach against an adversary's cities would produce such a large loss of life so as to break the will of the enemy, with *The Science of Military Strategy* explaining the concept as follows:[18]

> There are in principle two targets for a nuclear attack, military targets and urban targets. Politically, attacking military targets is comparatively more acceptable. Militarily it enables gaining the initiative, which is beneficial to controlling the war situation. But it requires comparatively high requirements for the number, precision, and destructive function of nuclear weapons.
>
> In order to effectively destroy an opponent's nuclear forces a preemptive nuclear attack is generally required. This is the choice commonly pursued by large nuclear countries with aggressive nuclear strategies. Targeting cities can cause great damage to an enemy society and a large loss of life, which creates the effect of strong shock while having comparatively lower requirements for the scale of the force of a nuclear attack, the capabilities of nuclear weapons, the timing of a nuclear attack, etc.

However, as restrained and undoubtedly logical as this approach might be at present, it reflects China as a small nuclear power when set against the much larger arsenals of the United States and Russia. It is an open question whether this restraint will continue as China emerges as a global power and seeks to use its military and economic might to intimidate neighbours into concessions.[19]

For India, the evolution of China's nuclear forces has particular significance and there should be a degree of concern—although not an excessive concern—as to whether China will adhere to its no-first-use policy

---

18. Ibid.
19. Ibid., n. 14.

and whether it will continue to see its nuclear arsenal as an instrument of last resort. China's willingness to support its territorial claims with aggressive military positioning could be a potentially ominous portent of changes that might be in the offing.

However, Chinese military writings and exposition of its nuclear strategy suggest that it is not intent of abandoning the no-first-use (NFU) policy. This is despite that, in its 2013 Defence White Paper, China omitted any mention of the NFU policy.[20] Inevitably, this sparked concern. Yet, it is suggested that this is perhaps premature and unwarranted. Evidence to support this latter contention is to be found in three documents:

- China's 2008 Defense White Paper:[21]

The Second Artillery Force is a strategic force under the direct command and control of the Central Military Commission (CMC) and the core force of China for strategic deterrence. It is mainly responsible for deterring other countries from using nuclear weapons against China and for conducting nuclear counterattacks and precision strikes with conventional missiles. The Second Artillery Force sticks to China's policy of no first use of nuclear weapons, implements a self-defensive nuclear strategy, strictly follows the orders of the CMC, and takes it as its fundamental mission to protect China from any nuclear attack. In peacetime, the nuclear missile weapons of the Second Artillery Force are not aimed at any country. But if China comes under a nuclear threat, the nuclear missile force of the Second Artillery Force will go into a state of alert, and get ready for a nuclear counterattack to deter the enemy from using nuclear weapons against China.

If China comes under a nuclear attack, the nuclear missile force of the Second Artillery Force will use nuclear missiles to launch a resolute counterattack against the enemy either independently or together with the nuclear forces of other services. The conventional missile force of the Second Artillery Force is charged mainly with the task of conducting medium- and long-range precision strikes against key strategic and operational targets of the enemy.

---

20. Anthony H. Cordesman with Joseph Kendall and Steven Colley, "China's Nuclear Forces and Weapons of Mass Destruction," *CSIS*, Working Draft: July 20, 2016.

21. Chinese State Council Information Office, "China's National Defense in 2008", http://www.china.org.cn/government/central_government/2009-01/20/content_17155577_9.html.

- China's 2010 White Paper argued that:[22]

China has never evaded its obligations in nuclear disarmament and pursues an open, transparent and responsible nuclear policy. It has adhered to the policy of NFU of nuclear weapons at any time and in any circumstances and made the unequivocal commitment that under no circumstances will it use or threaten to use nuclear weapons against non-nuclear weapon states or nuclear-weapon-free zones. China has never deployed nuclear weapons in foreign territory and has always exercised the utmost restraint in the development of nuclear weapons, and has never participated in any form of nuclear arms race, nor will it ever do so. It will limit its nuclear capabilities to the minimum level required for national security.

- China Military Strategy in 2015:[23]

The nuclear force is a strategic cornerstone for safeguarding national sovereignty and security. China has always pursued the policy of no first use of nuclear weapons and adhered to a self-defensive nuclear strategy that is defensive in nature. China will unconditionally not use or threaten to use nuclear weapons against non-nuclear-weapon states or in nuclear-weapon-free zones, and will never enter into a nuclear arms race with any other country. China has always kept its nuclear capabilities at the minimum level required for maintaining its national security. China will optimise its nuclear force structure, improve strategic early warning, command and control, missile penetration, rapid reaction and survivability and protection, and deter other countries from using or threatening to use nuclear weapons against China.

Summarising China's Nuclear Forces

China's nuclear arsenal is perhaps the most potent, outside that of the United States and Russia. It has steadily evolved, with the support of no fewer than 45 nuclear tests, into a sophisticated, survivable and flexible force encompassing sea, land and air-delivered systems. The Chinese inventory of missiles and warheads continues to grow in both reach and sophistication but the forces it has possibly earmarked for use against

---

22. "China's National Defense in 2010," People's Republic of China Information Office of the State Council, March 31, 2011, p. 35.

23. People's Republic of China Information Office of the State Council, "China's Military Strategy," *Xinhu*, May 26, 2015, Strategic Guideline for Active Defense, http://eng.mod. gov.cn/DefenseNews/2015-05/26/content_4586748.htm

India, while very potent, are not the apparent focus of the ongoing modernisation program of the overall arsenal. China's DF-21 and DF-26 missiles present a challenge to India's planners as do the cruise missiles launched from mobile land-based launchers as well as from submarines and the H-6 bomber. In the latter case, as with the wide array of Chinese SRBMs, India's challenge is complicated by the fact that the majority of such systems—perhaps the overwhelming majority—are intended for use with conventional warheads.

Supporting its missile and nuclear prowess is a well-considered, nuanced and inherently rational and realistic nuclear doctrine. China has traditionally eschewed nuclear sabre-rattling and has opted instead for its own version of credible, minimum deterrence. If estimates are to be believed, and China is not stockpiling a large number of hitherto unknown missiles and warheads, China has not embarked upon a nuclear arms race with either Russia or the United States. China's arsenal in numerical terms is relatively modest compared to that possessed by the former countries. Instead, China has created a flexible nuclear triad with an adequate, though not excessive, number of intercontinental range ballistic missiles capable of targeting even the United States. Against potential regional adversaries such as India and conceivably, Russia, it has chosen to induct new intermediate-range and medium-range ballistic missiles (MRBM) as replacements for its older systems rather than dramatically increase its arsenal. Combined with its doctrine of NFU and a counter-value targeting strategy, China's nuclear arsenal and strategy might be the ideal model for India to emulate.

India can take comfort in the rational approach China has adopted for nuclear strategy and doctrine. It cannot take comfort in the significant nuclear arsenal amassed by China nor in its modernisation of that arsenal and its associated delivery systems. Should China move away from its stated NFU policy or see nuclear weapons as instruments of intimidation to support military posturing for territorial claims, India would need to be ready to meet that challenge.

Pakistan's Nuclear Arsenal and Doctrine
For a country with a limited budget and with significant economic and physical constraints, Pakistan continues to expand its nuclear arsenal with

the production of more warheads, the deployment of more delivery systems and the establishment of a growing fissile materials production industry. Western analysis of commercial satellite images of both Pakistan army garrisons and air force bases reveal both mobile launchers and underground facilities that might be related to nuclear forces—though these could just as easily be dual-use facilities.

The Bulletin of Atomic Scientists estimates that Pakistan now has a nuclear weapons stockpile of 130–140 warheads.[24] This may perhaps be an overestimate as it seems to be predicated upon the optimal production of weapons-grade material from Pakistan's four reactors at the Khushab Nuclear Complex alongside the expansion of its uranium enrichment facilities. It is of interest that similar calculations for India completely ignore India's unsafeguarded power reactors. Nonetheless, with new ballistic missiles and cruise missile systems development, four plutonium production reactors, and with expanding uranium enrichment facilities, Pakistan has a fissile materials stockpile that will likely increase further over the next 10 years.

Yet, it is easy to exaggerate Pakistan's nuclear weapons production and intent. Moreover, looking purely at Pakistan's fissile production is an easy way to arrive at an overestimate of nuclear weapons and fissile materials stockpiles. The Bulletin of Atomic Scientists notes:[25]

> Estimating the size of the Pakistani nuclear warhead stockpile is fraught with uncertainty. A frequent mistake is to derive the estimate directly from the amount of weapons-grade fissile material produced. As of late 2015, the International Panel on Fissile Materials estimated that Pakistan had an inventory of approximately 3100 kg of weapon-grade (90% enriched) highly enriched uranium (HEU) and at least 190 kg of weapon-grade plutonium . This material is theoretically enough to produce 204–306 warheads, assuming that each warhead's solid core uses either 12–18 kg of weapon-grade HEU or 4–6 kg of plutonium.
>
> However, calculating stockpile size based solely on fissile material inventory is an incomplete methodology that tends to produce inflated

---

24. Hans M. Kristensen and Robert S. Norris, "Pakistani nuclear forces," *Bulletin of the Atomic Scientists* vol. 72, no. 6, 2016, pp. 368–376.
25. Ibid., p. 371.

warhead estimates. Instead, warhead estimates must take into account several factors, including: the amount of weapon grade fissile material produced, warhead design proficiency, warhead production rates, numbers of operational nuclear-capable launchers, how many of those launchers are dual capable, nuclear strategy, and statements by government officials. At their outset, estimates must take into account that not all of a country's fissile material ends up in warheads. Like other nuclear weapon states, Pakistan probably maintains a reserve of fissile material. Moreover, Pakistan simply lacks enough nuclear-capable launchers to accommodate 200–300 warheads; furthermore, all of Pakistan's launchers are thought to be dual capable, which means that some of them, especially the shorter-range systems, presumably are assigned to non-nuclear missions as well. Finally, official statements often refer to "warheads" and "weapons" interchangeably, without making it clear whether it is the number of launchers or the warheads assigned to them that are being discussed.

With these caveats in mind, the following Bulletin of Atomic Scientists must be taken with a slight degree of caution. Of particular note, the warhead yields should be viewed with scepticism as Pakistan probably has significantly higher yield weapons than indicated in the table below:[26]

Table 1.2

Type	NATO designation	Number of launchers	Year deployed	Range[1] (km)	Warhead x yield (kt)[3]	Number of warheads[2]
Aircraft	F-16A/B	~24	1998	1600	1 × bomb	~24
	Mirage III/V	~12	1998	2100	1 × bomb (or Ra-ad)	~12
Subtotal:		~36				~36
Land-based ballistic missiles	Abdali (Hatf-2)	n.a.	(2017)[4]	180	1 × low kt	n.a.
	Ghaznavi (Hatf-3)	~16	2004	250	1 × 5–12 kt	~16
	Shaheen-1 (Hatf-4)	~16	2003	750	1 × 5–12 kt	~16

26. Ibid., p. 369.

	Shaheen-1A (Hatf-4)	–	(2017)	900	1 × 5–12 kt	n.a.
	Shaheen-2 (Hatf-6)	~12	2014	1500	1 × 5–12 kt	~12
	Shaheen-3 (Hatf-10?)	–	(2018)	2750	1 × 5–12 kt	n.a.
	Ghauri (Hatf-5)	~24	2003	1250	1 × 5–12 kt	~24
	Nasr (Hatf-9)	~24	2013	60	1 × low kt	~24[5]
Subtotal:		~92				~92
Cruise missiles	Babur (Hatf-7)	~12	2014[6]	350[7]	1 × 5–12 kt	~12[8]
	Ra'ad (Hatf-8)	–	(2017)	350	1 × 5–12 kt	n.a.
Subtotal:		~12				~12
Total						~140

1. Range listed is unrefueled combat range with drop tanks.
2. There may be more missiles than launchers but since each missile is dually capable, this table assigns an average of one warhead per launcher unless noted otherwise.
3. Yield estimate is based on the range of yields measured in the 1998 nuclear tests. It is possible that Pakistan has since developed warheads with lower and higher yields.
4. After six test launches, the Abdali might be in the process of introduction within the army.
5. Each Nasr launcher has up to four missile tubes. But since Nasr is a dual-capable system and the primary mission probably is conventional, this table counts only one warhead per launcher.
6. For unknown reasons, the Babur has not been test-launched since 2012.
7. The Pakistani government claims the Babur range is 700 km, twice the 350-km range reported by the US intelligence community.
8. Each launcher has three missile tubes. But since Babur is a dual-capable system and the primary mission is probably conventional, this table counts only one warhead per launcher.

Delivery Systems

Pakistan has made some progress towards developing a nuclear triad with aircraft-delivered gravity bombs, a nascent air-launched cruise missile capability, a robust mobile, land-based ballistic missile capability, a probable land-based cruise missile capability as well as a limited submarine-launched cruise missile capability. While not yet a viable and survivable nuclear triad, it is beyond doubt a credible and potent deterrent force.

Nuclear-Capable Aircraft

As with most other nuclear powers, Pakistan's first nuclear weapons were air-delivered nuclear bombs. The original aircraft earmarked for this task appears to have been the F-16 A/B and now the later F-16 C/D variants. Pakistan possesses a substantial F-16 fleet and its potential for use as a nuclear weapons delivery platform was the cause of much concern. The Bulletin of Atomic Scientists notes that:[27]

Pakistan probably assigns a nuclear strike mission to select F-16A/B and Mirage III/V fighter squadrons. The F-16 was probably the first aircraft in the nuclear role, but the Mirage quickly joined the mission. The F-16A/Bs were supplied by the United States between 1983 and 1987. After 40 aircraft had been delivered, the US State Department told Congress in 1989: "None of the F-16s Pakistan already owns or is about to purchase is configured for nuclear delivery" and Pakistan "will be obligated by contract not to modify" additional F-16s "without the approval of the United States…"

Yet, there were multiple credible reports at the time that Pakistan was already modifying US-supplied F-16s for nuclear weapons, including West German intelligence officials reportedly telling Der Spiegel that Pakistan had already developed sophisticated computer and electronic technology to outfit the US F-16s with nuclear weapons . Delivery of additional F-16s, including the more modern F-16C/D version, were delayed by concern over Pakistan's emerging nuclear weapons program and withheld by the United States in the 1990s. But the policy was changed by the George W. Bush administration, which supplied Pakistan with the more modern F-16s. The F-16A/Bs are based with the 38th Wing at Mushaf (formerly Sargodha) Air Base, 160 km (100 miles) northwest of Lahore. Organized into the 9th and 11th Squadrons ("Griffins" and "Arrows," respectively), these aircraft have a range of 1600 km (extendable when equipped with drop tanks) and most likely are equipped to each carry a single nuclear bomb on the centerline pylon. Security perimeters at the base have been upgraded since 2014. Nuclear bombs are probably not stored at the base itself but kept at the Sargodha Weapons Storage

27. Ibid., pp. 371–372.

Complex 10 km to the south. In a crisis, the bombs could be flown in or the F-16s could disperse to bases near underground storage facilities to pick up the weapons.

The Pakistan Air Force's (PAF) substantial Mirage III/V fleet is probably no longer earmarked for the nuclear-strike role—if it ever had that role—and is already tasked with antishipping roles. With the addition of an aerial-refuelling capability to the Mirage fleet, the range and flexibility of the type are greatly enhanced and while this would theoretically serve for a potential nuclear delivery role, it is probable that this capability is much more relevant to the important antishipping role assigned to the aircraft.

The Mirage fighter-bombers are focused at two bases. Masroor Air Base, outside Karachi, houses the 32nd Wing with three Mirage squadrons: 7th Squadron ('Bandits'), 8th Squadron ('Haiders') and 22nd Squadron ('Ghazis'), while the other Mirage base is the Rafiqui Air base near Shorkot, which houses the PAF's 34th Wing with two Mirage squadrons: the 15th Squadron ('Cobras') and the 27th Squadron ('Zarras'). Whether directly related to nuclear weapons delivery or not, it should be noted that the Mirage III/V has been used in test-launches of the nuclear-capable Ra'ad air-launched cruise missile. The Bulletin of Atomic Scientists notes, referring to the Masroor air base:[28]

A possible nuclear weapons storage site is located five kilometers (three miles) northwest of the base and since 2004, unique underground facilities have been constructed at Masroor that could potentially be designed to support a nuclear strike mission. This includes a large underground facility within a high-security area and a possible alert hangar with underground weapons-handling capability. There are also rumors that Pakistan intends to make the Chinese-supplied JF-17 fighter nuclear-capable.

The most potent assets in the PAF fleet are the new F-16C/Ds based with the 39th Wing at Shahbaz Air Base outside Jacobabad. The wing converted from the Mirage III/V and has one squadron on strength—5th

---

28. Ibid.

squadron (Falcons). Shahbaz air base has undergone significant expansion, with numerous weapons bunkers added since 2004, though this might not only be related to nuclear weapons delivery but part of a general upgradation of facilities at the said base. The F-16 C/D remains Pakistan's most viable nuclear strike platform alongside its more conventional tasks.

Ballistic Missiles

The Pakistani ballistic missile force is substantial, robust and capable. With no fewer than six operational nuclear-capable ballistic missile types: the short-range Abdali (Hatf-2), Ghaznavi (Hatf-3), Shaheen-1 (Hatf-4) and NASR (Hatf-9), and the medium-range Ghauri (Hatf-5) and Shaheen-2 (Hatf-6), Pakistan's missile force is mobile, relatively modern and, once development of its longer-ranged systems is complete, capable of reaching the entire Indian land mass as well as the Andaman and Nicobar Islands. There should be a degree of caution exercised when comparing the number of missile systems and launchers—especially of the shorter-range types— and automatically inferring from them the number of Pakistani nuclear warheads. At least some, if not the majority, of Pakistan's ballistic missiles have a dual nuclear/conventional role and the latter ought not to be ignored.

With a range of systems at its disposal, Pakistan's missile force is now a highly flexible arm of the deterrent. SRBMs such as the Babur, Ghaznavi, Shaheen-1 and Nasr are housed in four to five garrisons near the Indian border with three other garrisons located further inland for medium-range systems such as the Shaheen-2 and Ghauri. Though Pakistan has undoubtedly inducted these systems, its testing program is somewhat limited with systems entering service after approximately two tests. This in and of itself is not of great importance but for Pakistan's longer-ranged systems, such as the Shaheen -2, the two development tests have been followed by only two user-associated tests thus far.

Of the short-range systems, the solid-fuel, single-stage Abdali (Hatf-2) has been in development for a long time with the Pentagon reporting in 1997 that the Abdali appeared to have been discontinued, but flight-testing resumed in 2002 with the last launch being in 2013. With a 180-km (111-mile) range of missile and carried on a road-mobile Transporter Erector Launcher (TEL), some such as the Bulletin of Atomic Scientist believe that the three-year gap in flight testing is indicative of technical difficulties. However, it is suggested that this need not be the case with Pakistan either believing testing was sufficient or that other missiles satisfied its requirements. Of interest, however, is the absence of user trials.[29]

One of Pakistan's first missile systems was the short-range, solid-fuel, single-stage Ghaznavi (Hatf-3) which was probably derived from the Chinese M-11 missiles procured by Pakistan in the 1990s. It is probable that the development of a nuclear warhead for the same has taken place. If the Hatf-3 is indeed derived from the M-11 or is a substantive copy of the same, its relatively short range of some 250-300 km suggests that it would be needed to be deployed close to the Indian border and is incapable of targeting Delhi, though cities in the Punjab and Rajasthan would come within its range.[30]

Chinese influence may also be seen in the Shaheen-1 (Hatf-4) which, as a re-engineered Chinese M-9 missile, is a single-stage, solid-fuel, ballistic missile with a maximum range of 750 km that probably entered service in 2003. A road-mobile system, a development of the Shaheen-1, known as the Shaheen-1A with a range of 900 km has been tested since 2012.[31]

The Nasr (Hatf-9), a short-range, solid-fuel missile with a range of only 60 km (37 miles) is easily the most controversial system fielded by Pakistan.[32] It was carried on a four-axle, road-mobile TEL on September 26, 2014 involved launching four missiles from a road-mobile quadruple box launcher. The debate over whether the Nasr is indeed nuclear capable is as yet unresolved. The missile has an exceedingly small diameter for a nuclear payload and, though one may indeed be possible, it should be asked whether or not Pakistan's tactical nuclear weapons (TNWs), in the low-kiloton range, might better be delivered by larger and longer-range systems with a longer range as the short-range of the Nasr makes it particularly vulnerable to interdiction efforts on the part of Indian air power.

Pakistan's Shaheen-2 is currently the longest-ranged system in service, with the range being variously reported as 2000 km or as 1500 km. The

---

29. Ibid., p. 372.
30. Ibid.
31. Ibid., p. 373.
32. "Week view No. PR94/2011-ISPR," (April 19, 2011). https://www.ispr.gov.pk/front/main.asp?o=t-press_release&date=2011/4/19

system became operational after a series of tests between 2003 and 2014, the last of which was by the Pakistan Army's Strategic Forces Command.[33] It is anticipated that at least fifteen of the six-axle, road-mobile TELs are in service, with between one and two missiles per launcher.[34]

Alongside the Shaheen-2, Pakistan's oldest nuclear-capable medium-range ballistic missile, the road-mobile, single-stage, liquid-fuel Ghauri (Hatf-5) continues to be retained in service. The system was test launched on April 15 2015 with the Pakistani government saying that the "launch was conducted by a Strategic Missile Group of the Army Strategic Forces Command" for the purpose of "testing the operational and technical readiness of Army Strategic Forces Command".[35] As a liquid-fuelled system, the extra time needed to fuel the missile before launch makes the Ghauri more vulnerable to attack than Pakistan's solid-fuel missiles. It is therefore probable that the Shaheen-2 and its successors will replace the Ghauri in service. It is of interest that this older system has been retained for this length of time when replacements are available, rather similar to India's retention of its Prithvi surface to surface missiles SSMs long after they were superseded by more modern missiles. The Ghauri was first tested in the 1990s and its continuation in service is indicative of the probable service life expected from MRBM, and intermediate-range ballistic missiles in the subcontinent.

Pakistan's missile program has an even longer-ranged Shaheen variant known as the Shaheen-3.[36] Pakistan conducted two test launches of the Shaheen-3 IRBM in 2015 with the Pakistani Government claiming the missile was capable of delivering a nuclear or conventional warhead to a range of 2750 km.[37] This would enable the missile to theoretically target the Andaman and Nicobar islands should it be positioned in the eastern parts of Pakistan close to the Indian border. More importantly, perhaps for the first

33. "Press release No. PR248/2014-ISPR," (November 13, 2014). https://www.ispr.gov.pk/front/main.asp?o=t-press_release&date=2014/11/13

34. National Air and Space Intelligence Center (NASIC), "Ballistic and Cruise Missile Threat," (2013). http://fas.org/programs/ssp/nukes/nuclearweapons/NASIC2013_050813.pdf

35. "Press release No. PR92/2014-ISPR," (April 15, 2015). https://www.ispr.gov.pk/front/main.asp?o=t-press_release&date=2015/4/15

36. "Press release No. PR61/2015-ISPR. Inter Services Public Relations," (March 9, 2015). https://www.ispr.gov.pk/front/main.asp?o=t-press_release&date=2015/3/9

37. Ibid., n. 23, p.373

time, the Shaheen-3 brings Israel within the range of Pakistani missiles, should it be based and launched from the Western parts of Balochistan. The road-mobile Shaheen-3 is carried on an eight-axle TEL purportedly supplied by China and was displayed publicly for the first time at the 2015 Pakistan Day Parade. It would be premature to consider the Shahneen-3 to be operational after only two test launches. If the usual Pakistani practice is followed, at least one user-associated test followed by induction and thereafter, a full user-test should be forthcoming.

Pakistan's ballistic missiles have emerged as a potent and viable arm of that country's nuclear deterrent force. Of interest to note is the premium placed by Pakistan on ensuring its missile force is road mobile. All missiles are on wheeled TELs with adequate cross-country mobility. Pakistan did not opt for either a silo-based or rail-mobile deterrent, perhaps in recognition of the vulnerability of the former mode of deployment and the geographical limitations faced by Pakistan in respect of the latter. The road mobility of Pakistan's TELs, combined with the varying ranges of the missile systems makes any effort at counter-force operations by India exceedingly difficult, if not impossible. This is particularly the case for the longer-ranged systems in Pakistan's arsenal though such operations may be somewhat practical for shorter-range systems such as the Nasr.

Cruise Missiles

Pakistan's research into cruise missiles is centred around two systems, both of which are said to be nuclear-capable—the ground-launched Babur (Hatf-7) and the air-launched Ra'ad (Hatf-8). It is conceivable that the Babur may be converted for use on ships or submarines but as yet no operational system in this regard has emerged. The Pakistani Government claims that the Babur and Ra'ad both have 'stealth capabilities' and 'pinpoint accuracy', and each is described as 'a low-altitude, terrain-hugging missile with high maneuverability'. Their relatively small size and the claim that they are nuclear capable suggests that Pakistan has had some success in miniaturising nuclear warheads for such systems—something that should be unsurprising, given the sophistication of Pakistan's nuclear program. The cruise missiles give Pakistan yet another option for nuclear weapons delivery though they are much slower than ballistic missiles and are considerably easier to intercept. The Babur is a ground-launched, subsonic, dual-capable cruise missile that has been test-launched approximately a dozen times with one of the last tests being in 2014. This should mean that the system is probably operational with the armed forces. The Bulletin of Atomic Scientists says that:[38]

> Its road-mobile launcher appears to be a unique five-axle TEL with a three-tube box launcher that is different than the quadruple box launcher used for static display. The Pakistani Government normally reports the range as 700 km (435 miles) (ISPR 2012b, 2012c), but the US intelligence community sets the range much lower, at 350 km (217 miles) (National Air and Space Intelligence Center (NASIC) 2013). Babur TELs have been fitting out at the National Defense Complex for several years and have recently been seen at the Akro garrison northeast of Karachi. The garrison includes a large enclosure with six garages that have room for 12 TELs and a unique underground facility that is probably used to store the missiles.

For airborne delivery, the second cruise missile under development is the air-launched, dual-capable Ra'ad which has been test-launched at least six times, most recently in February 2016 and could enter service shortly. Given that the test launches have been conducted from a Mirage III fighter-bomber, it could be that either this marks a potential revival of the nuclear delivery role for the ageing Pakistani Mirage fleet or this simply is a test phase where the missiles will eventually be fitted to much more capable aircraft such as the F-16C/D. The Pakistani government has officially stated that the Ra'ad "can deliver nuclear and conventional warheads with great accuracy" to a range of 350 km, and "complementing Pakistan's deterrence capability" by achieving "strategic standoff capability on land and at sea".[39] The Bulletin of the Atomic Scientists (BAS), on the assumption that the Mirage fleet will be designated as the carriers of the missile, suggests that a potential deployment site for the Ra'ad is the Masroor air base outside Karachi which houses several Mirage squadrons and which also includes

---

38. Ibid., n.23, 374.
39. "Press release No. PR16/2016-ISPR. Inter Services Public Relations," (January 19, 2016). https://www.ispr.gov.pk/front/main.asp?o=t-press_release&date=2016/1/19

"unique underground facilities that might be associated with nuclear weapons storage and handling".

Pakistan is undoubtedly desirous of creating a nuclear weapons capability for its navy—more than likely to be launched from a submarine. In 2012, the Pakistani navy established Headquarters Naval Strategic Forces Command with the intended purpose of developing and deploying of a sea-based strategic nuclear force.[40] This would, if it comes to fruition, enhance Pakistan's second-strike capabilities and confer a degree of flexibility to Pakistan's nuclear deterrent above and beyond which it currently possesses. None of Pakistan's naval vessels—whether surface ships or submarines currently have the capability of delivering ballistic missiles and as yet not been fitted with nuclear-capable cruise missiles. For the latter role, a ship or submarine-based version of the Babur cruise missile would be a probable candidate for adaptation to naval use. It is, however, unlikely that Pakistan would vest such a capability in its small surface fleet which, though expanding, is vulnerable to Indian naval superiority and particularly vulnerable to air attack, even under the protection of land-based air cover. Rather, any Pakistani sea-launched nuclear assets would likely revolve around the country's five conventionally powered submarines. Of these, the three Agosta-class vessels are the most likely and practical choice for carrying any Pakistani naval nuclear deterrent as these vessels are currently the most modern submarine assets in the Pakistan navy and possess enhanced endurance through its air-independent propulsion system. While lacking the flexibility of SSBNs, SSNs or SSGNs, and having less endurance, these vessels could be an adequate cruise missile carrier for Pakistan's second-strike deterrent purposes.

Pakistan's Nuclear Doctrine

Pakistan's nuclear posture and doctrine have moved from one of credible minimum deterrence to one of full-spectrum deterrence.[41] This has encompassed enhanced numbers of nuclear weapons as well as the development of a doctrine that may allow for the employment of nuclear

---

40. "Press release PR122/2012-ISPR," (May 19, 2012). https://www.ispr.gov.pk/front/main. asp?o=t-press_release&date=2012/5/19

41. A Conversation With Gen. Khalid Kidwai.. "Carnegie International Nuclear Policy Conference 2015." Carnegie Endowment for International Peace. Transcript, 4–5, March 23, 2015. http://carnegieendowment.org/files/03-230315carnegieKIDWAI.pdf

weapons as a tactical weapon in order to deal with a potential Indian incursion into Pakistani territory with the attendant risk of lowering the nuclear thresholds in the subcontinent. This is of course combined with a relatively survivable force of long-range missile systems capable of targeting Indian cities and which could serve as a potential deterrent to massive Indian counter-value retaliation. While Pakistan's doctrine dealing with TNWs will be dealt with in the relevant chapter, the country's nuclear redlines raise an important question as to whether Pakistan's nuclear doctrine is geared towards a tactical role or a strategic one:[42]

- **Spatial:** Indian armed forces occupying a large swathe of Pakistani territory;
- **Military**: Indian armed forces completely knocking out or comprehensively destroying a large part of the Pakistani armed forces;
- **Economic**: Any Indian attempt to economically strangle Pakistan;
- **Political**: Possibly, an attempt to militarily assist a secessionist movement in Pakistan to the extent that the said movement has a reasonable chance of success.

In the aforementioned scenarios, it is difficult to see how the use or threat of use of nuclear weapons by Pakistan against Indian cities is viable, given the inevitability of heavy Indian retaliatory strikes with the consequent destruction of Pakistan. An examination of the Pakistani arsenal—in particular, its recent emphasis on shorter-range systems— suggests that Pakistan believes that its TNWs represent the most viable instrument towards ensuring that its nuclear red-lines are not crossed.[43] In respect of Pakistan's concepts of full spectrum deterrence, the BAS says:[44]

How far Pakistan plans to go in terms of its development of a full-spectrum deterrent posture is unclear. It has provided no public statements

---

42. Sanjay Badri-Maharaj, "The Importance of Passive and Active CBRN Defensive Measures," *Institute for Defence Studies and Analyses: IDSA Issue Brief,* (October 17, 2016). https://idsa.in/issuebrief/importance-of-passive-and-active-cbrn-defensive-measures_sbmaharaj_171016, accessed on January 26, 2018.

43. "We have Low-yield N-weapons to Ward Off India's War Threat: Pakistan," *India Today,* October 20, 2015, http://indiatoday.intoday.in/articlePrint.jsp?aid=503185

44. Ibid., n. 23, p. 371.

about its intent. In 2015, however, Kidwai stated that "the program is not open ended. It started with a concept of credible minimum deterrence, and certain numbers [of weapons] were identified, and those numbers, of course, were achieved not too far away in time. Then we translated it, like I said, to the concept of full spectrum deterrence" in response to India's Cold Start doctrine. As a result, "the numbers were modified. Now those numbers, as of today, and if I can look ahead for at least 10 to 15 more years, I think they are going to be more or less okay." In terms of the required size of Pakistan's nuclear arsenal, Kidwai said, "we're almost 90, 95% there in terms of the goals that we had set out to achieve" 15 years ago.

Pakistan has not spelled out either a counterforce or counter-value doctrine and its nuclear strategy seems to be geared towards blunting India's conventional military superiority which might be used to retaliate for actions by Pakistani-assisted terrorist groups. However, unlike China, Pakistan has not spelt out a comprehensive doctrine nor has it detailed its thinking on either counterforce or counter-value targeting beyond its assertions that TNWs are intended as a response to India's 'Cold Start' doctrine.

This, it is submitted, is not necessarily an issue and extrapolating a broader doctrine from the aforementioned concepts, utterances and views leads to the inevitable conclusion that Pakistan's nuclear doctrine seeks to ensure the continued viability of its sub-conventional terrorist campaign against India while blunting an Indian military response thereto. Furthermore, should the aforesaid response materialise, its TNWs might be employed so as to achieve a relatively favourable situation on the battlefield, preventing the destruction of Pakistani military capabilities while simultaneously being insured against Indian counter-value retaliation by Pakistan's smaller force of nuclear weapons earmarked for use on its long-ranged ballistic missiles.

2
India's Nuclear Arsenal— Current and Future Deterrent

India's nuclear arsenal is shrouded in excessive secrecy. While some of this is inevitable, the complete lack of information on the Indian nuclear weapons inventory, delivery options and command and control is somewhat disconcerting. However, as of 2017, it can be safely said that the Indian arsenal—under the control of the Strategic Forces Command (SFC) is at present, land-based and consists of air-delivered weapons and land-based ballistic missiles. While India has made significant strides in developing a submarine-based deterrent, the INS Arihant and her K-4 missiles are a considerable distance away from attaining operational status. In the medium term, these systems will become relevant but at this juncture, India would plan its nuclear deployment and delivery systems around manned aircraft and a mix of short, medium and long-range ballistic missiles. It is also to be noted that with the Nirbhay cruise missile facing development challenges and the BrahMos system's nuclear payload (if any) being in the realm of pure speculation, Indian nuclear-armed cruise missiles cannot be counted on being part of the Indian arsenal at this juncture but are certainly prospectively so.

Given the fact that India has an avowed no-first-use policy—as discussed in a later chapter—this imposes a number of challenges for India to ensure the survivability of its deterrent. Having a nuclear triad is one way to ensure survivability but the individual components of this triad must themselves be sufficiently survivable to conduct their operations in the event of a first strike on India. To this end, issues of the number of delivery systems and warheads, the survivability of those assets in the event of a first-strike and the ability of those delivery systems to reach their targets and deliver an effective response are all issues to be considered. While there is little dispute in India about the necessity for strategic and sub-strategic warheads, the issue of tactical nuclear warheads is as yet unsettled, with some notable analysts not being in favour of such systems.

It is argued that India has made some progress towards developing a survivable and viable nuclear triad with the individual components of manned aircraft, road and rail mobile intermediate-range ballistic missiles (IRBMs) and intercontinental-range ballistic missile (ICBMs), submarine-launched ballistic missiles and land-based cruise missiles are largely in place though development work in some respects is still ongoing regarding the submarine and cruise missile components of the Indian triad. What is much less clear is whether adequate provisions have been made to build and deploy sufficient numbers of the delivery systems and to ensure that these systems are adequately protected in the event of a counter-force strike. This is not to say that India has not taken such steps, but the pervasive secrecy that permeates all aspects of the nuclear discourse in India makes certainty impossible.

Manned Aircraft
The Indian Air Force, with a force of some 230 Su-30MKIs, 45 Mirage 2000s and over 110 Jaguars, has many options for manned aircraft delivering nuclear gravity bombs. The weight, yield and dimensions of Indian gravity and/or glide bombs are not known; however, it might be anticipated that Indian weapons range between 250 and 1000 kg and can have a yield of between 15 kt and may be as much as 200 kt—the latter being fusion-boosted-fission weapons.

Indications are that the first Indian nuclear weapons design had a mass of about 1000 kg with a yield of 12–15 kt. However, subsequently, perhaps by 1982 (when rumours of a fresh round of nuclear tests were being circulated), the said weapon had been scaled down to a more manageable mass of between 170 kg and 200 kg.[1] Later it appears that a 100-kt fission

---

1.   George Perkovich, *India's Nuclear Bomb: The Impact on Global Proliferation* (London: University of California Press, 1999), p. 242.

weapon was later produced for aerial delivery with a mass of 200 to 300 kg.[2] If this is accurate, it would mean that India had perfected a relatively high-yield fission weapon with a relatively low mass for its class. It should also be noted that by the 1990s, fission-boosted-fission weapons had become available for air delivery.

While India had developed a stockpile of some 15–20 nuclear gravity bombs in the period 1974–1985—all of which were in the 15–20 kt range, India became an effective nuclear weapons state in May 1994. It might have been thought that this milestone would have been achieved earlier, and indeed it was certainly possible for this to be done. However, mating of the nuclear weapons with the delivery aircraft proved to be challenging.

India's first deployed air-delivered nuclear weapons were earmarked for use from the Jaguar strike aircraft. One would have assumed that in the 1980s and into the early 1990s, the Jaguar with an excellent navigation-attack system and a very good payload capacity would have been an ideal choice. However, the type's less than stellar flight performance combined with practical problems of ground clearance lead to the Mirage 2000 being chosen to perform this task with active trials of the system being undertaken in 1994.

Initial tests with the Jaguar IS—India's principal deep-penetration strike aircraft—found that the Armament and Research Development Establishment (ARDE)-designed bomb-pods were too heavy for the Jaguar and once fitted to the centerline pylon of the aircraft, the ground clearance of a mere two inches was deemed unsafe.[3] India then chose to use its Mirage 2000H/TH fleet for the nuclear delivery role. It was with this aircraft that India finally completed its development of a fully combat ready and deployable system for delivering nuclear weapons with the Indian Air Force (IAF) conducting acceptance trials. The ARDE developed bomb case, and the Terminal Ballistic Research Laboratory-developed implosion system were mated with a modified Mirage 2000 and successfully test-dropped at Balasore using a toss-bombing technique. The bomb, minus its plutonium core, was fused for an airburst and released over the ocean. With

---

2.   Bharat Karnad, Nuclear Weapons and Indian Security (New Delhi: Macmillan India Ltd, 2002), p. 320.

3.   Raj Chengappa, Weapons of Peace (New Delhi: Harper Collins Publishers India, 2000), p. 327.

this test, India has a reasonably reliable delivery system and by 1994, India now had an arsenal of at least a couple of dozen operational nuclear bombs.[4]

At least one of India's three IAF Mirage 2000 squadrons was tasked with the nuclear strike role—although it does not seem that this was its exclusive role given the limited number of aircraft available. One might expect that the 36 Dassault Rafales may find themselves supplementing and thereafter, supplanting the Mirages in the nuclear strike role.[5] It has also been speculated that the Su-30MKI fleet may have a nuclear strike role. This would not be unrealistic and the greater payload capacity offered by the Su-30MKI could eventually permit the carriage of air-launched nuclear-armed cruise missiles in the future. In fact, it has been suggested that the Su-30MKI has now supplanted the Mirage 2000 in the nuclear strike role.

It is of course preposterous to expect all Indian aircraft to be earmarked for the nuclear strike role. Rather, it is believed that certain squadrons have been given such a tasking in wartime with at least one squadron of each of the Su-30MKIs and Mirage 2000s being so employed. It might be expected that a degree of additional electromagnetic pulse (EMP) protection would be provided to these aircraft. However, given the fact that it is highly unlikely that whole squadrons can be permanently assigned to the nuclear strike role without compromising India's ability to conduct air operations in the event of hostilities, determining which aircraft needs to be given additional EMP shielding presents a challenge. It might be necessary for India to consider additional EMP shielding for a larger proportion of its air assets than would be necessitated by the number of nuclear weapons earmarked for aerial delivery.

India lacks a heavy bomber aircraft type equivalent to either the American B-52 and B-1B or the Russian Tu-22M3 and Tu-160 aircraft. It is interesting that India was offered the earlier Tu-22 as a replacement for the venerable Canberra bomber but for some reason declined the type—perhaps wisely as the aircraft proved less than successful in service. What is more surprising is that India has not moved towards obtaining an effective

---

4.   Ibid., pp. 382–384
5.   Shiv Aroor, "10 Reasons Why the Indian Rafale is Evolution Itself," *Daily O,* (July 04, 2017). http://www.dailyo.in/variety/rafale-aircraft-brahmos-nuclear-defence/story/1/18157.html, accessed on September 4, 2017).

strike aircraft perhaps, such as the Su-34 to augment its multirole aircraft which currently carries the dual responsibilities of conventional air combat tasks as well as a potential nuclear strike role. Given the finite—and none too generous—strength of the IAF, it is pertinent to ask if the procurement of specialist aircraft for a nuclear strike and possibly even their escort role are now a necessity.

As to survivability, India has constructed underground hangars in at least three airbases—Adampur, Hindon and Bareilly.[6] However, surface shelters in the form of hardened aircraft shelters (HAS) are not yet available for most of the Su-30MKI fleet. A proposal to build 108 new generation HAS with improved protection characteristics is currently pending.[7] HAS are not, strictly speaking, protection against a pre-emptive nuclear strike but may protect the aircraft to some degree against an airburst. It is also noted that Indian HAS lacks blast doors. While this is understandable in order to facilitate the rapid turnaround of aircraft, it does mean that protection is somewhat suboptimal. Should the IAF take its nuclear role seriously, then the question of improved HAS must be considered a priority. India's airbases do have one major advantage—munitions storage, fuel supplies and even command and control facilities are all underground. This enhances the survivability of key military assets in the event of a nuclear first-strike.

However, what does not pay sufficient attention to is the viability of the manned aircraft as nuclear strike assets against the intense and well-organised air defences of either China or Pakistan. There is a qualitative difference between delivering a relatively low-yield weapon against an army formation or even a smaller city as compared to delivering one against a hardened, heavily defended counter-force or countervalue target. In this regard, one aspect needs to be considered—air-delivered stand-off munitions with nuclear payloads. While it is as yet too early to speak of an Indian air-launched cruise missile capability, some analysts suggest that the use of nuclear glide bombs may provide a degree of stand-off capability

---

6. Mrigank Tiwari, "Unprecedented Security at Trishul Airbase," *Times of India,* (January 03, 2016). http://timesofindia.indiatimes.com/city/bareilly/Unprecedented-security-at-Trishul-airbase/articleshow/50430273.cms, accessed on September 4, 2017.

7. "India Plans Next Generation Bombproof Shelter for 108 Fighter Jets," *Sputnik News,* (July 03, 2017). https://sputniknews.com/military/201707031055187413-india-shelter-jets/, accessed September 04, 2017.

to attacking aircraft. Nonetheless, it is doubtful that manned aircraft will provide any more than secondary nuclear delivery systems.

Does India have Any Air-Delivered Nuclear Weapons Still in Service?

There is, as is usually the case with assessments of India's nuclear arsenal, a twist in the story of India's air-delivered weapons. India's entire fleet of Mirage 2000s is currently undergoing a major upgrade. In addition, as noted above, there are legitimate questions about the survivability of manned aircraft-carrying nuclear weapons. It is suggested that India's aircraft-based deterrent should be regarded as being in potential until stand-off munitions are introduced. This might be somewhat counter-intuitive, given the inherent value of the manned aircraft as a nuclear delivery system—and its inherent flexibility—but it must be noted that India does not have an unlimited number of aircraft in its inventory. Allocating a proportion of them to the dedicated nuclear strike role is not impossible but with declining force levels as well as an upgrade program in progress, it is probable that India's airborne nuclear strike capability is currently latent and will be reactivated once aircraft emerge from their upgrade process plus guided stand-off munitions become available.

Ballistic Missiles

India's first operational ballistic missiles of the Prithvi SS-150, SS-250 and SS-350 variants were relatively widely produced, with perhaps 180 of the SS-150 variant and 60 of the SS-250 and SS-350 variants being produced.[8] However, it is less clear on whether any of these variants has had anything more than a secondary nuclear role with anecdotal evidence suggesting that 4 SS-150s were armed with 15 kt fission warheads during the 1999 Kargil war.[9]

Development of the missile began in 1983. In its current configuration, the missile is 8.56 m long, 1.1 m in diameter and weighs 4000 kg. Unlike the later Indian missiles, the Prithvi family uses a single-stage, liquid propellant engine, which is essentially two liquid propellant motors side-by-side that

---

8.   Bharat Karnad, *India's Nuclear Policy* (Westport, Connecticut: Praeger Security International 2008), p. 78.
9.   Chengappa, n. 3, p. 437.

provide aerodynamic control as well as thrust vectoring. This engine control allows the missile to stop climbing when it reaches an altitude of 30 km, travel horizontally at this altitude and dive on its target at an 80° angle. The missile has a minimum range of 40 km and in its later variants, a maximum of 350 km.

The missile has a reported accuracy of 50 m circular error probable (CEP) against targets at 150 km. At present, it uses an inertial guidance system and is launched from a Transporter-Erector-Launcher (TEL) vehicle. It takes approximately 2 hours to prepare a missile for launch due to preflight fuelling and various support functions that must be accomplished. Two TEL vehicles require an average of 18 support vehicles that include warhead carriers, power suppliers, fuel carriers, cranes and others.

The Prithvi-I's first test flight was in 1988 and it officially entered service in 1994. By 1999, there had been 16 successful tests of this missile system. Further trials at user level were conducted from 2003. The missile was first deployed with the 333rd Indian Army Missile Group. Thereafter, the Indian army raised two more groups, the 444th Indian Army Missile Group and the 555th Indian Army Missile Group. Though the Indian army intended to deploy Prithvi as a viable tactical weapon with conventional warheads, more recent tests of the system have been reportedly conducted by the SFC. It should also be noted that the IAF operates a small number of Prithvi SS-250 variants and the navy, in its Dhanush missile, has two vessels equipped to launch these missiles.

However, the Indian land-based nuclear deterrent rests upon five variants of the Agni family of ballistic missiles which range from medium-range ballistic missiles (MRBM) (Agni-I) to limited-range ICBMs (Agni-V). All bar perhaps the Agni-V are in operational service with numbers as yet unknown but with production ongoing albeit at an apparently low rate.

The test of the Agni-V missile in its final deliverable configuration on December 26, 2016, represented a major step forward for India's strategic deterrence posture. Lost in the very legitimate emphasis on what the test means for India's nuclear deterrent, is the fact that the Agni-V represents the culmination to date of an evolutionary process in the development of India's ballistic missile capability, whereby one phase of development drew heavily on those versions of the missile that came before. The second test in this configuration took place on January 18, 2018.

There is one important point to note: India has used depressed and lofted trajectories to simulate ranges on its missiles. Details of the trajectories have not been disclosed extrapolations being made from the Notice to Airmen (NOTAM) warnings. This leads to a strong suspicion, with some foundation, that India has understated the range of its missiles from the Agni-II onwards. This trend continues with the words 'more than' being almost a permanent prefix to range figures of Indian missiles. Even more perplexing than the range estimates are the number of missiles produced and in service—particularly given the number of user trials from production batches.

The Agni Saga

The original Agni missile—formerly a 're-entry demonstrator' and which we can now term the Agni-TD—was tested on May 22, 1989. By its third test in 1994, the 2500-km-range missile had achieved a demonstrated range of 1450 km with a claimed CEP of 300 m.[10] However, what was the most remarkable aspect of this progenitor to the Agni missiles of the 21st century was that it was a hybrid, using the liquid-fuelled Prithvi-1 missile as the basis for its first stage coupled to a solid fuel booster reminiscent of, but not identical to, the booster of ISRO's SLV-3 launch vehicle. The Prithvi, which had entered bulk production by 1994, was a reliable system with propulsion based on India's stillborn 'Devil' SAM project of the 1970s and married to the proven SLV-3 booster, this low-risk approach enabled India to develop an IRBM capability at a relatively low cost, using proven technology.

However, it was soon realised that the Agni-TD was not a practical weapon owing in large part to its hybrid propulsion and the inherent problems of keeping such a system in a state of readiness or at least in a state of near-readiness. Moreover, it would appear that India, learning the lessons of the 1980s, decided against deploying its land-based deterrent in static-hardened silos and opted for mobile systems. The Agni-TD was not a mobile system and developing its successor required not only an improved missile but the development of a mobile launcher that could be deployed operationally. It should be noted that while unlikely, the Agni-TD could

---

10.   Raj Chengappa, "The Missile Man," *India Today*, April 15, 1994, pp. 40–42

have been weaponised. Admittedly, it was far from an ideal system but it appeared that its designers were always cognisant of the possibility of the need to weaponise it.

The Agni-II

First tested on April 11, 1999, the Agni-II had a range of anywhere between 2000 and 3000 km with all solid-fuel propulsion. Tested to a range of 2300 km with a 1000 kg payload in 1999, the Agni-2 established a pattern for Indian missiles—production and user trials would follow three consecutive successful technical trials.[11] The 1999 test was followed by one on January 17, 2001 and a third on August 29, 2004. Production of the Agni-II followed thereafter but it was not until 2009 that user trials began, the first two of which were complete failures due to quality control problems during manufacture. However, on May 17, 2010, the first user trial from a production batch was successfully completed, effectively marking the missile achieving operational status within the Indian arsenal.[12] This was followed by similar production batch trials undertaken by the SFC on September 30, 2011,[13] August 09, 2012, April 07, 2013[14] and on November 09, 2014. This means that the Agni-II has become the backbone of India's IRBM force. However, a test on May 04, 2017 failed. A subsequent test on February 20, 2018 was successful.[15]

11. Manvendra Singh, "Agni-II adds Firepower to N-Deterrence," *Indian Express*, April 12, 1999.

12. Y. Mallikarjun, "Agni-II Missile Test-Fired Successfully," *The Hindu*, (May 17, 2010). http://www.thehindu.com/news/national/Agni-II-missile-test-fired-successfully/article16302660.ece, accessed on September 05, 2017.

13. T. Subramaniam and Y. Mallikarjun, "Agni-II Soars in Success," *The Hindu*, (September 30, 2011). http://www.thehindu.com/news/national/agniii-soars-in-success/article2499781.ece, accessed on September 5, 2017.

14. "Odisha: Nuclear capable Agni-II missile successfully test fired," *IBN Live*, (April 07, 2013). https://archive.is/20130628175643/http://www.bharat-rakshak.com/NEWS/newsrf.php, accessed on September 05, 2017.

15. "India Successfully Test-Fires Nuclear Capable Agni-II Missile Off Odisha Coast," *News 18*, (November 09, 2014). http://www.news18.com/news/india/india-successfully-test-fires-nuclear-capable-agni-ii-missile-off-odisha-coast-724952.html, accessed on September 05, 2017. See also "India Test Fires Medium Range Nuclear Capable Agni-II Missile," *Economic Times*, (February 20, 2018) https://economictimes.indiatimes.com/news/defence/india-test-fires-agni-ii-missile-off-odisha-coast/articleshow/62993975.cms, accessed on March 02, 2018.

The Agni-II was India's first viable production IRBM and is mounted on a rail-mobile TEL with some suggestions that the TEL can be made road-mobile as well. In either case, the TEL provides the Agni-II with flexibility in deployment as well as survivability. Furthermore, the system can be deployed within 15 minutes. The Agni-II marked India's departure from liquid propellants to all solid-fuel systems. Furthermore, the Agni-II's reputed CEP of between 30 and 100 m at maximum range makes it an accurate system. Production of the Agni-II has been reported in 2001/02 but it is unclear as to which level of production has been achieved with estimates ranging widely. It is to be noted that in 1998, instructions were purportedly given to prepare production facilities for the Agni-II at the rate of one per month.[16] It is unclear whether such production levels have ever been achieved.

The Agni-I

In a curious twist, the Agni-II, which evolved from the Agni-TD, spawned the Agni-1. This 700-km-range MRBM was born out of an operational necessity for a missile with a longer range than the Prithvi to serve as a deterrent against Pakistan. The Agni-II was effectively re-engineered to create a smaller, lighter and road-mobile system that is both survivable and easily deployable. The Agni-1, therefore, could (at least conceptually) be deemed a single-stage Agni-II. Since its first test in 2002, it has undergone a series of user trials from 2007 onwards, the last two being on November 22, 2016 and February 06, 2018.[17] While the missile itself is an achievement of note, the road-mobile launch system should be considered of equal importance as it has evolved into the road-mobile TELs for the Agni-IV and the Agni-V.

The Agni-III

At a glance, the Agni-III bears no physical resemblance to the Agni-II and is of a very different configuration, renouncing the tall, slender form for a

---

16. "DRDO told to Test Upgraded Agni in August," *Deccan Chronicle,* July 15, 1998.

17. "India Successfully Test-fires N-capable Agni-I Ballistic Missile," *News 18,* (November 22, 2016). http://www.news18.com/news/india/india-successfully-tests-nuclear-capable-agni-i-ballistic-missile-1314397.html, accessed on September 05, 2017. See also "India Successfully Test-Fires Nuclear Capable Agni-1," *Times of India,* (February 06, 2018). https://timesofindia.indiatimes.com/india/india-successfully-test-fires-nuclear-capable-agni-1/articleshow/62801316.cms, accessed on March 02, 2018.

shorter but wider arrangement. With three stages, the Agni-III represents what might be termed an intermediate stage of missile development in India, part way between the Agni-II and the definitive Agni-V. Once again using a rail-mobile TEL, the Agni-III represents the largest missile to date that India has fired from such a launcher.

After a failed test in 2006, the Agni-III completed the now normal series of three consecutive technical trials on April 12, 2007, May 07, 2008[18] and February 07, 2010. Thereafter, the SFC conducted user trials of the system on September 21, 2012,[19] December 23, 2013, April 16, 2015[20] with the last being on April 27, 2017.[21] Like the Agni-II, a CEP in the 'two-digit' range (40 m being suggested) was claimed. The Agni-III has a stated range of more than 3500 km, but it bears a striking resemblance to the Soviet-era SS-20 IRBM, leading to the possibility that the range of the Agni-III could be as high as 5000 km.[22] While this has not been in any way verified or suggested further, the range of the Agni-III may be somewhat understated.

While in chronological terms, the Agni-IV succeeded the Agni-III, it is suggested that the Agni-III represents an entirely new missile family, unrelated to the Agni-II and its successor the Agni-IV. Rather, the Agni-III represents the precursor to the Agni-V which it closely resembles in size and configuration. It is of interest that on examination of the Agni-III TEL, there is a possibility that the vehicle is both road-mobile and rail-mobile. This continues a trend started with the Agni-I and Agni-II, which both possessed the ability to be launched from either road or rail-mobile

18. T. Subramanian and Y. Mallikarjun, "Agni-III test-fired successfully," *The Hindu*, (May 08, 2008). http://www.thehindu.com/todays-paper/Agni-III-test-fired-successfully/article15218480.ece, accessed on September 05, 2017.

19. Y. Mallikarjun, "Agni-III Test-Fired Successfully," *The Hindu*, (September 21, 2012). http://www.thehindu.com/news/national/agniiii-testfired-successfully/article3922230.ece, accessed on September 05, 2017.

20. "Agni-III Successfully Test Fired from Odisha Coast," *Economic Times*, (April 16, 2015). http://economictimes.indiatimes.com/news/defence/agni-iii-successfully-test-fired-from-odisha-coast/articleshow/46941664.cms, accessed on September 05, 2017.

21. "India Test-Fires Nuclear-Capable Agni III Ballistic Missile," *Economic Times*, (April 27, 2017). http://economictimes.indiatimes.com/news/defence/india-test-fires-nuclear-capable-agni-iii-ballistic-missile/articleshow/58396268.cms, accessed on September 05, 2017.

22. PTI "Agni III could have 5,000 km Range: Russian General," *The Hindu*, http://www.defencetalk.com/forums/missiles-wmds/indian-nuclear-missile-development-news-discussions-7241-11/, accessed on September 05, 2017.

launchers, though in the case of the Agni-II, road mobility seems to be debatable. Induction of the Agni-III reportedly began in 2011, but the unit designation and numbers inducted to date are unknown.[23]

The Agni-IV

With a range of 4000 km (or possibly more), the Agni-IV represents the successor to the Agni-II. Earlier known as the Agni-II Prime, the Agni-IV is no larger than its predecessor but has a significantly greater range and, being road-mobile, is even more flexible and survivable than the Agni-II. This reflects a greater use of lighter composites and improved solid-fuel propellants and improvements to the guidance system ensure that even at maximum range, the Agni-IV retains a 'two-digit' CEP but is a streamlined and noticeably better-engineered system as compared to the Agni-II, possessing a much longer range.

While its first test in December 2010 was a failure, technical trials on November 15, 2011, September 19, 2012[24] and January 20, 2014,[25] the latter in full user configuration, were deemed successful. Thereafter, the SFC commenced induction and carried out user trials on December 02, 2014[26] and November 09, 2015.[27] It is expected that the Agni-IV will supplement and then completely replace the Agni-II in production and become the mainstay of the Indian IRBM force. It is also noteworthy that there have been persistent rumours of a canister-launched version of the Agni-IV being contemplated. Its most recent test on January 02, 2017 did not garner

23. "India to Test Fire Agni-V by Year-End," *The Hindu*, (June 03, 2011). http://www.thehindu.com/sci-tech/science/India-to-test-fire-Agni-V-by-year-end/article13821309.ece, accessed on September 05, 2017.

24. "Long Range Strategic Missile Agni-IV Test-Fired," *The Hindu*, (September 19, 2012). http://www.thehindu.com/sci-tech/science/long-range-strategic-missile-agniiv-testfired/article3914340.ece, accessed on September 05, 2017.

25. T. Subramanian, "Agni-IV Missile Successfully Test Fired," *The Hindu*, (January 20, 2014). http://www.thehindu.com/news/national/agniiv-missile-successfully-test-fired/article5596563.ece, accessed on September 05, 2017.

26. "India successfully tests nuclear capable Agni IV missile," *The Hindu*, (December 03, 2014). http://www.thehindu.com/todays-paper/tp-in-school/india-successfully-tests-nuclear-capable-agni-iv-missile/article6656285.ece, accessed on September 05, 2017.

27. Rajat Pandit, "Ballistic Missile Agni-IV Test-Fired as Part of User Trial," *Times of India*, (November 09, 2015). http://timesofindia.indiatimes.com/india/Ballistic-missile-Agni-IV-test-fired-as-part-of-user-trial/articleshow/49720522.cms, accessed on September 05, 2017.

either the headlines or the attention of the December 26, 2016 test of the Agni-V, however, from a practical and strategic standpoint, the Agni-IV represents India's most viable deterrent weapon against China until the Agni-V enters full service.[28]

The Agni-IV entered service with the SFC in or around 2014, prior to its first user-associated trial in December 2014. Since that time, it may be assumed that the Agni-IV is in production and given its thus far trouble-free user-trials—three of which have now been conducted—it may also be inferred that the SFC is satisfied with the system and is increasingly comfortable with handling and operating the missile.

The system, being both rail and road mobile, is even more flexible and survivable than the Agni-II. In fact, the Agni-IV is, by virtue of its weight and relative ease of transportation, a versatile delivery system which can be transported more easily than the larger (though much more capable) Agni-V.

The Agni-IV has been fired out to its full revealed range of 4000 km at least twice (September 19, 2012 and January 20, 2014). It was fired out to 3500 km on November 09, 2015 and for about 3000 km on November 15, 2011 and December 02, 2014. With this demonstrated range, Chinese cities such as Beijing and Shanghai come within the range of the Agni-IV even if the missile is sited in Uttar Pradesh or Bihar. The combination of road and rail mobility gives unprecedented flexibility to the Agni-IV.

It is also noteworthy that there have been persistent rumours of a canister-launched version of the Agni-IV being contemplated. As with the Agni-V, a hermetically-sealed canister offers the prospect of keeping the missile ready to fire with a mated warhead. It is hoped that moves in this direction are taken with alacrity with positive indications emerging (the author has seen requests for launcher and canister components) that such a development will not be long in coming, increasing the already impressive flexibility of the Agni-IV.

With respect to warheads, the Agni-IV seems to be deployed with a fusion-boosted-fission weapon with a yield somewhere in the 150–500 kt

28. T. Subramanian, "Agni-IV missile successfully test fired," *The Hindu*, (January 02, 2017). http://www.thehindu.com/news/national/Agni-IV-missile-successfully-test-fired/article16977450.ece, accessed on September 05, 2017

range. Needless to say, this figure is arrived at by some interpretation of comments, but the well-informed nature of these comments makes them impossible to ignore as will be detailed later. It should be noted that the Agni-IV, with a relative nose-cone, would probably not be a viable choice for multiple independently targetable re-entry vehicles (MIRVs).

The Agni-V

While the first two launches of the Agni-V—on April 19, 2012[29] and September 15, 2013[30] respectively—were of the standard Indian uncanisterised missile, following the pattern set with the Agni variants I through IV, the tests on January 31, 2015, December 26, 2016 and on January 18, 2018 were of a canisterised system mounted on a road-mobile platform.[31] According to one report, by the usually well-informed Hemant Kumar Rout, Monday's test was what might be termed a 'contained test fire' to a range of 2500 km, probably at a depressed or lofted trajectory to simulate a longer range.[32] However, some analysis of the NOTAM issued prior to the launch suggests a splashdown zone between 4018 and 5123 km from the launch site. Given the fact that the Agni-V has already demonstrated a range of over 5000 km, this should not be a cause for any concern.

However, what should continue to raise eyebrows is the persistent suggestion, backed by calculations based on flight time, speed and altitude of the Agni-V, that the range of the missile is in reality anywhere between

29. Y. Mallikarjun, AMP and T. Subramanian, "Agni-V Propels India into Elite ICBM Club," *The Hindu*, (April 19, 2012). http://www.thehindu.com/news/national/agniv-propels-india-into-elite-icbm-club/article3330921.ece?homepage=true, accessed on September 05, 2017.

30. "India Test-Fires Agni V with Range as far as China," *Hindustan Times*, (September 16, 2013). http://www.hindustantimes.com/india/india-test-fires-agni-v-with-range-as-far-as-china/story-28IHgfrhxGgUt9XLNPRiwN.html, accessed on September 05, 2017.

31. Y. Mallikarjun and T. Subramanian, "Agni-V's Maiden Canister Trial a Roaring Success," *The Hindu*, (January 31, 2015). http://www.thehindu.com/news/national/maiden-canister-trial-of-agniv-a-roaring-success/article6841942.ece, accessed on September 05, 2017. See also Rajat Pandit, "India test-fires nuclear-capable ICBM Agni-V," *Times of India*, (January 18, 2018). https://timesofindia.indiatimes.com/india/india-test-fires-nuclear-capable-icbm-agni-v/articleshow/62550347.cms, accessed on March 02, 2018.

32. Hemant Kumar Rout, "India successfully test fires Agni-V missile for a reduced range," *New Indian Express*, (December 26, 2016). http://www.newindianexpress.com/nation/2016/dec/26/india-successfully-test-fires-agni-v-missile-for-a-reduced-range-1553219.html, accessed on September 05, 2017.

7500 and 8500 km—as claimed by Chinese analyst Du Wenlong.[33] It would be fair to term the Agni-V an ICBM because the range of 5500 km is the demarcation line between IRBMs and ICBMs in the normal use of the term, reflecting roughly the transatlantic distance between the Iberian Peninsula (or London) and the East Coast of the United States. Is India varying trajectories to simulate much longer ranges? This is a distinct possibility.

The Agni-V is the ultimate evolution of the Agni family so far. It not only combines the road mobility of the Agni-I and Agni-IV with the configuration of the Agni-III but also improves upon the latter redesigning the missile and making great use of maraging steel and composite materials to make the rocket motor. Moreover, improvements in the guidance system reputedly brought down the CEP to 'single-digits'. With these improvements in place, the Agni-V is now ready to enter production and induction into the SFC which will then undertake user trials—starting with 'user-assisted' trials and then, as with the case with Agni variants I-IV, the SFC will then take over subsequent trials.

Sea-Based Missiles

In 2009, the INS Arihant—the lead vessel of a class of at least three ballistic missile submarines (SSBN) was launched. The vessel, still undergoing evaluation and sea trials, although reports of its commissioning in August 2016, is an ambitious attempt to give India an operational and survivable nuclear triad.[34] Many Indian nuclear theorists and strategists have held that a force of SSBNs is essential for India to have a fully survivable nuclear deterrent and the development of the INS Arihant has largely been welcomed as a major step forward.

India is developing two SLBMs—the 750 km range K-15 and the 3500km range K-4 to be deployed aboard the Arihant class of SSBNs. The K-15 underwent at least 12 development trials from a submerged pontoon

---

33. "Agni-V can reach targets 8,000 km away: Chinese expert," *The Hindu*, (April 21, 2012). http://www.thehindu.com/todays-paper/tp-in-school/agniv-can-reach-targets-8000-km-away-chinese-expert/article3337202.ece, accessed on September 05, 2017.

34. Dinakar Peri, "Now, India has a nuclear triad," *The Hindu*, (October 18, 2016). http://www.thehindu.com/news/national/Now-India-has-a-nuclear-triad/article16074127.ece, accessed on September 05, 2017.

aimed at simulating a submarine.[35] However, on November 25, 2015, an unarmed K-15 was purportedly fired from the INS Arihant.[36] It should be stated that this has not yet been confirmed by Indian officials and no photographs have emerged of such a launch from the Arihant.

The K-4 was first tested on March 24, 2014 from a submerged pontoon.[37] Another pontoon launch followed on March 07, 2016.[38] Thereafter, it was reportedly tested from the INS Arihant itself on March 31, 2016.[39] It would be surprising if such a major development was not highlighted in some way but in any event, development of the K-4 is clearly well in progress. Four such missiles are to arm the Arihant class and the K-4 bears a striking resemblance to the land-based Agni-III dimensionally and in respect of its performance. It is to be noted that a pontoon-based test of the K-4 was reportedly aborted on December 17, 2017 after the battery was trained after the launch command was given.[40]

Despite reports of commissioning and submerged K-15 and K-4 missile launches, it is suggested that some degree of caution should be exercised when claiming that an Indian sea-based deterrent is operational. Indeed, it is very questionable whether the INS Arihant is fully commissioned as such an event would most likely be publicised. However, this is a matter of time rather than a question of whether this vessel will be commissioned. This

35. Ananatha Krishna M., "K-15 SLBM is a Beast with Gen-Next Tech," *New Indian Express,* (January 30, 2013). http://www.newindianexpress.com/nation/2013/jan/30/k-15-slbm-is-a-beast-with-gen-next-tech-445756.html

36. Violet Pereira, "N-capable Arihant submarine successfully test-fires unarmed missile," *Magalorean,* (November 26, 2015). http://www.mangalorean.com/n-capable-arihant-submarine-successfully-test-fires-unarmed-missile/, accessed on September 05, 2017.

37. Ankit Panda, "India Inches Closer to Credible Nuclear Triad With K-4 SLBM Test," *The Diplomat,* (May 13, 2014). http://thediplomat.com/2014/05/india-inches-closer-to-credible-nuclear-triad-with-k-4-slbm-test/

38. Franz-Stefan Gady, "India Successfully Tests New Ballistic Missile," *The Diplomat,* (March 22, 2016). http://thediplomat.com/2016/03/india-successfully-tests-new-ballistic-missile/, accessed on September 05, 2017.

39. Hemant Kumar Rout, "EXPRESS EXCLUSIVE: Maiden Test of Undersea K-4 Missile From Arihant Submarine," http://www.newindianexpress.com/nation/2016/apr/09/EXPRESS-EXCLUSIVE-Maiden-Test-of-Undersea-K-4-Missile-From-Arihant-Submarine-921990.html, accessed on September 05, 2017.

40. Manu Pubby, "Setback for Indian missile programme: Two failures in a week, submarine version stuck," *The Print,* (December 24, 2017). https://theprint.in/2017/12/24/setback-for-indian-missile-programme-two-failures-in-a-week-submarine-version-stuck/, accessed on January 10, 2018.

would complete the part of the third leg of India's nuclear triad. It is only when other submarines of the Arihant class are commissioned will India be truly deemed to have completed its subsurface-based nuclear deterrent. Three more such submarines—one of which is the INS Arighat—are in various stages of construction and the launch of the latter reportedly took place on November 19, 2017.[41] It should also be noted that the INS Arihant herself was out of commission for 10 months following an incident caused by sea water ingress following a hatch being left open, leading to fears of reactor contamination. Following checks, the vessel has returned to service.[42]

It may be in order to add a word on the possibility of India deploying a surface-ship-based deterrent. It is noted that at least two of the Indian navy's very lightly armed Sukanya class off-shore patrol vessels (OPVs)—the INS Subhadra and the INS Suvarna—have been fitted with storage, elevation and launching mechanisms for the Dhanush missile with a 350-km range.[43] The Dhanush is a ship-launched version of the Prithvi surface-to-surface missile and it is possible that its range could be enhanced by using a reduced payload warhead. However, while it is certainly conceivable that the Dhanush could be a viable nuclear delivery system, the Sukanya class OPVs are a decidedly odd choice for an operation launch platform being very weakly armed to the extent of being completely unable to defend themselves against even moderate levels of naval or air attack—being best suited to the maritime constabulary role. Rather, it is suggested that the Dhanush system provided the Indian navy and Defence Research and Development Organisation an opportunity to develop elevation, stabilisation and launch mechanisms at sea. This may have aided in the development of both the K-15 and K-4 systems.

41. Sandeep Unnithan, "From India Today magazine: A Peek into India's Top Secret and Costliest Defence Project, Nuclear Submarines," *India Today*, (December 07, 2017). http://indiatoday.intoday.in/story/india-ballistic-missile-submarine-k-6-submarine-launched-drdo/1/1104982.html, accessed on January 10, 2018.

42. Manu Pubby, "India's Only Nuclear-Armed Submarine is Back in the Water after Contamination Fears," *The Print*, (January 08, 2018). https://theprint.in/2018/01/08/indias-only-nuclear-armed-submarine-ins-arihant-is-back-in-the-water/, accessed on January 10, 2018.

43. "Indian Navy successfully test fires Dhanush missile: All you need to know," *India Today*, (November 26, 2015). http://indiatoday.intoday.in/education/story/dhanush/1/531950.html, accessed on September 05, 2017.

Furthermore, the Dhanush proved a useful target missile for India's ballistic missile defence system's early tests.

Cruise Missiles

Besides its ballistic missiles, India has a cruise missile program which, when completed, would give the country another option for the delivery of nuclear warheads. It must be clarified that India's cruise missile projects have to be divided into two—the BrahMos supersonic system and the Nirbhay subsonic system. While there have been multiple reports of the BrahMos being nuclear capable and/or fitted with a 20 kt warhead, it is suggested that this may not be entirely accurate—although the potential certainly exists for such an event.[44] Indeed, the BrahMos is set to experience something of a transformation. Initially claimed to be a 290-km-range missile, India's accession to the Missile Technology Control Regime enabled the system to be tested to its full range of 450 km against both land and sea targets. It is anticipated that a longer-ranged BrahMos—perhaps capable of ranges of up to 900 km—will be developed in air, sea and land-launched versions. It is possible that a nuclear warhead could be developed for such an extended range version although the principle task of the BrahMos would be a long-range precision attack.[45]

The Nirbhay, however, is intended to be nuclear capable, although it will also be an important component for convention payload delivery. It is India's first strategic cruise missile with a range exceeding 1000 km with a speed of between 0.8 and 0.9 Mach (speed of sound) with a launch weight of 1500 kg and a length of 6 m. The payload size of the missile is not yet known but there is speculation that it would be capable of carrying either conventional or nuclear warheads of 24 different types. It is intended to fly at very low altitudes of 20 m or less to evade radar detection using a terrain-following function which enables it to use mapped contours of the ground for both concealment and updating its inertial navigation system.

In contrast to ballistic missiles, cruise missiles can be cheaper, are much slower and use a different flight path entirely. They are also more flexible as, in the South Asian context, ballistic missiles are inextricably linked to

---

44. Karnad, n.8, p.82
45. Shiv Aroor, "'True' BrahMos Unleashed Today, Next 900-km Weapon," *Livefist Defence.* https://www.livefistdefence.com/2017/03/true-brahmos-unleashed-today-next-1000-km-weapon.html, accessed on September 05, 2017.

nuclear weapons and as such cruise missiles attract much less attention, making them useable weapons for the delivery of conventional warheads while retaining the ability to carry a nuclear payload.

Compared to the BrahMos missile already in service, the Nirbhay is longer-ranged (1000km + vs 290km) but slower and the BrahMos is considerably longer (8.4 m) and heavier (3000 kg). However, while the BrahMos is intended to cruise at higher altitudes and then complete its terminal run to target at a very low altitude of 10–15 m, the Nirbhay can complete much of its flight at these lower altitudes. The Nirbhay also has the ability to loiter and to pick out and engage a specific target in a multiple target environment.[46] In addition, it is very unlikely that the BrahMos has, at this stage, any ability to carry a nuclear warhead—its manufacturers specify a conventional payload only—although there has been some informed comment to the contrary. The Nirbhay has been tested four times to date with three tests being failures and the other being termed either a partial or complete success depending on which report is read:

The First Test

On March 12, 2013, when the missile took off from the launch pad successfully and reached the second stage of propulsion, travelling 15 minutes along its predicted path, it covered 30 percent of its intended 1000 km at a speed of 0.7 Mach. It then veered away from its trajectory forcing the missile to be destroyed in mid-flight. On this occasion, it was suggested that the fault was a defect in the inertial navigation system.[47]

The Second Test

On October 17, 2014, the second test of the missile was much more successful. All the test parameters were purportedly met and the missile completed all 15 waypoints. The missile covered a distance of more than 1000 km in a flight that lasted for over 1 hour and 10 minutes. It is to be noted though that the

46. T.S. Subramanian, "Nirbhay Likely to be Test-Fired in April," *The Hindu,* (March 07, 2012). http://www.thehindu.com/todays-paper/tp-national/nirbhay-likely-to-be-testfired-in-april/article2968219.ece, accessed on September 05, 2017.

47. Y. Mallikarjun and T. Subramanian, "Nirbhay Strays from Flight Path, Aborted," *The Hindu,* (March 12, 2013). http://www.thehindu.com/news/national/nirbhay-strays-from-flight-path-aborted/article4500527.ece, accessed on September 05, 2017.

missile did not manoeuvre as desired at low altitude. While the missile test was, therefore largely successful, it was not an unqualified success and should have raised questions about the missile's low-altitude performance. Yet, the test demonstrated the core capability of the Nirbhay missile.[48]

The Third Test

The third test of the missile took place on October 16, 2015. The missile was to be tested for its low-flying capability being brought down from 4800 to 20 m gradually and in stages. All initial critical operations such as booster ignition, booster separation, wing deployment and engine start were successfully executed and Nirbhay reached the desired cruise altitude. However, 11 minutes into the flight, after covering only 128 km, the missile crashed into the Bay of Bengal.[49]

The Fourth Test

The fourth test of the missile took place on December 21, 2016. Once again, there was a successful booster ignition and launch. Less than 4 minutes after lift-off, the missile veered off its intended trajectory and outside the safety zone, leading to it being destroyed in-flight. Initial reports suggest the flight control hardware and software failed to actuate the missile control services and that the engine lost thrust 2 minutes after takeoff.[50] The suggestion emerged that this test was rushed and did not follow advice.

The Fifth Test

Apparently stung by criticism that the third and fourth tests were rushed, the fifth test of the missile took place on November 07, 2017. This time the test was successful. The DRDO press release indicated that:[51]

48. "India Test-Fires Nuclear-Capable Nirbhay Cruise Missile," *Times of India*, (October 17, 2014). http://timesofindia.indiatimes.com/india/India-test-fires-nuclear-capable-Nirbhay-cruise-missile/articleshow/44845526.cms, accessed on September 05, 2017.

49. "Nirbhay, India's Indigenous Cruise Missile, Fails Test Midway," *NDTV*, (October 16, 2015). http://www.ndtv.com/india-news/nirbhay-indias-indigenous-cruise-missile-fails-midway-1233086, accessed on September 05, 2017.

50. T. S. Subramanian, "Nirbhay Missile Test 'an utter failure'," *The Hindu*, (December 21, 2016). http://www.thehindu.com/news/national/Nirbhay-missile-test-%E2%80%9Can-utter-failure%E2%80%9D/article16915750.ece, accessed on September 05, 2017.

51. "DRDO Conducts Successful Flight Trial of 'NIRBHAY' Sub-Sonic Cruise Missile," *Press Information Bureau*, (November 07, 2017). http://pib.nic.in/newsite/PrintRelease.aspx?relid=173291, accessed on November 07, 2017.

"The missile took-off in the programmed manner and all critical operations viz. launch phase, booster deployment, engine start, wing deployment and other operational parameters demonstrated through autonomous way point navigation. The guidance, control and navigation system of the missile is configured around the indigenously designed Ring Laser Gyroscope (RLG) and MEMS based Inertial Navigation System (INS) along with GPS system. The missile majestically cruised for a total time duration of 50 minutes, achieving the range of 647 km. The missile was tracked with the help of ground based radars and other parameters were monitored by indigenous telemetry stations developed by DRDO."

With this successful test, it is hoped that eventually, the Agni family will be joined by nuclear-armed versions of the Nirbhay cruise missile and the K-15 and K-4 SLBMs. It is interesting that India has developed, on a tight budget, without much fanfare or any significant degree of boasting, all the components for a viable, survivable and effective nuclear triad with all technical obstacles being overcome in a systematic manner.

Numbers of Missiles

Two issues frequently escape discussion when dealing with India's missile arsenal—quantities and production capacity.

The strength of the Agni missile force is obviously a closely guarded secret. It has been suggested that 334 and 335 missile groups which operate the Agni-1 and Agni-II missiles respectively, possess 8–12 TELs each. While it has been stated that another group has been raised on the Agni-III, its designation is unknown and whether the TELs are accompanied by vehicles which carry reload missiles is equally unclear. It would be very odd if the total production of Agni missiles still remained in the low single digits per annum. It is in light of Dr. S. Christopher's comments about the 2015 production meeting that only 20 percent of requirements is significant.[52] Though Dr. Christopher went on to indicate that production of the Agni-I and Agni-II missiles would be increased, the fact is that there appears to be

---

52. "India to Join ICBM Club Soon—Interview with Dr. S. Christopher," *NDTV,* (July 11, 2015). http://www.ndtv.com/video/news/news/india-to-join-icbm-club-soon-374683, accessed on September 07, 2017.

a significant disconnect between production and SFC requirements. As was noted earlier, as early as 1998, directions were given to prepare production for up to 12 Agni missiles per annum.[53]

Quantities of missiles seem to still be a mystery. American assessments suggest in the cases of the Agni-II and Agni-III systems, fewer than 10 launchers are operational. This may be on the basis of early reports suggesting that each missile group was to have only eight launchers.[54] This may not be accurate as these numbers do not consider road-mobile variants of the Agni-II and Agni-III nor do the numbers consider missiles and launchers that are kept in storage.

It has been suggested that at least two Agni-II missile trains are operational—perhaps with as many as eight launchers each.[55] Dr. Bharat Karnad argues that from the Agni-III onwards, the systems would not be rail-deployed but stored in hardened mountain tunnel complexes. This would make considerable sense to further reduce detection and also to enhance survivability.[56] It might be expected that ready-use and stored missiles would be so accommodated. Given the fact that at least two such complexes are already functioning, the conditions of storage and the maintenance of stored missiles must be examined on a continuous basis.[57]

To date, there have been twelve Agni-II tests, more than a dozen Agni-I tests, eight Agni-III tests and eight Agni-IV tests. As noted earlier, India has had the habit of initiating the deployment of missiles after three successful technical trials. Extrapolating production from these tests is problematic. If it is assumed that production commenced after the third

---

53. Op. cit. n. 16. The only other indication of production levels came in an interview Dr. Saraswat gave in 2012 to India Today where he said, "All I can tell you is that we will produce more than just 1 or 2 missiles a year." Sandeep Unnithan, "India has all the building blocks for an anti-satellite capability," *India Today*, (April 27, 2012). http://indiatoday.intoday.in/story/agni-v-drdo-chief-dr-vijay-kumar-saraswat-interview/1/186248.html, accessed on September 20, 2017.

54. "Ballistic and Cruise Missile Threat 2017," *Defense Intelligence Ballistic Missile Analysis Committee* http://www.nasic.af.mil/Portals/19/images/Fact%20Sheet%20Images/2017%20Ballistic%20and%20Cruise%20Missile%20Threat_Final_small.pdf?ver=2017-07-21-083234-343, p. 25

55. Karnad, n. 8, p. 101.

56. Ibid., pp. 101–102

57. Bharat Karnad, *Why India is not a Great Power (Yet)* (New Delhi: Oxford University Press, 2015), p. 375.

successful technical trial and that user trials would not involve testing more than one in five of any production batch, then it might be suggested that production of each type exceeds twenty missiles. This might also tally with the rough estimates available for the number of warheads held by India—if it is speculated that between twenty and two dozen of each of the Agni I through IV variants are in service to date, this would give India a deployable strength of perhaps 96 land-based missiles. Given that some estimates (which will be discussed in the following section) put the number of Indian nuclear warheads at between 110 and 130, the figure of 96 land-based ballistic missiles is not implausible—leaving room for aircraft-delivered weapons to be included in the overall total of deliverable warheads.

It is suggested that a conservative estimate of India's missile arsenal is as follows:[58]

- Agni-1: 1 Group with 12 launchers and 24 missiles,
- Agni-2: 1 Group with 12 launchers and 24 missiles,
- Agni-3: 1 Group with 12 launchers and 24 missiles,
- Agni-4: 1 Group with 12 launchers and 24 missiles with another 12 launchers and 24 missiles on order,
- Agni-5: 1 Group with 12 launchers with 24 missiles with another 12 launchers and 24 missiles on order.

Reliability of Missiles and Adequacy of Testing

While to date, user trials of the Agni-I, III and IV have been successful, the Agni-II has suffered three user trial failures despite its successful technical flight stage. The inevitable question that arises is whether the Agni-II was rushed into production after only three technical flights with the attendant question that arises is regarding the other missiles of the Agni family.

---

58. This is extrapolated on an estimated production of 1-2 missiles per year for the Agni-I and Agni-II post-developmental trials and a somewhat higher rate for the Agni-III and IV with Limited Series Production for the Agni-V assumed to have been started. The anticipated 48 launchers each for Agni-IV and -V have been gleaned from interviews and from a documentary on Transport Solutions India Limited which noted that a contract for forty-eight trailers—one for each Agni-V missile intended to be produced—was issued in 2015. See "Make In India— New Deal For Defence—Transport Solutions India, Episode 9, Segment 1," YouTube video, from 7:20 minutes onwards. https://www.youtube.com/watch?v=LIaQ3nOGmEI&t=640s (Accessible only to Indian users or through a VPN), accessed on March 19, 2018. It is also known that at least 16 Agni-V launchers are on order – see *DRDO Annual Report 2016 p. 39*

It is submitted that this is not necessarily the case. Depending on the type of missile, technical trials are to establish the performance parameters of the system. Once this has been established, there is no reason why production cannot commence, provided that tests from production batches are conducted to confirm the performance. The development of computer simulation also helps reduce the number of dynamic technical trials which are inevitably expensive to conduct. The Russian Federation has followed this development path with its RS-24 and RS-26 ICBMs being placed into production after two to three successful developmental flights with the RT-2PM2 ICBM being placed on experimental combat duty after only a single test.[59]

India's testing of missiles follows guidelines established in 2002 after a statistical analysis by the former chairman of ISRO, K. Kasturirangan, who conducted statistical analysis of failures of major systems, components and subsystems plus their performance in static tests. His conclusion was that 2–3 consecutive successful test-firings would meet the standards of reliability within the constraints of affordability.[60]

In the Indian context, where the production run of the Agni-II is unlikely to exceed 24 to date, the luxury of 10 or more technical trials is impractical. Moreover, given the fact that DRDO has very limited production facilities, simply obtaining sufficient missiles for 10+ technical trials requires putting the missile into production.

Of greater importance must be issues concerning the production and storage of the Agni-II inventory. Given the fact that the Agni-II has been in production for the longest period of time and missiles of this type would have spent the longest time in storage, there will inevitably be cause for concern on the part of the SFC.

The Agni-V is reportedly due to be followed by the Agni-VI which would have an even greater range and MIRVs.[61] In addition, a successor to the Prithvi and Agni-1, right now termed the Agni-1P, using technology

59. Robert S. Norris and William M. Arkin, "Russian Nuclear Forces," *Bulletin of the Atomic Scientists*, vol. 56, no. 4, 2000. https://www.highbeam.com/doc/1G1-63794409.html, accessed on September 05, 2017.

60. Karnad, n. 8, n. 114, p. 83.

61. Rajat Pandit, "Agni-V with China in Range Tested; Next in Line is Agni-VI, with Multiple Warheads," *Times of India*, (December 27, 2016). http://timesofindia.indiatimes.com/india/agni-v-with-china-in-range-tested-next-in-line-is-agni-vi-with-multiple-warheads/articleshow/56191362.cms, accessed on September 07, 2017.

from the Agni-IV is being designed.[62] It is hoped that these two projects will be pursued with alacrity and intensity.

What does the Agni saga tell us about the Indian ballistic missile program? Unlike almost any other DRDO project, the IRBM/MRBM/ICBM program has followed a path of constant product development and phased capability enhancement. This has meant that there is now a strong foundation in both design and systems engineering in respect of ballistic missiles with fabrication and construction facilities being able to deliver materials and products of sufficient quality. There has been a steady path of technological achievement—replacing liquid fuels with solid, improved guidance systems for accuracy and improved materials for lighter weights and greater ranges. While there have been delays and failures, the DRDO ballistic missile program has done remarkably well on a limited budget.

Two other missiles are worthy of mention—the hypersonic Shaurya canister-launched missile which was tested three times between 2008 and 2011—and the tactical support missile Prahaar which was tested in 2011. The Shaurya is purportedly a land-based version of the K-15 SLBM and offers a useful replacement for the Agni-1 as it covers ranges up to 700 km.[63] The Prahaar is perhaps the ideal replacement for the Prithvi SS-150—offering greater mobility, matching range and inherently greater flexibility.[64]

Despite the Shaurya and Prahaar offering distinct advantages over the existing Agni-1 and Prithvi SS-150 missiles, it is unclear as to whether either missile has entered production, much less induction into India's armed forces. Following its 2011 test, there was some indication that Shaurya was entering production but this is as yet unclear.[65]

---

62. Ajai Shukla, "New-Age Agni to boost Pak-Focused Nuclear Deterrent," *Business Standard*, (December 17, 2016). http://www.business-standard.com/article/economy-policy/new-age-agni-to-boost-pak-focused-nuclear-deterrent-116121601111_1.html, accessed on September 07, 2017.

63. T. Subramanian and Y. Mallikarjun, "India successfully Test-Fires Shourya Missile," *The Hindu*, (September 24, 2011). http://www.thehindu.com/sci-tech/science/india-successfully-testfires-shourya-missile/article2482010.ece, accessed on September 07, 2017.

64. "Prithvi Missiles to be Replaced by More-Capable Prahar: DRDO," *The Hindu Business Line*, (June 30, 2013). http://www.thehindubusinessline.com/news/prithvi-missiles-to-be-replaced-by-morecapable-prahar-drdo/article4866081.ece, accessed on September 07, 2017.

65. Subramanian and Mallikarjun, n. 63.

India's Warheads

Just as India's delivery vehicles can be divided into the manned aircraft and the ballistic/cruise missile categories, India's warheads must also be divided intending to be low-yield weapons for use against tactical targets and larger-yield strategic systems.

India's nuclear warheads are the subject of intense and often, contradictory speculation exists with experts such as Dr. Ashley Tellis being vociferous in suggesting only 15–20 kt warheads are deployed and deemed reliable. However, Professor Bharat Karnad, in some of his comprehensive work on the subject, notes that 100 kt fission weapons had been produced as early as the 1980s.[66] This would suggest that weapons in the range of 15–100 kt would be the main service types for the Indian nuclear arsenal, air or missile based.[67] The fact that the Indian government has officially only indicated that yields of 200 kt are deployable should not, especially considering the probability that 100 kt fission weapons being in existence, be doubted.[68]

It should also be stated that the yield of a weapon need not mean that it is fission, fusion-boosted-fission or fusion. The largest deployed fission weapon was the Mk.18 gravity bomb which, weighing some 8600 pounds, had a yield of 500 kt. Using some 60 kg of highly enriched uranium, 90 of these weapons were produced before being replaced by fusion weapons and converted into lower yield systems.[69] Outside the United States, the French deployed the 70-kt AN-22 fission bomb which weighed a mere 700 kg and the MR-31 fission warhead which armed S-2 IRBMs, which while also weighing 700 kg, had a yield of 120 kt.[70]

There is some anecdotal evidence for India developing fission weapons approaching these French weapons in yield. Indications are that the first Indian nuclear weapons design had a mass of about 1000 kg with a yield

66. Karnad, n. 2.
67. Ibid., p. 376.
68. "India capable of Building Nuke Deterrence upto 200 kilotons: Kakodkar," *Deccan Herald,* (September 24, 2009). http://www.deccanherald.com/content/27047/india-capable-building-nuke-, accessed on September 07, 2017..
69. Nuclear Weapon Archive, "Complete List of All U.S. Nuclear Weapons," ,http://nuclearweaponarchive.org/Usa/Weapons/Allbombs.html, accessed on September 19, 2017.
70. Nuclear Weapon Archive, "France's Nuclear Weapons: Development of the French Arsenal," http://nuclearweaponarchive.org/France/FranceArsenalDev.html, accessed on September 19, 2017.

of 12–15 kt. However, subsequently, perhaps by 1982 (when rumours of a fresh round of nuclear tests were being circulated), the said weapon had been scaled down to a more manageable mass of between 170 and 200 kg.[71] Later, it appears that a 100-kt fission weapon was produced for aerial delivery with a mass of 200–300 kg.[72] If this is accurate, it would mean that India had perfected a relatively high-yield fission weapon with a relatively low mass for its class. One would expect that missile warheads of similar designs and yields would be feasible.

With respect to boosted-fission weapons, the largest tested, to date, was the 720-kt Orange Herald device tested by the United Kingdom in 1957.[73] Given the fact that it is suggested that the fusion boosting failed to increase the yield, it is unclear whether this should be referred to as the largest fission bomb tested or the largest fusion-boosted-fission tested weapon.[74] The French had rather more success with deploying fusion-boosted-fission weapons with the 700-kg, 500-kt MR-41 warhead which armed the M1 and M2 SLBMs.[75]

That India might have fielded such fusion-boosted-fission weapons is borne out in two interesting sets of statements. Firstly, Admiral Arun Prakash in 2009 (at the height of the controversy generated by Dr. Santhanam's statements on the 1998 tests) stated:[76]

In the midst of the current brouhaha, we need to retain clarity on one issue; given that deuterium tritium boosted-fission weapons can generate yields of 200–500 kt, the credibility of India's nuclear deterrent is not in the slightest doubt.

71. Perkovich, n. 1.
72. Karnad, n. 2.
73. Nuclear Weapon Archive, "Britain's Nuclear Weapons: British Nuclear Testing," http://nuclearweaponarchive.org/Uk/UKTesting.html, accessed on September 19, 2017.
74. Visual Reverence, "Orange Herald," http://visualreverence.tumblr.com/post/85541430823/orange-herald-was-a-fusion-boosted, accessed on September 19, 2017.
75. Op.cit. n. 70.
76. Arun Prakash, "Strategic Policy Making and the Indian System," *Maritime Affairs* vol. 5, no.2, Winter 2009, pp. 22–31. On p. 22 Admiral Prakash responded to a query by the author by stating that weapons in the 200–500 kiloton yield were part of the Indian arsenal and assertions that India's reliable arsenal was limited to 20–25 kiloton weapons was "inaccurate by an order of magnitude".

More recently, an even more interesting comment was made by Dr. Avinash Chander in 2011 to the Business Standard newspaper in which he said: [77]

"Now we talk of [accuracy of] a few hundred metres. That allows a smaller warhead, perhaps 150-250 kilotons, to cause substantial damage."

To discount these two statements coming from two totally different perspectives—one by a former Chairman, Chiefs of Staff Committee and the other by the former Director-General DRDO—would be folly to say the least and could lead any analysis of India's nuclear arsenal to fall into serious error. The Indian design team has admitted that the trigger in the Shakti-1 thermonuclear device tested in 1998 was a fusion-boosted-fission device.[78] It should be noted that even a noted sceptic like Dr. Bharat Karnad, notes that India's boosted-fission capability is significantly more reliable than its thermonuclear capability.[79]

From the data gleaned from the French fission and boosted fission designs, it is clear that the weight of such weapons at even higher yields fits in easily with India's Agni family of missiles which have payloads ranging from 1000 to 1500 kg. Dr. Karnad asserts that Agni-I has been optimised for a 20–30-kt warhead, the Agni-II for a 90–150-kt warhead and the Agni-III for a 300-kt warhead.[80] However, issue should be taken with the first named missile as a 20–30 kt warhead ought not to approach 1000 kg (which is the payload of the Agni-I) and which runs counter to the reduced weight of both the 15–20-kt and 100-kt fission weapons

77. Ajai Shukla, "India Launches 5,000-km Range Agni-5 Missile Successfully," *Business Standard,* (April 20, 2012). http://www.business-standard.com/article/economy-policy/india-launches-5-000-km-range-agni-5-missile-successfully-112042002020_1.html, accessed on September 07, 2017.
78. Press Information Bureau, "Press Statement by Dr. Anil Kakodkar and Dr. R. Chidambaram on Pokhran-II tests," (September 24, 2009). http://pib.nic.in/newsite/PrintRelease.aspx?relid=52814, accessed on September 20, 2017. See also Press Information Bureau, "Pokhran—II Tests were Fully Successful; Given India Capability to build Nuclear Deterrence: Dr. Kakodkar and Dr. Chidambaram," (September 24, 2009 http://pib.nic.in/newsite/PrintRelease.aspx?relid=52813, accessed on September 20, 2017.
79. Karnad, n. 8, p. 68.
80. Ibid., p. 78.

developed in the 1980s.[81] Rather it is likely that the Agni-I has the same warhead as the Agni-II and is deployed with a warhead in the 150-kt range.

Does India Have or Need Thermonuclear Weapons?

The question as to whether India has any deployed thermonuclear weapons is a question that inevitably brings the disputed yield of the Shakti-1 thermonuclear test to the fore. This has sharply divided opinions among analysts with allegations, rebuttals and unfortunate forays into character assassination becoming part of the discussion. Rather more unfortunate is the tendency of aggressive Western advocates of containing or capping the Indian nuclear weapons program to use the disputed thermonuclear yield to one time ridicule India's capability while simultaneously pushing for more aggressive action aimed at coercing India.

If some Indian analysts are to be believed, thermonuclear weapons with yields of between 125 and 175 kt are readied for deployment.[82] However, there is little doubt that the controversy over the success of the Shakti-1 test would cause the user to have doubts as to the efficacy of these designs. This is further compounded by the fact that unlike fission or even boosted-fission weapons, the physics involved in the manufacture and development of thermonuclear weapons does not lend itself to single-test perfection of an entire scalable range of weapons design. This would inevitably mean that for India's SFC to be confident in the yield of these weapons, a resumption of nuclear testing would be required. The corollary to this would be that India might not be sufficiently confident to deploy such weapons.

However, Dr. Anil Kakodkar, former Chairman of the Atomic Energy Commission, in an interview with Karan Thapar of CNN-IBN, categorically stated that India had thermonuclear weapons. The text of part of that interview gives a different perspective:[83]

---

81. Perkovich and Karnad, n. 1 and n. 2.
82. Karnad, n. 57, p. 370.
83. "Use plural, India has thermonuclear bombs: Kakodkar," *CNN-IBN Interview Transcript*, December 13, 2009.

Karan Thapar: Let me put to you two or three critical issues. Given the fact that you have concluded several reviews, including one recently after the doubts were raised, the doubts continue. And given that there are doubts about India's one and only thermonuclear test do we need more tests?

Anil Kakodkar: Well, I would say no because the important point to note is that the thermo nuclear test, the fission test and the sub-kilotonne test all worked as designed. They are diverse.

In terms of detailed design, their content is quite different. And so we think that the design which has been done is validated and within this configuration which has been tested one can build devices ranging from low kilotonne all the way to 200 kilotonnes. And that kind of fully assures the deterrence.

Karan Thapar: You are saying that India doesn't need more thermonuclear tests but the truth is that all the established thermonuclear powers needed more than one test. Can India be the exception?

Anil Kakodkar: Well if you go by Dil Maange More, that's another story. But we are talking about a time where the knowledge base has expanded, the capability has expanded and you carry out a design and prove you are confident that on the basis of that design and that test, one can build a range of systems right up to 200 kilotonnes.

Karan Thapar: I want to pick up on that last point that you have just made. Given that doubts continue and given that there are going to be no further tests and you are not saying that there is any need for further tests—can you say India has a credible thermonuclear bomb?

Anil Kakodkar: Of course.

Karan Thapar: We have a credible thermonuclear bomb?

Anil Kakodkar: Why are you using singular? Make that plural.

Karan Thapar: The reason I ask is because Dr Santhanam writing in 'The Hindu' says that the thermonuclear device has not been weaponised even 11 years after the tests.

Anil Kakodkar: How does he know? He is not involved.

Karan Thapar: So you are saying to me that we have thermonuclear bombs—in the plural?

Anil Kakodkar: Yes.

Karan Thapar: With a yield of at least 45 kilotonnes each.

Anil Kakodkar: Much more than that.

Karan Thapar: Much more than that?

Anil Kakodkar: Yes. I told you we have the possibility of a deterrence of low kilotonne to 200 kilotonnes.

Karan Thapar: So when people like former Army chief, General Malik say, that because of the doubts in the public arena, the Army wants assurance of the yield and the efficacy of India's thermonuclear bomb, what is your answer to them?

Anil Kakodkar: I think that is guaranteed. The Army should be fully confident and defend the country. There is no issue about the arsenal at their command.

In effect, Dr. Kakdokar was indicating that the thermonuclear design had been weaponised and that the user could have confidence in its reliability. The question is whether these assurances are sufficient or the relationship between the warhead designer, the delivery system designer and the user sufficiently integrated to give the latter faith in those assurances. In this regard, an interesting anecdote is narrated by Dr. Karnad to indicate that the relationship between the warhead designers and the missile designers has improved to the point where, over a decade ago, S. K. Sikka, who was head of the thermonuclear weapons project was asked to reduce the diameter of a weapon intended to be fitted on an Agni variant by 5cm. His ready compliance with the same was deemed indicative of an improved relationship between design teams.[84]

Despite the credibility of the Indian deterrent being unaffected by a compromised thermonuclear capability, it is submitted that the development of thermonuclear weapons is an essential part of Indian weapons development, not to ensure the credibility of the deterrent but to make it more flexible. Thermonuclear weapons need not have higher yields than either fission or boosted-fission weapons—the French TN-75 fitted to the M45 SLBM having a yield of 100 kt—but they are inevitably lighter, with the 300-kt TN-80/81 warhead of the ASMP missile weighing a mere 200 kg.[85]

---

84. Karnad, n. 8, p. 82.
85. Op.cit. n. 70.

Thermonuclear weapons, relying on fusion for the majority of their yield, the primaries of fusion weapons can often use smaller quantities of fissile materials. Moreover if, as India has done, a fusion-boosted-fission primary is used, then the possibility of a variable yield weapon can be considered. Indeed, shortly after the 1998 tests, Dr. Frank Barnaby, writing in *Janes Defence Weekly*, suggested that an operational nuclear weapon could have variable yields of 5, 50 and 500 kt.[86] Such flexibility to obviate the need for India to maintain a separate inventory of fission weapons is to provide lower-yield options alongside the larger fusion-boosted-fission weapons.

Furthermore, if India is considering multiple warheads for its missiles—the purported Agni-VI for example—then the light weight of thermonuclear weapons would be essential.[87] For example, to accommodate six warheads, the French M4A and M4B SLBMs used M70/71 warheads which each had a weight of less than 200 kg and 175 kg respectively, but allowed each warhead to have a yield of 150 kt.[88] This model has also been followed by the British for their Trident D-5 SLBM force.[89]

Warhead Options?

To date, some twenty years after the 1998 nuclear tests, India has shown no inclination to resume nuclear testing. With this limitation what are India's warhead options?

Large fission weapons—in excess of 50 kt and up to, as Professor Karnad suggests, 100 kt—would perhaps involve the use of too much fissile material. While India's fission design capabilities are easily its most reliable, its fissile stocks might militate against opting for this route. Rather, there seems to be little doubt that the boosted-fission primary of the Shakti-1 test worked satisfactorily. In light of this, it is submitted that India's larger-yield weapons would be of the boosted-fission type. As

---

86. Frank Barnaby, "Trials provide data for range of weapon yields," *Jane's Defence Weekly,* May 27, 1998, p. 3.

87. "MIRVs to Make India's 'Agni' ICBM More Potent," *Sputnik,* (December 27, 2016). https://sputniknews.com/asia/201612271049036303-india-ballistic-missile/, accessed on September 19, 2017.

88. Op.cit. n. 70.

89. Nuclear Weapon Archive, "Britain's Nuclear Weapons: History of the British Nuclear Arsenal," http://nuclearweaponarchive.org/Uk/UKArsenalDev.html, accessed on September 19, 2017.

noted above, both Admiral Prakash and Dr. Chander suggest weapons with yields in the 150–250 kt range. It is also known that the payload capacity of the Agni series of missiles hovers between 1000 and 1500 kg. This relatively large payload for a monolith warhead would perhaps suggest that these missiles are indeed fitted with boosted-fission warheads. While it is true that boosted-fission warheads can achieve yields of 500 kt, the Indian nuclear establishment has claimed only yields of 200 kt since 1998, thus perhaps indicating an upper limit on the yield of India's deployed boosted-fission arsenal though not precluding the development and deployment of higher yield designs.

India has also examined the possibility of deploying MIRVs on later variants of the Agni family. A new missile—the Agni-VI will apparently test India's first MIRVs. However, deploying MIRVs will raise additional issues—namely, whether or not the number of launchers is adequate to ensure survivability. Insufficient numbers of launchers and missiles would lead to a disproportionate loss of warheads if MIRVs are deployed without a commensurate increase in the number of deployed missiles.

The choice for India is to find the correct compromise between both the advantages offered by MIRVed missiles and the requirement for larger numbers of missiles—albeit with single warheads. Whatever choice is made, India should increase the number of deployed missiles for credibility and survivability. MIRVs will place additional strain on the stocks of India's fissile materials and as such, the deployment of MIRVs will require India to increase its stocks of fissile materials and to increase its production of warheads. This may be part of the reason why India may be seeking thermonuclear weapons as, though there is no reason why fission or fusion-boosted-fission weapons can not be deployed as MIRVs, the yield of the fission weapons so employed would be limited and as fusion-boosted-fission weapons would inevitably be much bulkier for their given yield than thermonuclear weapons, it is debatable whether it is practical to use them in MIRVs.

Mated or De-Mated Warheads

For nearly a decade, the debate over whether India maintains a stock of fully mated nuclear warheads has been raging. Some analysts have suggested India's deterrent is "recessed". While this may have been true in the past,

India is reaching the stage where a deployed force of warheads mated to missiles is becoming increasingly likely. In 2003, a BBC report suggested that India would take between 8 and 12 hours to mate its warheads and retaliate to a first strike.[90] However, since then, with the creation of the SFC and a more streamlined process, it is probable that India does not need such a long period of time. Dr. Karnad suggested that, in 2008, part of the Indian arsenal was de-mated but a portion is in a "near-mated condition and almost operational".[91]

India could take this concept further and move towards a partially mated force with a limited number of weapons fully mated and either in a secure storage or deployed on patrol. In the alternative, mated systems could be kept stored and loaded on launchers on a rotating basis. As has been noted above, India is moving towards inducting canister-launched versions of the Agni-V and SLBMs aboard the Arihant class of SSBNs. It is also widely assumed that a canister launched version of the Agni-IV will eventually enter service. India's arsenal would then consist almost entirely of ready-to-fire missiles. With the submarine force, this will inevitably bring about issues of command and control and launch authorisation which were dealt with earlier.

Canister-launched missiles are effectively always in a ready-to-fire configuration which would make de-mated warheads completely impractical. This is even more so in the case of SLBMs which would require their warheads to be mated in advance before deterrent patrols. In both cases, challenges will emerge for refining command and control systems. An alternative deployment practice could be adopted for the land-based Agni missiles, whereby a proportion of de-mated missiles and warheads—perhaps even the majority of stock are kept stored in hardened facilities with only a limited number on patrol. This could allow India to minimise the costs of keeping fully operational systems while retaining the survivability and flexibility of its mobile, canister-launched systems. Whether this semi-recessed approach finds favour is as yet unknown but the option does offer some advantages and circumstantial evidence on the existence of hardened

---

90. Humphrey Hawksley, "India's Nuclear Muscle," *BBC World Service,* (January 11, 2003). http://news.bbc.co.uk/2/hi/south_asia/2646979.stm, accessed on September 18, 2017.

91. Karand, n. 8, p. 99.

mountain complexes for such systems which suggests that this is a distinct possibility.

In 2013, Shyam Saran, then a member of India's national security advisory board, made the following remarks:[92]

> If we look at the current status of India's nuclear deterrent and its command and control system, it is clear that at least two legs of the triad referred to in our nuclear doctrine are already in place. These include a modest arsenal, nuclear capable aircraft and missiles both in fixed underground silos as well as those which are mounted on mobile rail and road-based platforms. These land-based missiles include both Agni-II (1500 km) as well as Agni-III (2500 km) missiles. The range and accuracy of further versions for example, Agni V (5000 km) which was tested successfully only recently, will improve with the acquisition of further technological capability and experience. The third leg of the triad which is submarine-based, is admittedly a work in progress. We need at least three Arihant class nuclear submarines so that at least one will always be at sea. Submarine-based missiles systems have been developed and tested in the form of the Sagarika but these are still relatively short in range. It is expected that a modest sea-based deterrence will be in place by 2015 or 2016. There is also a major R&D programme which has been in place since 2005, for the development of a new, longer range and more accurate generation of submarine-based missiles which are likely to ready for deployment around 2020.

This statement is the closest 'official' remark on India's nuclear arsenal for some time. While Saran's comments relating to command and control and survivability are addressed in another chapter, his statements above are noteworthy for openly stating that India is moving inexorably towards a nuclear triad and if one were to read between the lines, possibly warheads mated on at least a proportion of India's missiles. Also of note is his claim that the Indian arsenal is "modest". This is a very vague word—perhaps deliberately chosen—and is also a relative

---

92. Shyam Saran, "Is India's Nuclear Deterrent Credible?," *Speech delivered at India Habitat Centre, New Delhi*, April 24, 2013.

word, "modest" compared to what? Nonetheless, his statements provide confirmation that India is moving towards a nuclear triad. What this triad will consist of is a matter of extensive debate on both the size of the required arsenal and its composition. It should be noted that much of the discussion on the size of the Indian arsenal has been taking place over a number of years—in some cases, a number of decades. The various commentators may not be in tune with the reality of 2017/18 but their rationales are valid.

Thoughts on the Size of the Required Indian Nuclear Arsenal

The Bulletin of the Atomic Scientists (BAS) in its 2017 report on India notes that India continues to modernise its nuclear arsenal, with at least four new weapon systems now under development to complement or replace the existing nuclear-capable aircraft, land-based delivery systems and sea-based systems. India, in their view was estimated to have produced enough plutonium for 150–200 nuclear warheads but has likely produced only 120–130 warheads. Acknowledging that, additional plutonium would be required to produce warheads for missiles now under development, the report indicated that India is reportedly building two new plutonium production facilities.[93] Its estimate of India's nuclear forces was as follows:[94]

Table 2.1. Indian Nuclear Forces, 2017

Type	North Atlantic Treaty Organization (NATO) designation	Number of launcher	Year deployed	Range[1] (km)	Warhead× yield (kt)	Number of warhead
Aircraft						
Vajra	Mirage 2000H	~16	1985	1,850	1 × bomb	~16
Shamsher	Jaguar IS/IB	~32	1981	1,600	1 × bomb	~32
Subtotal:		~48				~48
Land-based ballistic missiles						

---

93. Hans M. Kristensen and Robert S. Norris, "Indian Nuclear Forces, 2017," *Bulletin of the Atomic Scientists* vol. 73, no. 4, 2017, pp. 205–209.
94. Ibid., p. 206.

Prithvi-2	n.a.	~24	2003	350[2]	1 × 12	~24
Agni-I	n.a.	~20	2007[3]	700+	1 × 40	~20
Agni-II	n.a.	~16	2011[4]	2,000+	1 × 40	~16
Agni-III	n.a.	~8	2014?	3,200+	1 × 40	~8
Agni-IV	n.a.	n.a.	(2018)	3,500+	1 × 40	n.a.
Agni-V	n.a.	n.a.	(2020)	5,200+	1 × 40	n.a.
Subtotal:		~68				~68[5]
Sea-based ballistic missiles						
Dhanush	n.a.	2	2013	400	1 × 12	2
K-15	(Sagarika)	(12)	(2017)	700	1 × 12	(12)
K-4	n.a.	n.a.	?	~3,000	1 × ?	n.a.
Subtotal:		(14)				(14)
Total						~118 (130)[6]

1. Range listed is unrefuelled combat range with drop tanks.
2. US National Air and Space Intelligence Center has estimated the range as 250 km (155 miles) but we assume the range has probably been increased to about 350 km (217 miles) as stated by the Indian government.
3. Agni-I first began induction with the 334th Missile Group in 2004 but did not become operational until 2007.
4. Agni-II first began induction with the 335th Missile Group in 2008 but did not become operational until 2011.
5. The missile and warhead inventory may be larger than the number of launchers, some of which can be reused to fire additional missiles. This table assumes an average of one warhead for each launcher.
6. The number in parenthesis includes 12 warheads possibly produced for the first SSBN, but not yet operational, for a total stockpile of roughly 130 warheads.

Despite the purported stature of the BAS and the credibility given to its findings, there are serious issues with these estimates. As discussed earlier, there are serious questions if a single Indian combat aircraft is still tasked with the nuclear delivery role and certainly no Jaguars. Furthermore, there is as yet no indication that any of India's Prithvi surface-to-surface missiles are tasked for the nuclear delivery role—though admittedly, the potential for nuclear warhead deployment on those systems and the Dhanush exists— and seriously understates both the potential yield of India's warheads as well as the number of Agni missiles in service. It is passing strange that multiple trials of the Agni-III and Agni-IV are not reflected in the number of missiles in service. By the decidedly bizarre logic of the BAS team, seven successful Agni-III tests—four of which were user tests meaning only eight missiles are in service and six successful Agni-IV tests—three being user tests—mean that none are in service. These errors render the estimates provided by the BAS and similar organisations as decidedly unhelpful.

The Stockholm International Peace Research Institute (SIPRI) follows in a similar vein stating that at…

> "the beginning of 2017, India was estimated to have an arsenal of up to 130 nuclear weapons. This represented an increase in the size of the Indian nuclear stockpile from the 110–120 warheads estimated in the SIPRI nuclear data for 2016. India's Nuclear Doctrine is based on the principle of a minimum credible deterrent and no-first-use (NFU) of nuclear weapons, but there has been no official statement specifying the required size of the arsenal. India is gradually expanding the size of its nuclear weapon stockpile as well as its infrastructure for producing nuclear warheads."

While issue may be taken with the numbers, breakdown and details of the SIPRI and BAS estimates, given the possibility that India has probably produced fewer than 100 land-based medium and IRBMs, none of them as yet with MIRVs, we may reasonably speculate that the number of land-based missile warheads is the same as the number of missiles—that is, fewer than a 100. To these must be added any air-delivered weapons for which it might be estimated that between 20 and 40 aircraft have been earmarked. This brings us very close to the estimated size of the Indian arsenal given by Western analysts—between 110 and 130 with the potential that plutonium stockpiles for many more are held and with new production being undertaken each year.

This total is not deemed sufficient to ensure credible effective deterrence—or even credible minimum deterrence. Professor Bharat Karnad suggests that India was moving inexorably towards a total of some 200 warheads.[95] This would appear to be borne out by both India's existing stockpile and production capacity of fissile material. This is coupled with the relatively slow—but existing—production of ballistic missiles which, as production of the Agni-IV and Agni-V increases—will add to the number

---

95. Karnad, n. 8, pp. 89–93.

of land-based ballistic missiles available to the SFC. In addition, the pending induction of the INS Arihant and its K-15/K-4 missiles will further push the warhead total higher. This has found resonance with analysts such as Brigadier Gurmeet Kanwal who suggests that with potential losses from a first strike and with a margin of error for reliability, an Indian nuclear arsenal of no fewer than 200 weapons should be considered.[96]

Indian strategic writers, especially those dealing with nuclear issues, have different but usually well-reasoned arguments as to the ideal size and composition of an Indian deterrent arsenal. These range from the most modest figures of the late K. Subramanyam, a middle path which ranges from the modest forces espoused by General K. Sundarji to the perhaps more pragmatic but indubitably larger force levels suggested by such authors as Brigadier Kanwal, Brigadier Nair and to the maximalist and perhaps ideal force levels articulated by Dr. Bharat Karnad.

From India's official circles, the silence on the issue is deafening, leaving analysts to decipher from the writings of Indian experts the possible future shape of the Indian nuclear arsenal and where the current force stands in relation to the desired future force levels. It should be noted that any speculation with respect to a deterrent based upon high-yield thermonuclear weapons must perforce be viewed as being one effectively in potentia as aforementioned discussed, there are some legitimate questions as to whether India has deployed any thermonuclear weapons which can be realistically deemed reliable.

This does not hold true for either larger fission weapons or fission-boosted-fission weapons which form India's nuclear arsenal. In a 2016 article for the Carnegie Endowment For International Piece, Brigadier Kanwal examined the varying positions taken by analysts on India's nuclear deterrent dividing them into the "minimalist", "middle-path" and "maximalist" approaches to credible deterrence for India.[97] It should be noted that these are merely the opinions of analysts and writers. To date, India has made no public statements as to the intended size of its arsenal.

---

96. Gurmeet Kanwal, *Nuclear Defence: Shaping the Arsenal* (New Delhi: Knowledge World, 2001), pp. 133–137.

97. Gurmeet Kanwal, "India's Nuclear Force Structure 2025," *Carnegie Endowment for International Peace,* (June 30, 2016). http://carnegieendowment.org/2016/06/30/india-s-nuclear-force-structure-2025-pub-63988, accessed on September 07, 2017.

The Minimalist Approach

Krishnaswami Subrahmanyam was the most articulate advocate for minimalist deterrence. He believed that "a force of around 60 deliverable warheads could meet adequately India's need for a minimum deterrent."[98] For delivery of these 60 warheads, Subrahmanyam advocated the development of 20 Prithvi missiles and 20 Agni missiles. The remaining 20 warheads were slated for delivery by air force aircraft. Subrahmanyam argued that "if India were to develop a modest force of 20 Agni missiles, the India-China ratio in deterrence capability will still be higher than the present China-U.S. ratio."[99] Subrahmanyam did not see the need for SSBNs armed with SLBMs and did not make a major a major distinction between low-yield or high-yield weapons, instead emphasising the importance of solid-fuel missiles as delivery systems, stating unequivocally:

> Whether the warheads are of fifteen kilotons fission or 120-150 kilotons (thermonuclear warheads), both are bound to have a deterrent effect…. What is absolutely crucial for credible deterrence is the solid-fuelled missile of appropriate ranges. That is what India needs to concentrate on.[100]

Air Commodore Jasjit Singh also advocated a minimalist approach and suggested a time period of 15–20 years for the Indian arsenal to stabilise:

> "The exact size of the arsenal needed at the end-point will need to be worked out by defence planners based on a series of factors. But at this point it is difficult to visualize an arsenal with anything more than a double-digit quantum of warheads. It may be prudent to even plan on the basis of a lower end figure of say 2–3 dozen (survivable) nuclear warheads by the end of 10–15 years. It is necessary to keep in mind the fact that with

---

98. K. Subrahmanyam, "Nuclear Force Design and Minimum Deterrence Strategy for India," in Bharat Karnad ed., Future Imperilled: India's Security in the 1990s and Beyond, (New Delhi: Viking Penguin India, 1994), pp. 189–93.
99. K. Subrahmanyam, "China and Nuclear Rationale," *Economic Times*, July 26, 1997.
100. Ibid.

the passage of time, deterrence decay factors will lead to the requirement of a smaller arsenal rather than a larger one".[101]

Though he based his force structure on a triad for delivery, he felt that averred that pursuing an ICBM capability would not be necessary, advocating a deterrent with missiles ranging between 500 and 5000 km as being adequate for India's requirements. Echoing the Subrahmanyam parameters for nuclear force levels was Maharaja Krishna Rasgotra, a former foreign secretary, who held the view that:

"…some 30 bombs of Hiroshima strength committed against five major targets in Pakistan, 60 deployed against eight to ten targets in China, and another 30 held in reserve for contingencies and deployment at sea, should adequately meet the needs of minimum deterrence. This number (120 warheads in all) allows for possible losses in an enemy first strike and leaves enough for a devastating counterattack."[102]

Whether ICBMs are necessary or not, is a matter of policy. What should be noted is that missiles with a range of 3500–5000 km offer the ability to target all parts of China.

A Middle Approach

General K. Sundarji, perhaps the most articulate of early Indian nuclear strategists, advocated a pragmatic nuclear force structure of approximately 150 warheads mounted almost entirely on a Prithvi-Agni missile force.[103] Brigadier Vijay K. Nair suggested a force level of 132 nuclear warheads of different types, including weapons in the multimegaton range—clearly unrealistic for India without a resumption of nuclear tests on a significant basis.[104] Delivery systems would include manned aircraft together with

101. Jasjit Singh, "A Nuclear Strategy for India," in Jasjit Singh, ed., *Nuclear India*, (New Delhi: Knowledge World, 1998), p. 315.
102. Maharajkrishna Rasgotra, "Countering Nuclear Threats," in Brahma Chellaney, ed., *Securing India's Future in the New Millennium*, (New Delhi: Orient Longman, 1999), pp. 238–239.
103. Krishnaswamy Sundarji, "Imperatives of Indian Minimum Deterrence," *Agni*, May 1996, p. 21.
104. V. K. Nair, *Nuclear India* (New Delhi: Lancer International, 1992), pp. 170–82.

a fleet of 5 SSBNs with 16 SLBMs on each, and 48 land-based ballistic missiles—12 short-range ballistic missiles (SRBMs) and 36 MRBMs. Noting the need for reserves in the event of a first-strike by an adversary, Brigadier Nair wrote:

> "India must ensure adequate reserves to provide fail safe assurance of her strategy and yet maintain an adequate force structure after hostilities cease. An additional reserve of two weapon systems is required for each planed autonomous strike and a minimum of 20 percent of the entire force structure should be available for post-strike security imperatives." Out of a total requirement of 111 nuclear warheads for retaliatory strikes against Pakistan (seventeen targets) and China (eight targets), he felt that 37 warheads were required for strikes and an additional 74 as a "65 percent reserve for reliability." He added another 22 as a "post-war reserve," taking the total to 132 warheads.[105]

Rear Admiral Raja Menon (retired) recommended that India's nuclear arsenal should be based primarily on SSBNs from about 2020 onward. Until then, he felt that India's nuclear deterrent should be based only on ballistic missiles. Estimating that the modernised Chinese arsenal would comprise 596 warheads after 2010, Admiral Menon suggested that up to 2030, India should maintain an all-missile, land-based force of five regiments with twelve missiles each (survivability being ensured by concealment and rail-garrison mobility), with 50 percent of the missiles having up to four independently targetable warheads per missile. He felt that this arsenal would suffice to withstand the largest possible first strike launched by China and still leave enough missiles remaining to inflict unacceptable damage on China in a second-strike. Menon was of the view that India would need a number of hardened silos for additional survivability.

Interestingly, against Pakistan, he proposed a force of 200 cruise missiles, 36 of them nuclear-tipped, because cruise missiles are the less provocative—perhaps not adequately considering the relative ease of interception. He visualised a transition to an all sea-based deterrent by

---

105. Ibid.

2030 and suggested a nuclear force of six SSBNs, each armed with 12 SLBMs. In his view, each SSBN should carry at least 12 missiles and, as India has ambitions to create MIRVs, each missile could, in the future, carry up to 10 warheads with yields between 250 and 400 kt, writes Menon."[106]

The Maximalist Approach

R. R. Subramanian, a senior analyst at the Institute for Defence Studies and Analyses and a physicist by training, holds the view that India needs at least 425 warheads if the combined efficiency of the delivery systems is assumed to be 30 percent. By this, Subramaniam means that at 30 percent efficiency—30 percent of weapons hit and destroy the targets at which they were fired. So out of 425 warheads, approximately 125–130 warheads could be counted upon to destroy their intended targets. Of these, he estimates that 25–30 would be needed to target Pakistan and about 100 would target China. To assume that India's nuclear force would deliver an overall efficiency of only 30 percent is decidedly pessimistic though undoubtedly a useful basis for calculations.[107]

Bharat Karnad advocates the need for megaton-class thermonuclear weapons in the Indian arsenal. Dr. Karnad suggests that India's primary and secondary target lists could contain about 60 locations in China and Pakistan. In order to ensure, with a small degree of uncertainty, that each of these targets can be destroyed, targeting each location with four warheads is recommended. As it would take time to build a plutonium stockpile and to design and develop both the IRBMs and the SSBNs necessary for this targeting plan, Bharat Karnad, sensibly and realistically suggests that India's nuclear arsenal be gradually built up over a period of 3 decades to a total of 328 nuclear warheads, as given in Table 2.2.[108]

---

106. Raja Menon, "The Nuclear Doctrine: Yoking a Horse and Camel Together," *Times of India,* August 26, 1999.

107. Brigadier Kanwal's account of Subramanian's assessment was done by interview.

108. Bharat Karnad, "Going Thermonuclear: Why, With What Forces, at What Cost," *United Service Institution Journal* vol. 17, no. 3, July-September 1998, p. 315.

Table 2.2. Requirements for Nuclear Warheads.

Timeframe	Maximally Strategic* (warheads)	Minimally Tactical** (warheads)	Total (warheads)
2000–2010	57	30	87
2010–2020	131	40	171
2020–2030	268	60	328
Source. Bharat Karnad, "Going Thermonuclear: Why, With What Forces, at What Cost," *United Service Institution Journal* vol. 17, no. 3, July-September 1998, p. 315. *Intercontinentalballisticmissiles(ICBMs),IRBMs,SLBMs,SU-30sarmedwithN-gravitybombs (NGBs) and N-air-to-surface missiles (N-ASMs) and atomic demolition munitions (ADMs). **Jaguars and Mirage-2000s armed with NGBs and N-ASMs up to 2010 and SU-30s thereafter.			

The breakdown of the final figure of 328 nuclear warheads and the proposed delivery systems suggested by Bharat Karnad includes

- Four SSBNs with 48 SLBMs (presumably with a single warhead each),
- Forty SU-30s with 40 NGBs and 40 N-ASMs (maximally strategic) and 30 SU-30s with 30 NGBs and 30 N-ASMs (minimally tactical),
- Twenty-five ICBMs,
- Forty IRBMs,
- Twenty-five ADMs,
- Fifity reserve warheads.

Karnad suggests that 253 of the 278 non-reserve warheads should be thermonuclear. The remaining 25 should be atomic demolition munitions. He writes: "If a counter-cities or countervalue nuclear bombardment strategy is the only one that makes sense, then thermonuclear bombs, with megaton yields, are the most convincing instruments of this strategy."[109]

However, as discussed earlier, India's nuclear arsenal perhaps has reliable weapons of the fission-type with yields no larger than 100 kt and at most has fission-boosted-fission weapons with reliable yields of 200 kt with the possibility of yields of up to 500 kt. This renders his otherwise highly feasible force structure as eminently realistic. Of particular note is Karnad's inclusion of no fewer than 140 air-delivered weapons out of the 328 he suggests. This puts him at variance with the other analysts who have shown a preference for ballistic missiles.

109..Ibid.

Perhaps the most 'minimalist of the maximalists' is Lieutenant General Pran Pahwa (retired) who recommended in a study for the United Service Institution of India that India's deterrence should be based on 182 warheads.[110] His very cynical calculations are based on the survivability factor of India's arsenal and works on the assumption that China is likely to employ two warheads, each to destroy every Indian warhead, with efficiency as high as 70 to 90 percent.[111]

With this calculation, no more than 10–30 percent of Indian warheads would survive a Chinese counterforce first strike. If India had 182 warheads, China would need to fire 364 warheads to eliminate India's arsenal. Given a Chinese arsenal of about 200–250 warheads, a Chinese first-strike would leave about 36 Indian missiles unharmed and an equal number of Chinese missiles unlaunched. Since the numbers remaining would be matched, China would be deterred from launching a first-strike in the first place. This argument assumes a generous 80 percent success rate for China, and does not take into account the possibility that a Chinese first-strike is likely to combine countervalue with counterforce targets, thus enabling the survivability of even more Indian warheads.[112]

Brigadier Gurmeet Kanwal, one of the most nuanced of all India's nuclear thinkers, approaches the problem from first principles. Noting that soft area targets, such as the populated and industrial centres are likely to be the primary targets of India's countervalue targeting philosophy, would require a much larger number of missiles to destroy with a 90 percent assurance level. To destroy 10 countervalue targets in China, India would need a total of 40 nuclear warheads (at four 200-kt-warheads per target or ten20 kt weapons per target) to cause unacceptable damage if the CEP of the delivery systems was 1000 m and an assurance level of about 70 percent was acceptable.

Assuming a relatively modest level of assurance, Kanwal assumes an overall reliability of the whole system of 0.5–0.6, then 80 warheads must

110. Pran Pahwa, *Organisation and Employment of Strategic Rocket Forces* (New Delhi: United Service Institution of India, 1999), pp. 294–6.

111. Pran Pahwa, "Minimum Deterrent: Defining the Concept," *Tribune*, February 11, 1999. Gurmeet Kanwal, "India's Nuclear Force Structure," *Institute for Defence Studies and Analyses*, (September 2000). http://www.idsa-india.org/an-sept2-00.html, accessed on September 18, 2017.

112. Kanwal, n. 96.

actually be launched for about 40 warheads to be effectively delivered and explode over their targets. This means that India would need at least 80 warheads and delivery vehicles to survive a first-strike. Even if the maximum possible concealment and dispersion measures have been taken, including the emplacement of dummy warhead storage sites and dummy mobile missiles, up to 50 percent of the land-based nuclear warheads and delivery systems could be destroyed in a sustained and intense countervalue first-strike. Of the SLBMs carried by SSBNs, 80–90 percent may be expected to survive, should the SSBNs be at sea and protected by other surface and subsurface assets.

In Kanwal's assessment, India should therefore, plan to stock twice the number of land-based warheads and delivery systems that it expects to need. If 25–35 percent of India's deterrence is sea-based, a total of about 150 warheads must be stocked: 120 land-based warheads and about 30 warheads on SLBMs. In addition, India should maintain a prudent level of reserves for larger-than-anticipated damage in a first-strike, escalation dominance and unforeseen eventualities. Anticipating escalation dominance and war-termination strategies being dependent on India's ability to launch counter-recovery strikes and fresh strikes if necessary, Kanwal recommends adding one-third to the previously calculated required number of warheads to be adequate. Then in total, India needs 200 nuclear warheads for a minimum deterrence policy with a NFU strategy against China, assuming that this figure will also suffice for deterrence against Pakistan.[113]

In relation to the conventionally accepted figure of perhaps 110–130 weapons being in the current arsenal, it would appear that there is a significant shortfall in respect of any reasonably desirable figure for an Indian arsenal. However, this does not take into account the possibility of the use of either civil reactors being used for weapons-grade plutonium production or the use of reactor-grade plutonium with fusion boosting to eliminate pre-detonation problems. As will be seen later, the option of India diverting one or more of its unsafeguarded nuclear power reactors to weapons material production has the potential to substantially increase India's fissile material.

---

113. Ibid.

Tactical Nuclear Warheads: India's Choice

With estimates of Indian warhead yields ranging from 15 to 200 kt, with 100 kt fission and 200 kt fission-boosted-fission weapons being perhaps the most reliable high-yield weapons available to India, little consideration is given by Indian nuclear theorists and strategists to tactical nuclear weapons (TNWs)—of perhaps sub-kiloton to very low-kiloton yields—being part of the Indian arsenal. This is partly because of the inherent escalation between tactical and strategic nuclear use being cause for caution and also because of their questionable military utility to India.

At present, India's current inventory of weapons with yields of 10–20 kt would be more than adequate to destroy all types of tactical nuclear targets. However, such yields, in the context of the India–Pakistan battlefield fall into the 'overkill' category as opposed to truly tactical weapons. As will be discussed in another chapter, dealing with Pakistan's nuclear weapons presents challenges that can be best dealt by a combination of active and passive chemical, biological, radiological and nuclear measures plus the threat of 'massive' retaliation by India.

During the Pokhran II nuclear tests in May 1998, Indian scientists conclusively demonstrated the capability to design fractional kiloton weapons. The three smaller 'experimental' devices had yields of 0.2, 0.3 and 0.5 kt, as reported in the May 1998 issue of the Bhabha Atomic Research Centre newsletter. Hence, the capabilities declared by Indian scientists must be accepted. It follows that India is in a position to develop TNWs of fractional-kiloton yields although their manufacture and subsequent maintenance is extremely complex. To this must be added the inherent extreme caution to be exercised in the storage, handling and mating of these TNWs to their delivery systems.

The delivery of TNWs can be done by a combination of manned aircraft, Prithvi and perhaps later BrahMos, Prahaar and eventually Nirbhay missiles. Unlike the NATO/Warsaw Pact battlefield, it is difficult to conceive sub-kiloton nuclear shells for 155 mm artillery pieces as being practical.

Yet, it is questionable whether India has sought to incorporate such sub-kiloton weapons into its arsenal. Brigadier Gurmeet Kanwal has cogently argued that India's command and control issues associated with the deployment of

TNWs militate against their deployment by India.[114] Furthermore, their efficacy as retaliatory instruments—given India's NFU doctrine—is questionable as any Indian response to a tactical nuclear strike is to be disproportionate. As such, India has opted against TNWs with good reason.

Fissile Material Stockpiles: Correlation to Nuclear Weapons Stocks

It is an unfortunate, and for an analyst, frustrating fact that India's fissile material stockpile is the subject of much debate. Some of this is borne out of the inevitable uncertainty surrounding the Indian nuclear weapons program and its link to India's civilian reactor projects. However, a large and often contradictory debate has been raging by groups that might charitably be termed as having 'vested interests' in either understating or exaggerating India's fissile material stockpile. Pakistani estimates have tended towards extreme exaggeration while some of the estimates from the non-proliferation advocates in the West or supporters of the India–US civil-nuclear deal have tended towards underestimation to the extent of being somewhat implausible. New Delhi's stoic silence in this debate has contributed to uncertainty, especially as concerns over Pakistan's purportedly growing fissile material stockpile has raised much consternation in the West. This has had the effect of decreasing scrutiny of the potential for Indian flexibility in the production of fissile material. While this is undoubtedly useful for Indian geopolitical objectives, for an analyst, it is unfortunate that India has done such a remarkable job at obfuscation.

Estimates of the Indian fissile material stockpile must consider that India has effectively three nuclear reactor programs that are at once connected and separate. The first is the overtly military program which once consisted of two reactors—CIRUS and Dhruva, before the former's decommissioning in 2010. To date, no reactor has been built to take its place, leaving Dhruva as the sole surviving specific military reactor. In addition to these military reactors is India's large civilian reactor programme. Eight of these reactors have been kept out of international safeguard agreements and inevitably cause confusion in calculations of India's fissile material stockpile

---

114. Gurmeet Kanwal, "Does India Need Tactical Nuclear Weapons?," *IDSA May 2003,* http://www.idsa-india.org/an-may-03.html, accessed on September 19, 2017.

leading to varying estimates.[115] Indeed, one has to ask whether India has not tasked at least one or two of its civilian unsafeguarded reactors to replace the decommissioned CIRUS. India is under no obligation to reveal any such move, nor will it show any visible evidence of a change of use.

The Indian nuclear industry—categorised by 'safeguarded civilian', 'unsafeguarded civilian' and 'military' may be summarised as follows:[116]

Table 2.3. Civilian Nuclear Facilities under Continuous Safeguards

Type	Facility, Location	Purpose, Design Capacity
Thorium and uranium mines and mills	None—India's additional protocol does not apply to mines and mills	
Enrichment	None—India has not placed any enrichment facilities under safeguards	
Uranium conversion and fuel fabrication—natural uranium for pressurised heavy water reactor (PHWRs)	Nuclear Fuel Complex, Hyderabad: Uranium Oxide Plant (Block A)	Conversion to UO_2 (450 t/yr)
	Nuclear Fuel Complex, Hyderabad: Ceramic Fuel Fabrication Plant (Pelletising)(Block A)	Fuel fabrication (335 t/yr)
	Nuclear Fuel Complex, Hyderabad: Ceramic Fuel Fabrication Plant (Assembly)(Block A)	Fuel fabrication (300 t/yr)
	Nuclear Fuel Complex, Hyderabad: Gadolinia Facility	Zirconium alloy tubing and production
Uranium fuel fabrication—enriched uranium for light water power reactors	Nuclear Fuel Complex, Hyderabad: Enriched Uranium Oxide Plant and Enriched Fuel Fabrication Plant	Fuel fabrication using imported LEU (24 t/yr)
Heavy water production	None—India's additional protocol does not apply to its heavy water production	

115. Sharon Squassoni, "India's Nuclear Separation Plan: Issues and Views—CRS Report for Congress," *Congressional Research Service*, (December 22, 2006), pp. 20–21.
116. Kalman A. Robertson and John Carlson, "The Three Overlapping Streams of India's Nuclear Programs," *Harvard Kennedy School, Belfer Centre for Science and International Affairs*, (April 2016), pp. 13–19.

Power reactors— PHWRs	Rajasthan Atomic Power Station (RAPS1-6), Kota	PHWR, 90 MW, 187 MW, 202 MWx4
	Kakrapar Atomic Power Station (KAPS1-2), Surat	PHWR, 202 MWx2
	Narora Atomic Power Station (NAPS1-2), Narora	PHWR, 202 MWx2
Power reactors —light-water reactor (LWRs)	Tarapur Atomic Power Station (TAPS1-2), Boisar	BWR, 150 MWx2 (spent fuel to Tarapur storage)
	Kudankulam Nuclear Power Plant (KK1-2), Kudankulam	VVER-PWR, 917 MWx2A

According to media reports in June 2014, Russia has confirmed that India may reprocess the spent fuel from these reactors at PREFRE, rather than requiring return to Russia. See Vanita Srivastava, "India Has Right to Reprocess Spent Nuclear Fuel, Says Russia," *New Indian Express*, (June 9, 2014). http://www.hindustantimes.com/india/india-has-right-to-reprocess-spent-n-fuelrussia/, accessed on April 12, 2016.

Research reactors	None—India has not placed any research reactors under safeguards	
Fuel storage	Tarapur—Away from Reactor (AFR) Wet Spent Fuel Storage, Boisar	275 t spent fuel
	Tarapur—Nuclear power plant (NPP) site, Dry Spent Fuel Storage, Boisar	20 t spent fuel
	Other safeguarded spent fuel from PHWRs in storage	About 1500 t spent fuel[B]
Reprocessing and separated plutonium	Option to construct safeguarded reprocessing plants for PHWR fuel under US–India Nuclear Cooperation Agreement	
	Approximately 0.4 t of separated plutonium currently under safeguards, having been reprocessed at PREFRE-1, while the facility was under temporary safeguards[C]	
Other research centres	None—India's additional protocol does not apply to sites where India conducts nuclear fuel cycle-related research and development	

- See IPFM, "Plutonium Separation in Nuclear Power Programs," p. 57.
- See IPFM, "Plutonium Separation in Nuclear Power Programs," p. 54.

Table 2.4. Facilities that are used Primarily for Civilian Purposes and that are not Subject to Continuous Safeguards.

Type	Facility, Location	Purpose, Design Capacity
Thorium and uranium mines and mills	See Table 2.5 on military facilities below—in addition to being a source of nuclear material for India's military program, domestic mines are an important source for several reactors	
Enrichment	See Table 2.5 on military facilities— Rare Materials Plant (RMP) has both military and civilian applications	
Uranium conversion and fuel fabrication	Some facilities in Nuclear Fuel Complex, Hyderabad	For unsafeguarded PHWRs
	Plan for second Nuclear Fuel Complex, Kota	
	Trombay Fuel Fabrication	Small-scale production for Fast Breeder Test Reactor
Heavy water production— declared civilian as part of Separation Plan	Hazira	80 t/yr
	Thal-Vaishet	78 t/yr
	Tuticorin	49 t/yr
Power reactors— PHWRs	Tarapur Atomic Power Station (TAPS 3-4), Boisar	PHWR, 490 MWx2
	Madras Atomic Power Station (MAPS 1-2), Madras	PHWR, 202 MWx2
	Kaiga (KGS 1-4), Kaiga	PHWR, 202 MWx4
Power reactors — Fast Breeder Reactor (FBRs)	Prototype FBR, Kalpakkam	FBR, 500 MW (scheduled for April 2016)
Power reactors— other	Advanced Heavy Water Reactor	HWR, 300 MW (not yet operational)

- These reactors may be a source of tritium for nuclear weapons. See T. S. Gopi Rethinaraj, "Tritium Breakthrough Brings India Closer to an H-Bomb Arsenal," *Jane's Intelligence Review*, vol. 10, no. 1, January 1998; Mark Hibbs, "Indian PHWR Safeguards Offer Not Impressive, NPT States," *Nucleonics Week*, vol. 44, no. 16, April 2003.
- See R. K. Sinha, "Bhabha Atomic Research Centre Highlights: Reactor Technology and Engineering," *Bhabha Atomic Research Centre, India Department of Atomic Energy*, (2015), http://www.barc.gov.in/publications/eb/golden/reactor/toc/chapter1/1.pdf, accessed on April 12, 2016), p. 6.

Research reactors	Fast Breeder Test Reactor, Kalpakkam	FBR, 40 MWt
	Purnima reactor, Trombay	Small-scale U-233 LWR
	Kamini reactor, Kalpakkam	U-233 fuelled LWR, 30kWt
	Apsara reactor, Mumbai	LWR, 1 MWt (undergoing conversion from HEU fuel to LEU)
	Compact High Temperature Reactor, Trombay	U-233 and Th fuel (under construction)
Fuel storage	Rajasthan NPP site, Away from Reactor (AFR) Dry Spent Fuel Storage, Rajasthan	570 t spent fuel
	Spent fuel storage for unsafeguarded PHWRs to be reprocessed	2500–3600 t spent fuel
Reprocessing and separated plutonium	Kalpakkam Spent Fuel Reprocessing (KARP)	PUREX (used for both military purposes and reuse in civilian reactors), 100 t/yr spent fuel
	Tarapur Power Reactor Fuel Reprocessing (PREFRE-1 and 2) Center	PUREX (used to reprocess spent fuel from PHWRs for reuse in civilian reactors; temporary safeguards apply on 'campaign' basis), 100–150 t/yr spent fuel
	COmpact Reprocessing facility for Advanced fuels in Lead shielded cell reprocessing plant, Kalpakkam	Pilot plant for reprocessing spent fuel from FBRs, 12 kg/yr
	Tarapur Advanced Fuel Fabrication Facility	MOX fuel fabrication for various reactors

- Albright and Kelleher-Vergantini, "India's Stocks of Civil and Military Plutonium and Highly Enriched Uranium," pp. 2, 33.
- IPFM, "Plutonium Separation in Nuclear Power Programs," p. 57.
- This facility has tended to run well below its design capacity. Albright and Kelleher-Vergantini, "India's Stocks of Civil and Military Plutonium and Highly Enriched Uranium," p. 6.
- India has about 1.9 t of plutonium in FBR fuel as of 2014. See Albright and Kelleher-Vergantini, "India's Stocks of Civil and Military Plutonium and Highly Enriched Uranium," p. 10.

Table 2.5. Facilities that are Primarily used for Military Purposes.

Type	Facility, Location	Purpose, Design Capacity
Thorium and uranium mines and mills	Jaduguda Mill	200 t/yr
	Turamdih Mill	190 t/yr
	Tummalapalle Mill	220 t/yr
	More mills to enter operation in the next few years	
	Mines in Jharkland, Andhra Pradesh, Telangana, Karnataka, Meghalaya	
Enrichment	RMP, Bhabha Atomic Research Center, Mysore/Rattehalli (Karnataka)	Gas centrifuge enrichment for naval reactor fuel, LEU for Apsara reactor, possibly also for nuclear weapons, 15–25 tSWU/yr (capacity to produce 60–100 kg of weapons-grade uranium/yr from natural uranium feed)
	Apparent second RMP under construction at same site	Larger than original RMP
	Special Material Enrichment Facility, Khudapura (Karnataka) in initial stages of construction	Gas centrifuge enrichment for civilian and military purposes, larger than RMP
	Uranium Enrichment Plant, Trombay	Pilot-scale research on ultracentrifuges
	Laser enrichment research, various locations	
Uranium conversion and fuel fabrication— natural uranium	Uranium metals plant, Trombay	Fuel fabrication for CIRUS and Dhruva reactors
Heavy water production— not declared civilian as part of 'Separation Plan'	Baroda	17 t/yr
	Kota	85 t/yr
	Manuguru	185 t/yr
	Talcher	62 t/yr

- The military applications of enrichment include thermonuclear weapons and naval reactors.
- Albright and Kelleher-Vergantini, "India's Stocks of Civil and Military Plutonium and Highly Enriched Uranium," p. 20.

Research reactors	Dhruva, Mumbai	HWR, 100 MWt (historically a major source of weapons-grade plutonium for nuclear weapons)
	CIRUS, Mumbai	HWR, 40MWt (historically a major source of weapons-grade plutonium, despite being supplied by Canada in the 1950s on the condition that it only be used for peaceful purposes; shut down in 2010 as part of India's Separation Plan)
Naval reactors	Advanced Technology Vessel naval prototype PWR (HEU fuel), Kalpakkam	80–100MWt each
	INS Arihant SSBN with PWR (HEU fuel)	
	Two similar SSBNs under construction, two more planned	
Reprocessing	Trombay plutonium separation plant, Bhabha Atomic Research Center	400–700 kg weapons-grade plutonium separated as of 2014 PUREX, approximately 50 t spent fuel per year, including reprocessing weapons-grade plutonium from Dhruva, primarily for nuclear weapons
• Albright and Kelleher-Vergantini, "India's Stocks of Civil and Military Plutonium and Highly Enriched Uranium," p. 29. • See Albright and Kelleher-Vergantini, "India's Stocks of Civil and Military Plutonium and Highly Enriched Uranium." • IPFM, "Global Fissile Material Report 2015," p. 26.		

There is a caveat to these categories, however. Under the terms of the Nuclear Suppliers Group Waiver granted to India following the India–US Civil Nuclear agreement, there are only two categories—safeguarded civilian and military. It is a matter of debate as to whether the unsafeguarded civilian facilities are military or not, but technically, if they are not safeguarded civil, they are military. That would very much depend on whether India has chosen to make use of these facilities for its nuclear weapons program. This would inevitably cause all calculations on India's nuclear stockpile to go awry.

This inconsistency and occasional absurdity is where calculation of India's fissile stocks goes seriously awry. The Pakistani National Command Authority suggested that India had fissile stocks to make over 2000 weapons.[117] This estimate can be traced back to a 2014 assessment by Mansoor Ahmed, a Pakistani nuclear analyst.

By Ahmed's calculations, he estimated that at the end of 2013, India's fissile material stockpile included 800–1000 kg of weapons-grade plutonium, 2 metric tons of highly enriched uranium (HEU), and 15 t of reactor-grade plutonium.[118] Ahmed used the assumption that 4 kg of weapons-grade plutonium, 50 kg of HEU, or 8 kg of reactor-grade plutonium would be necessary to make one nuclear warhead although the type or yield was not specified. It might be conceivable that Ahmed was using the calculations normally employed for a 20 kt fission weapon (although his HEU calculations seem high for that). With these figures, he estimated that India could produce 250 warheads from weapons-grade plutonium, 40 from HEU (gun-type implosion devices, not thermonuclear weapons), and 1875 from reactor-grade plutonium—for a total potential of 2165 nuclear weapons.[119]

Ahmed's study further postulates that India is already working to install more than five FBRs which will increase its weapons-grade plutonium production capacity by 20 times to 700 kg every year. In addition, an expansion in its centrifuge enrichment programme will enable it to increase production of HEU for nuclear weapons to 160 kg every year. Should these calculations be accurate, India could theoretically produce approximately 80–90 plutonium-based and 7–8 uranium-based nuclear weapons every year.[120]

117. "India has Fissile Material for 2,000 Warheads: Pak Media," *Times of India,* (September 10, 2015) http://timesofindia.indiatimes.com/world/pakistan/India-has-fissile-material-for-2000-warheads-Pak-media/articleshow/48895568.cms,accessed on September 19, 2017.

118. Elizabeth Whitfield, "Fuzzy Math on Indian Nuclear Weapons," *Bulletin of the Atomic Scientists,* (April 19, 2017), http://thebulletin.org/fuzzy-math-indian-nuclear-weapons9343, accessed on September 19, 2017.

119. Ibid.

120. "Third Pakistani Nuclear Reactor Operational: US magazine," *The Nation,* (July 07, 2014) http://nation.com.pk/islamabad/07-Jul-2014/third-pakistani-nuclear-reactor-operational-us-magazine, accessed on September 19, 2017.

Pakistan was quick to cite Ahmed's study and claimed it "exploded the myth that Pakistan has the world's fastest growing nuclear weapons programme", with an otherwise farcical opinion piece in the *Tribune* claiming that India has increased the construction of nuclear facilities to stockpile weapons-grade material. The same *Tribune* opinion claimed that India can produce over 2600 weapons, while Pakistan could only produce 207.[121]

These calculations rather than being analysed for their possibility prompted a rather sarcastic response by the BAS which suggested a most generous estimate of 844 weapon equivalents if reactor-grade plutonium is considered, falling to a generous estimate of 219 if only the CIRUS and Dhruva outputs are considered with a more likely figure of 75–125 weapons equivalents being likely and one which coincides possibly with India's missile arsenal to date.[122]

In support of their contentions, the BAS suggested that, based on a 2015 study by the Institute for Science and International Security (ISIS) at the end of 2014, India likely possessed about 550 kg of weapons-grade plutonium, 100–200 kg of HEU intended for use in thermonuclear weapons and 2.9 t of separated reactor-grade plutonium. The ISIS study concluded that this fissile material was sufficient to produce about 75–125 nuclear warheads, ISIS arrived at this number mainly through an appraisal of India's probable weapons-grade plutonium stockpile, assuming that India would not use reactor-grade plutonium in nuclear warheads and that HEU would only be used to produce a handful of thermonuclear weapons at most. ISIS also considered that some plutonium is in weapons production pipelines or held in reserve, assessing that only about 70 percent of India's stockpile is available to be made into weapons. Consequently, assuming that it would take 3–5 kg of weapons-grade plutonium for each warhead, ISIS calculations yielded an arsenal that could range from 75 to 125 nuclear weapons.[123]

The biggest difference between these two estimates comes from their assessments of, and assumptions about, reactor-grade plutonium. The ISIS

121. A. Zaidi and H. Ehtisham, "The Indian threat is real," *The Tribune.pk*, (May 11, 2017). https://tribune.com.pk/story/1406430/indian-threat-real/, accessed on September 19, 2017.
122. Whitfield, n. 118.
123. Ibid.

study completely discounts the possibility that India would use reactor-grade plutonium in its nuclear weapons. Furthermore, its estimate of India's reactor-grade plutonium stockpile is also significantly lower than Ahmed's: 2.9 t as opposed to 15 t.

India's reprocessing plants have not had a particularly impressive record to date, although there is some evidence to suggest that Western estimates of their poor performance are greatly overstated.[124] This unfortunately, is a potential pitfall in using the estimates and calculations of India's capabilities.

The BAS suggests that by discounting reactor-grade plutonium entirely, India could possibly build some 219 weapons.[125] It further asserts that "that much, or even most, of India's HEU is intended for use in naval reactors rather than in nuclear warheads."[126] It is also clear that some of India's weapons-grade plutonium was already used in nuclear tests or is contained in process waste, which further reduces the estimate to between 75 and 125 weapons.

It is a legitimate question as to why would India wish to use reactor-grade plutonium for the production of nuclear weapons. Reactor-grade plutonium with its higher content of the Pu-240 isotope could produce pre-initiation in weapons so produced. However, Bharat Karnad asserts that reliable weapons with yields from low kiloton range to up to 20–40 kt with reactor-grade plutonium—comprising a fissile content of 66 percent—require a slightly higher critical mass than weapons-grade plutonium.[127] Furthermore, pre-initiation problems could be dealt with using the deuterium–tritium 'boosting' of fission devices.[128] The use of deuterium–tritium 'boosting' enables the manufacture of reliable and efficient weapons using reactor-grade plutonium with the said 'boosting'

---

124. Karnad, n. 8, p. 84. In an interview with Dr. Karnad, Dr. Iyengar refutes Ashley Tellis's assertions that India could not reprocess 55–60 kg of plutonium per year and said that figure had already been achieved.

125. Squassoni, n. 115.

126. While some of India's HEU will be used for these reactors undoubtedly, given that India's SSBN and SSN projects are moving at a ponderous pace, this assertion might be an overstatement.

127. Karnad, n. 8, p. 73.

128. Andre Gsponer and Jean-Pierre Hurni, "The Physical Principles of Thermonuclear Explosives, Inertial Confinement Fusion, and the Quest for Fourth Generation Nuclear Weapons," *Independent Scientific Research Institute Geneva-12, Switzerland,* (January 20, 2009), p. 17.

rendering such weapons virtually immune from pre-initiation problems. It would therefore mean that discounting India's stocks of reactor-grade plutonium is not necessarily wise when examining India's nuclear weapons potential.

This rationale has not found favour with Pakistani analysts. While it is undoubtedly true that Pakistani estimates will invariably fall on the higher side, it is not feasible to ignore India's civilian unsafeguarded reactors and their potential. Mansoor Ahmed, writing for the Belfer centre, after the BAS response, summarises the current and future Indian and Pakistani fissile material stocks and weapons equivalents as follows:[129]

Table 2.6. India-Pakistan Fissile Material Production Capacity Estimates (existing and projected)

	India	Pakistan
Production reactors	100 MWth existing 155 MWth planned	160–200 MWth
Breeder reactors	500–600 MWe existing 1200 MWe planned	Nil
PHWRs	2350 MWe existing 2800 MWe planned[252]	Nil
Reprocessing plants	350 tHM/year existing 1650 tHM/year planned	140 tHM/year Existing
Uranium enrichment	30,000–45,000 SWU/year existing 126,000 (planned)	15,000–45,000 SWU/year
Fissile material Stockpiles	3.1 t HEU (1.1-ton U-235) 0.7 t WG Pu 5.5 t RG Pu (separated) 11–14 t RG Pu (unseparated)	3.2 t HEU 0.19 t WG Pu No RG Pu

Sources: Zia Mian, et. al., "Fissile Materials in South Asia: The Implications of the US–India Nuclear Deal," (Princeton N.J., IPFM, Sept 1, 2006); International Panel on Fissile Materials, "Global Fissile Material Report 2015," (Princeton, N.J.: IPFM, December 2015); Government of India, Department of Atomic Energy, Annual Report, 2014-2015; von Hippel et. al, "Plutonium Separation in Nuclear Power Programs: Status, Problems, and Prospects of Civilian Reprocessing Around the World."; Prithviraj Chavan, Unstarred Question No. 389: Integrated Nuclear Recycle Fuel, Lok Sabha, 2010.

---

129. Mansoor Ahmed, "India's Nuclear Exceptionalism Fissile Materials, Fuel Cycles, and Safeguards," (Harvard Kennedy School, Belfer Centre for Science and International Affairs: Discussion Paper May 2017), pp. 51–53.

Table 2.7. Indian and Pakistani fissile material weapon equivalent potential

	India	Pakistan
WG Pu	0.59–0.79 t	0.19–0.21 t
R G Pu	5.5 t (separated) 11–14 t (unseparated)	0 t
HEU	3.2 t (1 t U-235)	3.1 t
Weapons Potential	148–198 (WG Pu) 688 (RG Pu separated) 1375–1759 (RG Pu unseparated) 50 (HEU) = 2261–2686	48–52 (WG Pu) 0 (RG Pu) 155 (WG HEU) = 207

Sources: Zia Mian et al., "Fissile Materials in South Asia: The Implications of the US-India Nuclear Deal," (Princeton N.J.: IPFM, Sept 1, 2006); International Panel on Fissile Materials, "Global Fissile Material Report 2015," (Princeton, N.J.: IPFM, December 2015).

Notes: This estimate considers 4 kg for WG Pu, 8 kg for RG Pu and 20 kg for WG HEU. Calculating the weapons potential for India's fissile materials presumes that: all of its unsafeguarded stockpile has military potential; India has yet to commission its first PFBR which keeps the proliferation potential of all of India's separated and unseparated weapon-usable plutonium stockpile intact; India has declared its unsafeguarded RG Pu stockpile as 'strategic'; India's reprocessing capacity is steadily increasing in size and efficiency; and India's unsafeguarded HEU stockpile can easily be scaled up to weapons-grade levels given, notwithstanding that its plans for a fleet of five nuclear submarines is far from complete.

From these tables, we can see that there is a wide divergence in respect of India's fissile material stockpile. Whether India has made any use of its civilian facilities for weapons-grade plutonium production is a matter of conjecture. This would inevitably lead to an exponentially higher demand for uranium for such reactors but such costs would be offset by eliminating the need to build and operate additional military reactors. This approach has evoked much speculation as analysts such as Bharat Karnad and, during the 1980s and 1990s, even non-proliferation advocates such as Leonard Spector have suggested that India has pursued this route.

Using PHWRs in the 'low burn-up' mode would inevitably require them to be refuelled more often, thus increasing the quantity of uranium for fuelling the reactors. To give an indication as to the quantitative difference in the uranium required, Ashley Tellis, writing in support of the India–US civil nuclear agreement at a time when concerns in this regard were raised, suggested the following figures, comparing fuel requirements for the dedicated military reactors, the civilian reactors and then examining the requirements for civilian reactors run for military purposes:[130]

Table 1. Estimated Amounts of Uranium Required for Producing Weapons-Grade Plutonium at Various Capacity Factors in India's Research Reactros

Reactor	Capacity Factor (%)	Thermal Power (MW)	Thermal Energy Output (MWD/ yr)	Average Discharge Bumup (MWD/ MTU)	Fuel Requirement (MTU/yr)	WGPu per year (kg)[a]
CIRUS						
	40	40	5,840	665	8.8	5.4
	40	40	5.840	1,000	5.8	5.1
	40	40	5,840	1,400	4.2	4.9
	50	40	7,300	665	11.0	6.7
	50	40	7,300	1,000	7.3	6.4
	50	40	7,300	1,400	5.2	6.1
	70	40	10,200	665	15.4	9.4
	70	40	10,220	1,000	10.2	9.0
	70	40	10,220	1,400	7.3	8.7
Dhruva						
	65	100	23,725	665	35.7	21.8
	65	100	23,725	1,000	23.7	20.9
	65	100	23,725	1,400	16.9	19.9
	75	100	27.375	665	41.2	25.2
	75	100	27,375	1,000	27.4	24.1
	75	100	27,375	1,400	19.6	23.0

a   PL production is calculated at 1 kg/1000 MWD of thermal energy output multiplied by a correction factor based on burnup level.

Note, MW, megawatt, MWD/yr, megawatt days per year. MWD/MTU, megawatt days per metric ton of anium.MTU/yr, metric ton of uranium per year.WGPu, weapons grade plutonium. Kg, kilograme.

130. Ashley Tellis, "Atoms for War? U.S.-Indian Civilian Nuclear Cooperation and India's Nuclear Arsenal," *Carnegie Endowment for International Peace,* 2006, pp.19–27.

Table 2. Estimated Fuel Requirements for Operational Pressurized Heavy Water Reactors

Reactor	MWe	Thermal Power (MW)	Annual Thermal Energy Output (MWD/yr)[a]	Annual Requirement (MTU/yr)	Date of Commercial Operation	National Decommis-sioning Date[b]	Fuel Needed 2006- Decom-missioning
RAPS-1 Rawatbhata, Rajasthan[c]	100	350	93,258	0.00	December 1973	?	0.00
RAPS-2 Rawatbhata, Rajasthan	200	690	183,759	27.43	April 1981	2011	137.13
RAPS-3 Rawatbhata, Rajasthan	220	760	202.502	30.22	June 2000	2030	725.38
RAPS-4 Rawatbhata, Rajasthan	220	760	202.502	30.22	December 2000	2030	725.38
MAPS-1 Kalpakkam, Tamilnadu	220	760	202.505	30.22	January 1984	2014	241.79
MAPS-2 Kalpakkam, Tamilnadu	220	760	202.502	30.22	March 1985	2016	302.24
MAPS-1 Narora, Uttar Pradesh	220	760	202,502	30,22	January 1991	2021	453.36
MAPS-2 Kapakkam, Tamilnadu	220	760	202,502	30.22	July 1992	2022	483.59
KAPS-1 Kakrapar, Gujarat	220	760	202.502	30.22	May 1993	2023	513.81
KAPS-1 Kakrapar, Gujarat	220	760	202.502	30.22	September 1995	2025	574.26
KAIGA-1 Kaiga, Karnataka	220	760	202.502	30.22	November 2000	2030	725.38
KAIGA-2 Kaiga, Karnataka	220	760	202.502	30.22	March 2000	2030	725.38
TAPS-2 Tarapur, Maharasthrra[d]	540	1,860	495,597	73.97	May2003	2036	2,219.09
TAPS-4 Tarapur, Maharasthrra	540	1,860	495.597	73.99	September 2005	2035	2,145.12
Total				478			9,972

a Assumes a capacity factor of 73 percent
b Assumes 30 year reactor life.
c Reactor virtually non-operational
d TAPS-3 went critical in May 2006, but is treated as operational for calculation purpose in this report.
Notes. Reactor identified in shaded rows have been offered for sateguards in India's March 2006 separation
    plan, MWe, megawatt-electronic, MW, megawatt, MWD/yr, megawatt days per year. MTU/yr metric
    ton of uranium per year. MTU, metric ton of uranium.

The unfortunate corollary to these conflicting figures means that estimates of Indian fissile material stocks and their disaggregation into civilian, military, weapons-grade and reactor-grade is largely a matter of conjecture.

Table 4. Comparison of National 220 MWe Reactor Fuel Requirement in Production of
Weapons-Grade Plutonium versus Electricity

Weapons-Grade Plutonum					
Capacity Factor (%)	Thermal Power (MW)	Thermal Energy Output (MWD/yr)	Average Discharge Burnup (MWD/MTU)	Fuel Requirement (MTU/yr)	WGPu per year (kg)[a]
73	750	202,502	665	304.51	186.30
73	750	202,502	1,000	202.50	178.20
73	750	202,502	1,400	144.64	170.10
79	760	219,146	665	329.54	201.61
79	760	218,146	1,000	218.15	192.85
79	760	218,146	1,400	156.53	184.08
Electrically					
Capacity Factor (%)	Thermal Power (MW)	Annual Thermal Energy Output (MWD/yr)	Average Discharge Burnup (MWD/MTU)	Fuel Requirement (MTU/yr)	WGPu per year (kg)
73	760	202,502	6,700	30.22	NA
79	760	219,146	6,700	32.71	NA

a Plutonium production is calculated at 1 kg/1,000 MWD of thermal energy output multiplied
    by a correction factor based on burnup level.
Note. MWe, megawatt-electric, WGFu weapons-grade plutonium. MW, megawatt. MWD/
    yr, megawatt days per year. MWD/MTU, megawatt days per metric ton of uranium per
    year. Kg. kilogram, NA, not applicable.

This is further complicated by the fact that India's Canada Deuterium Uranium PHWRs typically operate at relatively lower burn-ups of 6700 Mega-Watt days per ton (MWd/t) compared to LWRs, which run on higher fuel burn-ups of 33000–50000 MWd/t.[131] India's PHWRs, operating at normal capacity factors and an average burn-up of 6700 MWd/t, would therefore produce less of the more dangerous plutonium isotopes such as Pu-240 compared to LWRs, thus making the plutonium so produced more readily useable for nuclear weapons production.[132] As such, excluding these reactors from India's fissile material production capability may not be wise.

It should also be pointed out that India need not dedicate all eight of its unsafeguarded reactors to fissile material production. Given the fact that the burden of the India's weapons-grade plutonium production is now borne entirely by the Dhruva research reactor, allocating one or two reactors to fissile material production would significantly boost India's production of such material. A study of Tellis's estimates suggests that one reactor—even a small 220 MWe reactor—could be so tasked without becoming excessively costly.[133] This could potentially add 150–200 kg of weapons-grade plutonium per year to India's stockpile.[134]

To further complicate calculations, Dr. Karnad asserts that from 2001, India had operated some of its unsafeguarded PHWRs in "low burn-up" mode to bolster its fissile material stocks to the extent that by 2010–2012, sufficient fissile material would be on hand for 200 nuclear weapons.[135] He further states that plans suggest India desires a force of some 300–400 weapons by 2030.[136] With the potential use of the PHWRs to produce weapons grade plutonium or by using reactor-grade plutonium with deuterium-tritium 'boosting', India may well be on the way to reaching that target.

Is there a Capability Gap Between India and Its Potential Adversaries?

If one examines Indian capabilities and compares them to those of Pakistan

131. Op.cit. n. 126.
132. Perkovich, n. 1, pp. 429–430.
133. Tellis, n.130, pp. 20–23.
134. Zia Mian, et. al, "Plutonium Production in India and The U.S.-India Nuclear Deal," pp. 128–129.
135. Karnad, n. 8, pp. 92–93.
136. Karnad, n. 8, p. 84.

and China, one could be forgiven for possibly concluding that India is somehow at an inevitable disadvantage in terms of capability. However, this is possibly somewhat misleading.

At the outset, India's fissile materials production capability—of unsafeguarded weapons-grade plutonium—largely excludes the country's unsafeguarded nuclear power reactors. As has been detailed in the aforementioned text, the potential size of the Indian arsenal is dependent on whether India has chosen to earmark one or all of its unsafeguarded reactors for weapons purposes. In this respect, any 'gap' in fissile materials or warhead numbers is largely a product of deliberate restraint on the part of India.

With respect to warhead designs and yields, there is a cause for a degree of legitimate concern as, despite cogent and credible information suggesting reliable boosted-fission warheads being the issues as to whether India's warheads are sufficiently reliable and whether India's thermonuclear capability, with much greater uncertainty over the success of the Shakti-1 design, is in a position to manufacture deployable weapons do give cause for concern.

It must be categorically stated that China's deployable nuclear weapons designs have been robustly tested, with its thermonuclear capability being proven beyond any doubt. Furthermore, its incremental approach to the deployment of multiple warheads suggests a well-supported but not overly ambitious approach to nuclear weapons deployment. Compared to India's weapons, one may say without contradiction, that China is significantly ahead in terms of its weapons designs, the reliability of such designs and the capability to improve such designs.

Pakistan, on the other hand, is in much the same situation as India with doubts emerging over the yields of its 1998 nuclear tests. While it has been suggested that Pakistan received much assistance from China for its early weapons designs, it is as yet unclear whether assistance has been received to improve those designs beyond a certain point. Another source for potential assistance to Pakistan could conceivably come from North Korea which had previously supplied much missile technology to Pakistan in exchange for nuclear weapons designs. As North Korea has forged ahead with developing larger-yield and even thermonuclear weapons, the possibility of assistance to Pakistan in this regard is a distinct possibility. A Pakistani arsenal, qualitatively superior to India's, should not be acceptable and should any evidence of this nexus be obtained, India may want to reconsider its self-imposed moratorium on nuclear testing.

However, this is not to say that India needs to match China and Pakistan warhead-for-warhead in either quantity or yield. As has been detailed above, the Indian nuclear arsenal in terms of size and capability should be determined based on a clear understanding of the targets to be destroyed, the survivability of sufficient warheads after a first-strike and the ability of the warheads that are eventually used to achieve the desired effect on the intended targets. With these factors in mind, boosted-fission weapons would sufficiently suffice in respect of yield but whether India has deployed a sufficiently large nuclear arsenal is an open question.

Yet, it would be in error to think of India's nuclear weapons capability—in terms of quantity or warhead designs and yields as a 'gap'. That word, often in vogue with Indian analysts, is somewhat misleading. With nuclear weapons, as noted above, it is less about matching capabilities than about developing sufficient capabilities. If a 'gap' exists, it would be between India's desired levels of capability in terms of survivability, destructive power and targets to be engaged in the event of hostilities. Whether such a 'gap' exists is as yet unanswered but any suggestion that India needs to 'close' this 'gap' must be tempered with a clearer understanding as to whether such a 'gap' exists between the desired capabilities and the existing ones.

With respect to missiles, and other delivery systems, the perception that India is 'inferior' to China owing to the latter possessing ICBMs with ranges exceeding 10,000 km is again misleading, in this case exceedingly so. China has actively sought missiles that could target the Continental United States and has developed its capabilities accordingly. India, in contrast, has not sought such capabilities at least at present. To this end, the Agni series has been developed with certain performance characteristics. It should be noted, once again, China's view that the Agni-V has a range of some 8000 km and a very high re-entry speed—Mach 24—of the missile does suggest a range considerably greater than 5000 km. What would be unacceptable is if the Indian government caps the development of longer-range missiles in some misguided belief that such restraint would be appreciated internationally. That is patently absurd. Moreover, India's own missile capabilities are certainly theoretically capable of developing long-range systems, including ICBMs with ranges exceeding 10,000 km if necessary—a capability that has been tangentially displayed through the Indian satellite launch vehicle program, in particular its PSLV workhorse.

India's medium and intermediate-range systems are certainly comparable in technology and capabilities to their Chinese and Pakistani counterparts. However, India's SRBMs—all Prithvis at present—are decidedly unusual in that they are liquid-fuelled with the attendant drawbacks of a mobile system of that type. It is therefore puzzling that India has not pursued the development of its Prahar and Shaurya systems with any degree of intensity. India's cruise missile capability is an odd combination of the well-developed and advanced BrahMos system—probably only conventionally armed—and the still under development Nirbhay. In the sphere of subsonic long-range cruise missiles, India does lag behind in some way. India's submarine-launched ballistic missiles are as yet in their development phase and in this respect, India does lag far behind China. However, given the time taken for China to develop and deploy its current family of SLBMs, it is not surprising that India's efforts in this sphere are taking some time to fructify.

Yet, performance is the least of India's concerns with respect to missiles. The much greater issue that receives inadequate attention is that of quantities. As discussed, India has perhaps five groups, each of twelve launchers, of MRBMs and IRBMs. While not an insignificant capability, it is suggested that concerns for production of the Agni series of missiles has prompted some remedial action on the part of DRDO and it is hoped that the desired force levels can be achieved.

Conclusion

India's nuclear arsenal is still very much a matter of conjecture with higher or lower estimates being given depending on the inclination of the analyst concerned. Slowly and steadily, India has moved towards the deployment of a nuclear triad with land, sea and air-delivered components. In all three cases, however, the delivery systems are in a state of flux as new land-based missiles are introduced, aircraft await stand-off munitions and the first SSBN has yet to officially conduct a submerged firing of its main armament. India's cruise missile program has been noticeably less fruitful, consistent success being elusive. It should be noted that estimates of India's deployed missile arsenal are as yet relatively modest. It is possible that India could field somewhere in the vicinity of 100–120 MRBMs and IRBMs at present but any numbers significantly higher than that are speculative. While India's fissile stocks may allow for more weapons, delivery systems provide a limiting factor.

Nonetheless, it is important, as noted above, when considering and comparing India's capabilities to those of its potential adversaries to bear in mind the importance of India's targeting strategy which emphasises a countervalue as opposed to counterforce targets. When combined with India's second-strike doctrine, there is a need for a survivable arsenal— that India has sought to achieve through a combination of mobile missile systems and the existence of mountain secure and hardened storage facilities—combined with adequate numbers of missiles and warheads to achieve its desired effect.

India's warhead stockpile is largely a matter of its fissile material stocks and these, as has been previously noted, are very much dependent on how many, if any, of India's unsafeguarded power reactors have been diverted to produce weapons-grade plutonium. India's warhead designs and the reliability of the yields of its weapons have been the subject of intense debate. While doubts exist over the viability of India's thermonuclear weapons designs, which have undoubtedly been refined and improved over the two decades since the 1998 tests to rectify any deficiencies, the successful test of the boosted-fission primary in 1998 does give credence to the existence of a reliable and deployable arsenal based around boosted-fission weapons with substantial yields.

While it can be argued that India still has some way to go before achieving its optimum nuclear force structure, it is singularly unhelpful to think in terms of nuclear weapons or a missile 'gap' between India and its nuclear-armed neighbours. Rather, focus should be on achieving the force levels in terms of numbers and capability needed to inflict the desired level of damage to deter the use or threat of use of nuclear weapons by either neighbour.

3

Tactical Nuclear Weapons: Options for India?

—※—

In an early chapter, consideration was given to tactical nuclear weapons (TNWs) developed by Pakistan. In this chapter, some more examination will be done of the potential use of nuclear weapons on the potential battlefields likely on the Indian subcontinent. There is a distinction that must be drawn between any potential use of TNWs by Pakitan against India and the measures to be adopted therefrom, and any possible use of TNWs by China.

Indeed, the latter is somewhat more remote but it would be foolish to discount the possibility of such an event occurring. It should be noted that Dr Karnad has suggested that Atomic Demolition Munitions be part of India's arsenal. One would wonder if it is not as a hedge against China that such might be desirable. Much of this chapter will be dedicated to examining the India–Pakistan battlefield and various permutations of offensive operations that could take place and the doctrinal changes that have taken place post-2002. However, the advantages and disadvantages of TNWs in both the India–Pakistan and the India–China context will be explored.

The India–Pakistan Battlefield: Tyranny of Geography

Prior to Pakistan's development of TNWs—and nearly two decades ago—the author examined the South Asian battlefield.[1] The geography has not

---

1. Sanjay Badri-Maharaj, The Armageddon Factor: Nuclear Weapons in the India-Pakistan Context (New Delhi: Lancer, 2000), pp. 169–195—The relevant sections are summarised herein.

changed but with new thresholds defined, India is faced with a choice of either limiting any conventional military action or calling Pakistan's bluff. In this section, we will explore the old dynamic of the India–Pakistan battlefield and thereafter, we will examine the changes that have taken place post the introduction of the TNWs.

The Battlefield: Possible Theatres of Operations

An India–Pakistan conflict could take place in four major theatres, each varying in geography and, to a lesser extent, in climatic conditions. The theatres of operations are:[2]

- Along the Line of Control (LoC)—Northern Kashmir region,
- Southern Jammu and Kashmir and Punjab sectors,
- North and Central Rajasthan,
- South Rajasthan and Gujarat.

Each of these areas offers a mix of opportunities and challenges, and the Indian military would need to make an appropriate judgement as to the area most suitable for offensive operations. Over the years, India has shown a degree of adaptability in modifying its doctrine to suit the changed circumstances. For example, in 1987, the Army conducted a massive military exercise, 'Brasstacks', which outlined what was then a new doctrine. No longer would it concentrate on operations in Punjab, as it had during the 1965 war. Under the new doctrine, it would deploy powerfully armoured formations in the Rajasthan sector with the aim of bisecting Pakistan at its weakest point in the Sindh Province. This model is now clearly unworkable as any such existential threat would cross Pakistan's spatial threshold. Nevertheless, the risk of TNW use is at its highest in this sector.

India has, in acceptance of a changed reality, abandoned the 'Brasstacks' concept. The Indian Army will not attempt to make major territorial gains. Instead, it will concentrate on occupying small stretches of territory and in the process take care not to cross Pakistan's spatial threshold. The territory occupied would not threaten Pakistan's existence, but would be enough to force Pakistan to commit its forces where they will be met and engaged by

---

2. M. Thomas, "An Analysis of the Threat Perception and Strategy for India," *Indian Defence Review*, January 1990, p. 63.

superior Indian firepower—in some ways this concept as early as the mid-1990s, presaged the development of the Cold Start Doctrine. By altering its offensive doctrine and possibly opening up new areas for possible offensive action—such as along the LoC—India has sought to nullify Pakistan's threat of nuclear weapons use. This presents challenges of its own in that India's mechanised forces cannot be adequately employed along the LoC and emphasises the need for infantry and artillery formations to be adequately prepared.

Further evidence of change can be found in India's attempt to reduce the time taken to commence military operations. Concerned at the lengthy mobilisation witnessed during Operation 'Parakram', India has made a significant progress in reducing the time taken to prepare and conduct offensive operations. Despite official denials of its existence, the 'Cold Start' proactive military doctrine seems to be the current incarnation of this approach, aiming to commence military operations within 48 hours of the orders being given, and limiting territorial aims while seeking to engage and inflict attrition on the Pakistani armed forces. It is a fully legitimate question to ask whether this risks crossing the Pakistani 'military threshold' for nuclear use. What, for example, would Pakistan deem 'unacceptable damage' to its military forces? It is, therefore, submitted that Pakistan's threat to use TNWs in the event of its forces being decimated is a bluff which, in the event of hostilities, India must be willing to call. In this regard, both passive and active chemical, biological, radiological and nuclear (CBRN) measures assume importance.

When looking at these theatres of operations, it must be borne in mind that the LoC in the Northern Kashmir region is not an internationally recognised border. It should also be noted that Punjab and Kashmir are politically very sensitive areas for the political establishments in both countries. It is, therefore, hardly likely that any major loss of territory in either of these two areas would be acceptable. To this end, military operations in these regions will be the most intensely contested with both sides keen to avoid a loss of territory much more than make major gains.

In the Southern Jammu and Kashmir and Punjab sectors, stretching down into North and Central Rajasthan, there are a series of extremely formidable obstacle defences, which are called ditch-cum-bunds by the

Indians and canals by the Pakistanis. These defences, combined with the existing natural ground features, make large-scale mechanised operations virtually impossible.[3] These linear defences are extremely formidable since the ditch-cum-bunds are liberally laced with diffused and well-concealed concrete bunkers which have considerable defensive firepower and are difficult to locate, even with thermal imaging.[4] This effectively limits operations to defensive positions with only a local offensive capability. It is possible that major operations could be carried out if either side is willing to suffer the inevitable losses in equipment that would ensue.

The Rajasthan and Gujarat regions present an entirely different scenario. In the Northern/Central Rajasthan theatre, considerable scope exists for the large-scale use of mechanised formations in the desert and semi-desert sectors. It is in these sectors, the Thar Desert and the Rann of Kutch that the major armoured battles of the next India–Pakistan war are likely to be fought. It is, therefore, not surprising that a complete Indian Strike Corps is earmarked for use primarily in this area.

The Thar Desert and the Rann of Kutch also present the best possible place for tactical nuclear warfare. The barren desert areas are ideal as the so-called collateral damage could be reduced. Moreover, any meaningful Indian gains in this area, which are beyond the major river lines, would threaten the very existence of the Pakistani state, thus prompting Pakistan to actively consider using nuclear weapons in the event of a major Indian breakthrough.

On the other hand, since the Indian Strike Corps will be operating in this area, so will be the bulk of India's formidable Corps of Army Air Defence (CAAD). This means that any Pakistani attack against a major Indian formation would be met with heavy resistance from the extremely dense and sophisticated CAAD assets—not to mention fighter squadrons from the Indian Air Force (IAF). Therefore, any Pakistani attack stands a good chance of being repelled without reaching their targets.

India could also reduce the risk of nuclear retaliation by limiting its advance to the major river lines, or between 60 and 80 km in the North/Central Rajasthan sectors. This would mean that the existence of Pakistan

---

3. Ibid.
4. S. Bhaduri, "The Artillery Division—Part II," *Indian Defence Review*, April 1992, p. 118.

would no longer be threatened while India would still occupy chunks of territory. Pakistan would probably be less willing to cross the nuclear threshold for such a limited Indian advance.

It is unlikely that either India or Pakistan would initiate nuclear warfare in either the Punjab or Kashmir regions purely for tactical gain. Indeed, for Pakistan, the use of such weapons in Kashmir would almost certainly alienate the Muslim population of the Kashmir Valley. In the case of Punjab, Pakistan's military and political elite are largely drawn from that province and as such, it is extremely unlikely that they would take a risk as large as this for limited tactical gains. From a purely military standpoint, it should also be pointed out that the ditch-cum-bund defences and their network of concrete bunkers would probably survive a nuclear attack. This would render a nuclear attack in this sector virtually useless.

Therefore, the only area in which nuclear weapons would be tactically useful is in Rajasthan and Gujarat—for reasons which have already been given. Yet, that land, especially in the Thar Desert sector of Rajasthan, is of virtually no strategic importance. Would any militarily sane nation risk revealing the full extent of its covert nuclear program unless its very existence was threatened? The answer is clearly no. Therefore, if India limits its territorial gains in this area, Pakistan would have no reason to resort to nuclear weapons.

There is one wild card in this scenario—the LoC. If India were to launch a major assault along the LoC—would Pakistan use nuclear weapons? An examination of a possible war scenario will perhaps illustrate Indian planning more clearly.

War Scenario

In 1987, the Indian Army conducted a massive military exercise, 'Brasstacks', which outlined what was then a new tactical doctrine. No longer would the Indian Army concentrate on operations in Punjab, as it had during the 1965 war, but would deploy massively powerful armoured formations in the Rajasthan sector with the aim of bisecting Pakistan at its weakest point in the Sindh province.

This has been the model most often used and quoted by scholars in the literature available on possible war scenarios. Moreover, it has been further argued that thanks to Pakistan's nuclear capability, an Indian offensive in the Sindh that met with success would be answered by a Pakistani nuclear strike. Since defences in Punjab are strong, it was argued that as India's military superiority was hardly overwhelming, the nuclear factor may be creating an environment where war was almost impossible.

This model is, however, obsolete and far from creating a certain conventional stalemate, has simply led to the Indian Army rethinking its tactical doctrine. No longer will the Indian Army attempt to make major territorial gains, but it will concentrate on occupying a small stretch of territory, not enough to threaten Pakistan's existence, but enough to force Pakistan to commit its forces where they will be met by superior Indian firepower which will then inflict maximum attrition. The reason for this, in part, lies in the risk of nuclear warfare, but the main reason lies in the fact that previous wars in 1965 and 1971 have shown that major territorial gains are unlikely in a short war.

It is likely that if a major Indian offensive occurs, it will occur in Kashmir. Never before has the Indian Army attempted any offensive in Kashmir, but this time, thanks to the massive influx of troops into the State, an Indian offensive along the LoC is very possible. It could be argued that these troops are primarily for counter-insurgency operations. However, this does not explain why the formations coming into Jammu and Kashmir are bringing their artillery with them. Any fighting in Kashmir will centre around a clash of infantry and artillery and as such, the induction of substantial artillery assets into the region must be seen as significant.

At the outset, one thing must be made clear. In the past, neither India nor Pakistan believed that anything would be decided in a war lasting less than 4 weeks. India based its plans on a period of intense fighting lasting 6–8 weeks followed by a period of major, but less intense fighting lasting up to four more weeks. War wastage reserves are calculated on this basis and so if a war lasts only 2 weeks or thereabouts, the most that can be hoped for is for heavy attrition of the enemy forces. However, since then, there has been an emphasis on shorter duration conflicts with a desire to achieve realistic objectives within a 14 day period.

India has therefore moved away from the Brasstacks plan of bisecting Pakistan in the Sindh and threatening Islamabad with encirclement to a more modest objective of destroying as much of the Pakistani military as possible. Pakistan's nuclear weapons provide some deterrence against any Indian move to make deep thrusts into its territory and against any possible bisection of Pakistan, they are of limited use in a war aimed solely at inflicting maximum attrition against Pakistani military forces.

The Indian Army has two Strike Corps, two Corps and one Corps assigned to the Rajasthan and Punjab sectors respectively. The Strike Corps are described in an earlier section, but each is composed of one armoured division and several infantry divisions and supporting units. Each will also have an artillery division attached. A third Strike Corps—21 Corps is deployable as needed.

In the Brasstacks model, these were the two formations Pakistan was most concerned about and their continued presence in the Rajasthan and Punjab sectors will ensure that Pakistan cannot consider any major troop redeployments in either sector. Under the current plans, India intends not to advance more than 60–80 km in the North/Central Rajasthan sector and only up to the major river lines in South Rajasthan/Gujarat, Pakistan's existence would hardly be threatened.

However, it must be remembered that India and Pakistan will be fighting a political war as much as a military one and any loss of territory is considered a major political embarrassment. This means that Pakistan would invariably have to attempt a counterattack against the Indian forces occupying any of its territories. Its forces would then be drawn into a battle of attrition against Indian forces, a battle that they would lose. If the current buildup of air defence assets, upgrading of armour and antitank munitions and the increase in artillery within the India army is seen in the light of this post-Brasstacks tactical doctrine, it is abundantly clear that India is building up its forces to ward off any Pakistani counterattack, inflicting devastating losses on the attackers.

In the Southern Jammu and Kashmir and Punjab sectors, the huge fixed fortifications described previously effectively limit the scope of any Indian operation. India is highly unlikely to attempt a major offensive in this sector for two reasons. The first is the extent of the fortified defences in this sector, but the second is far more significant and goes to the core of Pakistan's vulnerability versus India.

The real vulnerability of Pakistan lies, not in a lack of 'strategic depth', but in the fact that so many of its major population centres and politically and military sensitive targets lie very close to the border with India. As was mentioned earlier, this negates the tactical use of nuclear weapons in the Punjab sector in particular. However, should India threaten Lahore, for example, Pakistan could be compelled to attempt a nuclear strike against an Indian civilian target. As such, it is hardly likely that India would want to risk a major advance in Punjab. Aims in this sector would be limited to holding Pakistani forces in a defensive deployment pattern while inflicting maximum attrition with 2 Corps and 21 Corps.

Along the LoC, however, the situation is very different. One of the consequences of the Kashmir insurgency is that India has transferred several divisions to the area to reinforce the troops already there and bringing the total troop strength in this sector to over 250,000. The Indian divisions and brigades also brought their supporting artillery with them and this combination—which is far in excess of what is needed for defensive operations—enables Indian planners to contemplate a major offensive along the LoC with every chance of success.

The importance of the term LoC cannot be understated. Pakistan clings to the illusion, in official pronouncements at any rate, that its part of Kashmir is not really part of Pakistan. As such, it has always refused to recognise the LoC as the international border with India. This is something that India intends to exploit to the fullest. Pakistan, on the other hand, appears to work on a different strategy. From the time of the 1965 and 1971 wars, up until India's Brasstacks exercise, the emphasis was placed on the static defence of the LoC and the border. However, in light of India's substantially enhanced offensive capabilities, Pakistan realised that this 'stand and fight' doctrine would lead to serious Indian penetration of Pakistani territory with the Pakistani army being unable to manoeuvre to meet the threat. Counterattacking formations would then be destroyed piecemeal.

Pakistan has therefore adopted a new strategy—the Riposte. This is remarkably simple in concept, in that Pakistan would accept the loss of territory in Indian penetrations, but would conduct a limited advance along narrow fronts with the aim of occupying territory near the border to a depth of 40–50 km. Pakistan believes that this would give it a bargaining chip to be used in the aftermath of a ceasefire brought about by international pressure after 3–4 weeks of fighting. The Pakistanis, to some extent, still assume that India will attempt deep penetrations into the territory. Moreover, it appears that though the Pakistani army is well prepared for this new doctrine, there is an inadequate appreciation of the threat posed by Indian air power to the attacking formations. Some planning has been based on the highly unrealistic assumption of local air superiority and as such, these plans may go seriously awry.

So what will a future India–Pakistan war look like? There are a number of good books on the 1965 and 1971 wars and some excellent accounts of the tactical thinking behind Exercise Brasstacks are available. These, however, are not of much use at present. However, perhaps the best and most realistic war scenario was painted by defence journalist Pravin Sawhney in the Asian Age newspaper in November 1994.[5]

Holding formations in both India and Pakistan can man their forward defensive positions and fortifications in less than 24 hours. However, Corps-level reserves with large stockpiles of munitions will take between 24 and 72 hours for mobilisation after being given their orders. In this regard, both armies will be evenly matched in the first 24 hours since the Pakistani units have to travel a shorter distance to their forward positions.

Pakistan's Army Reserve North (ARN) is based in the Kharian/Mangla complex and would need to travel only 200 km to its forward concentration areas or even their assembly areas, where regrouping before an offensive is done. This could be done on extremely short notice and is consistent with Pakistan's preconceived offensive plans as outlined in the Riposte doctrine. Army Reserve South (ARS), which is based in the Multan area, can also be available for operations in a similar time. While many of India's formations may take up to 72 hours to be fully deployed, two out of India's three Strike Corps, 1 Corps and 2 Corps, are so positioned as to match the mobilisation timings of ARS. As of now, it is not known if the third Strike Corps and 21 Corps will be available at such a short notice.

India could, in theory, disrupt the early deployment of ARN if the Indian Army's Northern Command denies deployment space with the pre-

---

5. P. Sawhney, "If Pakistan and India Go to War," *The Asian Age*, November 12–13, 1994, p.13.

emptive mobilisation and deployment of Northern Command's theatre reserves. In 1994, Sawhney was unconvinced that this was possible owing to the employment of so many units of the Indian Army on internal security duties in Jammu and Kashmir. However, since 1994, the number of paramilitary units in Jammu and Kashmir has grown and the Indian Army has deployed almost 30,000 men from its Rashtriya Rifles battalions. These would take at least some pressure off the regular army in counterinsurgency operations. Moreover, the number of regular army troops in the state seems to have grown. These could provide the Indian Army with sufficient troops in theatre to deny Pakistan's ARN deployment space, thus neutralising any advantage Pakistan had in this regard.

The problem with assessing whether or not Indian troop strength is adequate to the task of neutralising ARN's deployment is that the internal security situation in Jammu and Kashmir is very variable. It is possible that the paramilitary forces and the Rashtriya Rifles will free a large number of troops for conventional operations. Moreover, it is possible that up to three divisions, with over 40,000 men, could be moved from the China border without seriously degrading India's defences against a Chinese assault. These troops are held by Central and Eastern commands and have actually been earmarked for out-of-theatre operations.

In the case of ARS, the IAF has the potential to cause havoc with their deployment by beginning an intensive interdiction campaign in the Gujarat (Punjab)–Sialkot–Gujranwala area. However, this would make India the aggressor in any conflict. Sawhney argues that this would make the Indian government reluctant to permit this; however, this is not at all certain. The Indian Government may well engineer incidents to give an excuse, however flimsy, for the IAF to begin such an interdiction campaign.

In order to further reduce the risk of a Pakistani nuclear strike, it is possible that India, through the United Nations, might make certain pledges to Pakistan. These might include a pledge not to deliberately attack a civilian target, to refrain from attacking civilian nuclear installations and a promise not to initiate the use of weapons of mass destruction unless attacked with such weapons. India could also make it clear that it would abide by these terms only if Pakistan agrees to do the same. Should Pakistan not agree, India would probably assume that a nuclear strike would be forthcoming.

Let us for the moment assume that India does not deny ARN deployment space and that the Indian government does not sanction the launching of pre-emptive air strikes. Both India and Pakistan will have a relative parity in manpower and combat formations at the beginning of any conflict. India will be able to bring up some very large combat formations from central and eastern India, but Pakistan would be almost fully committed. A force of three infantry divisions plus some independent brigades under 11 and 12 Corps would be transferable from the Peshawar and Quetta areas respectively, but with very little artillery and armour. Moreover, if there is any serious escalation of fighting in Afghanistan, Pakistan may be less willing to denude its Afghan border of all regular army formations.

The Indian objectives in the Northern sector, in Jammu and Kashmir, are somewhat unclear. The Indian Defence Review Research Team argued that the capture of Skardu to cut off the main glacier zone in Baltistan would be a major objective. Moreover, a strong offensive aimed at capturing Muzaffarabad from the North and the South of the Jhelum, and the neutralisation of the Haji Pir (Bedori) Bulge would have to be undertaken. The Indian Army would also attempt to capture the Mirpur-Mangla Complex with the view of presenting a clear and present threat to the Pakistani national capital region. Finally, to cope with the threat posed by ARN, Indian formations would make a penetration into the Sialkot sector with the sole aim of bottling up and denying deployment space to the Pakistani formations, thus ensuring its eventual destruction.[6]

The scenario described above leads to the question as to whether Pakistan would launch a nuclear strike in response to the threat posed to its national capital. The Indian Defence Review Research Team does not answer this question in any way. Pravin Sawhney describes a far more detailed scenario which, while essentially similar in concept, seems to differ in some major details.

Sawhney, in his scenario, argues that the Indian Army would have a choice—attacking into either Ladakh–Baltistan or into Pakistan-occupied Kashmir and that the army would prefer an ingress into the latter along the LoC. He also argues that the main thrust would be in the Jammu division

---

6.   IDR Research Team, "Operational Scenario Alpha," *Indian Defence Review,* July 1992, p. 22.

between Poonch and Chamb with a secondary thrust into the Tithwal–Keran sectors.

Northern Command might also suggest that a limited offensive be conducted to the west of Zoji La in the Dras–Kargil sectors. The aim here would be to cut off the lines of communications of the Pakistani brigade based near the Shingo and Indus Rivers. These operations will call for troops specially trained and equipped for operations in mountainous and hilly terrain and to this end, the three divisions previously earmarked for use against China would be invaluable. Moreover, select formations from these forces already send divisional reconnaissance groups into Kashmir for terrain familiarisation. That these divisional reconnaissance groups have been conducting terrain familiarisation for quite some time gives rise to the idea that India has been planning for a major offensive in the Jammu and Kashmir sector for a long time.

Pravin Sawhney assumes that the attack in Kashmir would be launched first with two mountain divisions concentrated to begin operations in the directions of Jhanghar–Mirpur and Nowshera–Bhimber with the ability to switch between the two. A third division would be allocated to the Mendhar–Kotli–Mirpur axis in two columns. Pakistan would probably understand that some move was afoot at this stage to the sector defended by 19 Infantry Division. The Pakistanis would then move the 7 and 9 infantry divisions based at Peshawar to assist in their defence. However, it is not certain that these two divisions would be available entirely since the Afghan border is volatile at the best of times and the situation in Afghanistan is very fluid.

Nonetheless, assuming these formations begin an eastward movement, Pakistan's ARS would start mobilising at Multan. At this stage, India's three Strike Corps would begin a forward movement. The plan as envisaged by Indian planners is for 1 Corps to face ARN and 2 and 21 Corps to face ARS.

The offensive would begin in the Ladakh sector with two brigades attacking from Kargil along with two brigades from the Northern Kashmir-holding division tasked with straightening the LoC in the Tithwal–Bugina bulge sector. The three mountain divisions mentioned earlier would then commence their offensive which would probably face extremely stiff resistance from the Pakistani infantry divisions facing them. Compared to the dashing manoeuvre warfare employed during the Brasstacks exercise, the current Indian Army high command is fully convinced that their present offensive plans would be more akin to the 'meat-grinding' assaults of the Second World War.

As Pakistan's strategic depth was eroded around Islamabad and with its Army Head Quarters at Rawalpindi fixed on the worsening situation at Mirpur, ARN would be committed to action. ARN would attempt an offensive aimed at the Jammu–Pathankot corridor while crossing the river Ravi aimed at threatening Gurdaspur–Pathankot.

These operations would be met by India's 1 Corps which would engage ARN in a savage battle of attrition, forcing Pakistan to move 9 division to the Mirpur sector, where the Indian offensive continues, while 7 division will move along with 30 Corps to reinforce ARN. In the meantime, the Indian and Pakistani air forces would engage in their own battle of attrition, with the former waging a heavy counter-air offensive while engaging in a massive offensive-air-support operation for the Indian Army.

With the Indian offensive overcoming its opponents in the Kashmir region and ARN, and its reinforcements, engaged with India's 1 Corps in a battle of attrition, Pakistan's army high command would prefer that ARS be kept out of action as long as possible. However, since the whole object of the Indian plan is to inflict heavy attrition on Pakistan's armed forces, it would be essential for ARS to be neutralised.

Sawhney believes that India would use its Desert Corps (12 Corps) to draw ARS into action. 12 Corps would launch a limited offensive aimed south of Rahim Yar Khan to which ARS would respond with a thrust to its north. The Indian Holding Corps, with their Re-organized Army Plains Infantry Divisions (RAPIDS), would probably find themselves under heavy pressure from the powerful ARS. At this stage, with ARS fully committed, India would spring its trap with 2 and 21 Corps, along with massive air support, launching out together along a very narrow front aimed at punching through 31 Corps and falling on the soft underbelly of ARS which would then be destroyed in detail.

In this scenario, the fighting which has lasted between 2 and 4 weeks has left Pakistan's armed forces severely depleted, if not almost destroyed. ARS has been destroyed along with the Pakistani formations in the

Rajasthan/Gujarat sector. Indian forces have made gains along the LoC, severely eroding Pakistan's strategic depth in the region of Islamabad and ARN and its reinforcing formations have been mauled by 1 Corps, Indian Holding Corps and the IAF.

What is significant is that Pakistan would not have suffered any major territorial losses. No Indian offensive actually seized much land and in no case was the existence of Pakistan actually threatened. While nuclear threats and counterthreats might be traded, Pakistan would probably not feel quite so compelled to go nuclear as it would if its very survival was at stake.

India's gamble is that with such a mauling of its military capability and since Pakistan has neither the money nor the resources to re build such a large and powerful military machine again, Pakistan might be far more amenable to a permanent settlement of the Kashmir dispute and other outstanding matters. Since India would hold a major advantage in that, Pakistan could no longer rival India militarily, such a settlement would probably go in India's favour. At least that is the Indian plan. Whether or not any permanent settlement over Kashmir can be achieved after such a war remains a matter for speculation.

The most important point to note in this scenario is that in no case would India be seeking to seize large areas of Pakistani territory. Pakistan's existence will not be endangered so would Pakistan risk using nuclear weapons on the battlefield? Having said this, it should further be pointed out that there is a lot of room for misinterpretation in this scenario. For example, will Pakistan be able to distinguish between a limited Indian advance and a full-scale invasion? At what stage would Pakistan consider its existence to be threatened?

After discussions with a number of retired Indian officers—specifically about this question of misinterpretation—the only answers that could be provided revolved around the fact that a limited Indian penetration would be along a broad front and have limited depth while a full invasion would have areas of narrow but deep penetrations into the Pakistani territory. The officers believed that Pakistan would have no difficulty in differentiating between the two and as such, the question of misinterpretation did not arise. However, now that Pakistan has developed TNWs, the above scenario is only partially realistic.

The Cold Start Doctrine

The so-called 'Cold Start Doctrine' evolved after the 2001/02 military stand-off following a series of Pakistani terrorist attacks, including one on the Indian Parliament. India's frustration at not being able to launch a swift military response, owing to its long mobilisation period, made the Indian Army examine its doctrine with the hope of evolving one that would enable the country to achieve its political and military aims in a short war without running the risk of crossing Pakistan's nuclear red lines. The premise of the doctrine was based on two major elements: readjustments were carried out to enhance the offensive operations' capability of 'Pivot' corps (previously designated Holding corps), so as to make it possible to launch offensive operations virtually from a 'cold start' to deny Pakistan the advantage of early mobilisation, plus Strike Corps cantonments were moved closer to the border, enabling them to deploy much more quickly.

The second element of the Cold Start doctrine envisages the fielding of a number of 'integrated battle groups' (IBG) each of division size and raised from within existing forces. Each IBG would be capable of launching limited offensive operations to a shallow depth, to capture a long swathe of territory almost all along the international boundary. Any success achieved by the IBGs could be exploited by one or more Strike Corps, where possible, but without crossing Pakistan's nuclear red lines. India would then try to use the captured territory as a bargaining chip to force Pakistan to end its support to terrorist forces operating against India.[7]

The overall objective would be to destroy the Pakistan Army's war-waging potential through the application of what Brigadier Gurmeet Kanwal termed "asymmetric firepower" from ground forces (through long-range medium guns, rocket launchers and surface-to-surface and cruise missiles) and through concerted air strikes directed against Pakistani forces on the battlefield. Brigadier Kanwal notes that the logic behind the generation of massive asymmetries of firepower is necessary given the difficulties inherent in drawing into battle and destroying Pakistan's strategic reserves (ARN

---

7. Gurmeet Kanwal, "India's Cold Start Doctrine and Strategic Stability," *Institute for Defence Studies and Analyses*, (June 01, 2010). https://idsa.in/idsacomments/IndiasColdStartDoctrineandStrategicStability_gkanwal_010610, accessed on October 23, 2017.

and ARS) through deep manoeuvre in a short, limited war. To this end, the most effective way of destroying these formations—which form the bulk of Pakistan's offensive capability—is through asymmetric firepower.[8]

The 2001/02 stand-off taught the Indian Army many operational and logistics lessons. Undoubtedly, the most important lesson that emerged was the need to reduce the excessively long time period that India's three Strike Corps needed to mobilise for war. At that time, Kanwal argues, by the time the three Strike Corps were ready to be launched across the border, the international community had prevailed on India to give General Musharraf an opportunity to prove his sincerity in curbing cross-border terrorism. In an interview with Praveen Swam, General S. Padmanabhan, India's Chief of Army Staff (COAS) during Operation Parakram stated:[9]

"You could certainly question why we are so dependent on our strike formations," he said, "and why my holding Corps do not have the capability to do the same tasks from a cold start. This is something I have worked on while in office. Perhaps, in time, it will be our military doctrine…"

Since then, Indian Army planners have worked hard to reduce the mobilisation time and come up with a new doctrine for offensive operations that would achieve the desired military objectives without risking escalation to the nuclear level.

After deliberation at length during the biannual conference of the army's Commanders in Chief in April 2004, chaired by General N C Vij, the COAS, the adoption of the 'Cold Start' doctrine that is to be executed by 'Integrated Battle Groups' was announced. But, in perhaps typical Indian Army obfuscation General V K Singh, then COAS, said during a media interview:[10]

"There is nothing called 'Cold Start'. As part of our overall strategy we have a number of contingencies and options, depending on what the aggressor does."

---

8. Ibid.
9. Praveen Swami, "War and Games," *Frontline,* (February 15, 2002). http://www.frontline.in/static/html/fl1903/19030040.htm, accessed on October 23, 2017.
10. Manu Pubby, "No 'Cold Start' doctrine, India tells US," *Indian Express,* (September 9, 2010). http://archive.indianexpress.com/news/no--cold-start--doctrine-india-tells-us/679273/, accessed October 23, 2017.

Yet the name 'Cold Start' has continued. Accepting that India does not have overwhelming military superiority, the doctrine seeks to leverage India's modest superiority in conventional forces to respond effectively and efficaciously to Pakistan and to restore a conventional option to India in light of Pakistan's nuclear 'red-lines'.

As indicated before, this doctrine augmented the Indian Army's offensive power which had been monopolised by the three large strike corps with eight division-sized IBGs. These eight battle groups would be prepared to launch multiple strikes into Pakistan along different axes of advance with heavy air support and bringing concentrated firepower to bear. At the same time, the 'pivot corps', augmented by additional armour and artillery, would both man defensive positions and undertake limited offensive operations as necessary. All elements would engage in continuous operations, day and night, until their military objectives were achieved. With the objective of the military operations being to make shallow territorial gains, 50–80 km deep, it is hoped that this would avoid nuclear red-lines—along the lines as outlined in the early scenario detailed above.[11]

It would appear that the Cold Start doctrine envisages, according to Kanwal, 3–5 IBGs entering Pakistani territory within 72–96 hours from the time the order to mobilise is issued. The emphasis on speed has two objectives. The first is, of course, the military objective as outlined earlier. However, equally important is the political objective of achieving a result before either China or the United States could intervene either diplomatically or more vigorously on Pakistan's behalf. In the case of the former, the spectre of military action cannot be ruled out. The Cold Start doctrine also seems to have the aim of preventing the Indian civilian leadership halting military operations prematurely whether due to external pressure or lack of resolve. This latter distrust of the resolve of the Indian civilian leadership is interesting and perhaps reflects a lack of either understanding or empathy with the compulsions they face.

---

11. Gurmeet Kanwal, "Cold Start: India's Pro-active Offensive Operations Doctrine for War in the Plains," http://gurmeetkanwal.com/ArticleDetails.aspx?id=391, accessed on October 23, 2017.

Therefore, compared to the earlier doctrines, the perceived advantages of the Cold Start doctrine over its predecessor are fivefold. As Walter Ladwig III explains:[12]

First, forward-deployed division-sized units can be alerted faster and mobilized more quickly than larger formations. If the battle groups and the pivot corps start closer to the international border, their logistics requirements are significantly reduced, enhancing their maneuverability and their ability to surprise. Second, even though division-sized formations can "bite and hold" territory, they lack the power to deliver a knockout blow. In the minds of Indian military planners, this denies Pakistan the "regime survival" justification for employing nuclear weapons in response to India's conventional attack. Furthermore, under Cold Start, the Indian Army can undertake a range of responses to a given provocation rather than the all-or-nothing approach of the Sundarji doctrine. Third, multiple divisions, operating independently, have the potential to disrupt or incapacitate the Pakistani leadership's decision-making cycle.

In the opinion of Indian planners, when the Pakistani military is faced with offensive thrusts in as many as eight different sectors, it would be hard-pressed to determine where to concentrate its forces and which lines of advance to oppose. In a conflict of limited duration, India would be hard-pressed to leverage the numerical superiority of its conventional forces to achieve a decisive outcome as neither its qualitative nor quantitative superiority is overwhelming. To this end, increased emphasis is put on the rapid mobilisation of forces in an effort to quickly attain realistic military objectives. Fourth, having an additional eight units—each of division size—plus three strike corps— capable of offensive action significantly increases the challenge for Pakistani intelligence's limited reconnaissance assets to monitor the status of all the IBGs, improving the chance of achieving surprise.[13]

The question is how prepared is India to implement the Cold Start Doctrine. Even before the 2001/02 confrontation, India was moving

12. Walter C. Ladwig III, "A Cold Start for Hot Wars?," *International Security* vol. 32, no. 3, (Winter 2007/08), pp. 158.http://www.mitpressjournals.org/doi/pdf/10.1162/isec.2008.32.3.158, accessed on October 23, 2017.

13. Ibid.

towards improved coordination between forces and shortening its mobilisation times. For example, In May 2001, Exercise Vijayee Bhava was launched by the Indian Army, which involved some 50,000 troops to improve coordinated operations between the army and the air force. One of the major objectives of this operation was to reduce the mobilisation time drastically to 48 hours. Apparently, the exercise was successful in achieving this objective. In this respect, Exercise Vijayee Bhava can be considered to be a trial run of the Cold Start Doctrine as, according to the Cold Start doctrine, IBGs will be well forward from the existing garrisons. Conducted in the Bikaner and Suratgarh area, Exercise Vijayee Bhava was conducted with the stated aim of reducing mobilisation time which it claimed to have cut down to just 2 days from 27 days in *Operation Parakaram* in 2001–02.[14]

This was followed by *Operation Sudarshan Shakti'*—India's largest war games in two decades in which nearly 60,000 troops and 500 armoured vehicles participated and thereafter, 2 Corps *(Strike Corps, Kharga)* conducted 'Exercise Brahmashira' in Rajasthan to practice swift multiple offensives deep into enemy territory.

Refining its techniques, many of the elements of the Cold Start Doctrine were tested during Exercise Sudarshan Shakti in 2011. 'Sudarshan Shakti' was the outcome of a study undertaken by the Army on how to initiate transformation and maintain continuous offensive capabilities with a networked headquarters supported by intelligence, surveillance, and reconnaissance acting as the nerve centre of operations. The improvements in weaponry had also given an added impetus to revising existing military doctrines.

The Indian military conducted the exercise in the Barmer-Jaisalmer sector, Rajasthan. It was a 15-day exercise, started in mid-November 2011 and ending in early December 2011, aimed to strengthen the war-fighting capabilities of the Indian Army's Southern Command 21 Corps (Strike Corps) and the IAFs South Western Air Command. Exercise Sudarshan Shakti was spread over the huge geographical area in the deserts of Barmer, Jaisalmer, Pokhran and Pachpadra.

---

14. Suman Sharma, "Army Mobilization Time: 48hrs," *DNA India*, (May 16, 2011). http://www.dnaindia.com/india/report-army-mobilisation-time-48-hours-1543679, accessed on October 23, 2017.

Almost 50,000 troops along with 500 main battle tank (MBTs), 120 artillery guns, various missiles, rockets, combat aircraft, airborne early warning and control system, Battlefield Surveillance Radars, Weapon Locating Radars and attack helicopters took part in the Exercise. Troops of the 31-Armoured Division of the Indian Army and a battalion of the Assam Regiment also participated in this exercise. The Indian Army also utilised the Army Aviation Corps and medium-lift transport helicopters for logistical transport operations.

Exercise Sudarshan Shakti also sought to adopt new technologies such as precision munitions, advanced surveillance systems, space and network-centricity. One of the aims of this exercise was to ensure infusion of the latest technology with the weapons and troops while providing real-time information of the battle front to the field commanders. The exercise was held to help validate the Southern Command's war-fighting concepts while working towards a 'capability-based approach' relying on a series of transformational initiatives, concepts, organisational structures and absorption of new technology.[15]

In a sense, these exercises have sought to refine the Cold Start Doctrine. The use of combined air-land assets is indicative of the importance that air power plays in the viability of the Cold Start Doctrine and the emphasis on mechanised formations, their deployment and their operations suggests that India continues to place emphasis on its armour for achieving results. This will have particular significance should a nuclear red-line be crossed as India's armoured units, as will be discussed later, are the best adapted Indian formation for fighting in a CBRN environment.

There are many unknowns, however, in respect of communications networks, effective coordination of close air support in operations where friendly and enemy forces are in close proximity. Moreover, are India's night-fighting capabilities adequate to ensure unhindered operations on a 24/7 basis? While India's armour has made significant strides in this direction, infantry units still lack adequate quantities of night-vision devices and night sights for weapons to enable unimpaired operations—although

15. Subhash Kapila, "Indian Army Exercise Sudershan Shakti-Revalidation Of Cold Start War Doctrine," *South Asia Analysis Group*, (December 10, 2011) https://web.archive.org/web/20120104045741/http://southasiaanalysis.org/papers49/paper4809.html

the infantry is quite capable even without such devices of fighting at night but with reduced effectiveness. An additional weakness that is slowly being addressed—with the recent contract for 100 K-9 self-propelled guns—is the absence of self-propelled artillery with Indian strike formations. Even the order for 100 K-9s will be inadequate to satisfy the needs of all three Strike Corps, much less the eight integrated battle groups.

More pressing concerns include the gradual drawdown in available aircraft for close-air -support operations. The withdrawal of the MiG-23BN and MiG-27 fleets leave a gap in the Indian air power that is difficult to plug with the existing assets despite the superior survivability, weapons and targeting systems on those aircraft. Quantity can only partially be replaced by quality and the removal of close to 200 aircraft from the IAF inventory may make it difficult to sustain the tempo of air operations necessary to achieve optimum results from the Cold Start doctrine.

The scale of the challenge facing the IAF to optimally participate in the Cold Start Doctrine cannot be overstated. The IAF has a requirement to supplement and eventually replace much of its fighter fleet with light (MiG-21), single-engine medium (Mirage 2000 and MiG-23/-27) and twin-engine medium (MiG-29 and Jaguar) aircraft being either available in too few numbers or being phased out. Of these types, the MiG-21 is on track to being partially replaced by the Tejas while upgrades to the Mirage 2000, MiG-29 and Jaguar fleets plus the purchase of 36 Rafales are in progress.

The Air Support Challenge

The IAF has an effective strength of 31 combat squadrons, operating 34 combat squadrons in total. These include 11 squadrons of the Su-30MKI, three each of the MiG-29 and Mirage 2000 (currently undergoing an upgrade), six of the Jaguar (at the initial stage of an upgrade process) and six of the MiG-21Bison. In addition, two upgraded MiG-27 squadrons continue to serve alongside the equivalent of half a squadron with the Tactics and Air Combat Development Establishment. It is believed that three squadrons continue to operate older MiG-21s and non-upgraded MiG-27s—one each of the MiG-21bis, MiG-21M and MiG-27—but these will be phased out in the near future, possibly by the end of 2017 or in early 2018.[16]

It is to be noted that the peak strength of the IAF was approximately 39.5 combat squadrons, with four MiG-23MF/-BN and six MiG-27ML squadrons forming the core of the strike assets and some 17 MiG-21 FL/M/MF/bis squadrons forming the bulk of the air defence units. These were, at the time, complemented by the Jaguar, Mirage 2000 and MiG-29 squadrons, which added a high-technology cutting edge to an otherwise mediocre force. Since then, the MiG-21 and MiG-27 squadrons have been in decline and the MiG-23 phased out completely.

Table 3.1

Type	Sqadron No.	No. of Sqadrons
MiG-29	28, 47, 223	3
Mirage 2000H	1, 7, 9	3
MiG-21 Bison	3, 4, 21, 23, 32, 51	6
Sukhoi-30 MKI	2, 8, 15, 20, 24, 30, 31, 102, 106, 220, 221	11 + 3 to be formed.
HAL Tejas	45	*1—not yet operational*
MiG-21Bis	26	1
MiG-27 UPG	10, 29	2
MiG-27 ML	22	1
MiG-21 M/MF	37	1
Jaguar IS	5, 6, 14, 16, 27, 224	6
		34 + one not yet operational

The IAF desires strength of some 42 combat squadrons by the period 2027–2032 to meet the contingencies of a two-front war.[17] Assuming a practical strength of 31 squadrons (the three remaining MiG-21M/bis and MiG-27 squadrons being discarded), there is an immediate

16. Sanjay Badri-Maharaj, "The Indian Air Force's Declining Squadron Strength—Options and Challenges," *Institute for Defence Studies and Analyses—Issue Brief,* (November 03, 2017). https://idsa.in/issuebrief/the-indian-air-force-declining-squadron-strength_sbmaharaj_031117, accessed on November 06, 2017.

17. "IAF to reach full squadron strength by 2032: Air chief," *Indo-Asian News Service,* (October 05, 2017). http://economictimes.indiatimes.com/articleshow/60958636.cms?utm_source=contentofinterest&utm_medium=text&utm_campaign=cppst, accessed on November 01, 2017.

requirement for 11 more to meet its desired force levels by 2027. To date, three more Su-30MKI and two Dassault Rafale squadrons are on order with two squadrons of Tejas MK.1 fighters supplementing them. All this will add some seven squadrons to the IAF. However, six squadrons of MiG-21Bison and two MiG-27UPG will be phased out by 2025.[18] If no new aircraft are ordered, it is possible that the IAF would be left with 30 combat squadrons by 2025—an overall deficiency of 12 squadrons when set against its desired strength. Subsequently, one Jaguar squadron is due to be retired by 2027, which would mean an overall deficiency of 13 squadrons by 2027.[19]

Although making up this shortfall by 2027 poses significant challenges, the IAF is not without options. It had planned to acquire an additional of five squadrons of Rafales and undoubtedly would still like to do so if permitted. To compensate for this shortfall and to cater for future replacements for aircraft, such as the Jaguar and eventually the MiG-29 and Mirage 2000, India has two active plans to bolster force levels. One of these plans involves the procurement of new single and twin-engine fighters, with the latter taking priority. The other involves the procurement of four squadrons of the Tejas Mk.1A variant.

In considering new aircraft for the IAF, it is very easy to overlook one combat role that is not going to be easily met by the supersonic aircraft under review and that is the role of close air support. While the Tejas and larger aircraft such as the F-16, Rafale, Gripen and others are capable of delivering ordnance against ground targets, they are neither optimised nor ideal for the close-air-support tasks currently fulfilled by India's MiG-27s and MiG-21 M/MFs. One option could have been for the IAF to consider an armed modified version of the BAE Hawk but this has been rejected.

Close air support will be augmented with the arrival of attack helicopters in the form of the HAL Light Combat Helicopter and the AH-64 Apache augmented by armed Rudra helicopters but there remains an unfilled gap left by the loss of the MiG-27s and MiG-21s. It is conceivable that the Tejas in its Mk.1 and Mk.1A variants could be tasked for such a

18. "India will continue to operate the MiG-21 fighters until 2025," *Itar-Tass*, (October 09, 2013). https://www.rbth.com/economics/2013/10/09/india_will_continue_to_operate_the_mig-21_fighters_until_2025_30019, accessed on November 01, 2013.
19. IAF, n. 17.

role as could whatever single-engine fighter type might be selected as a replacement for the MiG-23/-27. In conjunction with attack helicopters, these will be tasked with the close support task.[20] Whether these forces will prove sufficient to provide the air support necessary to make the Cold Start Doctrine work in the face of what would inevitably be intense Pakistani air opposition depends on force levels.

As to whether the Cold Start doctrine is in any way neutralised by Pakistan's TNWs is debatable. As will be discussed later, effective active and passive CBRN measures can mitigate the effects of a nuclear strike on a military formation—much more so if the weapon used is one of a sub-kiloton yield. Pakistan may perhaps be using the vagueness of its nuclear red-lines and thresholds to confuse Indian decisions-makers so as to preclude an Indian military response. On the other hand, should India choose to act militarily, its best option is the combination of speed and multiple strike formations offered by the Cold Start doctrine and its evolutions that will inevitably emerge.

The Cold Start Doctrine is a work-in-progress. Its successful implementation could have major ramifications for strategic stability in South Asia. Optimists might suggest that it would have a stabilising influence in the sense that it will build confidence in the Pakistan Army that India has no desire to dismember Pakistan through large-scale Strike Corps-led offensive operations deep into the country. On the other hand, the doctrine provides India with a viable option for launching low-risk shallow-thrust offensive operations in the plains in response to any major provocation.[21]

To date, India's initial military response has been limited to the areas across the LoC in Jammu and Kashmir. However, the Cold Start Doctrine offers the prospect that should Pakistan choose to escalate a situation by launching retaliatory strikes in areas across the international boundary, India could implement its Cold Start Doctrine and with little notice of impending operations—thanks to faster mobilisation, launch several divisional-size IBGs into Pakistani territory at multiple locations across the Western front.

This inevitably brings the discussion to that of Pakistan's nuclear thresholds and its TNWs. As a caveat, it should be noted that Pakistan's conventional forces are far from negligible and despite the intentions of Cold Start and India's existing conventional military superiority over Pakistan, it is still an open question as to whether that superiority is sufficient and able to be brought to bear on Pakistan in a rapid enough fashion to ensure that Pakistan's conventional forces are overwhelmed as quickly as possible. Yet, Pakistan has been sufficiently alarmed about India's capability that they have developed TNWs.

Pakistan's Nuclear Thresholds and TNWs

Pakistan has openly touted its TNWs as a direct response to India's Cold Start Doctrine. Whether it is workable or not, it has altered the nuclear thresholds under which Indian forces have to operate.

Pakistan's nuclear 'red-lines' have not been clearly defined. It is important to note that regardless of definition, there is always a degree of uncertainty with respect to nuclear weapons employment. This ambiguity is by no means surprising, but in the discourse on Pakistan's Nuclear Doctrine four thresholds have been identified:[22]

- **Spatial:** Indian armed forces occupying a large swathe of Pakistani territory;
- **Military**: Indian armed forces completely knocking out or comprehensively destroying a large part of the Pakistani armed forces;
- **Economic**: Any Indian attempt to economically strangle Pakistan;
- **Political**: Possibly, an attempt to militarily assist a secessionist movement in Pakistan to the extent that the said movement has a reasonable chance of success.

None of these thresholds are, however, well defined. For instance, it is difficult to imagine any country using nuclear weapons to break an economic blockade. Indeed, the viability of such a response is questionable as retaliation

---

22. "Nuclear Black Markets: Pakistan, A.Q. Khan and the rise of proliferation networks—A net assessment," *International Institute for Strategic Studies: Nuclear policy,* (May 02, 2007) https://www.iiss.org/publications/strategic%20dossiers/issues/nuclear-black-markets--pakistan--a-q--khan-and-the-rise-of-proliferation-networks---a-net-assessmen-23e1, accessed on October 23, 2017.

would inevitably follow. Similarly, the political threshold lacks credibility in the absence of a clearer description of what the target of a nuclear weapon would be. Is Pakistan concerned about an Indian military intervention in support of an independent Baluchistan a la Bangladesh? This lack of clarity and, it is suggested, implausibility renders the political threshold somewhat suspicious. This also holds true, and to a greater extent, for the military threshold. Where does the threshold for 'comprehensively destroying a large part' of Pakistan's armed forces lie? The spatial threshold is perhaps most easily understood and as such also the easiest to incorporate into operational planning by the Indian military. However, it must also be noted that Pakistan's e spatial and military thresholds cannot be deemed separate. Can India occupy a large swathe of Pakistani territory without inflicting significant attrition upon the Pakistani armed forces? It is submitted that the two cannot be separated as one is certainly contingent upon the latter.

The other thing that is not entirely clear is how Pakistan's intended use of TNWs will actually work in practice. Retired Lt General Lodhi suggests that Pakistan has several options:[23]

- a public or private warning;
- a demonstration atomic test of a small atomic device on its own soil (preferably at weapon-testing laboratories);
- the use of (a) nuclear weapon(s) on Pakistan's soil against foreign attacking forces;
- the use of (a) nuclear weapon(s) against critical but purely military targets on foreign soil, probably in thinly populated areas in the desert or semidesert, causing the least collateral damage.

This is very vague but nonetheless provides a glimpse into Pakistani thinking. The question that is unanswered is what types of nuclear weapons would be used for these tasks. It is not entirely clear if Pakistan's objectives could be met by the use of very low-yield weapons which may inflict relatively insignificant damage but running the risk of attracting retaliation from India could be disproportionate. This raises the spectre of Pakistan's TNW doctrine being seriously flawed.

---

23. Sardar F. S. Lodhi, Pakistan's Nuclear Doctrine," *Defence Journal April 1999* http://www.defencejournal.com/apr99/pak-nuclear-doctrine.htm, accessed on October 23, 2017.

It is interesting to note, however, as have Dr G. Balachandran and Kapil Patil at the IDSA, that:[24]

"Neither the Pakistan government nor any of its major military or civil officials have ever admitted to the possession of a TNW or enunciated the conditions under which such alleged TNWs will be used. However, the most commonly assumed usage of TNWs by Pakistan is against Indian troops on Pakistani soil. Even this supposition is based on reported discussions between Indian and Pakistani Track II participants at one or more of the numerous such dialogues at various venues across the globe, incidentally none of which has been held either in India or Pakistan."

Basic Flaws in Pakistan's Doctrine

Writing in the Indian Defence Review, Brigadier Pillalmarri Subramanyam highlighted certain major flaws in Pakistan's Nuclear Doctrine. Firstly, he notes, Pakistan's assumption that its untested TNWs will work as designed and cause an unacceptable degree of damage—sufficient to deter Indian forces is misplaced. If Pakistan is intent on using very low-kiloton or sub-kiloton devices, then the chances of significant damage being caused to Indian mechanised formation are reduced. Against infantry formations, operating in the open, the physical results would certainly be greater but it is debatable whether the strategic impact would be the one desired by Pakistan as India's offensive power resides in its mechanised formations.

Secondly, Pakistan's assumption that the use of TNWs against Indian forces, be it on Pakistan soil or in the thinly populated desert or semi-desert areas of India will localise the nuclear conflict zone. Pakistan hopes that this will not attract disproportionately massive/punitive retaliation. It is suggested this is completely flawed. Once the nuclear threshold is crossed, there is the risk of escalation whereby retaliation against Pakistan which, according to the Indian Nuclear Doctrine, would be 'massive', though in practice might just be 'disproportionate. Disproportionate retaliation by

---

24. G. Balachandran and K. Patil, "Revisiting India's Nuclear Doctrine," *Institute for Defence Studies and Analyses* (March 27, 2017). https://idsa.in/idsacomments/revisiting-india-nuclear-doctrine_gbala-kpatil_270317, accessed on October 23, 2017.

India could bring about precisely what Pakistan seeks to prevent by using TNWs if its nuclear thresholds are crossed.

Thirdly, the credibility of Pakistan using TNWs on its own soil in a deteriorating situation, perhaps when Indian forces are likely to breach or have already breached Pakistan's main defence lines, is at best dubious. Should these defence lines not be restorable by conventional means, then with Indian forces already in contact with Pakistani forces, perhaps within the proximity of Pakistani cities, is Pakistani intent on using TNWs with the attendant risks, even with sub-kiloton weapons of collateral damage to civilian targets?

It is debatable whether sub-kiloton or very low-kiloton weapons would have the requisite impact to blunt or deter a concerted effort by Indian mechanised forces. Against bridgeheads or mass non-mechanised infantry formations in the open, the effects could be different. It has been suggested that Pakistan would have to use a 30-kt weapon on its own soil as this is the minimum required, to render 50 percent of an armoured unit ineffective. To put this in perspective, should a 30-kt weapon be detonated over Lahore, anywhere between 50,000 and 350,000 people could be killed depending on where the weapon was used. It is debatable whether Pakistan would be blasé about using a weapon of such yield.[25]

Brigadier Subramanyam raises an issue that is not directly related to Pakistan's TNW doctrine when he notes that Pakistan is not unaware of its own internal security problems and while it is probable that security around nuclear weapons sites is heavy, the number of jihadi groups operating within the country must give cause for concern. Furthermore, Pakistan is reported to have delegated the authority to launch these weapons to lower level field commanders for timely decisions in combat. This raises the dual possibilities of either an appropriation of a portion of the TNWs by jihadi groups or an inadvertent or unauthorised use of TNWs. Moreover, the two possibilities are not mutually exclusive as radical elements within the Pakistani officer corps could pose a threat of unilateral TNW use with the delegated command posing a possible risk in such circumstances.

25. Pillalmarri Subramanyam, "Pakistan's Tactical Nuclear Weapons and India's Response," *Indian Defence Review Net Edition*, (October 30, 2016). http://www.indiandefencereview.com/news/pakistans-tactical-nuclear-weapons-and-indias-response/0/, Accessed on October 23, 2017.

He concludes that it is therefore questionable as to whether Pakistan will benefit substantially from deploying and integrating TNWs. It is suggested, that for Pakistan, such weapons will at best serve as a psychological deterrent and at worst, potentially increase the risk of Indian escalation. Associate Professor C. Christine Fair in a 2015 article of hers opined that the TNWs conferred only limited utility to Pakistan concluding:[26]

"Even if Pakistan fully inducts these weapons in its arsenal, it still has an army that can't win a conventional war against India and nuclear weapons it cannot use. This leaves only an industrial farm of terrorists as the only efficacious tool at its disposal. And given the logic of the above scenario, India and the international community should consider seriously calling Pakistan's bluff. The only logical Pakistani response to a limited offensive incursion is to accept the fait accompli and acquiesce."

Yet India cannot afford to take the possibility of TNW use by Pakistan lightly. While the issue of whether India should deploy similar weapons is debatable, what is clear is that India must prepare its forces for operations in a CBRN environment so that India can call the Pakistani nuclear bluff.

Calling Pakistan's Nuclear Bluff—Preparedness is Key

Even before the Indian Army conducted surgical strikes against terrorist targets in Pakistan-occupied Kashmir (PoK) on the night of September 28–29, 2016, Pakistan has long been fond of rattling its nuclear sabre. It is true that Pakistan's purported development and deployment of TNWs and the means to deliver them poses challenges for any potential Indian conventional military response to an act of extreme provocation that may occur. But India is not without options and can indeed take steps to avoid crossing whatever Pakistan's nuclear red-lines may be. Nevertheless, given the relative lack of clarity about what those nuclear red-lines are, India may find itself faced with the choice of either abandoning a conventional military option or preparing, should the need arise, to call Pakistan's nuclear

---

26. C. Christine Fair, "Pakistan's army is building an arsenal of "tiny" nuclear weapons—and it's going to backfire," *Quartz India*, (December 21, 2015). https://qz.com/579334/pakistans-army-is-building-an-arsenal-of-tiny-nuclear-weapons-and-its-going-to-backfire/, accessed on October 23, 2017.

bluff. Should India choose the latter, the key to calling Pakistan's nuclear bluff lies in ensuring that the Indian armed forces are prepared to meet the threat of TNW use by Pakistan. This involves taking both adequate passive measures to mitigate the impact of a TNW attack and active measures to intercept delivery vehicles aimed at Indian targets—formations in the field or target further inland.

Pakistan has used the threat of nuclear weapons use to effectively blunt the prospect of Indian conventional military operations, allowing Pakistani freedom of action while constraining India's response to limited reprisals. It is argued that effective preparation—employing both active and passive defensive measures against CBRN attack—confers on India sufficient freedom of action to permit conventional military operations should that option need to be exercised.

The Indian Army's Readiness for CBRN Warfare[27]

The Indian Army consists of 13 Corps-sized formations with a total of 37 divisions and a number of independent brigades. The cutting edge of the Army is centred on three Strike Corps—each built around an armoured division. The three Strike Corps—1, 2 and 21—are composed of an armoured division (33, 1 and 31, respectively) and two infantry divisions with supporting units. In addition to these formations, the Army has five Independent Armoured Brigades, fifteen Independent Artillery Brigades, seven Independent Infantry Brigades, one Independent Parachute Brigade, three Independent Air Defence Brigades, two Independent Air Defence Groups and four Independent Engineer Brigades.

India has understood that its previous operational doctrine, which emphasised the use of its three Strike Corps, was inadequate to meet the changing realities of the India–Pakistan battlefield. To this end, the previously designated 'Holding Corps' along the India–Pakistan border have been renamed as 'Pivot Corps'. And they have been reinforced with the

---

27. Sanjay Badri-Maharaj, "The Importance of Passive and Active CBRN Defensive Measures," *Institute for Defence Studies and Analyses: Issue Brief,* (October 17, 2016), https://idsa.in/issuebrief/importance-of-passive-and-active-cbrn-defensive-measures_sbmaharaj_171016, accessed on October 23, 2017.

addition of eight IBGs, which are of division size and combine mechanised infantry, armour, artillery and aviation assets. The IBGs are to work in conjunction with the IAF to conduct offensive military operations and be available for operations within 48 hours of the order being given. This reorientation of assets has increased the offensive capability of the previous defensively orientated formations and has also made them considerably more flexible.

To enable India to call Pakistan's nuclear bluff and further to enable its combat formations to operate effectively under the backdrop of TNW use, the Indian Army has to give priority to passive and active CBRN measures. Passive CBRN measures involve protecting personnel and equipment from the effects of CBRN use, while active measures involve the interception of the delivery systems of CBRN agents before they can inflict damage on their intended targets. The extent to which India has undertaken such measures is discussed below.

Passive CBRN Defensive Measures

India's 63 armoured regiments and 26 mechanised infantry battalions have significant levels of protection from a CBRN attack. The Arjun, T-90 and T-72 tanks all have CBRN protection systems. The BMP-1 and BMP-2 force conveys that the mechanised infantry units have CBRN protection systems. And each BMP comes with two TDP-1 decontamination kits. It is, however, unclear if India has maintained and replaced life-expired filters on these vehicles or refurbished and/or replaced ageing decontamination kits. In addition, India has also deployed a number of indigenously developed CBRN reconnaissance and decontamination vehicles. Of note, however, is its continuing reliance on towed artillery, which is far more difficult to operate in CBRN conditions; the lack of appropriate self-propelled artillery is a major deficiency. The latter point cannot be overemphasised as trying to operate towed artillery in a CBRN environment is not only difficult but also could place an excessive physiological strain on artillery crews operating in high ambient temperatures. That said, respiratory protection is feasible as even the primitive and claustrophobic respirators used in World War 1 were employed by artillery crews during chemical bombardment during hot summers, which although not comfortable, were not debilitating.

With respect to infantry formations in the 1980s, the army began some tentative preparations for CBRN warfare. A quantity of CBRN equipment was imported from the Union of Soviet Socialist Republics, but these proved to be useless in Indian environmental conditions. Following that, in 1987, the Defence Research and Development Organisation (DRDO) produced prototypes of CBRN suits, decontamination suits, facelets, overboots and CBRN tents. This equipment has entered production and is in service with the armed forces. From 1987 onwards, the Army, through its College of Military Engineering, began running familiarisation courses in CBRN warfare, while DRDO scientists have conducted theoretical courses at the brigade level. Over time, this became practical training.

The Ministry of Defence has allocated priority to the indigenous production of CBRN gear. This has also involved the participation of the private sector in the manufacture of CBRN suits. India seems to have purchased 50,000 S6 and S10 respirators and No.1 Mk3 suits from the United Kingdom in the 1980s (the types being identified through photographic evidence), 150,000 Draeger Kareta Nova respirators in the early 1990s, and subsequently, a larger order of 334,000 full sets of individual protective equipment (IPE) with CBRN suits and locally produced variants of the Kareta Nova respirator.[28] Further purchases have included 40,000 new model CBRN suits in 2011 with a subsequent order for 50,000 Mk.V suits being placed.[29] As CBRN IPE has a limited shelf life and in order to retain CBRN readiness levels, India would need to replace life-expired items, refurbish them where possible and ensure proper storage of equipment. The latter point is of particular importance given India's climate, which could be detrimental to the integrity of CBRN respirators if special care is not taken in storage, preventative maintenance and periodic thorough refurbishment. A recent order for over 30,000 sets of IPE from

---

28. Shahid K. Abbas, Top of Form "Brahmos anti-ship missile to be produced in 2003," Bottom of Form *Rediff.com*, (June 01, 2002). http://www.rediff.com/news/2002/jun/01war11.htm, accessed on October 23, 2017.

29. "Indian Army May Soon get Bio-Chem Suits," *Rediff.com*, (May 11, 2011). http://www.rediff.com/news/report/indian-army-may-soon-get-bio-chem-suits/20110511.htm, accessed on October 23, 2017.

the United States is perhaps the precursor to the adoption of a new model of IPE gear.[30]

To the extent that research has thus far permitted, it is suggested that, at present, India has an adequate stock of CBRN gear for individual protection of its infantry units. Older equipment is now making way into training establishments and new production replacing IPE sets that have become life-expired. Decontamination equipment, locally designed and manufactured, is also available in some quantity but on a scale that is far from lavish. However, it is a matter of conjecture whether the army's towed artillery crews are issued with or trained to operate in CBRN gear.

Despite all the above, the exact status of CBRN preparedness and training in the Indian Army remains unclear. For instance, it is unclear as to whether training and equipment have gone down to the battalion level. It is certainly the case that outside of CBRN exercises, Indian troops do not carry CBRN haversacks. Since the late 1990s, some exercises have been conducted with troops in full CBRN gear and decontamination vehicles in operation—the latest being in April 2016. However, these exercises have not been widely publicised and their extent is not clear. Nevertheless, it is clear that the foundation for reasonably strong passive CBRN measures has been laid in the Indian Army. It remains to be seen if the threat of Pakistani TNWs will provide further impetus in this regard. It should also be noted that the IAF has also initiated measures to operate in a CBRN environment. Some decontamination exercises have been carried out and recently, a repair and refurbishment facility has been established for CBRN gear. However, once again, it is unclear if these efforts amount to anything more than basic familiarisation measures or a much more serious impetus towards protecting aircrew as well as ensuring effective IAF operations in a CBRN environment.

Active CBRN Defensive Measures

The Corps of Army Air Defence (AAD) possesses one of the largest arrays of medium and short-range air defence systems of any army in Asia. At

---

30. Arkadev Ghoshal, "India to Procure Anti-Chemical, Anti-Nuclear Suits from US for Rs 480 crore," *IB Times*, (May 12, 2017). http://www.ibtimes.co.in/india-procure-anti-chemical-anti-nuclear-suits-us-rs-480-crore-726410, accessed on October 23, 2017.

present, AAD has, in pride of place, two Air Defence missile groups—501 and 502—equipped with Kvadrat SA-6 surface-to-air missiles. In addition, there are 23 regiments with Bofors L-40/70 towed antiaircraft (AA) guns, four with ZSU-23/4 self-propelled AA guns and a similar number with Tunguska systems, 11 composite regiments equipped with a combination of ZU-23-2 guns and Igla 1M missiles. These are complemented by a number of mobile point-defence missile regiments with OSA-AKM SA-8b and Strela-10M SA-13 missile units. Two regiments of Akash surface-to-air missiles (SAMs) are on order, with delivery already in progress. Despite the size of the Corps of AAD, given its possession of only two medium-range SAM groups and an increase in the number of mechanised units needing protection (the eight IBGs for example), the Army's air defences are quantitatively inadequate to ensure adequate protection to formations. Thought must, therefore, be given to expanding the number and quality of air defence assets, in particular, holding formations must be adequately provided with appropriate air defence resources. While it is appreciated that strike formations will perhaps be priority targets, TNW strikes on static formations—such as pivot corps—can not be ruled out.

Any Pakistani TNW strike would need to be delivered either by manned aircraft, cruise missiles or ballistic missiles. At present, the Indian Army air defence is geared to defend against threats from manned aircraft and, to a lesser extent, subsonic cruise missiles. It is neither structured nor equipped to deal with TNWs delivered by ballistic missiles. Furthermore, other than the Akash and SA-6 systems, the equipment available is designed primarily to ward off an attack from low-flying aircraft. The army currently lacks any ability to detect or intercept even short-range ballistic missiles such as Pakistan's Nasr and certainly not the M-9 and M-11 missiles also in service.

While it is indisputable that ballistic missile defence systems should be a priority for India for the defence of critical military and civilian targets—cities, airbases, strategic weapons complexes and critical supply depots for vital stores and fuel—it is also important that India considers some limited defensive capability for its military formations. The Indo-Israeli medium-range surface-to-air missile (MRSAM) currently being tested for the IAF could offer the requisite capability. To this end, the MRSAM testing programme should include testing against a ballistic missile target.

The Indian Army has placed substantial orders for the type and should participate with the IAF in testing the system against ballistic missile targets. Of importance is that the Indian formations—whether mobile or static—will need to enhance radar surveillance assets available as existing systems are not only ageing but also geared up towards attacks by manned aircraft and to a lesser extent by cruise missiles. Reorienting the army air defence network to detect and engage ballistic missiles will present a challenge and will require greater integration of the army radar network with that of the IAF.

Furthermore, to evaluate its current systems—in particular, the Akash—against missiles such as the Nasr, India should carry out exercises aimed at evaluating the ability of its radars to detect missiles such as the Nasr and the interception capability of the Akash. Early in its development, it was widely speculated that the Akash would have some capability against ballistic missiles but thus far, none has been demonstrated.

The idea of using SAMs against missiles is not as far-fetched as it may first seem, as the United States and Russia have tested a variety of SAMs—HAWKs and V-750 SA-2s among them—against ballistic missile targets. It is probable that there will need to be some changes to the Akash algorithms, which are optimised for aircraft intercept but the experiment would be worth the effort and would give additional confidence to the ADA.

Against cruise missiles, the India army is in need of significant inductions of quick-reaction SAMs (QRSAMs). At present, the Akash and SA-6 systems, while capable of cruise missile interception, are not designed for quick reaction. The sole assets available to the army in this regard are the regiments equipped with OSA-AKMs which are not only ageing but inadequate in number to cope with a growing potential threat. The existing AAA guns, while possessing not inconsiderable capability against cruise-missiles, are overdue for replacement by faster firing systems. The Strella-10M systems which form the bulk of the short-range SAM units of the Indian Army lack meaningful capability against cruise missiles and are in need of either a major upgrade or augmentation by more advanced systems with a new QRSAM presently under testing.

While the use of TNWs in the event of an India–Pakistan conflict is a situation that is best avoided, India cannot be held hostage to Pakistani provocations and the consequent loss of life in Pakistani-sponsored and abetted terror attacks. Pakistan's willingness to raise the spectre of nuclear weapons use has thus far shaped much of the narrative. Despite the surgical strikes of September 28–29, 2016, India's response to Pakistan continues to be constrained by the threat of TNW use—whether realistic or not.

While it is not even remotely being suggested that India should seek to launch a major military offensive against Pakistan, to ensure that it retains the flexibility for an escalating response, India will need to pay more attention to both passive and active defensive CBRN measures with a view towards negating as much of the impact of Pakistan's TNWs as may be practical. Progress has already been made in respect of the former, it is now necessary to build on that progress while working towards improving active CBRN defences. It is unfortunate that Indian military discourse on the subject is limited to sound-bites and minimally informative press releases.

The reticence of the Indian armed forces to highlight their CBRN preparedness is a two-edged sword. On one hand, it does ensure that there are no misapprehensions about India moving towards an aggressive nuclear warfighting doctrine and on the other hand, it could embolden Pakistan into thinking that the Indian military is inadequately prepared for CBRN warfare, overestimate the effect that the use of such weapons would have on the Indian forces and with the potential for dire miscalculations. A bit more clarity could go a long way towards assuaging such concerns.

Are TNWs Viable for Either India or Pakistan?

Brigadier Gurmeet Kanwal, an opponent of India's deployment of TNWs, has been one of the few to examine the potential positives and pitfalls of India deploying TNWs. His arguments remain the most cogent and coherent on the subject emanating from India to date. Although this perhaps delves into territory veering away from the technical nature of this chapter, the importance of the discourse to the issue of India's development of TNWs warrants such a diversion. Brigadier Kanwal notes that supporters of TNWs suggest that:[31]

---

31. Gurmeet Kanwal, "Does India Need Tactical Nuclear Weapons?," *Institute for Defence Studies and Analyses*, (May 2003). https://www.idsa-india.org/an-may-03.html, accessed on October 23, 2017.

- They deter the use of TNWs by the enemy.
- They provide flexible response over the whole range of possible military threats.
- They offer nuclear military options below the strategic level.
- They help to defeat large-scale conventional attacks.

If we follow the conventional logic, strategic nuclear targets are either countervalue or counterforce targets. Countervalue targets include major enemy cities and industrial centres and these are the ones that generate the 'terror' of the 'balance of terror' through the threat of causing millions of civilian casualties. Counterforce targets primarily comprise the nuclear assets of the adversary including delivery means, bases, nuclear warheads and missile storage sites, command and control elements and early warning and targeting infrastructure. While the aim of selecting countervalue targets has generally been to maximise deterrence, counter-force targets aim to degrade the enemy's capability to make optimum use of his nuclear forces. Thus, military planning for the use of nuclear weapons, in the eventuality that deterrence fails, includes a judicious mix of both countervalue and counterforce targets in first use as well as retaliatory strikes. The question is whether the risk of the former deters the latter.

On the other hand, Kanwal notes, tactical or battlefield nuclear targets are normally those that are either located within the tactical battle area (TBA) or have a direct bearing on it. Besides the enemy's forces, tactical targets include such military infrastructure as important bridges and choke points on the transportation systems, airbases and communications centres—including but not limited to:[32]

- locations of headquarters and adjacent communications centres;
- bridgeheads established by a 'break-in' force on a defensive obstacle system to facilitate a 'break out';
- Leading 'combat groups' forming the spearheads of an 'operational manoeuvre group' or an Indian or Pakistani Strike Corps— ARN or ARS in the case of Pakistan;
- defence fortifications and nodal/strong points, to facilitate a breakthrough;

---

32. Ibid.

- mechanised forces—deployed for defence, assaulting, laying off in the harbour or being transported to the TBA;
- surface-to-surface missiles and rocket artillery positions;
- self-propelled and towed medium artillery regimental gun areas;
- logistics support areas.

Some or all of the abovementioned targets may be close to areas with civilian populations—particularly true in the case of Pakistan. However, collateral damage can be minimised by using a low air-burst nuclear weapon. This has the advantage of enabling troops on foot to transit through 'ground zero' of a low air burst within 30 minutes to 1 hour of the explosion and troops in armoured fighting vehicles can do so almost immediately. On the other hand, it would require a ground-burst nuclear explosion with fractional kiloton yields to accurately hit point targets such as an individual missile launcher (if detection permits engagement before launch). Such a weapon would inevitably produce a large amount of fallout and would require special precautions to protect ground troops from adverse effects. These passive measures have been discussed earlier in this chapter but suffice it to reiterate that India has taken some positive steps in this regard.

Pakistani Nuclear Strikes on Tactical Targets
However, there is an undeniably close link between nuclear weapons and a nation's conventional military capacity. If a nation's conventional potentiality is relatively low vis-à-visa nuclear-armed adversary, that nation is likely to adopt a 'first use' strategy to thwart a conventional military offensive that may threaten to undermine its territorial unity and lead to its break up. This is the place that Pakistan finds itself in nowadays. Pakistan may use or threaten to use TNWs against India's mechanised forces within Pakistani territory. Even with India having relatively modest military aims in respect of holding Pakistani territory, given India's conventional superiority (no matter how slender the edge may be), Pakistan has based its national security strategy on the first use of nuclear weapons to prevent its comprehensive military defeat and its possible disintegration as a nation. It is for this reason that Pakistan will not accept India's offer of a bilateral no-first-use (NFU) treaty.

With respect to the Indo-Pak context, Kanwal elaborates that Indian advocates of TNWs presuppose that if Pakistan's nuclear thresholds are crossed, Pakistan would not hesitate to use nuclear weapons against India's mechanised forces inside Pakistani territory with little risk of General Sundarj's appropriately phrased 'opprobrium quotient', since the use of nuclear weapons could be justified as a defensive measure of the last resort.[33] Such advocates argue that in response, India should employ only TNWs on Pakistani forces, rather than raise the nuclear ante. There is some merit in this argument as will be discussed later in this chapter but it is neither entirely accurate nor wrong.

In an earlier incarnation—not superseded by subsequent revisions—of the Indian Army's doctrine as published by the Army Training Command, it was stated that:[34]

> *The Indian Army believes in fighting the war in enemy territory. If forced into a war, the aim of our offensive(s) would be to apply a sledgehammer blow to the enemy. The Indian Army's concept of waging war is to ensure a decisive victory and to ensure that conflict termination places us at an advantageous position.*

In the event of hostilities with Indian military operations being conducted in the plains, whereby India pursues a proactive offensive strategy involving one or more Strike Corps plus the Integrated Battle groups with substantial air support, Kanwal postulates that it is probable that India's mechanised formations are likely to achieve major operational level gains in 3–5 days and strategic gains soon thereafter. Pakistan may then be forced to commit its strategic reserves, either or both the ARN and ARS and risk their destruction in detail or, in the alternative, chose to exercise its nuclear option.

Indian analysts in favour of India developing TNWs are of the view that Pakistan is likely to resort to the early use of nuclear weapons if it can justify their use as a defensive measure set against advances made by Indian mechanised forces. Kanwal's view—with which the author partly

---

33. Ibid.
34. "National Security", Fundamentals, Doctrine and Concepts—Indian Army (Shimla: HQ ARTRAC, 1999), pp. 11–12.

agrees—is that the corollary to this argument is that India's conventional superiority against Pakistan will stand largely negated and the Indian military leadership will either have to face the consequences of a possible nuclear strike from Pakistan or confine itself to launching only tactical-level limited offensives with shallow objectives so as to avoid crossing Pakistan's supposed nuclear threshold.

Such an approach could play into Pakistan's strategic aims, whereby that country could continue to support its 'proxy war' without the fear of significant Indian retaliation. There is also the possibility of Pakistani offensive actions in areas such as the Rann of Kutch on one pretext or the other, as it did in the summer months of 1965. Pakistan may view the Indian NFU doctrine as providing it with some degree of protection, emboldening Pakistan to seek a tactical advantage.

The Indian Army would be left with the option to plan to seize a long though narrow strip of Pakistani territory virtually all along the front without ringing Pakistan's nuclear alarm bells by launching a number of limited, shallow objective offensives. These operations while having the potential to inflict substantial damage on opposing forces will not achieve decisive results and are unlikely to compel Pakistan to change its conduct.

Kanwal argues that perhaps India's only realistic option would be to call Pakistan's nuclear bluff and plan to launch Strike Corps operations to achieve strategic gains in as early a timeframe as is militarily possible. Such action would need to be combined with a declaratory policy that a nuclear strike against Indian soldiers, even if they are deep inside Pakistani territory, will constitute the use of nuclear weapons against India and will, argues Kanwal, invite massive countervalue and counterforce punitive retaliation against Pakistan, drawing inspiration from General Sundarji who wrote in 1992 that:[35]

> *If the damage suffered by Indian forces (due to a Pakistani nuclear strike) is substantial, national and troop morale would demand at least a quid pro quo response. There might even be a demand in some quarters for a quid pro quo plus response.*

35. General Krishnaswamy Sundarji, "Nuclear Deterrence Doctrine for India," *Trishul* vol. 5, no. 2, December 1992.

This does not factor in the growing impatience with Pakistan within India. Following the Kargil war, the subsequent attacks on the Parliament and Mumbai, should India and Pakistan find themselves at war, it is possible that Indian public opinion will accept nothing short of the final dismemberment of Pakistan in case that country chooses to cross the nuclear Rubicon and launches a nuclear strike, even if it is on Indian forces. It is interesting that Sundarji did not explicitly call for a massive retaliatory response. One might suggest that General Sundarji's view was that India should respond in kind to a Pakistani nuclear attack or at worst respond in an enhanced manner to such an attack. This falls short of calling for a countervalue response to a TNW attack and certainly for massive retaliation, though not ruling out punitive retaliation.

Kanwal's argument is that even if Pakistan still persists with its stated policy of launching nuclear strikes on Indian forces inside Pakistan and India decides to reciprocate in kind with nuclear strikes on Pakistani forces rather than an all-out decapitating strike, this escalation control will be extremely difficult to manage.

It is suggested that this may not be entirely accurate. While there is a risk of escalation, controlling the same is feasible. There is, of course, the possibility of nuclear exchanges eventually graduating to massive strikes. However, this is not necessarily automatic.

Kanwal's argument suggests that India has only a viable response to a Pakistani nuclear strike, whether on Indian cities or military forces, whether inside Pakistan or not, and that is massive punitive retaliation with the full force of India's nuclear capability. However, it is suggested that this approach is perhaps too rigid and perhaps, as will be discussed later, a more nuanced approach is necessary.

In contrast to Kanwal, there are some Indian analysts in favour of Indian TNWs. Brahma Chellaney justifies the use of TNWs and his arguments are as follows:[36]

---

36. Brahma Chellaney, "Nuclear Deterrent Posture," in Brahma Chellaney, ed., Securing India's Future in the New Millennium, (New Delhi: Orient Longman Limited, 1999), pp. 209–214.

"Some Indian analysts have arbitrarily judged tactical weapons as immoral and dangerous, and sought only mass killer strategic weapons for their country. India's deterrent posture logically implies that wars can still be fought along traditional, just lines, with nuclear weapons primarily aimed at an opponent's armed forces than his civilian population. In this kind of counter-force strategy, tactical weapons would have to play an important role. If the deterrent ever failed, such small weapons for local defence could ensure that non-combatants do not become the first targets in counter-city offensives and also permit leeway for nipping further hostilities. Through an economy of force, tactical nukes could potentially diminish an enemy's military might, including his strike forces."

"Without tactical weapons, a failed deterrent situation could uncontrollably spark counter-city attacks, wreaking limitless destruction After failing to deter an adversary from committing aggression, efforts have to shift to force him to halt aggression. Such intra-war deterrence or compellence can succeed if responses are judiciously modulated to allow for only a stage-by-stage escalation, with opponent's civilian population held hostage but not under attack to nations that have disputed frontiers—such as India, Israel, China and Pakistan—and to Russia, tactical nukes cannot but be an integral component of defence (India's deterrent force) has to be structurally and doctrinally established in a manner to allow for possible bargains to be struck at any step of the escalation ladder."

Kanwal, being the foremost opponent of Indian TNWs, suggests that the main weakness of this argument is that if the Pakistani ruling elite, dominated as it is by the military establishment, believes that India would not respond with countervalue and counterforce strikes to a tactical nuclear strike on its armed forces in the field, it would be tempted to launch such a strike during the early stages of a conventional conflict.

On the other side of the spectrum, there are some Indian analysts who remain wholly unconvinced of this logic as they believe that Pakistan is a rational nuclear power and will not be cavalier about risking the destruction of their country by using weapons. Pravin Sawhney, for example, argues:[37]

---

37. Pravin Sawhney, "How Inevitable is an Asian Missile Race?," *Jane's Intelligence Review*, January 2000, pp. 32.

"Pakistan knows a nuclear counter-strike would be devastating to its existence. Considering Pakistan's nuclear policy, weaponisation options and (that) command and control of nuclear assets are likely to be the sole responsibility of the General Headquarters; the chances of a war escalating to nuclear level would be a professional, conservative and well thought through decision. A pre-emptive nuclear strike or an early employment of nuclear weapons in a conventional war is ruled out."

This, it is suggested, is a remarkably naïve approach to take for planning for conflict. A well-thought-out and professional approach can just as easily lead to a wrong decision as a hasty and arbitrary approach. India must consider what Pakistan can theoretically do, not what it is likely to do.

A greater limiting factor on Indian employment of TNWs can be the inherent problems the decentralised control necessary for their effective employment on the battlefield can pose. This is not beyond solution, however, and even here, while some may argue that the problems are not worth the effort, it is suggested that given the fact that whether tactical or strategic, Indian nuclear weapons are to be used in retaliation against a first-strike, there is no reason why control needs to be devolved to battlefield level. Retaliation could and should be authorised at the political level as before.

In his 2013 speech, Saran reiterated the stated rejection of Indian doctrinal or strategic change as a response to Pakistan's development of TNWs. A limited nuclear war, he stated, was not possible—"a contradiction in terms"—and whether the first weapon used was strategic or tactical was "irrelevant from an Indian perspective." He also described how India, since 1998, had taken steps to move toward a triad of land, air and submarine-based nuclear forces and delivery system "to conform to its declared doctrine of NFU and retaliation only." India had also created a survivable command and control infrastructure and secure communications. He further asserted that the Indian armed forces were involved in the strategic decision-making process, but argued that the "exclusive military management of strategic forces" was not necessary for a "credible nuclear deterrent." More importantly, he reiterated that:[38]

---

38. Shyam Saran, "Is India's Nuclear Deterrent Credible?," Speech given at the India Habitat Centre, New Delhi April 24, 2013.

...the central tenet of [India's] nuclear doctrine [was] that India will not be the first to use nuclear weapons, but that if it is attacked with such weapons, it would engage in nuclear retaliation which will be massive and designed to inflict unacceptable damage on the adversary.

Conceptually, TNWs have always been problematic and posed challenges for any country choosing to develop and deploy them. In the India–Pakistan context, the issue is still poorly understood. In looking at the various viewpoints on the subject, we can see there is a divergence of opinion with each author and analyst putting forward his own interpretation on the subject.

Unfortunately, there are many uncertainties and, as Kanwal rightly argues, even basic issues become highly subjective. Analysts coming to definitive conclusions are doing so in large part on their own assumptions, preferences and judgements on political, technical and military aspects of the TNWs problem. However, so many uncertainties exist that basic issues are really matters of judgement. Yet, these may have no basis in fact. Whether India chooses to develop nuclear weapons or not, the advantages and disadvantages of such weapons need to be more clearly understood.

The Tactical Use of Nuclear Weapons: Advantages and Disadvantages[39]
Having looked at the areas in which nuclear weapons might be applied, it is now appropriate to examine the 'pros' and 'cons' of using nuclear weapons on the South Asian battlefield. The first question that has to be answered is how nuclear weapons can be used tactically. The arguments for and against the Indian development of TNWs have been expounded at some length in an earlier chapter but while that addressed the rationale of Pakistani TNWs and the option for an Indian response to the same, the actual employment of the same will be worth exploring in some detail.

Like the American, Russian and the Chinese armed forces, the Indian and Pakistani military establishments, since the tests of May 1998, are likely to eventually have access to weapons in the very low yield—0.1–4 kt—range. However, in the past, the nuclear weapons most likely to be used on the South Asian battlefield might range between 5 and 20 kt owing to

---

39. Badri-Maharaj, n. 1.

difficulties in miniaturisation. These weapons are fairly large—by Western battlefield standards—and it is extremely difficult to differentiate between 'tactical' and 'strategic' nuclear weapons in the India–Pakistan context. However, Pakistan's development of TNWs—with smaller yields now presents an additional challenge to the Indian forces as such weapons can be more easily employed without significant risk to civilian targets.

For the defending forces, either Indian or Pakistani, nuclear weapons might be used to block attacking units crossing obstacles—for example, rivers. To this end, the defending forces would adopt a mobile defence posture, which would present a difficult target for a retaliatory nuclear strike. The nuclear weapons would be used as the attacking force concentrates to overcome a defensive position or obstacle. This would require a degree of advanced warning to the defending units and this might be detected.

As far as offensive operations are concerned, these would necessarily be planned around the use of nuclear weapons. The attacking forces would remain dispersed and only concentrate rapidly to attack. The objective of this is to present as few worthwhile nuclear targets as possible. In addition, the attacker would aim to destroy the enemy's nuclear capability and, perhaps more importantly, the controlling headquarters.

In order to perform these tasks, in both defence and offence, the armies must possess mobile reserves and strike formations with a preponderance of armour and mechanised infantry and possess excellent intelligence. In this regard, both the Indian and Pakistani armies have such forces in sizeable numbers, the Indian Strike Corps and RAPIDS and Pakistan's ARN and ARS. This mechanisation was carried out as part of the evolving conventional military doctrine, but as can be seen, also prepares both armies for the use of battlefield nuclear weapons in South Asia.

However, there are a number of very serious constraints that mitigate against the battlefield use of South Asia. The first, and perhaps the most important, of these, is the stigma attached to being only the second country in the world to use nuclear weapons. Certainly India, for example, would be very much restrained from using nuclear weapons in the initial stages of any attack on Pakistan. Similarly, Pakistan would be very wary of using nuclear weapons for a tactical gain. Both sides would only use nuclear weapons in the event of their very existence being threatened, not just to gain a battlefield advantage.

In addition to this, there are limitations to the success of a nuclear strike on an enemy position. A Pakistani attack on an Indian Strike Corps, as mentioned earlier, would be met by intense anti-aircraft fire—in addition to Indian fighters. This does not apply, at least not to the same extent, to an Indian attack on a major Pakistani formation, owing to the limited variety of air defence weapons available to the Pakistani army.

An attack on a well-dispersed, mechanised combat force would not be catastrophic. Armoured vehicles in both armies are designed to operate in nuclear, biological, chemical (NBC) conditions and furthermore, unless the unit is almost at the centre of the blast (Ground Zero) it is highly possible that the MBTs and armoured personnel carriers would provide a significant protection from the blast and radiation effects. This means that the principal offensive formations of both armies would be rather less vulnerable targets than would be ideal. The holding formations—heavily dug in and in well-constructed concrete bunkers and behind the ditch-cum-bund and canal defences—would be more vulnerable. However, even these, with the protection afforded by the fixed defences might not suffer as much as hoped as these defences would probably survive a nuclear strike. The most vulnerable units would be lone battalions or brigades in isolated areas. Moreover, weapons in the 0.1–4 kt range would be of little utility against these fortifications and substantial portions of the defences may be able to survive blasts up to 20 kt.

There is also a major problem of providing intelligence to friendly forces in the area of a nuclear blast. It is unlikely that either army would want to have sizeable numbers of friendly forces caught either at the centre or in the vicinity of a nuclear strike. In order to prevent this, instructions for dispersal, issuing of protective equipment and constructing shelters would have to be given. There may also have to be large-scale issues of NBC protective gear and decontamination and monitoring equipment. Moreover, medical units would also have to be alerted to the possibility of the use of nuclear weapons so as to cater for battlefield casualties.

These preparations would probably be noticed by the enemy, thus eliminating the essential element of surprise. In addition, given the fact that only the Southern Rajasthan/Gujarat sectors are really suitable for tactical nuclear warfare, the disastrous effects of using NBC gear on combat efficiency would have to be taken into account. While an examination of

CBRN readiness has been discussed in some detail above, there is still the question as to whether adequate studies on the effect of heat on protected troops have been undertaken by India. Of course, whether this has been done or not, the need to protect personnel must take precedence over any deleterious effects on the performance of troops in combat. It is known that India's newer CBRN gear has tried to factor in the issue of troop comfort in high-ambient temperatures but it would still be a challenge for infantry to operate in protective gear while carrying out offensive operations.

Perhaps India's approach is correct. The ultimate deterrent to the tactical use of nuclear weapons is the threat of massive retaliation. In the absence of a clear nuclear doctrine, neither side is fully aware of where the nuclear threshold lies. Would either India or Pakistan risk a concentrated nuclear attack on each other's cities in retaliation to a nuclear strike on a battlefield target? This is hardly likely, however, in the absence of clearly stated policies and nuclear doctrines, such a miscalculation cannot be ruled out. Ultimately, there is a cogent argument that tactical nuclear restraint revolves around the vulnerability of South Asian population centres—civilians will pay the price for any nuclear miscalculation on the battlefield with severe casualties. Yet, despite the advantages and disadvantages of nuclear weapons on the India–Pakistan battlefield, it is still a matter of concern as to whether this risk of a civilian nuclear Armageddon is sufficient to prevent the possibility of the employment of TNWs. As we have discussed, Pakistan's approach seems to be a graduated scale of nuclear escalation with a few to deter any Indian conventional military response. Pakistan seems to doubt the credibility of India's response to TNW use involving retaliation on cities. It is, therefore, suggested that maybe the adoption of an articulated calibrated response to Pakistan and its threats regarding TNWs' use may be necessary.

A Calibrated Response against Pakistan?

One of the questions that repeatedly emerge in any discussion of Pakistan's nuclear TNWs is whether the Indian Nuclear Doctrine is credible in the event of TNW use. Writing in the IDSA, Dr Balachandran and Kapil Patil outlined a debate over doctrinal review as follows:[40]

---

40. Balachandran and Patil, n. 24.

"In the current Indian context, the only pressing reason could be the change in the adversary's capabilities, namely the reported Pakistani acquisition of Tactical Nuclear Weapons (TNWs). Pakistan's acquisition of a TNW such as the Hatf IX missile, with a range of 60 kilometres and capable of carrying a nuclear warhead of an appropriate yield, has attracted widespread attention in various Indian debates on strategic stability. It has been argued that Pakistan's acquisition of TNWs has lowered the deterrence threshold and thereby affected the overall strategic stability in the region. Emphasising this change in India's strategic environment, the proponents of doctrinal review argue that India's existing doctrine is ill-suited to deter Pakistan from using TNWs against India."

The question as to the credibility of India's threat to retaliate 'massively' (with its implied meaning of attacks on cities and countervalue targets) continues to be raised despite India having never clarified what it means by 'massive retaliation'. Former Research Fellow at the IDSA, Col. (retd) Dr Ali Ahmed, notes that:[41]

India's deterrent posture is based on an assurance of inflicting 'unacceptable damage' as punitive retaliation in case of a Pakistani nuclear first use of any sort—either on Indian territory or on Indian forces 'anywhere'. The declaratory nuclear doctrine of 2003 has it that such a retaliation would be 'massive'. That the term carries some significance can be discerned from the use of the word 'very heavy' by the former Chairman Chiefs of Staff Committee to describe India's likely nuclear reaction. It echoes General Padmanabhan's warning during Operation Parakram that: "The perpetrator of that particular outrage shall be punished, shall be punished so severely that the continuation of any form of fray will be doubtful."

Questioning the utility of such an approach, Dr Ahmed suggests that a "tit-for-tat" response pattern be adopted, suggesting that a non-punitive retaliatory approach could contain a conflict and also allow India to retain

---

41. Ali Ahmed, "Tit for Tat: A Nuclear Retaliation Alternative," *Institute for Defence Studies and Analyses*, (October 03, 2011). https://idsa.in/idsacomments/TitforTatANuclearRetaliationAlternative031011, accessed on October 23, 2017.

moral ascendency internationally after Pakistani first-use on the battlefield. Dr Ahmed suggests that this way incentivises:[42]

"…limitation even in a nuclear war. This can be done by following a 'tit for tat' strategy at lower levels of nuclear use. It would involve imitative strikes that would leave the onus to escalate on Pakistan, as also denying it any intended gains. India's variegated capability, increasing numbers of nuclear weapons over time and second strike capability would ensure escalation dominance thus deterring Pakistan from upping-the-ante."

This certainly has attractions but would require India to develop TNWs and refine a nuclear war-fighting doctrine beyond mere CBRN readiness. Whether India wishes to take this approach is debatable, given the current antipathy towards the development of TNWs.

However, set against this is the viewpoint advocated by Dr G. Balachandran and Kapil Patil, who examined the Indian Nuclear Doctrine both for its wording and its intent and noted the following:[43]

However, the use of TNWs by Pakistan against Indian troops in Pakistani territory cannot under any circumstances be considered as a first strike. It will have no effect on India's second strike capabilities. Therefore, India's current nuclear doctrine does not call for an automatic massive retaliation for Pakistan's use of TNWs against Indian troops on Pakistani soil. However, this does not mean that such an attack will go unanswered. The doctrine does state in unambiguous terms that "nuclear weapons will only be used in retaliation against a nuclear attack on Indian Territory or on Indian forces anywhere." It does not define the level of such retaliation; only that a nuclear attack, which is not a first-strike, will be met with nuclear retaliation. In short, the apprehension that the Indian nuclear doctrine calls for an automatic reflexive massive retaliation for use of TNWs by Pakistan on Pakistani soil is totally unjustified. Such a use of TNWs will be met with a nuclear response. But the size and intensity of the response will be a political decision depending on the circumstances surrounding such use.

---

42. Ibid.
43. Balachandran and Patil, n. 24.

> In the absence of any Pakistani doctrine on the use of TNWs, it will not be possible for India to define its response to such an attack.

This suggests that the Indian Nuclear Doctrine, as discussed earlier, is inherently flexible and does not necessarily need revisiting, given Pakistan's TNWs. However, the counterpoint to this argument is whether the interpretation given by Balachandran and Patil is the one which is accepted by Islamabad in its calculations. This raises the important question as to whether perceptions on the opposing sides of the border are in sync with each other or does there exist such a divergence of views that a misunderstanding or misinterpretation could have a devastating cascading effect.

The question that thus remains is how India responds to the potential of TNW use by Pakistan, possibly or even probably on its own soil, without embarking on the process of developing TNWs of its own with all their complications of storage, command and control. It is suggested that perhaps as opposed to the path suggested by Dr Ahmed which suggests retaliation in kind—presupposing weapons of similar yield and similar target selection—his "tit-for-tat" approach be combined with the fact that a flexible response need not mean retaliating with similar weapons. Rather a combination of a 'tit-for-tat' and punitive response could be adopted, whereby India responds to a Pakistani TNW use against, for example, Indian forces on Pakistani territory, with weapons of yields no smaller than 5 kt and against twice the number of targets attacked by Pakistan but restricting retaliation to similar military concentrations. This path is a compromise, to be sure, may present India with a viable retaliatory path.

This approach tries to accommodate the need for effective and heavy retaliation with the desire to avoid nuclear escalation. Furthermore, it avoids the need for India to squander fissile material developing sub-kiloton weapons with limited destructive power. Yet, it cannot be understated that by moving in this direction, India is inexorably moving towards developing a nuclear warfighting doctrine. Any form of calibrated response will still need Indian conventional forces to continue military operations against Pakistan and in doing so, running the risk of either becoming a target of Pakistani TNWs or having to operate in a contaminated environment. In every practical sense, a calibrated response to Pakistan would inevitably involve India taking active and passive CBRN measures and making its preparations in this regard a matter of high priority.

China: Calibrated Response Once Again

China has been described by Brigadier Kanwal as a status quo nuclear power with a long-standing territorial and boundary dispute with India. In spite of the Border Peace and Tranquillity Agreement of 1993 and the confidence-building measures agreed upon in 1996, the Line of Actual Control continues to remain ill-defined and ambiguous. 'Clarification' still appears to be a distant goal as China is apparently in no hurry for further progress on this issue. China's continuing nuclear and missile collusion and defence cooperation with Pakistan, its support to the military regime in Myanmar and increasing activities in the Bay of Bengal, its attempts to isolate India in the ASEAN Regional Forum and its relentless efforts to increase its influence in Nepal, Bhutan and Bangladesh and its hysterical rantings over the recent confrontation in Bhutan point to its aim of the strategic encirclement of India. China's arsenal as described before is considerably larger than India's but as Air Commodore Jasjit Singh stated:[44]

> *The non-strategic category of weapons, which constitutes*[45] *96 percent (if warheads on SLBMs are taken into account, the proportion drops to a little over 93 percent) of China's nuclear arsenal, even after 34 years, have relevance only for China's immediate neighbours.*

As has been discussed, China's force of ICBMs and IRBMs, while considerable, is not enormous. However, it has deployed a large number of medium-and short-range nuclear-tipped missiles and nuclear-capable aircraft in Tibet. Given that China has already signed a de-targeting agreement with Russia and the United States, it is probable that these deployed nuclear weapons constitute a 'threat-in-being' to India and could be either used as weapons of intimidation or destruction.

---

44. Jasjit Singh, "A Nuclear Strategy for India," in Jasjit Singh, ed., *Nuclear India*, (New Delhi: Knowledge World in association with Institute for Defence Studies and Analyses, 1998), pp. 268.

45. Christine Fair, n. 26.

Also, China has lately modified its original NFU doctrine. Surprisingly, China's military strategists do not consider the use of nuclear weapons in their own territory as violating their NFU (no-first-use) doctrine. Kanwal writes that:[46]

"Though China has never bothered to clarify the ambiguities inherent in this stand as it suits its purpose to play a guessing game, it can be deduced that since China clearly considers Taiwan as its own territory, the use of China's nuclear weapons during a war over Taiwan would not violate its no-first-use doctrine. As a corollary, Indian analysts are justified in concluding that as China has not renounced its claim over Arunachal Pradesh, or for that matter is still to recognise Sikkim, it may seriously consider the first use of tactical nuclear weapons during a border conflict with India in the future."

It is probable that China's concept of fighting a 'limited war under high-tech conditions' includes a nuclear warfighting strategy. In these circumstances, there is the possibility that India may face a Chinese first-use of nuclear weapons in the event that China seeks to dislodge Indian troops from areas claimed by China or in the event that a Chinese commander believes that Indian forces have obtained a decisive or even significant conventional advantage on the battlefield. India may wish to ensure that collateral damage in Tibet is avoided for political reasons, although in the event of the nuclear threshold being crossed that may be of little consequence. However, a greater concern is that nuclear use could result in the long-term contamination of the Himalayan water sources which lead into the Indian plains. It is therefore in India's interest to ensure that nuclear weapons are not used in any future conflict in such a way as to affect the Himalayan watershed. This poses the question as to how any Chinese threat of TNWs use could be countered in an effective, non-escalatory and yet credible manner by Indian forces.

Two approaches to this problem can be taken. One would be that India retaliates in kind on China's forward troops, firepower assets, headquarters, logistics support areas and communication choke points

---

46. Ibid.

and avoid escalating the conflict by targeting Chinese cities which could prove to be counterproductive as China has a superior nuclear arsenal. The second option is to do the opposite. In the unlikely event that China employs battlefield nuclear weapons against Indian Army positions, assets or infrastructure on the grounds that it is justified in using them on the territory that it claims, India's option would be to retaliate massively against Chinese cities and economic centres on China's well-developed eastern seaboard. The argument to the latter would be that an articulated policy of escalation would deter any TNWs use.

It is a moot point whether the loss of a single Chinese city would be acceptable to the proponents of the first use of battlefield nuclear weapons within the Chinese Central Military Commission—it obviously would not be acceptable but it may or may not deter the use of battlefield nuclear weapons. The credibility of such a response by India is deeply suspicious. Nonetheless, the prospect of losing cities could be a deterrent to China's use of TNWs on the battlefield.

China has been working towards developing tactical, low-yield and enhanced-radiation weapons since the 1980s. The People's Liberation Army started exercises featuring the simulated use of TNWs in offensive and defensive situations beginning in 1982. Reports of Chinese possession of TNWs remained unconfirmed in 1987. In 1988, Chinese specialists tested a 1–5 kt nuclear device with an enhanced radiation yield, advancing the country's development of a very low-yield neutron weapon and laying the foundation for the creation of nuclear artillery. India has to consider if these Chinese capabilities warrant a re-examination of India's heretofore neglected tactical, low-yield weapons capability and its development as a viable response to the possible Chinese use of such nuclear weapons.[47] It should be noted, however, that as in the case of Pakistan's TNWs, the efficacy of low-yield or sub-kiloton weapons, even enhanced-radiation weapons against troops in well prepared and hardened defences would be highly suspicious and the impact could be averted by proper CBRN defensive precautions— passive measures for troop protection and combat effectiveness and active measures aimed at reducing the chance of a successful delivery

47. Swaran Singh, "China's Nuclear Weapons and Doctrine," n. 39.

of a TNW on an Indian position. Enhanced air defences and, perhaps, limited antimissile defences will also be needed.

It is suggested that India adopt a flexible response option and not summarily reject the same. It is difficult to predict with any degree of certainty what course a future war may take. If limited retaliation emerges as a better alternative under the prevailing circumstances, the options would be to launch retaliatory nuclear strikes of the required yield (10–20 kt) from suitable platforms (combat aircraft or Prithvi missiles) against Chinese targets in the TBA or at multiple points of India's choosing against major Chinese military targets in the Lanzhou, Chengdu and Yunnan Military Regions as a disproportionate yet, not an intemperate response. In either case, it is essential that a retaliatory strike capability with a survivable nuclear force is available, particularly, as it is likely that China may seek to adopt a limited counterforce approach.

Much more than in the case of Pakistan, this last sentence takes on great importance. India's strategic nuclear arsenal, aimed at countervalue targets in China, must not only be survivable but also must be reliable and available in sufficient numbers so as to inflict catastrophic damage on both the Chinese urban centres and their infrastructure as well as on China's industrial capacity and its capability for post-attack recovery. This is not to say that India's approach should be one of 'massive retaliation' to any Chinese TNW use, but given the spectre of nuclear escalation, it is suggested that India prepare itself for such a contingency, should it arise. It should be noted that the discourse on possible Chinese TNW use is far less extensive as compared to that regarding Pakistani TNW use. Furthermore, CBRN preparedness discussions in the Indian military have tended to emphasise the Pakistani threat as against the potential Chinese one. While this is understandable and indeed quite logical, it is suggested that CBRN preparedness should be as thorough as possible for Indian forces facing both China and Pakistan. This is particularly so for defensive measures such as hardening of facilities and providing protective gear to personnel.

Conclusion

Against either Pakistan or China—and indeed, both—it is clear that India's Nuclear Doctrine is perhaps inadequately understood or articulated. It is suggested that India needs to emphasise that its existing doctrine is flexible and allows for a calibrated response. Perhaps, some adjustments to the language would be inevitable to provide for adequate clarity in this regard. It is also clear that India may not be envisaging nuclear strikes against cities as a response to the use of TNWs on the battlefield.

In this regard, India needs to articulate its calibrated, disproportionate response thoroughly. The shadow of nuclear escalation following the use of TNWs is a clear and present danger. Given the vulnerability of Indian cities to a nuclear attack, it would be folly to risk such major escalation without considering more calibrated responses to the battlefield use of nuclear weapons. This does not necessarily mean that India should develop TNWs but rather for lower-yield weapons, develop and elucidate a policy of calibrated retaliation where any attack would be met with a disproportionate response but not necessarily the one which would involve massive retaliation. The debate over whether India should develop TNWs, as it is currently articulated, , is a somewhat irrelevant one. Rather, it is the refining of a response doctrine that is clear, credible and understood by the adversary that is of importance. In this regard, India has much to do.

One aspect of the TNW debate that cannot be overemphasised is the need for adequate passive and active CBRN measures to be part of India's preparations. To date, though there has been some progress in this regard, insufficient clarity is available for Indian passive CBRN measures to be seen as an adequate message to Pakistan that any threat of use of TNWs would not have the impact that they desire upon Indian forces. Moreover, while India has conducted CBRN defensive exercises during the course of major manoeuvres, there has been a dearth of information, discussion, debate and direction in the public discourse on such measures. While a degree of secrecy is desirable, a complete absence of information serves to unnecessarily obfuscate the issue of what should be an essential part of Indian military preparations.

4

Ballistic Missile Defences for India: An Essential Asset

──────※──────

The discourse surrounding the possibility of an Indian Ballistic Missile Defence (BMD) System is unfortunately lost in the cacophony of debate—most ill-informed and some nonsensical—as to the 'separate' nature of the Indian system. It is suggested that this is a singularly unhelpful approach to assessing the Indian BMD program as well as its eventual impact. Rather than viewing the Indian BMD system as a separate and 'destabilising' component of India's force architecture, the BMD concept should be examined within the wider and more important parameters of the Indian strategic air defence network and its gradual modernisation and expansion to deal with a wider variety of targets. If looked at in this context, India's BMD efforts are much more of an attempt to improve the range of targets that can be engaged by its air defence network.

It should be noted that the present Indian air defence network is undergoing a substantial upgrade process. Unfortunately, the current air defence network has a large number of obsolete systems that will mean that the upgrade process will be a time-consuming one. Yet, the gradual upgradation of the air defence network will also facilitate the integration of the BMD system when it becomes available. It should also be stated that the present state of Indian indigenous BMD efforts has been somewhat exaggerated. While the program has achieved tangible successes, its exoatmospheric component is some way from entering service and India will probably field an imported system to cater for exoatmospheric interception for some time to come.

A question that is frequently raised in any discussion of Indian BMD systems is that of whether the deployment of such systems would be destabilising to the region and could prompt either Pakistan or China to increase the development and deployment of nuclear weapons and delivery systems. It is submitted that this is a completely unwarranted fear and certainly not one which should deter India from developing and deploying an effective BMD system. To date, even without India deploying such a system, Pakistan has embarked upon a substantial increase in the quantity and quality of its nuclear weapons and ballistic missiles. China has had its own compunctions and has pursued a path of weapons development and deployment without any regard for Indian security concerns. In effect, neither Pakistan nor China has needed the so-called excuse or 'provocation' of Indian BMD development to seek to build and enhance their nuclear arsenals and ballistic missile inventories. In fact, it would be fair to suggest that India has been responding to the challenge posed by these increased arsenals by building its own deterrent as well as seeking to develop a BMD system to provide a veneer of security against the threat of either Pakistani or Chinese ballistic missiles. As such, any notion that an Indian BMD system would be 'destabilising' is completely erroneous as strategic stability already stands vitiated.

Strategic Air Defences in India

India, with its vast airspace, maintains an advanced Air Defence Ground Environment System. This system, along with the civilian air traffic control, is responsible for the detection, identification and, if necessary, the interception of aircraft in Indian airspace. The air defence network is also in the process of being upgraded to cater for ballistic missile threats. Before examining the system in detail, a quick overview is in order. India's air defence network is essentially divided into two parts—the Air Defence Ground Environment System (ADGES) and the Base Air Defence Zones (BADZs). These two components are closely linked and share information relating to air defence tasks. The ADGES consists of an array of radars along the Western and Northern Borders as well as a network of mobile systems in the North East and South of the country. Southern India is still peculiarly ill-served by air defence sensors.

The ADGES network is responsible for the overall airspace management and detection of intruders. The ADGES also controls and coordinates the air defences for large area targets. The BADZs, as the name implies, are tasked with the defence of high-value targets—airbases, nuclear installations and key military installations. The BADZ is a scaled-down ADGES network, limited to an arc of 100 km. The BADZ is a far more concentrated air defence environment than the ADGES and provides the only gap-free air defence cover in most sectors. In addition to these networks, India is now establishing an anti-tactical ballistic missile screen—with new radars and weapons. It is not clear whether this will be incorporated into the BADZs or whether it will comprise a separate network. This ATBM screen is slowly taking shape and news of its structure is still awaited. It is noteworthy that India's traditional concern has been its vulnerability to low-level aerial attacks in areas without adequate radar coverage. This is slowly changing to reflect the multiplicity of threats at all altitudes which can emerge.

Interception Assets

India's air defences currently rely on a mix of MiG-21/-23/-29 and Mirage 2000 interceptors and 38 squadrons of surface-to-air missiles (SAM). The SAM units comprise 30 squadrons of SA-3b Pechoras and 8 squadrons of SA-8b OSA-AKM systems and are deployed to protect key airbases as well as some major military/industrial centres. Though the SAMs are old, they have been updated periodically and, when operating as part of the BADZ, are deployed in such a manner as to minimise their shortcomings. In addition, a large number of L-40/70 radar-directed 40 mm anti-aircraft guns and man-portable Igla-1M SAMs are deployed to provide a 'last-ditch' tier of 'hard-kill' defences. It should be pointed out, however, that this system is geared up to the defence of point targets and not for overall area defence. It also lacks a viable capability against ballistic missiles. With this in mind, the Indian Air Force (IAF) has begun a substantial modernisation of its strategic air defences but while progress has undoubtedly been made, strategic SAM defences remain weak. The IAF is in the process of inducting eight squadrons of Akash SAMs and has sought to upgrade sixteen of the Pechora squadrons.[1] In addition, at least nine squadrons of a 70 km-range medium-range surface-to-air missile are being procured with the possibility that several more squadrons may follow which, in conjunction with future Akash procurements, could replace the entire Pechora force.[2] Replacement of the OSA-AKM is in progress with three squadrons of SPYDER SAMs being delivered and a new Quick Reaction SAM under development.

India's air defences are heavily reliant on a force of Su-30MKI interceptors—14 squadrons of which will form the backbone of the IAF in years to come. Augmenting these are three squadrons each of MiG-29s and Mirage 2000s, which are currently undergoing a deep upgrade aimed at enhancing their capabilities—not least of which is their air defence potential. Finally, six squadrons of MiG-21 Bison aircraft complete the Indian interceptor force and these aircraft are set to serve at least until 2024.

Indian Air Defences: Sensor Network

The Indian ADGES employs a three-tier detection network. While this system is currently in the process of a major modernisation program, the basic structure of the ADGES network will remain unchanged. The first layer, rather surprisingly, consists of Mobile Observation Posts (MOPs). These remain among the most reliable of the early-warning mechanisms available to the IAF. The MOPs consists of two-man teams equipped with a high frequency/very high frequency (HF/VHF) radio set and field glasses. The personnel in the MOP are very well versed in the visual identification of aircraft as well as their general direction of flight. The MOPs are scattered along the borders at random intervals, ranging between 25 and 45 km. The

---

1. Vivek Raghuvanshi, "Indian Excludes Foreign Vendors From Its Air-Defense Upgrade," *Defense News*, (June 13, 2016). https://www.defensenews.com/global/asia-pacific/2016/06/13/indian-excludes-foreign-vendors-from-its-air-defense-upgrade/, accessed on November 08, 2017. See also Chethan Kumar, "Six new Akash squadrons to give IAF missile muscle," *Times of India*, (February 17, 2015). https://timesofindia.indiatimes.com/india/Six-new-Akash-squadrons-to-give-IAF-missile-muscle/articleshow/46269673.cms, accessed on November 08, 2017.

2. Ajai Shukla, "Army Orders Surface to Air Missile, Making it the First Tri-Service Weapon," *Business Standard*, (September 26, 2017). http://www.business-standard.com/article/economy-policy/army-orders-surface-to-air-missile-making-it-the-first-tri-service-weapon-117092500988_1.html, accessed on November 08, 2017.

MOPs usually give the first warning of airborne intrusion, the general direction of the attack and, more often than not, the number of aircraft and their type. The MOPs are assisted in this task by personnel from the Indian police forces and Railway Protection Force, who are given some training in aircraft identification. These agencies report via a communications system based on both HF/VHF radio sets as well as telephone lines. A more advanced communications system based on fibre optic cables and satellite communications is also available to assist the MOPs in reporting to the radar picket line.

The radar picket line, which lies about 150 km behind the MOPs, consists of a number of radar clusters. These comprise three radar stations separated at a distance of the sum of their radii. The equipment issued to these clusters generally comprises one license-made Soviet ST-68/U and two P-18/-19 radars. These are then flanked by two P-12/-15 radars. The ST-68/U acts as the Control and Reporting Centre. This may have changed somewhat as the ST-68U, which was plagued with some nagging development problems, has largely replaced older Soviet-made equipment. Moreover, India has been license-producing the French designed TRS-2215D 3-D surveillance radar for a number of years and has derived an indigenously built radar—PSM-33 Mk.2 from it. These have probably supplanted most of the older Soviet-bloc equipment. It should be pointed out that these radars are all long-range surveillance types with ranges in excess of 300 km and a good performance against targets flying at all altitudes—even those employing electronic countermeasures. These radar pickets are responsible for giving accurate information on the intruding force to the Air Defence Control Centres (ADCC) located behind the radar picket line. The picket line and the ADCC are separated by a first layer of air defence weapons which are the first to engage the intruders.[3]

The backbone of the Indian ADGES is the THD-1955 3-D long-range surveillance radar. This radar, originally of French design, has been license produced in India for a number of years. This radar, though somewhat elderly, still has sterling performance characteristics and is capable of maximum detection ranges of up to 1000 km, though, in peacetime, the

---

3. Jayant Baranwal, *SP's Military Yearbook 1992-93* (New Delhi: Guide Publications, 1993), p. SS13.

IAF usually limits its power to a 400 km detection range. These form the core of the ADCCs. ADCCs also keep in touch with the BADZ control centres.

The BADZ is a scaled-down version of the ADGES configuration and is geared towards the defence of key airbases and other high-value targets. The BADZ is limited to an arc of 100 km, compared to the hundreds of kilometres in the case of the ADGES system. Like the ADGES, the BADZ consists of three layers. The first of which is the mobile observation posts, followed by a mixed layer of weapons and their associated radars along with a picket line of low-level radars. These are in turn supported by anti-aircraft artillery batteries. This network is controlled by an ST-68U radar. The BADZ provides comprehensive and gap-free coverage over its assigned area of responsibility. Some observers have likened the BADZ setup to the defence pattern of a carrier battle group. Any aircraft attacking a vital military target, therefore, not only has to get past the ADGES but also the far more formidable BADZ. This has serious implications for the attacking force.

Upgrading the System

The process of replacing the legacy radars of the IAF is slowly making progress. A critical element in this is the Arudhra version of the Elta M-2084 radar. Orders for 34 radars of this type were placed in 2009 and between direct supply and production of an Indian version of the same, this radar will become the backbone of the new air defence network. The Arudhra will act as an early warning and target engagement radar as opposed to the airspace surveillance/air traffic management radars, which currently dominate the IAF's inventory. The IAF will be able to employ the Arudhra-EL/M-2084 to provide early warning of inbound tactical ballistic missiles and cruise missiles, whether air-launched, ground-launched or perhaps even launched from the surface or subsurface assets. Installation of these radars will take place in and around Jamnagar, Mumbai and the National Capital Region, to begin with.[4]

---

4. Prasun Sengupta, "Arudhra MPR Is EL/M-2084 MMR: Seeing Is Believing," *Trishul-Trident*, (June 04, 2011). http://trishul-trident.blogspot.com/2011/06/arudhra-mpr-is-elm-2084-mmr-seeing-is.html, accessed on November 08, 2017.

Technically speaking, the AESA-based EL/M-2084 represents a quantum leap in technology for the IAF—especially compared to the PSM-33 and TRS-2215D radars that it will replace. It merges all land-based radar functions—weapons location, air surveillance and air defence functions, inclusive of the cruise and tactical ballistic missiles. The M-2084 is able to detect and track incoming targets and, in the case of missiles and other such projectiles, can calculate the anticipated impact and launching points, subsequently passing on target data to the relevant air-defence weapons systems. As an initial step, this system would enable India to detect and potentially engage incoming tactical ballistic missiles but would not be able to cope with longer range systems.[5]

The sensor network will be completed with a series of low-level and medium-level radars. Low-level surveillance is to be catered by a total of 67 low-level air transportable radars, including 19 180 km-range, three-dimensional THALES-built Ground Smarter GS-100 radars, which were ordered in November 2009. Six of these were supplied directly and the remaining thirteen being license-assembled by Hindustan Aeronautics Limited. Each radar will be accompanied by operational and communication shelters, an energy subsystem, a mobility subsystem and personnel living quarters—making them virtually self-contained units. These will augment the 34 active phased-array EL/M-2084 medium-power radars detailed above.[6]

In addition, a series of Indian developed systems including the Defence Research and Development Organisation (DRDO)-developed and Bharat Electronics Ltd.-built S-band Aslesha three-dimensional micro-radar, the Army-specific Bharani manportable radar, and 30 (20 more to be ordered) 180 km-range Rohini S-band central acquisition radars. The Aslesha, which weighs 250kg, uses low-probability-of-intercept frequencies to look out for terrain-hugging tactical unmanned aerial vehicles (UAVs) over mountainous terrain out to 50 km. The IAF has to date ordered 21 of them, and first deliveries took place in January 2008. In contrast, the Bharani is a

---

5. Vimal Bhatia, "IAF to Deploy New Radar near Border Areas," *Times of India*, (October 02, 2011). https://timesofindia.indiatimes.com/city/jaipur/IAF-to-deploy-new-radar-near-border-areas/articleshow/10204373.cms, accessed on November 08, 2017.
6. Prasun Sengupta, "IAF's Multi-Phase IACCCS Being Enhanced," *Trishul-Trident*, (January 22, 2012). http://trishul-trident.blogspot.com/2012/01/iafs-multi-phase-iacccs-being-enhanced.html, accessed on November 08, 2017.

two-dimensional L-band gap-filler system now in series-production for the Army. It has a range of 40 km and can track up to 100 airborne targets. To date, 16 Bharanis—meant to be used in conjunction with VSHORADS/MANPADS—have been ordered and deliveries are in progress. In addition, also under delivery are 29 THALES Reporter tactical control radars for the Army's upgraded ZU-23 and L70/40 air defence guns.[7]

The IAF has a total of 3 A-50 Phalcon airborne early warning (AEW) platforms, supplemented by three ERJ-145-based Netra AEW systems developed by DRDO. The IAF is now gearing up to induct new-generation S-band long-range surveillance radars (LRSR) and it is also hoping to acquire an additional nine ELTA Systems-built L-band EL/M-2083 'Airstar' aerostat-mounted high-power radars to add to the two already in service, but to date, no progress has been reported in this regard. For the LRSR requirement, a competition is presently underway between the ELTA Systems-built EL/M-2288 AD-STAR, THALES-built Ground Master 400, and SELEX Sistemi Integrati's RAT-31SL.[8] Twenty Ground-Master 400 systems were ordered in 2009 for the IAF.[9]

These new radar acquisitions will be integrated with the IAF's existing 32 new mobile control and reporting centres, 12 ADCC, 24 air defence direction centres and some 40 terminal weapons control centres along India's western and north-eastern borders. This will enable the slow but progressive replacement of the above-mentioned existing ST-68U gapfiller radars and related 19ZH6 command-and-control consoles, P-18/NRS-12 and P-19 gap-filler radars. It is anticipated that the LRSR will replace the THD-1955 radars but this is some way from happening. In the interim, new inductions will enable the replacement of the P-30/NRS-20, P-37 and P-40 gap-filler/target engagement radars, and THALES-built TRS-2215D and BEL-built PSM-33 Mk2 airspace surveillance radars, all of which were inducted in the 1970s and 1980s.[10]

Both the Indian Army and navy are desirous of obtaining aerostat-mounted EL M-2083 radars. In the army's case, the intention is to acquire

---

7. Ibid.
8. Ibid.
9. "Electronic Weapons: Instant Radar," *Strategy Page*, (February 21, 2009), https://www.strategypage.com/htmw/htecm/articles/20090221.aspx, accessed on November 08, 2017.
10. Sengupta, n. 6.

six such systems to enable the Corps of Army Air Defence to detect and track both ballistic missiles and terrain-hugging cruise missiles launched from Pakistan, while the Indian Navy is reportedly asking for two EL/M-2083s. Capability wise, the 1700 kg EL/M-2083 'Airstar' is mounted inside the 240 feet-long aerostat that is perched at altitudes of up to 4000 ft, and uses electronically-steered multibeam techniques to detect terrain hugging airborne targets—combat aircraft, helicopters, cruise missiles and UAVs—at ranges of up to 300km, while the trajectories of ballistic missiles can be accurately plotted up to 500km away. There has been a renewed emphasis on acquiring these systems on the part of all the three services despite some earlier delays in additional purchases of the type.

These systems would enhance India's TBM defences and cruise missile defences but would offer little by way of assistance in the detection of longer-ranged ballistic missiles which would require radars of considerably greater capability and which have yet to enter service with the Indian armed forces. Yet to see India's BMD efforts as something separate from its overall air defence modernisation program is to miss the very essence of that program which seeks to completely transform the Indian air defence network from a 1980s vintage system to a state-of-the-art one. This is somewhat different from the approach taken in the United States where the BMD system is distinct from the limited air defence system available for the defence of that country owing to a significantly reduced aerial threat. In contrast, the IAF must cater for manned aircraft, short- and long-range cruise missiles as well as tactical and strategic ballistic missiles. The integrated air command, control and communications system (IACCCS), as described below will be an important component of establishing defences against these threats.

The Integrated Air Command, Control and Communications System

Phase 1 of the IAF's IACCCS. which seeks to provide a layered, hardened and in-depth air defence command, control and communications network achieved full operational capability by June 2012 with the operationalisation of the Air Force Network (AFNET)digital information grid which is IAF-owned, -operated and -managed fully secure and reliable network.

According to Prasun Sengupta, the integrated air command, control and communications (IACCC) is being established under a two-phase programme at a cost of Rs 16,000 crore is designed to achieve a robust, survivable network-centric C4I3 infrastructure that will receive direct real-time feeds from existing space-based overhead reconnaissance satellites, ground-based and aerostat-mounted ballistic missile early warning radars and high-altitude-long-endurance unmanned aerial vehicles and manned airborne early warning and control platforms. In summary, the IACCCS gives the IAF an automated command and control system for air defence operations as undertaken by the IAF. IACCCS operations will use AFNET enabling the integration of all ground-based and airborne sensors, air defence weapon systems and command and control nodes enabling a coordinated and efficient response to any aerial threat from any sector.[11]

The IAF has also sought to enhance its airspace management and surveillance capabilities to cater for both peacetime and wartime exigencies. To this end, Sengupta states, the IAF has initiated a multiphase $1.3 billion programme under which a state-of-the-art joint civil/military sub-continental airspace control system is being developed using the following fundamentals: the unity of effort, common procedures, and simplicity. The IAF's terminal area air traffic services and airfield management expertise and en route airspace/air corridor management are also being upgraded. It is hoped that the final result will be the creation of a vastly expanded air defence identification zone (ADIZ) and provision of a real-time recognised air picture. The upgraded ADIZ will extend the IAF's airspace management and surveillance coverage (using ground-based sensors) up to 500 NM away from India's territorial boundaries. When fully implemented, new-generation ATCR-33S and SIR-S primary/secondary surveillance radars and their related joint air traffic control and reporting centres will be operational at IAF airbases in Adampur, Agra, Ambala, Bagdogra, Bareilly, Bathinda, Bhuj, Bidar, Chabua, Chandigarh, Gorakhpur, Gwalior, Halwara, Hasimara, Hindon, Jaisalmer, Jamnagar, Jodhpur, Jorhat, Kalaikunda, Nal, Naliya, Pathankot, Pune, Sirsa, Suratgarh, Tezpur, Uttarlai, Yelahanka and Zopuitlang in Lunglei district in southern Mizoram.

11. Ibid.

The IACCCS can be further integrated with the army and navy radar networks and with the civilian airspace surveillance system and to enable the provision of an integrated air situation picture for operators to carry out Air Defence roles. It is the intention of the IAF that all of its assets—air, ground and, eventually, space—would be connected to create total situational awareness of a region. For the first time, the IAF will be close to achieving a complete level of integrated coverage of all of India's airspace. This will not only dramatically enhance basic air defence operations but also will provide an essential first step in which a BMD detection, tracking and engagement system is to be built. To this end, the IACCCS will also coordinate the early warning and response and interception aspects of India's planned layered, ground-based, two-tier BMD network that is now is in the development stages and but which depends heavily on the IACCCS.

Communications for the IACCCS is provided through the fibre-optic network-based AFNet, which replaces the IAF's troposcatter-based communications network. This system was developed at a cost of Rs 10.77 billion in collaboration with US-based Cisco Systems Inc, HCL Infosystems Ltd and Bharat Sanchar Nigam Ltd (BSNL). It incorporates the latest traffic transportation technology in the form of internet protocol packets over the network using multi-protocol label switching. A large voice-over-internet-protocol layer with stringent quality of service enforcement will facilitate robust, high-quality voice, video and conferencing solutions. Having established these critical components, the IACCCS can now be integrated with a large number of new-generation ground-based radars that are now in the process of being delivered or are on order. These radars will be able to deal with airspace surveillance in search of airborne targets (such as manned aircraft, ballistic and cruise missiles, attack helicopters and unmanned aerial vehicles), or coastal surveillance or ground surveillance. This would enable India to mount a coordinated response to an attack from any direction and through any medium.[12]

Cruise Missile Defences

The challenge of defending against cruise missiles has assumed as much importance in the Indian context as BMD. While the existing SAMs and radars

12. Ibid.

have some capability against cruise missiles, the deployment of the Chinese ground-launched CJ-10/DF-10A and air-launched K/AKD-20 land-attack cruise missiles (LACM) and against the Babur (a DF-10A clone) and Ra'ad LACMs of Pakistan has spurred interest and urgency in the development of an effective cruise missile defence system which would be significantly more effective than the existing network of ageing radars and SAMs.

To this end, the initial steps to develop an effective CMD system are being taken. A version of the Astra-2 BVRAAM is also being modified for use with the ground-based Quick Reaction Surface-to-Air Missile (QR-SAM) system and its maiden test-firing took place on June 4, 2017, followed by another on July 3, 2017.

The Mach 1.8 QR-SAM will have a range of between 3 km and 30 km in range, and an intercept ceiling from 30 m to 6 km in altitude, with 360-degree coverage in azimuth. While the IAF-specific variant of the QR-SAM will be employed exclusively for cruise missile defence, for the Indian Army, a QR-SAM regiment will comprise a Regimental Command Post Vehicle, one S-band 90 km-range air-defence tactical control radar for volumetric airspace surveillance, and three batteries, each of which will include a Battery Command Post Vehicle, a 120km-range C-band active phased-array Battery Surveillance Radar and four Combat Groups (CG). Each CG, in turn, will comprise an X-band 80 km-range active phased-array Battery Multi-Function Radar, plus a 16 km-range optronic fire-control system and four Missile Launch Vehicles (MLV), each of which will carry six canister-encased missiles.[13]

As for the CMD network's projected deployment sites, two villages in the Alwar and Pali districts of Rajasthan have been selected for the first two QR-SAM Squadrons. Prasun Sengupta claims that Rajasthan's State Forests Department has cleared the acquisition of 850 ha of land in Khoa in Alwar district, and 350 ha in Rupnagar for installing a CMD grid that will protect the western and southern approaches to India's National Capital Region. He further states that site selection work for a similar CMD grid meant for Jamnagar and Mumbai is now in progress.[14]

---

13. Prasun Sengupta, "Poised for A Hattrick," *Force India October 2017*. http://forceindia.net/cover-story/poised-for-a-hattrick/, accessed on November 08, 2017.
14. Ibid.

The Role of the IACCCS in the Indian BMD Network

Dealing with manned aircraft and cruise missiles is well within the technological capacity of India's existing systems which have undergone periodic upgrades as needed. However, the need for a BMD system—encompassing both exoatmospheric and endoatmospheric interception assets presents a completely different challenge and has presented the IAF and DRDO with a number of technological and practical constraints. At the outset, it has to be reiterated that to date, India has not deployed any BMD systems and its capability is still nascent though steady progress has been made. Few efforts have been made to analyse the progress made to date and link it to other air defence developments. One of the few to have undertaken this is Prasun Sengupta.

Prasun Sengupta suggests that the most challenging and contentious part of the IACCCS' implementation roadmap is the two-tier BMD component. He notes that while the ground-based, airborne and space-based tools required for giving early warning of inbound hostile ballistic/cruise missiles are already being acquired from both indigenous sources and abroad (primarily Israel), the process to acquire and deploy an interception capability—the active 'hard-kill' component—antiballistic missiles and their fire-control systems—is going to take some considerable time. At the current rate of progress, it is unlikely that the initial components of such a two-tier BMD network, comprising both endoatmospheric and exoatmospheric missile interceptors, are unlikely to be commissioned before 2022.[15] It is probable that the initial Indian BMD system will be comprised of a mixture of imported and domestic BMD interceptors and radars.

At present, that for fire-control purposes, the BMD system sues ELTA Systems-built EL/M-2080 'Green Pine' ground-based active phased-array L-band long-range tracking radar (LRTR). Two of these radars were supplied in late 2001 under the US $50 million 'Project Sword Fish' to the DRDO by the ELTA Systems Group subsidiary of Israel Aerospace Industries.[16] This has led to some confusion as some have assumed the name

---

15. Sengupta, n. 6.
16. "India acquires Green Pine radars from Israel," *Press Trust of India,* (June 28, 2002), https://timesofindia.indiatimes.com/india/India-acquires-Green-Pine-radars-from-Israel/articleshow/14351441.cms, accessed on November 08, 2017.

'Sword Fish' to be a DRDO-developed radar. India did write 3 million lines of software code for the Battle Management/Command, Control, Communications & Intelligence (BM/C^{3}I) centre, the hub of software and hardware systems.

Furthermore, transmission links to the interceptor missile are based on jam-proof code-division multiple access (CDMA) technology with multiple data transmission links having been set up so that if one is jammed the others could function. In addition, Sengupta notes that Israeli inputs were sought and obtained for designing and fabricating the BM/C^{3}I centre, which not only acts as the DRDO's primary BMD engagement simulator but also is being used for evolving BM/C^{3}I concepts, for defining BMD goals and developing a BMD doctrine, for evaluating candidate systems architectures, for serving as the principal prototyping-cum-validation tool for the BMD's BM/C^{3}I algorithms and for defining the human role in the BMD battle. The BMD's endoatmospheric element makes use of the THALES Raytheon-supplied S-band Master-A engagement radar. [17]

BMDs for India: Interceptor Missiles

India's efforts to obtain a ballistic missile interception capability date back to between 1996 and 1998. News began leaking out about the deployment from 1998 onwards of an Anti-tactical Ballistic Missile (ATBM) screen. This system was to comprise the Russian S-300V ATBM (SA-12) and India's own 'Akash' missile, which has a considerable ATBM capability. In March 1997, the Indian press confirmed these reports, stating that one S-300V squadron was being purchased, with more to come in the future. These reports proved to be incorrect and as far as is known, no variant of the S-300 has entered Indian service. The S-300 saga illustrates some of the many pitfalls of Indian defence reporting and coverage where, apparently, definitive reports of acquisitions turn out to be completely false. This has the dual effect of confusing analysis while simultaneously decreasing the credibility of analysts who, in good faith, believe such media reports.

India's quest for a BMD system has had many false starts and, while still very much a work in progress, has made some tangible steps towards

---

17. Sengupta, n. 6.

the development of a viable system. Early efforts focused on evaluating the potential of the Akash SAM to intercept short-range ballistic missiles. To date, this remains a potential development but has never been demonstrated. Other efforts included stillborn attempts to acquire S-300 PMU-1 and S-300V systems from Russia, as noted above and Arrow-2 systems from Israel.

More recently, there has been a more determined effort to acquire five squadrons of S-400 SAMs from Russia which do have a potential BMD role, especially in the variants sought by India. However, to date, the contract for the said systems has not been signed though the prospects of a contract appear hopeful with contract signing possible as early as late December 2018.[18]

India's indigenous efforts at developing a BMD system has had the misfortune of being plagued by a series of misstatements by DRDO officials which claimed deployment readiness when it was evident that the Indian system was more of a proof-of-concept technology demonstration until later versions of its endo- and exoatmospheric interceptors became available.[19]

DRDO itself has acknowledged that its first efforts were not the definitive versions of the interceptor missiles and as such, it was surprising to see claims of the system being deployable when this was patently not so. Such unfortunate statements have had the effect of obfuscating DRDO's genuine progress.

C4ISR

DRDO's overall BMD C4ISR architecture is intended to consist of both over the horizon and X-band fire control radars, which detect and track incoming missiles, a mission control centre (MCC) that fuses input (which may also come from satellite-based sensors), processes it and then sends orders for engagement to launch control centres (LCCs) situated up to a 1000 km away via mobile communication terminals (MCTs). According to

---

18. Pravin Sawhney, "Decks Cleared For the Contract Signing of S-400 ADMS in December," *Force India*, (October 17, 2017). http://forceindia.net/decks-cleared-contract-signing-s-400-adms-december/, accessed on November 08, 2017.

19. "Missile defence shield to be ready in three years: India," *Dawn*, (December 13, 2007), https://www.dawn.com/news/280120, accessed on November 08, 2017.

Saurav Jha, the LCCs then orchestrate the final launch sequence with the mobile interceptor sitting nearby.

Repeated tests of the two-tier system, including the latest Prithvi Defence Vehicle (PDV) test, has given enough confidence to DRDO to recommend the freezing of the current configuration for Phase-I. Both the radars and the LCCs receive and send information via target update transmitters based on the CDMA technology. According to Jha, the MCTs of the MCC are themselves connected via an IP wide area network, data links for the entire setup also include fibre optic communication channels and line of sight relays.[20]

A deployed Indian BMD system would consist of several launch vehicles, radars, LCCs and the MCC. Using a secure communication system, the MCC and perhaps, secondary sites would be used to link a geographically widespread network. The MCC is the heart of the BMD system. It is a software-intensive component which receives information from radars and satellites which is then processed by ten simultaneously running computers. The MCC is then connected to all other elements of the system through a wide area network. The MCC would perform tasks such as target classification, target assignment and interception success assessment deciding the number of interceptors required for the target for an assured kill. After performing all these functions, the MCC assigns the target to the LCC of a launch battery. The LCC computes the necessary time required and the optimal window for launching the interceptor based upon information received from a radar based on the speed, altitude and flight path of the target.[21]

While experimental versions of tracking and fire-control radars are available for testing, India would need to establish production facilities for these radars. To date, there is little indication that any progress has been made in this regard, reflecting either a desire for a refined system to be finalised for production or concern that these may still need to be imported. Currently, India uses the imported radars mentioned earlier and has not placed future orders for additional systems

20. Saurav Jha, "Hit-to-Kill Successfully Demonstrated By DRDO's PDV Interceptor," *Delhi Defence Review*, (February 25, 2017). http://www.delhidefencereview.com/2017/02/25/hit-kill-successfully-demonstrated-drdos-pdv-interceptor/, accessed on November 08, 2017.

21. T. S. Subramanian, "Smashing Hit," *Frontline*, (December 22, 2007–January 04, 2008). http://www.frontline.in/static/html/fl2425/stories/20080104242512300.htm, accessed on November 08, 2017.

Endoatmospheric Interceptors

The Advanced Air Defence (AAD)

The AAD system is an antiballistic missile designed to intercept incoming ballistic missiles in the endoatmosphere at altitudes of 15 and 30 km. It is a single-stage, solid-fuelled missile. Its guidance is based on an inertial navigation system, with midcourse updates from ground-based radar and has an active radar homing in the terminal phase. It is 7.5 m (25 ft) tall, weighs around 1.2 t (1.2 long tons, 1.3 short tons) and a diameter of less than 0.5 m (1 ft 8 in).[22]

Compared to the exoatmospheric systems, the AAD has been tested often and against relatively realistic targets. On December 06, 2007, AAD successfully intercepted a modified Prithvi-II missile acting as an incoming ballistic missile enemy target. The endoatmospheric interception was carried out at an altitude of 15 km. The AAD was launched when the Prithvi reached an apogee of 110 km (68 mi). The AAD with the help of midcourse updates and its terminal seeker manoeuvred itself towards the target and scored a hit on the target at an altitude of 15 km and at a speed of Mach 4. Ground and ship-based radars detected formation of a large number of tracks, signifying that the target had broken into multiple pieces, which were confirmed by thermal cameras located on Wheeler Island.[23] This was followed on July 26, 2010, when the AAD was successfully test-fired from the Integrated Test Range at Wheeler Island.

On March 06, 2011, India launched its indigenously developed interceptor missile from the Odisha coast. India successfully test-fired its interceptor missile which destroyed a 'hostile' target ballistic missile, a modified Prithvi, at an altitude of 16 km over the Bay of Bengal. The interceptor, AAD missile positioned at Wheeler Island, about 70 km across sea from Chandipur, received signals from tracking radars installed along the coastline and travelled through the sky at a speed of 4.5 Mach to destroy it. The interceptor missile had its own mobile launcher, a secure data link for interception, independent tracking and homing capabilities and

---

22. "Interceptor Missile Scores 'Direct Hit'," *The Hindu*, (December 07, 2007). http://www.hindu.com/2007/12/07/stories/2007120761241800.htm, accessed on November 08, 2017.
23. Subramanian, n. 21.

sophisticated radars.[24] Another test was conducted on February 10, 2012.

Finally, on November 23, 2012, India again successfully test-fired its homemade supersonic AAD interceptor missile from a defence base off the coast of the eastern state of Odisha. The test-firing was part of India's efforts to create a missile defence shield against incoming enemy missiles. The AAD interceptor missile, which was fired from the Wheeler Island off the Odisha coast, successfully destroyed an incoming ballistic missile mid-air launched from the Integrated Test Range in Chandipur, about 70 km from the Wheeler Island.[25]

The Upgraded AAD: The definitive endoatmospheric interceptor

On April 06, 2015, an improved AAD was tested. The missile was launched from a canister for the first time and the composite rocket motor fired successfully. The upgraded AAD improves over the AAD as it has a bigger warhead, improved manoeuvrability and a higher hit-probability. The test, however, was unsuccessful. As the missile was in-flight, one of the subsystems malfunctioned causing the interceptor to veer away from the flight path resulting in the failure of the mission.[26]

On November 22, 2015, the upgraded AAD was successfully tested. The antiballistic missile took off at 9.40 a.m. from the A. P. J. Abdul Kalam (Wheeler) Island soon after it received the command to waylay and destroy an incoming electronically simulated target missile. Conditions similar to the launch of a target missile from Balasore were simulated electronically and upon receiving its coordinates, the interceptor missile, travelling at a supersonic speed, engaged and destroyed the 'virtual target' in mid-flight.[27] The first test against a live target took place on May 15, 2016. During this test, DRDO officially reported that the upgraded AAD interceptor intercepted and destroyed a Prithvi ballistic missile

---

24. "Interceptor Missile Test Fired Successfully," *NDTV.com*, March 06, 2011.

25. "India Successfully Test-Fires AAD Missile Interceptor," November 23, 2012.

26. Y. Mallikarjun, "Interceptor Missile Test Off Odisha Coast Fails," *The Hindu*, (April 06, 2015). http://www.thehindu.com/news/national/intercepter-missile-test-odisha-coast-wheeler-island-drdo/article7073662.ece?ref=sliderNews, accessed on November 08, 2017.

27. Y. Mallikarjun, "Upgraded Interceptor Missile Successfully Hits Virtual Target," *The Hindu*, (November 22, 2015). http://www.thehindu.com/news/cities/Hyderabad/upgraded-interceptor-missile-successfully-engages-electronically-simulated-target-missile/article7905298.ece, accessed on November 08, 2017.

fired from a ship.[28] However, some reports suggest that the intercept failed with the upgraded AAD failing to launch, much less intercept the target.[29]

A further test took place on March 01, 2017 when the upgraded AAD interceptor achieved a terminal intercept of the target missile at an altitude of 15 km. A further test on December 28, 2017, achieved a hit-to-kill (HTK) intercept at an altitude of 15 km.[30]

The upgraded AAD configuration for these tests was similar to what would be offered for production and deployment. This test achieved both an actual intercept of an incoming ballistic missile target as well as an explosive intercept, as the pre-fragmented warhead onboard the upgraded AAD was detonated using the missile's radio proximity fuze.[31] The upgraded AAD was initially guided by its onboard inertial navigation system which received continuous updates about the incoming target's trajectory from ground-based radars through a secure data link. Subsequently, a radio frequency seeker in the upgraded AAD's nose cone section tracked the target while an intercept course was plotted by its onboard computer.[32]

To summarise, as compared to the exoatmospheric interceptors, development of the AAD and the upgraded AAD endoatmospheric interceptor missiles has witnessed greater urgency, with the AAD being test-fired on December 06, 2007; March 06, 2009; March 15, 2010; July 26, 2010; March 06, 2011; February 10, 2012 and November 23, 2012. As has been detailed above, upgraded AAD missile's test-firings commenced

28. "India Successfully Test-Fires Supersonic Interceptor Missile," *Tribune India*, (May 15, 2016). http://www.tribuneindia.com/news/nation/india-successfully-test-fires-supersonic-interceptor-missile/237107.html, accessed on November 08, 2017.

29. T. S. Subramanian, "Interceptor Missile Mission a 'Failure'," *The Hindu*, (May 23, 2016), http://www.thehindu.com/news/national/Interceptor-missile-mission-a-%E2%80%98failure%E2%80%99/article14333898.ece, accessed on November 08, 2017.

30. DDR Staff, "DRDO's AAD Ballistic Missile Defence Interceptor Heads Toward Induction With Latest Test," *Delhi Defence Review*, (December 29, 2017). http://www.delhidefencereview.com/2017/12/29/drdos-aad-ballistic-missile-defence-interceptor-heads-toward-induction-with-latest-test/, accessed on January 10, 2018.

31. Saurav Jha, "DRDO's AAD Endo-atmospheric Ballistic Missile Interceptor Hits Bullseye," *Delhi Defence Review*, (March 01, 2017). http://www.delhidefencereview.com/2017/03/01/drdos-aad-endo-atmospheric-ballistic-missile-interceptor-hits-bullseye/, accessed on November 08, 2017.

32. Ibid.

on April 06, 2015 and were followed by test firings on November 23, 2015; May 15, 2016, March 01, 2017 and December 28, 2017.

In the future, it is expected that the upgraded AAD will be supplemented with the AD-1 and AD-2 missiles. Prasun Sengputa noted that the Mach 8 AD-1 would feature an all-composite rocket motor casing, MEMS-based redundant micro-navigation system, as well as a new-generation imaging infrared seeker (IIR) sensor that employs semiconductors using indium gallium nitride and aluminium gallium nitride alloys for the Research Centre Imarat (RCI)-developed 1024-element staring focal plane arrays operating in the ultraviolet bandwidth that give better solar radiation rejection. Its flight trajectory is shaped through aerodynamic control out to an altitude of 35 km and a distance of 200 km when used for intercepting re-entry vehicles (RVs) flying at 9 km/second. Both the upgraded AAD and AD-1 are able to sustain up to 30 G. This makes them unstable at an altitude of over 35 km.[33] Fire-control cues for the AAD missile are provided by the DRDO-developed, 400 km-range Arudhra S-band active phased-array medium-power radar, for which orders worth Rs 800 crore have already been placed with Larsen & Toubro, while TATA Power's Strategic Electronics Division has been contracted for the upgraded AAD's transporter erector launcher vehicle.

Despite this, the AAD system is still five years away from maturing, pending the availability by 2020 of a full instrumented theatre missile defence (TMD) test range costing Rs 1000 crore that will be co-located at Machilipatnam in Andhra Pradesh and at Rutland Island in the Andaman and Nicobar islands.[34] The upgraded AAD, when deployed, would give India an effective capability against tactical ballistic missiles but its intercept ceiling to date has been tested only to 15-16km as against its stated maximum ceiling of 25-30km. This could limit its efficacy to intercepting conventionally armed ballistic missiles as a nuclear warhead may detonate at an altitude between 15 and 30 km. It would be instructive to see if the upgraded AAD is tested to higher altitudes.

---

33. Sengupta, n. 13. See also Prasun Sengupta, "AAD Endo-Atmospheric Interceptor Headed For Systems Maturity," *Trishul-Trident Blogspot*, (January 01, 2018). http://trishul-trident. blogspot.in/2018/01/aad-endo-atmospheric-interceptor-headed.html, accessed on January 10, 2018.
34. Ibid.

The version of the Long Range Tracking Radar used in the May 2017 upgraded AAD mission is an L-band array that can track a ballistic target with a radar cross section (RCS) of 0.1 m^2 from over 1500 km away. The Multi Function Control Radar, which is an S-band array has a tracking range of over 370 km for a target with an RCS of 0.3 m^2. These detection figures may be sufficient to detect a re-entry vehicle but this is debatable.[35]

As can be seen, India has made tangible and realistic progress towards developing an endoatmospheric interception capability. The use of a modified Prithvi missile as a target missile simulating missiles with a range of up to 600 km presents a viable test for the upgraded AADs efficacy. However, against longer-range missiles and RVs, some refinement is necessary. The fact that the Prithvi target missile does not have a detachable re-entry vehicle, the upgraded AAD is as yet untested against such a small target. Furthermore, there has been no testing of the system against a mass or swarm attack. Until such tests are carried out, the efficacy of the upgraded AAD system will be theoretical rather than demonstrated and one hopes that steps are taken to ensure that such tests are conducted before declaring the system fully operational. Nonetheless, the upgraded AAD represents a tangible success for DRDO and it presents a useful and sound platform upon which future progress can be based as India seeks to refine its missile interception capability.

ExoAtmospheric Interceptors

India's efforts to develop an exoatmospheric interceptor have been markedly slower than those made in respect of their endoatmospheric interceptors. This has made any claim of either phase-1 or phase-2 of India's BMD system being ready for deployment somewhat incredible. To date, only four tests of exoatmospheric interceptors have been carried out, two of which were with what can best be described as a proof of concept demonstrator, based on the liquid-fuelled Prithvi SSM. This is an impractical system for deployment as an interceptor missile and as such, India has opted to move away from that towards a potentially more efficient and effective system. A critical aspect for successful exoatmospheric interception is target detection. Sufficient warning time must be available for a successful intercept. India is yet to develop

---

35. DDR Staff, n. 30.

or deploy a missile early warning radar suitable for the detection of longer-ranged missiles and lacks space-based radars. Until the time these systems are developed and deployed, India's exoatmospheric interception capability will remain somewhat limited.

India's requirements for an exoatmospheric interceptor have acquired a degree of urgency with the IAF identifying multiple targets which need to be protected. To this end, as will be discussed later, India and Russia are negotiating for the sale of S-400 TMD systems to India specifically for the purpose of providing a degree of protection for vital areas and potential targets within India. The procurement of the S-400 would provide India with a considerable degree of exoatmospheric interception capability as one version of the system is capable of interception at altitudes of up to 185 km, approximating the performance of the US Terminal High Altitude Area Defense (THAAD) system.

India's efforts have not been insubstantial in this regard with intercepts achieved at the altitudes of 47 km, 75 km and most recently 97 km, with the existing PDV missile purportedly having the capability to intercept targets at altitudes exceeding 150 km and itself being the precursor for the second phase of development aimed at producing an interceptor with an interception ceiling of 300 km. Yet, India's progress in this respect has been slow. Only four tests have been conducted of exoatmospheric interceptor missiles over an 11-year period. This could be due to the greater technological challenges faced in the development of these missiles or it could also be due to the greater priority assigned to the AAD and upgraded AAD endoatmospheric interceptor missiles.

The Prithvi Air Defence (PAD) Missile

The first test of India's indigenous BMD was the test of the PAD missile in November 2000. During this exercise, a PAD missile successfully intercepted a modified Prithvi-II missile at an altitude of 47 km The Prithvi-II ballistic missile was modified successfully to mimic the trajectory of M-11 missiles.

A second test took place in March 2009, when India conducted a test using ship-launched Dhanush missile (naval version of the Prithvi missile) as the target simulating a missile with a range of 1500 km. Swordfish (the

LRTR) radar was used for tracking and destroyed using a PAD missile at an altitude of 75 km.[36]

Following the 2009 test, DRDO made claims that India has completed phase 1 of the project capable of engaging targets at 2000 km range and that it is in the process of developing missiles to tackle targets at 5000 km range. These claims ought not to be taken seriously considering that India's exoatmospheric interception systems are as yet seriously deficient. While some capability has been demonstrated, it is impractical for India to consider the deployment of an ad hoc system that would be costly and relatively ineffective.

The exoatmospheric stage of the Indian BMD system went through two phases—the first where the exoatmospheric interceptor was effectively a re-engineered Prithvi SSM and the second where a new and much more capable exoatmospheric interceptor was fielded. Initially, as stated above, the two-tiered BMD system consisted of the PAD, which demonstrated the ability to intercept missiles at altitudes of 47–75 km. To date, the Indian system has been tested on target missiles based on the Prithvi SSM modified for longer ranges and smaller radar cross sections. For exoatmospheric interceptions, it is essential that this target missile be replaced by one with a separating re-entry vehicle to properly test the interceptor missile.

The PAD, using a liquid-fuelled interceptor was impractical from a fuelling and storage perspective. The corrosive liquid fuel used in the Prithvi missile makes storage of a fully-fuelled missile impossible beyond a 5-year period. Storing the missiles in an unfuelled state is not merely impractical but defeating for the purpose of a BMD defence system which needs to be ready to intercept a target at short notice and which may need to be stored in a ready-to-use form for prolonged periods. The liquid-fuelled PAD cannot, for example, be considered for canister launch. To this end, India has moved forward with a much more advanced and practical system.

---

36. Air Marshal Narayan Menon, "Ballistic Missile Defence System for India," *Indian Defence Review Vol 27.3 July–September 2012* http://www.indiandefencereview.com/spotlights/ballistic-missile-defence-system-for-india/, accessed on November 08, 2017.

The PDV

For exoatmospheric interceptions, the PAD has been replaced by the much more capable PDV missile which is intended to carry out interceptions up to an altitude of 150 km. On April 27, 2014, the first PDV was successfully tested against an electronic target. This simulation seemed to be intended to validate the parameters of the interceptor missile rather than to achieve an actual interception and as such has to be viewed as a test launch rather than an actual engagement.[37] Furthermore, it was used to validate the interceptor's integration with the detection, tracking and automated launch control systems

This was followed by an actual interception on February 11, 2017, when a target missile was engaged in a successful HTK intercept at an altitude of 97 km. While this is a considerable achievement, unlike the earlier instances when claims of near deployment were being made, DRDO issued a much more nuanced statement indicating the requirement for more tests and a more effective detection system were emphasised upon, though the capability of the PDV was undeniable.[38]

Saurav Jha, in a detailed report on the interception, noted that the HTK interception achieved by the exoatmospheric 'PDV' was a major achievement for the Indian BMD program. By achieving an exoatmospheric intercept at an altitude of 97 km, the February 11 test validated among other things, an improved guidance algorithm used for this test mission, as the incoming missile target had deviated significantly from what would have allowed an intercept along a typical minimum energy trajectory (MET). He noted that the PDV interceptor had to hit the target at the far end of its engagement envelope and at a lower altitude than what a 'standard' MET intercept would have entailed.[39]

This test, Jha further notes, could indicate the maturity of the onboard IIR, the responsiveness of the divert and attitude control system (DACS)

37. "India Successfully Test-Fires New Interceptor Missile," *Outlook India,* (April 27, 2014). https://web.archive.org/web/20140428163936/http://news.outlookindia.com/items. aspx?artid=838755, accessed on November 08, 2017.

38. M. Somasekhar, "India's 'Interceptor' May Make Ballistic Missile Shield Real," *The Hindu Business line,* (February 12, 2017). http://www.thehindubusinessline.com/news/indias-interceptor-may-make-ballistic-missile-shield-real/article9537665.ece, accessed on November 08, 2017.

39. DDR Staff, n. 30.

used by the PDV's kinetic kill vehicle (KKV) as well as the sensor fusion achieved by various tracking systems involved in the mission. The February 2017 test, unlike the 2014 one was used to prove the efficacy of the KKV used by PDV by destroying an actual incoming warhead in an HTK mission.

Compared to the PAD, which Jha describes essentially as a high endoatmospheric system with a maximum ceiling of around 85 km, the PDV is a genuine exo-atmospheric interceptor capable of destroying targets at altitudes of up to 150 km.[40] In addition, instead of using a radio frequency seeker like the PAD, the PDV uses a strap-down IIR seeker developed by DRDO's RCI with a 128 x 128 focal plane array.[41] This IIR seeker enables the interceptor to discriminate against missile warheads and decoys. The PDV's inertial guidance package includes a ring-laser gyroscope which enables its solid-fuelled booster to move towards the estimated point of interception as calculated by ground-based radars until the KKV is released and the integral IIR seeker takes over in the terminal phase track the RV. After which, the KKV steers itself continuously to plot a collision course with the incoming RV. In the February 2017 test, Jha reports that the KKV managed to smash right into the central portion of the RV.[42]

Acknowledging that a new interceptor in the class PDV requires a new MRBM class target missile for effective trials, DRDO developed a new target missile. This used a two-stage target, comprising a new solid-fuelled second stage that sits atop a liquid fuelled Prithvi booster first stage. This target missile successfully simulates the 3–4 km/sec re-entry speeds of a 'hostile' ballistic missile approaching from more than 2000 km away. This new target missile provides a considerably more realistic challenge for the PDV as compared to that used in the PDV and AAD tests which would invariably have been limited in range and performance.

Prasun Sengupta notes that the PDV will take at least a decade to mature. It is designed to intercept MRBMs (with atmospheric re-entry speeds of 5 km/second) more than 500km away at an altitude of 150 km. The PDV will cruise at Mach 5, but will be required to attain a peak

---

40. Ibid.
41. Ibid.
42. Ibid.

terminal speed of Mach 11—made possible by the divert thruster placed on top of the second stage. This divert thruster will generate high lateral acceleration for the 'end-game'. Both the warhead and divert thruster will be fired simultaneously towards the target once they are within the acquisition range of the PDV's IIR.[43]

A critical aspect of a layered approach to BMD is the verification of the modularity of the systems involved. This would allow the use of different interceptors—with varying interception parameters—with the same command and control network which would inevitably lead to cost-effectiveness through interoperability. The February 2017 PDV test validated the successful integration of the PDV interceptor with DRDO's ground-based automated response network that has been used for the AAD and upgraded AAD interceptors and which forms the mainstay of the two-tier BMD scheme.[44]

The PDV, as an exoatmospheric interceptor is larger and has more on-board fuel than the AAD and its successor, the upgraded AAD endoatmospheric interceptor. Unlike the PAD, the PDV booster uses solid propellants which have high burn rates and can function effectively in temperatures ranging from −40° to 50°C. This has required special casting for the propellants developed by DRDO's High Energy Material Research laboratory (HEMRL) which has required significant improvements in metallurgy.

Recognising the inherent deficiencies in the PAD, which cannot be stored in a ready-to-launch role, the PDV is also designed to have a shelf life of 10–15 years before overhaul and its propulsion systems have a high margin for safety while retaining quick reaction capability. This makes the system suited, when fully developed, to being deployed in a ready-to-launch mode, slaved to an automated launch mechanism. Furthermore, PDV's propulsion systems are robust enough to withstand being moved, facilitating deployment of the system as a mobile platform. Jha notes that the DACS on board the PDV's KKV is fuelled by hypergolic propellants, with high thruster valves which can precisely control the flow of propellant to the rocket engines used for KKV steering.[45]

---

43. Sengupta, n. 13.
44. DDR Staff, n. 30.
45. Ibid.

While its development cycle is still a work in progress, once the development of PDV is successfully complete, it would signal the maturing of Phase-1 of India's BMD program which is designed to provide credible capability against theatre ballistic missiles (TBM) launched from up to 2000 km away. Moreover, as Jha has pointed out, the PDV gives an indication that India has low earth orbit capabilities through the PDV. As the PDV is but a step towards another and more capable exoatmospheric interceptor with the capability to intercept RVs at altitudes exceeding 300 km, India has the building blocks, though as yet in their dispersed and unassembled stages, to deploy an antisatellite system. However, this is some way into the future.

Importing the S-400

There is a possibility of a disconnect between DRDO and the capability desired by the IAF. Though the IAF had decided to acquire TMD assets in 1996, it was the MoD-owned DRDO which proposed an indigenous solution, for which it initiated the development of the PAD/PDV family of exoatmospheric interceptor missiles and AAD/upgraded AAD family of endoatmospheric interceptor missiles. As we have noted for target acquisition-cum-engagement, two EL/M-2080 'Green Pine' active phased-array L-band long-range tracking radars (LRTR) were ordered in late 1998 from Israel Aerospace Industries (IAI), along with two THALES-built Master-A Multi Function Control Radars and a TMD simulation test bed from Israel's Tadiran Electronic Systems, all systems being delivered by 2001/02.

A sense of urgency has infused the RCI and its associated Sensors Research Society, which have accelerated their efforts to develop a TMD system using the upgraded AAD endoatmospheric interceptor described above and which is specifically designed for neutralising the Pakistan Army's solid-fuelled single-stage DF-11 (Hatf-3/Ghaznavi) 280km-range tactical ballistic missiles and the liquid-fuelled single-stage Hatf-5/Ghauri-1/Nodong-1 IRBMs of North Korean origin, both of which are conventionally armed. Presently, the Pakistan Army deploys two Missile Groups each of the Ghauri-1 and Ghaznavi (grouped under two separate Artillery Brigades, these being the Hyderabad-based Missile Brigade South comprising Missile Groups 25, 35 and 40; and the Sargodha-based Missile

Brigade North comprising the 14, 28 and 47 Missile Groups).[46] As noted above, the AAD has evolved into the upgraded AAD and has been tested against realistic targets, leading to a potentially deployable system by 2022.

However, as has also been noted, India's exoatmospheric interception systems are as yet in their infancy and will require a significant period of time before being ready for deployment. It was in light of this that a Russian offer for their new S-400 system has come to the fore.

Sengupta claims that in 2015, a combined team from IAI and Russia's JSC Almaz-Antey MSDB made an unsolicited presentation to the IAF on an improved version of the new S-400 'Triumph' LR-SAM that would make use of IAI's latest EL/M-2090U Ultra high frequency-band active phased-array LRT.[47] The IAF, being impressed with the said system, began making hectic plans for procuring such a system for TMD within as short as space of time as possible. With the IAF projecting a requirement defending a total of 12 strategic sectors against inbound TBMs, IRBMs and MRBMs, the Indian government approved the purchase of five squadrons of the type.[48]

In order to satisfy the IAF's more urgent TMD requirements, Sengupta notes that Russia has proposed to the IAF two hypersonic missiles, the 77N6-N and the 77N6-NI. These have top speeds of 7 km/second and are the first SAMs of Russian origin to possess inert warheads, that is, warheads that do not contain any explosives and instead, are 'hittile', meaning they will destroy inbound TBMs, IRBMs or MRBMs by sheer force of impact.[49] Sengupta further notes that these systems will have a revolutionary element in the form of their on-board nose-mounted, Ka-band millimetre-wave active phased-array radar seekers and their real-time target discrimination algorithms required for fire-control and guidance of the HTK interceptors. To this end, the radar seekers have been designed with a rigid mount and

46. Sengupta, n. 13.
47. Ibid.
48. "Defence Acquisition Council okays purchase of Russian air defence missile systems," *Press Trust of India*, (December 17, 2015). http://www.dnaindia.com/india/report-defence-acquisition-council-okays-purchase-of-russian-air-defence-missile-systems-2156916, accessed on November 08, 2017.
49. Andrei Kislyakov, "Russia to roll out new hypersonic missiles," *Russia Beyond*, (December 18, 2012). https://www.rbth.com/articles/2012/12/18/russia_to_roll_out_new_hypersonic_missiles_21107, accessed on November 08, 2017.

narrow beam to provide precise angle metric accuracy. This combination of metric accuracy, wide bandwidth, and high Doppler-resolution capabilities makes for effective sensors enabling real-time target discrimination. This enables the sensors to provide accurate identification-processing estimates of motion differences caused by mass imbalances on real and threat-like targets—filtering decoys from actual threats.[50]

As has been noted, the IAF projects an ultimate requirement for 12 batteries of the S-400, with each battery using four TELs, each housing four canister-encased LR-SAMs, plus 14 long-range tracking radars. This would enable the protection of a total of five strategic sectors in northern, western and southern India. Depending on how the IAF's five squadrons are configured—how many batteries to comprise each squadron—the five soon to be ordered squadrons might be sufficient to cover the areas envisaged by the IAF, failing which further imports of the system may be required to satisfy India's BMD needs.[51]

Should India require the protection of large metropolitan areas, it will need an area defence BMD system rather than the point defence BMD systems currently being offered. In this sense, the long range of the S-400 system proved attractive to the IAF. Furthermore, it is anticipated that at least some BMD protection will be afforded to the defence of India's nuclear forces as well as critical command and control nodes. Assuming that two squadrons of BMD systems should provide an adequate defence for the national capital region, it is inevitable that additional squadrons would be needed for the defence of Mumbai and the nuclear storage facilities around Bhabha Atomic Research Centre and in the south of the country.

Will an Indian BMD system be Effective?

This is perhaps the most difficult question to answer at present in respect of India's BMD efforts since the system is not yet deployed and is as yet in development. However, if we are to predicate an analysis based on the anticipated performance characteristics of the AAD and the PDV—based largely on what has been demonstrated to date—the short answer must be 'it depends'.

---

50. Sengupta, n. 13.
51. Ibid.

If the intention of the Indian BMD system is to provide a complete level of protection against all incoming missiles from either Pakistan or China, whether from land-based IRBMs or from SLBMs, then the answer is almost definitely no, with 'almost' being included simply because predicting the future is always uncertain. Neither the PDV nor the AAD is likely to be deployed in either the numbers required to provide such a level of defence and lack the performance to provide the requisite level of protection needed to be deemed a national BMD network.

The BMD systems under development have achieved a degree of success against low RCS targets mimicking SRBM, MRBM and IRBM RVs. However, they have not been tested against an actual RV as yet. Thus, their efficacy remains somewhat questionable. Moreover, in terms of the ceiling, range and speed of the existing systems in development, they appear to be designed for TMD than for defence against a multifaceted strike involving both theatre and longer-ranged systems.

On the other hand, if the intention is to develop a system that could intercept conventionally armed ballistic missiles aimed at military targets and a limited number of IRBMs or MRBMs armed with nuclear warheads aimed at a small number of vital military and civilian targets, then it is possible that as the PDV and AAD systems evolve, they will be capable of meeting such a challenge. This is particularly true if the system is configured to intercept an isolated or rogue launch of a missile or perhaps a small group of missiles from Pakistan.

The cost of deploying a BMD system is also a factor which will necessarily constrain the deployment of any Indian system. It would be impossible for India to deploy a nationwide system and at best, India would be able to deploy a limited defence system catering for the defence of a select number of cities and military targets. In such a limited defensive role, it is possible that an Indian BMD system could be moderately effective. Nonetheless, much work needs to be done and it would be very premature to suggest that the system would be effective against even these threats. It is unfortunate that some ill-advised statements on the part of Drs Saraswat gave the impression of the system being available for deployment when it is clearly not.

China's BMD Efforts

Pakistan has moved neither towards the development nor the purchase of a BMD system. However, China has made some significant steps towards the development of an indigenous BMD system which will supplement the existing inventory of S-300 and derivatives thereof that form a significant part of China's air defence network. To date, China has expressed its vociferous opposition to the deployment of BMD systems in East Asia and has remained somewhat guarded about its own intentions in this regard. While it has kept a few secrets about its ability to intercept satellites, its BMD efforts have attracted less attention but have made substantial progress with a number of successful interceptions being reported over the course of the last eight years, though details are limited.

To date, the extent of China's capabilities is unclear but it is known that four exoatmospheric interceptions have been conducted—one in 2010, 2013, 2017 with the last being in February of 2018. Details of the last test, conducted on February 05, seemed to indicate that the interception took place at an altitude of approximately 62 miles (approximately 100km), and involved a system tentatively called the DN-3.[52] This would make the system similar in general performance to the Indian PDV project. In fact, one school of thought suggests that China's efforts in respect of BMD systems were in part a response to India's BMD research, with one scholar expressing astounded disbelief that India could have such a system but not China.[53]

However, it is suggested that China's BMD efforts, which may include BMD systems based aboard naval vessels, are aimed at deploying a relatively effective defence against India's nuclear deterrent.[54] This may

52. Jeffrey Lin and P. W. Singer, "China Shot Down Another Missile in Space," *Popular Science*, (February 13, 2018). https://www.popsci.com/china-space-missile-test, accessed on March 17, 2018.

53. Wang Ting, "Agni V and China/India Ballistic Missile Defense," (presentation, Carnegie Endowment for International Peace, n.d.), http://carnegieendowment.org/files/Wang_Ting%20Presentation.pdf. The presentation took place during the week of October 2, 2012. See Sarah Weiner, "Recap: 'China-India Nuclear Crossroads'," *Center for Strategic and International Studies*, (October 9, 2012). http://csis.org/blog/event-recap-china-india-nuclear-crossroads.

54. Minnie Chan, "China Plans Sea-Based Anti-Missile Shields 'for Asia-Pacific and Indian Ocean'," *South China Morning Post*, (February 08, 2018). https://www.cnbc.com/2018/02/08/china-plans-sea-based-anti-missile-shields-for-asia-pacific-and-indian-ocean.html, accessed on March 17, 2018.

not be implausible as India does not seem intent on deploying either a large number of delivery systems or warheads. A large-scale deployment of BMD systems could create some difficulties for Indian planners and would inevitably require an increase in the number of missiles and warheads to preserve India's deterrent against China. Chenming Zhou commented that:[55]

China's mid-course anti-missile system is powerful enough to shoot down missiles from North Korea and India, though it's not clear whether it could intercept an ICBM from the US if they start firing at each other.

As will be discussed later, China and Russia have been vociferous in their condemnation of American efforts to deploy THAAD and SM-3 systems in East Asia. However, coinciding with a tripartite BMD exercise conducted by South Korea, the United States and Japan, China and Russia conducted a joint BMD exercise in December 2017.[56] It is not clear, however, if any actual interceptions were carried out by either the Russian or Chinese systems so deployed and it appears that China's BMD efforts are not being conducted with the level of urgency that is apparent with the United States and its allies.

Nonetheless, China, like India, has some level of incentive to deploy a limited BMD system with coverage limited to a few selected cities, leadership site, military installations and perhaps particularly vulnerable infrastructure such as the Three Gorges Dam.[57] This would be significantly less expensive, though not inconsiderable in cost. Moreover, as a two-tier system is probably more efficacious, it is possible that China might be prompted to examine such a system. It should be noted that thus far, China does not appear to have articulated plans for any two-tier BMD system but

55. Ibid.
56. Franz-Stefan Gady, "China, Russia Kick Off Anti-Ballistic Missile Defense Exercise," *The Diplomat*, (December 12, 2017). https://thediplomat.com/2017/12/china-russia-kick-off-anti-ballistic-missile-defense-exercise/, accessed on March 17, 2018.
57. Brad Roberts, "China and Ballistic Missile Defense: 1955 to 2002 and Beyond," *IDA Paper P-3826*, September 2003, p. 21, n. 80, http://www.dtic.mil/cgi-bin/GetTRDoc?AD=ADA418710 (citing Wan Yung-Kui, "Can the Chinese Armed Forces Successfully Protect the Three-Gorges Dam?," *Hong Kong Tangai*, No. 31 [October 15, 1993], pp. 72–80.)

such a step would be well within their technical and financial capabilities.

Bruce MacDonald and Charles Ferguson, writing for *Arms Control Today*, suggest that China might have an incentive to focus on the development of endoatmospheric interceptors (in the class of India's AAD system) which could simplify the interception process, reducing cost at the expense of long-range efficacy. As a practical, deployable system, endoatmospheric interceptors have some advantages although it would inevitably mean that defence is limited to point defence rather than area defence. MacDonald and Ferguson note that:[58]

> The cost of a robust defense would be substantial, so the number of such sites would likely be limited to a few high-priority locations, but certainly those that provided protection to senior officials would qualify. The radars and interceptors for such point defenses would be different from those used for broad-area defense, with interception taking place within the atmosphere much closer to the attacking missile's target rather than outside the atmosphere. The atmosphere strips away the chaff and decoys that help hide the nuclear warhead from radar detection, making warhead detection and tracking much easier. At this point, however, the nuclear warhead is very close to its target and still moving quite fast.

It is of interest to note that MacDonald suggests that China's BMD efforts are geared towards its ASAT research program, a factor which in his view outweighs even the threat of Indian nuclear weapons. In an interview to *Asia Times*, MacDonald's views were summarised in the following manner:[59]

---

58. Bruce W. MacDonald and Charles D. Ferguson, "Chinese Strategic Missile Defense: Will It Happen, and What Would It Mean?," *Arms Control Today*, (November 2015), https://www.armscontrol.org/ACT/2015_11/Features/Chinese-Strategic-Missile-Defense-Will-It-Happen-and-What-Would-It-Mean?utm_source=Arms+Control+Association+E-Updates&utm_campaign=114a736ce4-The_November_2015_ACT_Issue_Features&utm_medium=email&utm_term=0_0bf155a1a2-114a736ce4-79430281#notes, accessed on March 17, 2018.

59. Doug Tsuroka, "China Pursuing Missile Defenses; Indian Nukes are Main Worry," *Asia Times*, (January 19, 2018). http://www.atimes.com/article/china-pursuing-missile-defenses-indian-nukes-main-worry/, accessed on March 17, 2018.

At the same time, MacDonald stresses that China's hidden motive in pursuing missile defense is that such activities can be used to develop anti-satellite (ASAT) weapons. "ASAT weapons are the single biggest reason for China to pursue a missile defense program," MacDonald said, noting that this factor even outweighs Chinese concerns about India's nukes.

MacDonald and Ferguson also argue that China may seek to deploy BMD systems to protect its IRBM and ICBM force, rendering them somewhat more survivable than might otherwise be the case to preemptive strikes.[60] This, it is submitted, may not be entirely convincing as the current generation of Chinese IRBMs and ICBMs are road-mobile which vests them with a high degree of survivability. Moreover, the practicality of deploying BMD systems alongside IRBMs and ICBMs may not be particularly practical.

However, there are factors which may militate against the deployment of any significant BMD system. Two such factors are detailed by MacDonald and Ferguson as follows:[61]

Incurring large costs for the deployment and operation of an effective system. Developing and deploying an effective strategic missile defense system would be expensive. A number of academics in China made reference to the cost of deployment, with a few calling strategic ballistic missile defense "a money-burning program" and "a hole with no bottom."

Contradicting past Chinese position on strategic missile defense. Actual deployment of a missile defense system would represent a major shift in Chinese policy.

Yet, even considering these constraints, there are several cogent factors which suggest that China will continue BMD research with a view to deploying a limited BMD system, and, as suggested by MacDonald and Ferguson, such a limited deployment is likely because:[62]

---

60. MacDonald and Ferguson, n. 58.
61. Ibid.
62. Ibid.

- It would provide China with a plausible cover to continue testing its kinetic-energy Anti-satellite weapons (ASAT) system. This suggests that a limited nationwide or regional defence would be more likely than a point defence although the latter cannot be ruled out. Point defence would not provide much cover for an ASAT testing program.
- It would send a strategic message to India, Japan and the United States, in that order, that China is capable of defending itself and overcoming major technical obstacles to do so.
- It would enhance China's regional prestige and sway, providing a 'technological merit badge' of recognition for achieving such a difficult technological task.

It is difficult to find any fault with these reasons as they are all valid and make perfect strategic sense. In fact, one may simply replace India for China and the same reasons are equally applicable to India's efforts to develop and deploy BMD systems. It is therefore submitted that China's BMD research will be driven by its own strategic perception, as should be India's efforts.

Implications for the Indian Deterrent

Any Chinese BMD system will perforce have implications for the Indian nuclear deterrent. However, it is submitted that BMD systems are not destabilising in and of themselves and should be seen as the inevitable consequence of the development of ballistic missiles. Nonetheless, there are implications for the Indian nuclear deterrent which need to be considered as the Indian nuclear arsenal evolves.

This goes beyond merely a consideration of an increase in the number of missiles and warheads to be deployed but might require a recalibration of the composition of the arsenal, its deployment pattern and possibly even the types of missiles and warheads to be deployed by India to create its deterrent. Indeed, it is possible that in order to be 'credible', India's deterrent may not be quite so 'minimum' as it moves to ensure the former. It is suggested that India should respond to Chinese BMD efforts in the following ways:

- Re-examine the potential target list and adopt a revised, geographically diverse targeting plan;

- Reevaluate the number of warheads that need to survive a first-strike as well as any moderately effective BMD system, making any adjustments necessary in production capacity of warheads as needed from such a reevaluation;
- Consider force increments in respect of the force of IRBMs deployed against China as well as perhaps earmarking part of the MRBM to serve in that capacity as well;
- The deployment of SSBNs with longer-ranged SLBMs needs to be accelerated with emphasis on deploying a viable, sustainable force of SSBNs, capable of reaching any target in China from secure Indian waters;
- Concurrent with steps 3 and 4 above, research into MIRVs must take a higher degree of priority with the objective being, in spite of any Chinese BMD system, for an adequate number of warheads to penetrate the defences to ensure the destruction of the requisite targets;
- Consider enhancing the role of cruise-missile-based nuclear warheads with an emphasis on a combination of long-range air-delivered systems as well as long-range ground-based systems.

Inevitably, as defences evolve, so must the deterrent and as we have noted the potential constraints on any Chinese BMD system, it is submitted that none of the above measures will either result in an escalation in regional tensions or be excessively costly to the Indian exchequer as many of these programs are already at work and might merely need to be scaled up to meet the challenges so presented. There are some views that suggest that BMD is inherently destabilising to a nuclear deterrent. It is submitted that this view is perhaps an exaggeration as shall now be explored in detail.

Are BMD Systems Destabilising?

One of the arguments that is often used against the development or deployment of BMD systems lies in the perception that they are somehow destabilising to the concept of mutually assured destruction or in the alternative may provoke an arms race with one side trying to deploy more warheads and delivery systems so as to overwhelm any BMD efforts. There is some merit to these arguments but, it is suggested, these are somewhat overstated.

Indian BMD efforts have, as has been shown, geared towards the dual threat of conventionally armed ballistic missiles as well as nuclear-armed systems. Furthermore, it seems to be developing its BMD systems as an adjunct to its strategic air defence network. Resource constraints would suggest that India would not be able to deploy more than a limited BMD network, perhaps protecting a limited number of critical targets and maybe one or two major cities. It may be able to deploy a more robust defence against short-range ballistic missiles that might be used against its airbases or other military targets. Moreover, no BMD system is 100 percent effective and this is especially true for a nascent system like India's.

The 'destabilisation' argument gained traction when the United States withdrew from the 1972 Anti-Ballistic Missile Treaty (ABM) Treaty and the subsequent decision of then President George W. Bush to deploy a less than mature Ground-based Midcourse Defence (GMD) system. This system, reportedly deployed at a cost to date of US $40 billion, has displayed a low level of effectiveness.[63] As Sebastien Roblin put it:[64]

> Or at least so one hopes—which brings us to the not very trivial issue of accuracy and reliability. There have been a total of seventeen test intercepts using some form of the GMD interceptors, the first dating back to 1996. Only nine have been successful. This equates to a 53 percent success rate.
>
> Now, it would be reasonable to suppose that many of the failures came during the prototype stages of the GMD tests, and since then the bugs have been ironed out. But actually, *three of the four* last interception tests, which took place between 2010 and 2014, have failed.
>
> Non-interception tests have a better track record, but even so, the last non-intercept test in January 2016 also had a malfunction in one of the four rocket thrusters, causing it to go off course by a distance "20

---

63. David Willman, "$40-Billion Missile Defense System Proves Unreliable," *La Times,* (June 15, 2014), http://www.latimes.com/nation/la-na-missile-defense-20140615-story.html, accessed on March 16, 2018.

64. Sebastein Roblin, "America's Missile Defenses Against North Korea Have a Big Problem (They Only Work Half the Time)," *National Interest,* (May 27, 2017). http://nationalinterest.org/blog/the-buzz/americas-missile-defenses-against-north-korea-have-big-20872?page=show, accessed on March 16, 2018.

times greater than expected." The cause was apparently a circuit board malfunction possibly struck by a loose object. Troublingly, the Missile Defense Agency mischaracterized this test as a success, even though the malfunction would have clearly prevented the missile from hitting an actual target under operational conditions.

Many of the GMD interceptor failures are due to mechanical breakdowns and software errors. If the causes of those breakdowns can be corrected, perhaps the success rate would rise. However, the Los Angeles Times reports that there are no plans to upgrade the earlier generation interceptors, which failed to work! Furthermore, new model interceptors are being produced for operational use without undergoing testing.

Finally, analysts argue that the tests are being performed under ideal conditions: only one missile at a time approaching from an anticipated direction without use of decoys and countermeasures. If the missiles fail under these conditions, they may perform even worse when used under more realistic conditions.

However, it is suggested that against the limited number of IRBMs or ICBMs capable of being fielded by countries such as North Korea, the GMD system might fare somewhat better. More success has been achieved with the land-based THAAD system and the naval SM-3 missile, both of which have demonstrated a degree of success against theatre ballistic missiles.[65]

Russia and China expressed concern over this concerted BMD effort on the part of the United States. However, while both countries have made efforts to improve their delivery systems and to introduce more modern missiles and MIRVs, neither has dramatically increased their nuclear arsenals and there is little evidence to suggest that either country is intent on doing anything more than force modernisation with perhaps incremental increases in deployed warheads.

This has not stopped the clamour over the potential destabilising effect of BMD systems. Indeed the policy group Arms Control has opined:[66]

---

65. Boris Toucas, "Ballistic Missile Defense: Proceed With Caution," *ArmsControl.org*, (November 2017). https://www.armscontrol.org/act/2017-11/features/ballistic-missile-defense-proceed-caution, accessed on March 16, 2018.

66. Ibid.

Yet, efforts to obtain a capability to reliably shoot down advanced ballistic missiles would almost certainly trigger a renewed arms race with the greatest powers. It would not only increase the risks of a misunderstanding, but also justify a surge in modernized nuclear stockpiles and delivery systems, harming prospects for nuclear disarmament. Potential adversaries would use an ambitious U.S. missile defense policy as a pretext to infringe on existing multilateral regimes if they believe that such accords will eventually become obsolete anyway due to technologically driven developments. For instance, this could be used by Russia to justify formal withdrawal from the Intermediate-Range Nuclear Forces Treaty and deployment of more short-range ballistic missiles in Kaliningrad.

For the same reasons, an increased level of ambition for missile defense programs would harm the prospects for U.S.-Russian talks on strategic stability. Instead, a competition on missile defense systems accompanied by a diversification of offensive arsenals would encourage new, therefore unstable weapons concepts and doctrines, fueling the risk of misunderstanding. Russia's delivery of the advanced S-300 air defense systems to Iran and Russian efforts to field S-400 area defense capabilities against air and missile threats have spread alarm within NATO, worried that anti-access/area denial capabilities might give Russia tactical superiority in disputed areas, such as the Baltic Sea, Black Sea, and Syria. Notably, these concerns have been high in peacetime, a period during which Russia never activated them against NATO assets. This suggests that any U.S. sense that relying more on missile defenses will lead to increased stability and security could vanish as China and Russia also invest in this sector and start implementing similar strategies.

It is submitted, however, that these concerns are somewhat overwrought and that to date, one has seen neither a significant increase in the Chinese or Russian nuclear arsenals nor an increase in their already ongoing BMD activities. It is noteworthy that Russia maintained the only operational strategic ABM system in the world for decades with the A-35 and later A-135 ABM systems. The latter system continues to be in service while an upgraded A-235 system was recently tested with a view to an improved interception of ICBMs.[67] Russia's families of S-300, S-400 and S-500 SAMs have always had an important TMD role and Russia has felt neither constrained nor compelled to justify their development and deployment.

It is therefore hard to see how the deployment of a limited BMD system on the part of the United States would destabilise the strategic balance between Russia and the United States or China and the United States. This has not stopped either China or Russia from complaining bitterly at every BMD step taken by the United States. Indeed, even the deployment of THAAD systems to the Korean peninsula and Japan prompted the *South China Morning Post* to report on the Chinese and Russian reactions as follows:[68]

> In Beijing, Foreign Vice-Minister Zhang Yesui summoned the US and South Korean envoys to protest the THAAD deployment, saying it would "seriously damage" China's strategic security interests and undermine the balance of security in the region. Neither would it be conducive to maintaining peace and stability in Northeast Asia, Zhang said.

> The Russian foreign ministry said in a statement: "This missile defence system tends to undermine stability in the region….We hope that our partners will avoid any actions that could have irreparable consequences." Russian media quoted Yevgeny Serebrennikov, the deputy chair of the arms committee in the upper house, as saying Russia could respond by deploying missile and ground units in the country's eastern regions.

Given the fact that America's BMD efforts—either through THAAD, the SM-3 and GMD—pose little threat to the Russian and Chinese arsenals, especially as the latter expands, it would appear that at present, the concerns raised by the Russian and Chinese governments might be

---

67. Kyle Mizokami, "Moscow's Defender: Russia Tests Modernized Ballistic Missile," *Popular Mechanics*, (February 21, 2018). https://www.popularmechanics.com/military/weapons/a18567468/moscows-defender-russia-tests-modernized-ballistic-missile/, accessed on March 16, 2018.

68. Laura Zhou, "China and Russia Criticise THAAD Missile Defence System as Destabilising Region," *South China Morning Post*, (July 09, 2016). http://www.scmp.com/news/china/diplomacy-defence/article/1987103/china-and-russia-criticise-thaad-missile-defence-system, accessed on March 16, 2018.

exaggerating. Nonetheless, with some 44 GMD systems currently deployed along with several hundred SM-3 missiles of various types deployed on the US and allied warships plus a growing force of THAAD launchers, the United States has invested heavily in BMD systems. Russia is, perhaps in response, accelerating its S-400 and S-500 strategic SAM projects which have substantial TMD capability while continuing work on its A-235 strategic BMD system. It is therefore very difficult to see how the deployment of the American BMD system has in fact been destabilising despite the concerns expressed in that regard.

In the India–Pakistan–China context, what impact would India's development and deployment of a BMD system potentially have?

It is submitted that Pakistan's nuclear build-up has been continuing without regard for Indian BMD systems. It is therefore unlikely that either Pakistan's missile or warhead production capacity can be significantly enhanced or even needs to be enhanced to deal with the limited nature of any possible BMD network that India could deploy. In respect to China, its arsenal of MRBMs and IRBMs could overwhelm any BMD network should China choose to employ such ballistic missiles in significant quantities. In fact, it is more a question as to whether any deployment of a BMD system on the part of China could affect India's credible minimum deterrent and compel it to produce more Agni missiles and warheads in order to overcome such a defence. As has been noted above, the solution to the latter problem lies in the expansion of the already existing programs.

Conclusion

India's air defence and BMD networks are closely linked to each other. As the IAF seeks to modernise the effective but rapidly ageing air defence network, the addition of the task of BMD, and, as noted, CMD, falls naturally within the IAF's ambit. As has been noted, the IACCCS is making considerable progress and new radars are being inducted to provide a degree of detection capability against theatre ballistic missiles, although their efficacy is suspicious against ICBMs.

In relation to BMD interceptors, India has adopted a two-fold approach, combining indigenous efforts with pending imports of the S-400 system. It has placed emphasis on developing a viable endoatmospheric interceptor in the form of the AAD and its upgraded AAD successor, with reasonably satisfactory results to date against realistic targets. To complete its envisaged two-tier BMD network, India's work on exoatmospheric systems has made relatively slower progress with initial efforts on the PAD being supplanted by the newer PDV version. With further tests, a viable and comprehensive BMD system may be in place between 2022 and 2027. However, this system will at best provide a limited capability against small-scale attacks and its efficacy will depend on its scale of deployment. The deployment of an Indian BMD system does not pose any significant threat to the viability of the increasingly advanced Chinese arsenal and it is unlikely that it will pose anything more than a limited defence to the significantly smaller Pakistani arsenal.

5
India's Military Space Efforts: An Important Yet Underappreciated Asset

———※———

One of the least appreciated aspects of India's nuclear construct is one which is not specifically intended for the same. India has made considerable progress in the use of satellites for military purposes and, while to date, India has not deployed any dedicated space-based early-warning systems to complement its intended land-based missile defence radars, it has made some progress in developing secure communications and surveillance satellites.

India's satellite saga began in the 1970s while its development of effective launch vehicles achieved its first success in 1980 but gained much more traction in the 1990s. India does not have a dedicated space program, and its use of space technology for military purposes is decidedly secretive and probably makes extensive use of dual-purpose satellites for military functions. While a specialised military space program is perhaps currently not cost-effective, it is suggested that India needs to make more effective use of its existing assets, with perhaps some accretion in the number of satellites.

At the outset, it should be noted that India's capability of launching satellites into both Polar Synchronous Orbit, through the Polar Satellite Launch Vehicle (PSLV), and Geostationary Orbit, increasingly through various iterations of the Geostationary Satellite Launch Vehicle (GSLV), does offer potential benefits to the Indian missile program, to date, India has not chosen to overtly use technology from its space program to enhance the capabilities of its missiles. This was, in the past, to ensure that the Indian Space Research Organisation (ISRO) did not fall foul of arms control regimes such as the Missile Technology Control Regime (MTCR) of which India was not then a member. With India now getting a membership to the MTCR, the opportunity now exists for somewhat greater collaboration. India's space program's launch vehicles and its ability to launch multiple satellites into orbit offers potential technologies which could be used to enhance the range of India's missiles as well as assist in its development of MIRVs for the said missiles. In the past, there has been some speculation that India's SLV systems could be morphed into ballistic missiles. The trajectory of the Indian ballistic missile program to date suggests that any such concern is unwarranted.

Nonetheless, in respect of its nuclear posture, aside from enhancing its conventional forces through improved communications and surveillance, the opportunity exists for India to explore the use of space technology as has been done by other nuclear powers to enhance its early warning capabilities and to possibly explore the idea of space-based weapons.

Military Use of Satellites: Foreign Powers Lead the Way

The use of satellites for military purposes began in 1958 when the United States launched the communications satellite SCORE which transmitted a prerecorded message from space. Since then, more than 2000 military satellites, the first of which were experimental and others later operational, have been launched by the USA and USSR and its successor states.

Since then, China, the United Kingdom, France, Germany, Japan, Italy and Israel have all endeavoured to deploy satellites which can be used for military purposes. Many of these are dual-tasked, such as the Italian COSMO-SkyMed system.

As of 2016, the United States has the largest fleet of satellites in orbit with 589, followed by China with 181 and Russia with 141. India currently stands in seventh place with some 42 satellites in orbit.[1] While the number of satellites may be of importance in and of themselves, the challenge of making effective use of the data obtained therefrom by the military is critical.

---

1. "India Has the World's 7th Largest Satellite Fleet," *Times of India*, (September 09, 2016) https://timesofindia.indiatimes.com/india/India-has-the-worlds-7th-largest-satellite-fleet/articleshow/54222923.cms, accessed on March 03, 2018.

These satellites enable a dedicated military communications networks with a degree of immunity from jamming, interference and deception. They have further branched out into such spheres as surveillance, early warning, intelligence gathering as well as navigation. In the surveillance and navigation spheres, the use of dual-purpose systems—such as the American Global Positioning System (GPS) and the Indian integrated reception system (IRS) series allows for a filtered sharing of data with the civilian market.

Communication satellites have revolutionised warfare, making network-centric warfare possible. These satellites enable high-speed communications allowing soldiers deployed on battlefields direct communications with command centres, dramatically improving their situational awareness. The United States, for example, is trying to establish a Global Information Grid to connect all military units and branches of service to further the concept of network-centric warfare. This concept is the corner-stone of new military doctrines employed by the United States and may be considered instructive for India as the United States Department of Defence noted in its 2001 Report to Congress that:[2]

- A robustly networked force improves information sharing.
- Information sharing enhances the quality of information and shared situational awareness.
- Shared situational awareness enables collaboration, self-synchronisation, enhances sustainability and speed of command.
- Speed of command, in turn, dramatically increases mission effectiveness.

In addition, intelligence gathering is also an invaluable application of space technology for military or other security-related purposes. Reconnaissance satellites provide high-quality imagery to military establishments and, increasingly, the civilian market. While the United States, Russia, France, Israel and Germany continue to operate dedicated military surveillance satellites, others have followed the dual-purpose path.

---

2. "Network Centric Warfare Department of Defense Report to Congress," (July 27, 2001). *Department of Defence,* http://www.dodccrp.org/files/ncw_report/report/ncw_main.pdf, accessed on March 03, 2018.

China, like India, has sought to make use of its extensive and increasingly sophisticated network of Yaogan remote sensing satellites. Some thirty of these satellites were launched between 2006 and 2016. Most of these are optical imaging satellites but several have synthetic aperture radar (SAR) systems fitted and others are apparently for the gathering of electronic-intelligence.[3] China also makes use of its Zi Yuan satellites which are nominally earth-resource satellites for military purposes.

Space detection systems have found much favour with the United States and Russia leading the way. During the Cold War, as the Soviet Union moved towards an intercontinental ballistic missile (ICBM)-based nuclear deterrent, the United States Air Force developed a space-surveillance and missile-warning system which aims to enable worldwide space-based detection and tracking of potential missile launches with the ability to classify and differentiate objects in space. The satellites of the Defense Support Program use an infrared sensor to detect heat from missile or booster plumes set against the relatively cool background of the Earth's surface. These satellites, launched into a 22,000-mile geosynchronous orbit, are designed to detect strategic ballistic missiles in the early stage of launch of their flights and were first fielded in the 1970s.

American space-based sensors provide the first level of immediate missile detection. Some satellite sensors also accomplish nuclear detonation detection—enabling detection of possible nuclear weapons tests. Most recently, the deployment of the space-based infrared system (SBRIS) GEO-3 in January 2017, and GEO-4 being deployed in 2018—have brought the total of the SBRIS systems in service to 10, marking a continuing commitment to space-based detection systems by the United States.[4]

The Soviet Union, and later the Russians, have followed suit and have continued, like the United States to deploy and improve space-based detection systems. In 2017, for example, the EKS-2, the second of six new early warning satellites was launched into orbit. The EKS system of

3. Rui C. Barbosa, "China continues Build Up of Yaogan-30 constellation," *Nasa Spaceflight*, (December 26, 2017). https://www.nasaspaceflight.com/2017/12/china-continues-yaogan-30-build-up/, accessed on March 03, 2018.

4. William Graham, "Atlas V Launches with SBIRS GEO-4," *Nasa Spaceflight*, (January 19, 2018). https://www.nasaspaceflight.com/2018/01/atlas-v-sbirs-geo-4-launch-cape-canaveral/, accessed on March 03, 2018.

satellites is intended to replace the earlier OKO system which made use of US-K, US-KS and US-KMO satellites.[5] Other than the United States and Russia, to date, no other country seems to have deployed space-based early warning systems though China is reportedly working on such systems and Japan is reputedly doing the same.

Satellites are also extensively employed in the signals intelligence (SIGINT) role. The United States deployed a large number of SIGINT satellites deployed in low-earth, highly-elliptical and geosynchronous earth orbit. The Soviet Union did likewise, and China has followed suit with at least some of its Yaogan satellites being fitted with appropriate equipment.

In the field of navigation, however, the use of satellites for both civilian and military tasks has now become commonplace. The GPS/Navstar, the European Galileo, Russian Global Navigation Satellite System and the Chinese Beidou systems are now in widespread use. In all cases, their civilian accuracy is slightly degraded as compared to data made available to the military but the dual-use systems embodied herein have obviated the need for a dedicated series of military navigation satellites.

While satellites are an important aspect of the application of space technology to military needs, it is also important to recognise the increasing possibility of the deployment of antisatellite weapons and possibly space-based weapons in the medium to long-term future.

Nuclear weapons being based on satellites have been conceptually viable for a considerable period of time. The Soviet Union, for example, experimented with a Fractional Orbiting Bombardment System based on the old SS-9 ICBM. The United States Defense Support Program was developed in response to this potential threat. Since the deactivation of the Soviet system, the spectre of such a system being deployed by another power—North Korea being named as a possible contender—has lurked as a distinct possibility. However, while the capacity for any of the nuclear powers to deploy such a system is probably there, to date, there has been a desire to refrain from deploying such space-based weapons. The prospect of

---

5.   Curt Godwin, "Soyuz Rocket Successfully Delivers Eks-2 Early-Warning Satellite To Rare Orbit," *Spaceflight insider,* (May 25, 2017). http://www.spaceflightinsider.com/organizations/roscosmos/soyuz-rocket-successfully-delivers-eks-2-early-warning-satellite-rare-orbit/, accessed on March 03, 2018.

orbiting bombardment systems is fraught with danger and it is perhaps not an option that would be attractive to most nuclear weapons states.

In contrast, there has been a renewal of interest in antisatellite weapons. These weapons were considered during the 1980s with the United States and the Soviet Union trying to deploy usable systems. The United States experimented with the ASM-135 missile fired from a fast-climbing F-15 fighter to destroy satellites. The Soviet Union developed a counterpart using MiG-31D interceptors. In addition, the Union of Soviet Socialist Republics also used ground-based directed-energy weapons to blind US satellites and deployed IS-A 'Satellite Fighters' using Polyot, Tsyklon-2A and Tsyklon-2 rockets.

More recently, interest in the anti-satellite (ASAT) weapons revived with the Chinese conducting tests in 2005 and 2007 of a kinetic energy interception system—the SC-19. In 2013, there was a reported test of a ground-based interceptor for ASAT use. The United States conducted a successful satellite intercept in 2008 when a RIM-161 SM-3 missile intercepted a USA-193 reconnaissance satellite which was decaying in orbit. In 2015 and 2016, Russia conducted tests of a direct ascent ASAT interceptor missile called the PL-19 Nudol which is based on the A-235 anti-ballistic missile (ABM) system.

India's Efforts

On the June 10, 2008, the then Defence Minister A. K. Antony announced the formation of an Integrated Space Cell under the aegis of the Integrated Defence Services Head Quarters which would act as a single entity to facilitate integration among the Armed Forces, the Department of Space and the ISRO, operated jointly by the three service arms, the Defence Research and Development Organisation (DRDO) and the ISRO. While India has not yet developed a dedicated space command—such as the Russian Space Forces or the United States Space Command—India does make extensive use of space technology for its military needs but has chosen the path of dual-use satellites to fulfil its requirements.[6]

---

6. "India sets up Integrated Space Cell," *NDTV*, (June 10, 2008). https://web. archive.org/web/20080614000739/http://www.ndtv.com/convergence/ndtv/story. aspx?id=NEWEN20080052615, accessed on March 03, 2018.

Indian Satellites with Military Applications

India today has some 14 operational satellites dedicated to remote sensing, making the Indian Remote Sensing (IRS) series the largest civilian remote-sensing constellation in orbit. All of the IRS satellites are placed in polar sun-synchronous orbit, being launched by the PSLV, making both the satellites and launch vehicle entirely Indian. The IRS satellites provide data in a variety of spatial, spectral and temporal resolutions, some having a spatial resolution of 1 m or below with definite military applications.

An early experiment in this regard was the Technology Experiment Satellite (TES) which was launched in October 2001. The TES had a panchromatic (PAN) camera capable of producing images of 1 m resolution and was perhaps India's first ostensible reconnaissance satellite. This does not mean that the earlier IRS satellites did not have military applications but rather reflects the greater military utility of the lower resolution afforded by the TES.[7]

One of the more recent satellites with clear military applications was the Radar Imaging Satellite 2 (RISAT-2) which has a SAR purchased from Israel Aerospace Industries (IAI). It has a day-night, all-weather monitoring capability and has a resolution of 1 m, enabling it to track ships at sea. The RISAT-1, launched later than the RISAT-2, was also fitted with a SAR system and augments the former in surveillance tasks.[8]

The CARTOSAT family of satellites—a subset of the IRS family—is probably the most capable of India's military satellites. The CARTOSAT-2A is a dedicated military satellite whose capabilities are as yet unclear but it is capable of being steered to enable the imaging of any particular area with greater frequency. It reportedly has a resolution of 2.5 m.

Its predecessor—the CARTOSAT-2—carries a state-of-the-art PAN camera that can take black and white photographs in the visible region of the electromagnetic spectrum. The swath covered by these high-resolution PAN cameras is 9.6 km and their spatial resolution is 80 cm. CARTOSAT-2 can be steered up to 45° along as well as across the track and is capable of providing scene-specific spot imagery. Its successor, CARTOSAT-2B offers multiple spot scene imagery.

---

7. Air Marshal Anil Chopra, "India's Military Space Program," *South Asia Defence and Strategic Review* http://www.defstrat.com/india%E2%80%99s-military-space-program, accessed on March 03, 2018.
8. Ibid.

In 2017, the CARTOSAT-2E was launched. This provided scene-specific images with a spatial resolution of less than 60 cm and marked a remarkable improvement in India's satellite imagery. The latest member of the CARTOSAT family, the CARTOSAT-2F, was launched in January 2018. It has four MX detectors with band-pass filters between 450 and 860 nm which can deliver imagery at a 2-m ground resolution along a 10-km swath. While its principal tasks are for disaster management, cartography and environmental monitoring, its military applications are evident.[9] One might expect further improvements in follow-on satellites.

Aside from remote sensing satellites, ISRO has fielded a wide variety of communications satellites. The Indian National Satellite System (INSAT) series of satellites has provided transponders for communications for several decades. Of the 24 satellites put into orbit, 11 are currently operational with ISRO making more use of the GSLV, as opposed to the French Ariane rocket, as the reliability of the GSLV improves. INSAT-4F, also known as GSAT-7, is a dedicated military communications satellite with the Indian Navy making extensive use of the satellite to facilitate communications between its ships. GSAT-6, launched in 2015, also purportedly provides secure communications to several strategic end-users in India.

More recently, India has completed all the building blocks for its own satellite navigation system. Six Indian Regional Navigation Satellite System (IRNSS) satellites are currently in operation, providing the foundation for the development of an Indian navigation satellite system—NAVIC. This will provide both a standard positioning service for civilian users and an encrypted positioning service for military users.

While six satellites are sufficient to start the NAVIC system, an attempt to place a seventh satellite into orbit failed in 2017. This satellite, which was to replace the earliest member of the family—IRNSS-1A—was to provide the necessary redundancy for the NAVIC system. There are plans, however, to increase the number of satellites to 11, thus increasing the coverage area.

Indian Military Use of Satellites

India's employment of satellites for military purposes has been gradually

---

9. "Cartosat-2f," *Spaceflight 101*, http://spaceflight101.com/pslv-c40/cartosat-2f/, accessed on March 03, 2018.

revealed. In 2016, half a dozen ISRO satellites were used to obtain ground information for the surgical strike carried out by the Indian Army against terrorist targets in Pakistan-occupied Kashmir (PoK). Prior to this, the Indian Navy used the GSAT-7 to assist its search and rescue operations and was able to seamlessly network some 60 ships and 75 aircraft during the 2014 Theatre-level Readiness and Operational Exercise conducted in the Bay of Bengal.[10]

Shortly after the 2017 launch of the CARTOSAT-2E, it was revealed that some 13 satellites were being used for surveillance purposes. This number is set to grow as newer versions of the IRS series begin to enter service. However, barring a few examples, none are dedicated military satellites, being used for both civilian and military purposes.[11]

India's National Technical Research Organisation (NTRO) which is controlled by the Research and Analysis Wing, India's premier intelligence agency, makes extensive use of IRS, RISAT and CARTOSAT data to aid it building a comprehensive intelligence picture.

India also has a nascent ASAT capability though it has not been demonstrated to date. In 2017, an Indian exoatmospheric ballistic missile interceptor, the PDV, achieved an interception at an altitude of 97 km.[12] This is not adequate as yet for an ASAT system but demonstrates a potential capability similar to that of the Israeli Arrow-3 missile. The interception of a satellite, however, is different to that of a ballistic missile. The successful intercept achieved by the US Navy using an ABM system points to a potential dual purpose. In India's case, it has also been suggested that a modified Agni-5 missile could serve as a viable ASAT weapon with the propulsion system mated to a dedicated kill-vehicle.[13] However, without a dynamic test, India's ASAT capability is at best theoretical.[14]

10. Chopra, n. 7.
11. Surendra Singh, "Military using 13 Satellites to Keep Eye on Foes," *Times of India,* (June 26, 2017). https://timesofindia.indiatimes.com/india/military-using-13-satellites-to-keep-eye-on-foes/articleshow/59314610.cms, accessed on March 03, 2018.
12. Chopra, n. 7.
13. Rajat Pandit, "After Agni-V Launch, DRDO's New Target is Anti-Satellite Weapons," *Times of India,* (April 21, 2012). https://timesofindia.indiatimes.com/india/After-Agni-V-launch-DRDOs-new-target-is-anti-satellite-weapons/articleshow/12763074.cms, accessed on March 03, 2018.
14. Harsh Vasani, "India's Anti-Satellite Weapons," *The Diplomat,* (June 14, 2016). https://thediplomat.com/2016/06/indias-anti-satellite-weapons/, accessed on March 03, 2018.

Is India Moving in the Right Direction?

The closest India has come to outlining a vision for the use of space technology to enhance its military was the Indian Air Force (IAF) Defence Space Vision 2020, which outlined ways to harness satellite resources to significantly boost India's defence preparedness. The Defence Space Cell is a step in the right direction but, a decade later, it is time to look again at whether there is a need for a much more focused organisation. Outlined in 2011, the Defence Space Vision focused on military space applications in the spheres of intelligence, reconnaissance, surveillance, communications and navigation. It envisaged the need for several dedicated military satellites as well as the need for a specialised Aerospace Command under the auspices of the IAF.

While the IAF would be the natural service to foster an Aerospace Command, without a clear vision, resources and a path forward, it is submitted that such an organisation would be little more than an entity to enable networking and perhaps a certain amount of planning. Will the Aerospace Command, for example, have control of the satellites to the extent of adjusting orbits where necessary? Furthermore, as all three services have a need for both satellite intelligence and communications, is it necessary to place such an Aerospace Command under the control of a single service?

These are fundamentally administrative questions but at this juncture, India needs to ascertain whether it requires a constellation of specialised built-for-purpose military satellites or whether the current dual-use satellites are a more cost-effective way of using resources. This latter point cannot be understated as India will not be able to afford the prodigious duplication of effort that parallel civilian and military satellite programs would envisage. It is worth remembering that the reconnaissance satellite concept was created and developed at a time when civilian imaging satellites were at best in their infancy. Nowadays, civilian satellites can offer imagery rivalling that of dedicated military satellites.

With improved resolutions, the line between civilian and military satellites is being increasingly blurred, especially when it relates to quality imagery. The IRS, CARTOSAT and RISAT dual-use satellites are effectively used by the Indian military. At this point, perhaps concentrating on an improved image resolution, secure data transmission and processing is perhaps the order of the day rather than incurring the expense of dedicated military satellites.

This does not preclude the need for prioritising military imagery requirements, but it does pose the question as to whether the expense of dedicated satellites is needed. This expense could be justified if it was the intention to create a global system of near-constant surveillance along the lines of that developed by the United States. In practical terms, however, it is unlikely that this would be cost-effective for India, though the need for such a constellation of satellites could emerge in the medium-term. It is not possible to transpose the path adopted by the other powers directly onto India's requirements in this regard. For a decision on the need for dedicated military surveillance satellites, India must first define which areas it needs to keep under constant observation and the systems required to do this. If this remains limited to China, Pakistan and the Indian Ocean and Arabian Sea regions, it is not inconceivable that the dual-purpose satellites currently in use could suffice for this purpose.

With respect to military communications, the needs of the services in terms of transponders must be quantified. Just as the Navy is satisfied with the GSAT-7, the other two services may require similar satellites of their own to ensure secure communications with additional transponders from civilian satellites, with necessary security being used for redundancy. It is unlikely, therefore, that any more than a few dedicated military communications satellites will be needed and even then, the number and type would need to be specified. With respect to navigation, however, it is suggested that the dual-use IRNSS system must be made operational as soon as practicable. The need for dedicated military navigation satellites is not envisaged nor may it be practical especially given the emergence of the IRNSS system as a viable navigational asset.

There may be, however, a growing requirement for dedicated military early-warning satellites as the missile threat from both China and Pakistan grows. Indeed, satellites may offer the only means of launch detection for India. In addition, there may be a requirement for dedicated SIGINT satellites which can bolster intelligence gathering capabilities. In neither of these spheres, India has shown any appreciable sense of urgency. This is particularly evident in the failure of India to embrace the urgency of space-based missile warning systems to enhance its ballistic missile early-warning network. It is strange that despite considerable effort in the development of land-based interceptors and radar systems, India has been so reluctant to develop space-based early warning capabilities.

Finally, India has to give consideration to develop a viable and working ASAT capability and demonstrating the same. With three countries already having done so, India would merely be demonstrating a needed military capability. This may require a degree of innovation and adapting the existing MRBM or IRBM systems for the ASAT role as has been done by China. Technologically, this should be well within India's capabilities but failing a dynamic test, India's capabilities will continue to remain theoretical and this is clearly not adequate.

In conclusion, while India has not developed the desired Aerospace Command, its military space capabilities are not inconsiderable. What is lacking is a sense of direction, a clear statement of military space requirements and a closer relationship between the military and space authorities. It is perhaps in this regard that the Defence Space Cell can come into its own and facilitate and foster this relationship with a view eventually morphing into a tri-service Space Command. How this will interact with the Strategic Forces Command is a matter of medium-term concern as the latter's preparations to contend with first-strikes from either Pakistan or China would depend at least in part on an effective early warning system.

6
Responding to a Nontraditional CBRN Attack

India faces not only the risk of traditional nuclear attacks but also from the potential use of nuclear weapons through nontraditional means. These could include a terrorist strike using a nuclear weapon of low yield or a so-called 'dirty bomb' or even an attack involving either a nuclear or non-nuclear generated electromagnetic pulse. Another potential method of attack could be the possible sabotage of a nuclear power plant with the potential for radioactive release. Strictly military or retaliatory measures will not necessarily deter such attacks. In this case, a combination of active measures to detect and prevent such attacks and passive measures to deal with the impact of such attacks may have the best prospects of deterring or at the very least containing such attacks. To this end, it is important to determine how well prepared India is to respond to the impact of such attacks so as to minimise damage. Into this sphere, we must assess the civil defence capabilities and emergency response systems of the Indian state. It will be shown that while the Indian state has significant deficiencies in its response mechanisms, it is far from impotent.

As noted above, the types of nontraditional chemical, biological, radiological and nuclear (CBRN) attacks may be broken down as follows:

- A nuclear or non-nuclear-generated electromagnetic pulse (EMP) aimed at disrupting military and/or civilian activities, networks, operations and infrastructure;
- The use of CBRN agents by a non-state actor aimed at creating either a mass casualty event or significant civilian fear and panic as well as disruption to society; or with the aim to stretch emergency, relief and economic resources with a view towards destabilisation of a state or to divert resources away from any military or diplomatic effort;

- The sabotage of a chemical or nuclear power plant aimed at causing casualties and disruption through the release of radiation, radioactive materials or chemical agents.

In none of the above scenarios do any of the conventionally accepted concepts of deterrence work effectively. Furthermore, with non-state actors as possible perpetrators, even the risk of retaliation may not prove sufficiently credible to deter such attacks. While efforts to prevent such nontraditional CBRN attacks would take the route of intelligence gathering, appropriate threat perception and prediction as well as the interception and/ or interdiction of hostile entities intending to perpetrate such attacks, the ultimate guarantee of casualty minimisation as well as impact reduction lies in the Indian state being prepared to neutralise the effects of such attacks. This can take the form of both proactive preventative measures or adequate disaster response mechanisms to deal with and minimise the deleterious effects of such attacks. Unfortunately, despite some significant progress, India's capabilities in this regard—which can be broadly described as civil defence measures are as yet wholly inadequate and in need of improvement.

Potential Threats

An EMP attack

In a recent commentary for the Institute for Defence Studies and Analyses, Group Captain Atul Pant, noted that the intense burst of electromagnetic energy can be triggered by nuclear and non-nuclear means.[1] In 1962, during the 'Starfish Prime' high-altitude nuclear test, the United States observed the effects of the EMP produced by a high-altitude nuclear burst. Electrical equipment some 1400 km away was affected by the EMP produced by this explosion and no fewer than seven satellites were damaged by the effects so produced.[2] Further refinement and studies by the former Soviet Union and

---

1. Atul Pant, "EMP Weapons and the New Equation of War," *Institute for Defence Studies and Analyses*, (October 13, 2017). https://idsa.in/idsacomments/emp-weapons-new-equation-of-war_apant_131017, accessed on November 09, 2017.
2. Scott Stewart, "Gauging the Threat of an Electromagnetic Pulse (EMP) Attack," *Stratfor Worldview*, (September 9, 2010). https://worldview.stratfor.com/article/gauging-threat-electromagnetic-pu...

the United States showed that high-altitude EMP effects could damage underground cables, making the potential disruptive and destructive power of a nuclear-generated EMP a potentially potent weapon of war.[3] The possibility of complete disruption and destruction of electrical grids, electronic equipment, communication networks and vehicles offers a strong argument in favour of developing and using such a weapon. However, there is a significant downside. Plotting the impact zone of the EMP generated by a high-altitude nuclear blast is difficult to predict and the possibility of an EMP pulse so generated damaging friendly forces or even devastating the nation employing the said device acts as a major deterrent of the effective weaponisation of the same.[4] To date, this has not become a viable weapon of war.

Rather, the focus has been placed on localised, non-nuclear EMP weapons which would have an effect over a much smaller area. It is believed that such weapons are in service with several North Atlantic Treaty Organization (NATO) countries, Russia and China and India have made significant progress in the development of offensive 'E-Bombs' since 2011.[5] These weapons have the potential of severely disrupting military operations by inflicting damage to vehicles, weapons and electronic equipment. Military hardware can be hardened against EMP effects, though widespread hardening to any significant degree may be impractical. Nonetheless, military establishments by using Faraday cages, stockpiling additional spares and refining responses to such attacks can mitigate the effects of the same. It is known that nuclear command and control systems in India are hardened against EMP effects and it might be expected that some degree of protection is being accorded to military communications networks, air defence networks and select weapons systems either through hardening or by storing them underground to mitigate the effect of either a nuclear or non-nuclear EMP attack. Though the efficacy of such measures may be tested, reality may prove otherwise.[6]

3.   Edward E. Conrad et al., "Collateral Damage to Satellites from an EMP Attack," *Defence Threat Reduction Agency*, (August 2010). http://www.dtic.mil/dtic/tr/fulltext/u2/a531197.pdf

4.   Pant, n. 1.

5.   Jatinder Kaur Tur, "India Developing E-bomb to Paralyze Networks," *Times of India*, (August 29, 2013). https://timesofindia.indiatimes.com/india/India-developing-E-bomb-to-paralyze-networks/articleshow/22127411.cms, accessed on November 09, 2017.

6.   "Is India's Nuclear Deterrent Credible?," Speech by Shyam Saran at the India Habitat Centre, New Delhi, April 24, 2013.

However, the effects of a non-nuclear EMP attack on India's civilian infrastructure are potentially devastating. Civilian targets such as urban data and communication centres, stock exchanges, factories and other centres of gravity could be attacked by e-bombs along with power grids and transportation hubs.[7] While the area affected by such an attack would necessarily be limited owing to the more limited intensity of the EMP generated by non-nuclear means, any such attack could seriously disrupt the Indian economy. Though communication systems with their increased redundancy may be less vulnerable, the spectre of industries and commercial centres being crippled by such attacks would give pause for thought to any business and government and preventative measures would need to be considered. As Group Captain Pant expressed it:[8]

India is vulnerable to EMP attacks, given the presence of technologically capable neighbouring rivals and adversaries. India should conduct a formal evaluation of the regional EMP threat and work towards building EMP resilient data and communication structures, both for civil and military requirements. There may also be a need to devise contingency plans and procedures for EMP attacks.

To date, however, India has not openly discussed or detailed any of its contingency plans for dealing with an offensive EMP strike—whether against military or civilian targets. It is known that New Delhi has established a series of bunkers to protect important communications and data networks in the event of either a direct nuclear strike or an EMP strike.[9] It is believed that at least some of these facilities are earmarked for the protection and security of vital industries and commercial data, thus providing some degree of insurance in the event of an EMP strike.

---

7.   "Developing Threats: Electro-Magnetic Pulses (EMP)," *Tenth Report of Session 2010–12*, United Kingdom House of Commons, (February 08, 2012), https://publications.parliament. uk/pa/cm201012/cmselect/cmdfence/1552/1552.pdf.
8.   Pant, n. 1.
9.   "New Delhi Prepares for War, Plans Underground Bunkers Against WMD Attacks *Sputnik,* (October 17, 2016). https://sputniknews.com/asia/201610171046419397-india-war-bunker/, accessed on November 09, 2017.

The Use of CBRN Weapons by Non-State Actors

The most notorious instance of the use of CBRN weapons by a non-state actor was the 1995 Sarin attack on the Tokyo subway network by the Aum Shinrikyo religious cult. Using liquid sarin contained in packets wrapped in newspaper, the attack killed 12 people and caused nonfatal injuries to over 4000.[10] With relatively few fatalities, the chemical attack produced and affected out of all proportion to the number of deaths, reflecting the inevitable value of the panic and general disruption to life and business that ensues during and in the aftermath of such attacks.

To date, there have been no repeat chemical weapon attacks, though there were a number of biological weapons scares with packets of anthrax being sent via the postal service in the United States in the aftermath of the September 11, 2001 terrorist attacks. These killed five people and infected seventeen others but once again, had an impact completely out of proportion to the number of people physically affected.[11] The psychological impact was severe and disruptive.

A potentially more destructive and disruptive version of a CBRN attack is the radiological dispersal device (RDD) or so-called 'dirty bomb'. This works on the principle of using an explosive device to spread radioactive material over a wide area, contaminating people and infrastructure with the aim of causing both casualties and panic. To date, there has been no instance of a 'dirty bomb' being used but the scenario is one which is all too plausible for potential terrorist attacks.

In the spring of 2016, Georgian authorities made a number of arrests and destroyed several networks which had been attempting to smuggle small quantities of the radioactive and fissile Uranium 235 isotope.[12] Furthermore, in August 2017, Indonesia police foiled an alleged plot by Islamist terrorists to detonate a 'dirty bomb' after converting the slightly radioactive Thorium

---

10. Amy E. Smithson and Leslie-Anne Levy, "Chapter 3—Rethinking the Lessons of Tokyo," *Ataxia: The Chemical and Biological Terrorism Threat and the US Response* (Report). Henry L. Stimson Centre. pp. 91, 95, 100. Report No. 35.

11. "Amerithrax or Anthrax Investigation, U.S.," *Federal Bureau of Investigation*, https://www.fbi.gov/history/famous-cases/amerithrax-or-anthrax-investigation, accessed on November 09, 2017.

12. Simon Shuster, "Inside the Uranium Underworld: Dark Secrets, Dirty Bombs," *Time*, (April 10, 2017). http://time.com/4728293/uranium-underworld-dark-secrets-dirty-bombs/, accessed on November 09, 2017.

232 isotope into the highly radioactive and fissile Uranium 233 isotope.[13] While the prospects of this plot succeeding without highly specialised equipment and expertise were extremely low, it reflects the potential of this class of weapon and the relative ease of obtaining radioactive material.

Indian concerns over the possible terrorist employment of a 'dirty bomb' have led to studies and simulations by Bhabha Atomic Research Centre (BARC) and while the measures taken to deal with the same will be dealt with later in this chapter, K. S. Pradeepkumar, head of emergency preparedness for the said BARC was of the strong view that a 'dirty bomb' was mainly a disruptive weapon:[14]

> *...is not in terms of a casualty or a serious injury we are worried about a dirty bomb, or what is called a radiological dispersal device. The concern is about the fear it may inject into the people because very large number of people will believe that they are all affected because they are all contaminated. It causes disruption.*

Pradeep Kumar noted that, in the event of a 'dirty bomb' being detonated, depending on the size of the explosive blast, the nearby area of 30–50 m from where the device is detonated can have a high level of contamination, beyond which there may be a cigar-shaped area where the spread of contamination will take place. This area could be over 80 m, depending on the explosive and the radioactive material used.[15] Beyond that, the risk of contamination diminishes.

In these circumstances, it can be seen that a 'dirty bomb' is not a mass casualty weapon but rather a weapon which derives its main impact from the fear it generates, the disruption it causes and the cost of decontaminating the area and people which may be affected. To date, there has fortunately not been any use of such a weapon so that both estimates of its physical and

---

13. Tom Allard and Agustinus Beo Da Costa, "Exclusive: Indonesian militants planned 'dirty bomb' attack—sources," *Reuters,* (August 25, 2017). https://www.reuters.com/article/us-indonesia-security/exclusive-indonesian-militants-planned-dirty-bomb-attack-sources-idUSKCN1B51FW, accessed on November 09, 2017.

14. "Does India Face A 'Dirty Bomb' Threat? Top Nuclear Scientist Explains," *Press Trust of India,* (May 10, 2016). https://www.ndtv.com/india-news/does-india-face-a-dirty-bomb-threat-top-nuclear-scientist-explains-1404739, accessed on November 09, 2017.

15. Ibid.

psychological effects are as yet theoretical, simulations being able to deal with the former.

However, it is a potentially significant weapon in the hands of non-state actors and puts additional strains on intelligence agencies, entry and exit port authorities, who have to intensify screening efforts and in-country monitoring for not only the potential theft of radioactive material but also the monitoring of key areas. Radiation and radioactive material detection devices have already made their debut in India since the time of the 2010 Commonwealth games with both mobile and static systems being deployed to guard against any contingency. Four such detectors were procured and placed in service with the Delhi police marking an important but still minimal step forward.[16]

Sabotage of Chemical or Nuclear Facilities

India has the unfortunate distinction of being the host country of the worst industrial disaster in history. On the night of December 02–03, 1984, the release of methyl isocyanate gas affected over half a million people in Bhopal, Madhya Pradesh.[17] The immediate death toll from the release was over 2000, with nearly 4000 deaths being directly related to the gas release.[18] Government data suggests that over 558,000 people suffered injuries as a result of the accident, with nearly 4000 permanently injured or disabled as a direct consequence of the same.[19] While there was no evidence or insinuation of sabotage in the Bhopal incident, the number of deaths and injuries, direct and indirectly caused by the incident, is indicative of the potential for a replication of the same in the event of a deliberate act of sabotage.

---

16. Sruthjith K. K., "Delhi Gradually Ushering in CWG Juggernaut," *Economic Times*, (September 27, 2010). https://economictimes.indiatimes.com/delhi-gradually-ushering-in-cwg-juggernaut/articleshow/6632785.cms, accessed on November 09, 2017.

17. Roli Varma and Daya R. Varma, "The Bhopal Disaster of 1984," *Bulletin of Science, Technology and Society* vol. 25, no. 1, 2005, pp. 37–45.

18. "Madhya Pradesh Government: Bhopal Gas Tragedy Relief and Rehabilitation Department, Bhopal," Mp.gov.in. Archived from the original, (May 18, 2012). https://web.archive.org/web/20120518020821/http://www.mp.gov.in/bgtrrdmp/relief.htm

19. A. K. Dubey, "Bhopal Gas Tragedy: 92% Injuries Termed 'Minor'," *First14 News*, (June 26, 2010). https://www.webcitation.org/5qmWBEWcb?url=http://www.first14.com/bhopal-gas-tragedy-92-injuries-termed-minor-822.html

For chemical incidents, the National Disaster Management Authority (NDMA) has outlined a comprehensive set of guidelines but notes that the prospect of an incident occurring has risen due to the rapid industrialisation that has taken place in India, noting the following:[20]

> With rapid economic development, there has been spread of chemical industries—small, medium and large—across the country. However, there is a relatively higher presence along the west coast, largely due to the proximity to raw materials and ports. Gujarat alone is estimated to contribute around 53 percent to the total production in the country, followed by Maharashtra, which contributes nine percent. The other major producing states include Uttar Pradesh (UP), Tamil Nadu (TN), Madhya Pradesh (MP), and Punjab. On the other hand, in the case of heavy chemicals segment, especially inorganic chemicals, fuel availability is a determining factor, and hence there is a concentration of these companies around power plants. Due to the regional concentration of chemical companies in certain pockets, the chemical hazard has increased many folds. The growth of chemical industries has led to an increase in the risk of occurrence of incidents associated with hazardous chemicals (HAZCHEM). These events occur due to mishaps or failures in industry and affect the industrial functions, property and productivity. While the common causes for chemical accidents are deficiencies in safety management systems or human errors, or natural calamities or sabotage may also trigger such accidents. Chemical/ industrial accidents are significant and have long term impact on the community and environment. It leads to injuries, pain, suffering, loss of lives, damage to property and environment. Hence, a robust plan and mitigation measure needs to be adapted to overcome the hazard.

While there has been only mass casualty nuclear incident—Chernobyl in 1986 (Fukushima in 2011 produced 37 nonfatal injuries)—the potential for an act of sabotage creating a release of radioactive materials is a possibility that cannot be ignored. However, it should be noted that much more than in the chemical industry, nuclear facilities have heavy physical security and nuclear reactors are protected by containment domes of reinforced concrete.

---

20. National Disaster Management Plan, May 2016, p. 26.

This makes the prospect for success of a terrorist attack on a nuclear power plant or facility as being somewhat remote.

These incidents come under the ambit of nuclear and radiological emergencies. The Indian NDA defines a Nuclear or Radiological Emergency (NRE) as follows:

A nuclear and/or radiological emergency (NRE) is an incident resulting in, or having a potential to result in, exposure to and/or contamination of the workers or the public, in excess of the respective permissible limits (see NDMA's guidelines for NRE). These emergencies are classified into five broad groups as follows:[21]

An accident taking place in any nuclear facility of the nuclear fuel cycle including the nuclear reactor, or in a facility using radioactive sources, leading to a large-scale release of radioactivity in the environment;

A 'criticality' accident in a nuclear fuel cycle facility where an uncontrolled nuclear chain reaction takes place inadvertently leading to bursts of neutrons and gamma radiation (as had happened at Tokaimura, Japan);

An accident during the transportation of radioactive material;

The malevolent use of RDD or IND by terrorists;

A large-scale nuclear disaster resulting from a nuclear weapon attack, which would lead to mass casualties and destruction of large areas and properties. Unlike a nuclear emergency, the impact of a nuclear disaster is beyond the coping capability of local authorities and calls for handling at the national level.

The latter incident is likely to be the result of either a state-launched nuclear strike—in which instance retaliation, as well as mitigation efforts, would be necessary—or the employment of a nuclear weapon by a non-state actor in which case mitigation efforts would take precedence over any potential retaliation. As will be noted later, in the event of the former scenario, there would be a difference in response in the event of early warning being made available—as in the case of a conventional conflict which later escalates

---

21. Guidelines on Management of Nuclear and Radiological Emergencies as listed in Annexure-I of the NDMA National Disaster Management Plan 2016

into a nuclear one—in which case the mobilisation of auxiliary services to augment the National Disaster Response Force (NDRF), Atomic Energy Regulatory Board (AERB) and other agencies might lend useful assistance, as against a surprise attack which would require the immediate response by unassisted first response agencies (especially in the case of a terrorist strike using a nuclear weapon) augmented by national assets. It is in this latter case where India's state response units may be inadequate.

With respect to the nontraditional class of incident—either deliberate or accidental—the NDMA goes on to state that the International Atomic Energy Agency categorises NREs into two broad categories—a) nuclear and b) radiological:[22]

- A nuclear emergency refers to an emergency situation in which there is or is presumed to be, a hazard due to the release of energy along with radiation from a nuclear chain reaction (or from the decay of the products of a chain reaction). This covers accidents in nuclear reactors, 'criticality' situations in fuel cycle facilities, nuclear explosions or any other situation where an explosion releasing radiation occurs.

- All other emergency situations which have the potential hazard of radiation exposure due to the decay of radioisotopes are classified as radiological emergencies.

India's contingency planning envisages the management of any NRE through a combination of preventing an incident from occurring and adequately preparing for such emergencies. Inevitably, the management of an NRE must be conducted through a series of thoroughly planned, established and rehearsed mechanisms, both structural and non-structural. These must further be conducted in a manner that will minimise risks to health, life and the environment, and where possible, property. The planning of these mechanisms is within the purview of the NDMA but the nodal agency will invariably be the one most closely involved with the incident—the Indian Atomic Energy Regulatory Body. Current disaster management plans in India envisage eight types of nuclear/and radiological emergency scenarios encompassing a wide range as listed below:[23]

---

22. Ibid.
23. *National Disaster Management Plan May 2016*, (New Delhi: NDMA, 2016), pp. 26–27.

- accidents in nuclear power plants and other facilities in the nuclear fuel cycle,
- 'criticality' accidents,
- accidents during transportation of radioactive materials,
- accidents at facilities using radioactive sources,
- disintegration of satellites during re-entry,
- nuclear/radiological terrorism and sabotage at nuclear facilities,
- state-sponsored nuclear terrorism,
- explosion of nuclear weapons.

The physical security of India's nuclear facilities is entrusted to the Central Industrial Security Force (CISF) which has deployed a mix of quick reaction teams, sentries and electronic surveillance mechanisms to protect these facilities.[24] The CISF is tasked as being the first responder to any incident, whether sabotage, accident or direct attack on nuclear facilities.[25] However, given the CISFs wide mandate and numerous other tasks, some have suggested that India might want to consider establishing a dedicated nuclear security force.[26] The containment of an incident, however, requires inter-agency and departmental collaboration between the NDMA, the Department of Atomic Energy (DAE), the AERB and the first responders—the CISF and the relevant Fire and Emergency services, supported by the NDRF as well as an effective coordination mechanism to maximise response efficiency.

The Civil Defence Capabilities of the Indian State

Any consideration of India's response to a nontraditional CBRN attack must cater for the ability of the country to marshal its resources and expertise to deal with the effects of such an attack. However, even discussions of the implications of nuclear weapons in the India–Pakistan context mention of

---

24. Rahul Wadke, "Nuclear Plant to Have Eye in the Sky," *Hindu Business Line,* (April 02, 2017). http://www.thehindubusinessline.com/news/science/nuclear-plant-to-have-eye-in-the-sky/article9612475.ece, accessed on November 09, 2017.

25. "DAE, CISF Review Security of Nuclear Power Plants," *Times of India,* (April 30, 2011). https://timesofindia.indiatimes.com/india/DAE-CISF-review-security-of-nuclear-power-plants/articleshow/8122343.cms, accessed on November 09, 2017.

26. Rajeswari Pillai Rajagopalan, "India's Nuclear Security: Strengths and Gaps," *Observer Research Foundation,* (June 14, 2017). http://www.orfonline.org/research/india-nuclear-security-strengths-gaps/, accessed on November 09, 2017.

the civil defence capabilities of either state. It is generally assumed that the civil defence services in both countries will be rapidly overwhelmed by a nuclear attack and would be as good as useless. This may well be true—we have yet to find out—however, in India's case, the state has had enormous experience in dealing with some of the most catastrophic natural disasters known to man. While these may not approach the magnitude of a nuclear attack, they provide an interesting insight into the strengths and weaknesses of the Indian disaster management apparatus. Furthermore, the Indian state has slowly evolved as having a yet imperfect but nonetheless viable capability for dealing with the lower level casualties that might be caused by either a CBRN strike by a non-state actor or an incident caused either by accident or by deliberate action at a nuclear or chemical facility. In no case will any of these incidents compare to a limited, much less all-out, nuclear exchange but an analysis of these capabilities will provide the best indication of how India might respond to a nontraditional CBRN strike or incident.

Control of any response to a disaster lies in the hands of the NDMA. This body, in turn, has control of the professional core of India's civil defence capability, namely the NDRF, which maintains 12 specialist disaster response battalions. These units include specialist CBRN teams which are capable of dealing with the effects of both a nuclear disaster at a power plant and the effects of a 'dirty bomb' or other terrorist nuclear strike. To these must be added the Indian Fire and Emergency Services which are invariably the first responders to any incident. These latter forces are severely undermanned and underequipped and despite being reasonably effective in urban areas, are in dire need of both reinforcement and overhaul while in rural areas their presence is minimal.

India maintains and trains a sizeable civil defence force and has laid down a reasonably comprehensive set of procedures and regulations governing civil defence operations in the event of war. While many of India's state governments do not implement these plans in peacetime, the fact that these plans exist and are periodically reviewed cannot be ignored. Moreover, as will be shown, the plans lay emphasis on rapid emergency measures rather than on a well-developed peacetime infrastructure. In addition to the civil defence organisation, India spends considerable money on a reserve body called the Home Guards (HGs) and on the National

Cadet Corps. These organisations do receive a modicum of civil defence training but their efficacy is debatable.

The NDMA: The lynchpin for Success

The NDMA is part of the Indian internal security ministry—the Ministry of Home Affairs. Its main task is to coordinate response to natural or man-made disasters and for capacity-building in disaster resiliency and crisis response.[27] The NDMA was established through the Disaster Management Act enacted by the Government of India in December 2005 and has the Prime Minister is the ex officio chairperson of it.[28] The NDMA is responsible for framing policies, laying down guidelines and best practices and coordinating with the State Disaster Management Authorities with the aim of ensuring a holistic and effective approach to disaster management.[29] Governance of the NDMA is through a four-member board chaired by the Prime Minister of India with the remainder of the board members being subject matter experts in such areas as planning, infrastructure management, communications, meteorology and natural sciences. The current members have expertise in disaster management.

Operationally, the NDMA is managed by its Vice-Chair on a day-to-day basis while being organised into the following divisions, each of which is tasked with ensuring efficacy:[30]

- Policy and Planning,
- Mitigation,
- Operations and Communications,
- Administration,
- Capacity Building.

The NDMA seeks to equip and train other government officials, institutions and the wider national community in mitigation and response

---

27. National Disaster Management, "NDMA Vision," http://www.ndma.gov.in/en/about-ndma/vision.html
28. National Disaster Management, "Evolution of NDMA,"http://www.ndma.gov.in/en/about-ndma/evolution-of-ndma.html
29. National Disaster Management Authority, "Functions and Responsibilities," http://www.ndma.gov.in/en/about-ndma/roles-responsibilities.html
30. Disaster Management Act, [December 23, 2005.] no. 53 (2005).

during a crisis situation or a disaster. To this end, it operates the National Institute of Disaster Management, which develops practices, delivers practical training and organises rehearsal drills for various disaster management scenarios. It also equips and trains disaster management cells at the state and local levels.[31]

The NDMA works in conjunction with the Lal Bahadur Shastri National Academy of Administration and Sardar Vallabhbhai Patel National Police Academy to impart training to Indian Administrative Service and Indian Police Service in planning and incident response as these two groups are often at the forefront of handling any disaster. It further monitors and develops guidelines for the local firefighting services across the country although the implementation of the same is a state responsibility.[32] The NDMA also collaborates with the Ministry of Health and Family Welfare in developing emergency health and ambulance services with a special focus on capacity-building in dealing with mass casualty at local hospitals with some success to date.[33]

The NDMA, as the major and overarching entity tasked with disaster management, is mandated to lay down the policies, plans and guidelines for Disaster Management to ensure a timely and effective response to disasters. The NDMAs responsibilities are thus to:[34]

- lay down policies on disaster management;
- approve the National Plan;
- approve plans prepared by the Ministries or Departments of the Government of India in accordance with the National Plan;
- lay down guidelines to be followed by the State Authorities in drawing up the State Plan;
- lay down guidelines to be followed by the different Ministries or Departments of the Government of India for the Purpose of integrating the measures for prevention of disaster or the mitigation of its effects in their development plans and projects;

31. "Capacity Building and is bhavin Training," National Disaster Management Authority.
32. National Disaster Management Authority, "Fire Services," http://www.ndma.gov.in/en/fire-services.html
33. National Disaster Management Authority, "Trauma Care," http://www.ndma.gov.in/en/capacity-building/trauma-care.html
34. National Disaster Management Authority, "NDMA Roles and Responsibilities," http://www.ndma.gov.in/en/about-ndma/roles-responsibilities.html

- coordinate the enforcement and implementation of the policy and plans for disaster management;
- recommend provision of funds for the purpose of mitigation;
- provide such support to other countries affected by major disasters as may be determined by the Central Government;
- take such other measures for the prevention of disaster, or the mitigation, or preparedness and capacity-building for dealing with threatening disaster situations or disasters as it may consider necessary;
- lay down broad policies and guidelines for the functioning of the National Institute of Disaster Management.

The NDMA is impressive on paper but has not always had an impressive track record. It came in for harsh censure during the devastating floods in Uttarakhand in 2013 with a task force, constituted under the chairmanship of the former agriculture secretary P. K. Mishra to review the Disaster Management Act pointing to lack of functional integration between NDMA and the home ministry. In particular, the NDMA's National Executive Council was criticised as being ineffective and the task force recommended its dissolution and the streamlining of the entire NDMA setup.

This criticism was undoubtedly deserved. Indeed, despite a reasonably good performance during Cyclone Phailin, where in conjunction with other central and state agencies, it successfully minimised the loss of life, the task force's most damning indictment of the NDMA called it "a think tank without any link to ground realities" and further recommended the redesign of the NDMA structure to ensure greater objectivity and transparency in the selection of members stating:[35]

"Though the NDMA has certain achievements to its credit, like issue of useful guidelines, its present structure is not conducive for carrying out the tasks it has been mandated to perform under the Act. There is a

---

35. Deeptiman Tiwary, "NDMA has failed to achieve objectives, task force says," https://timesofindia.indiatimes.com/india/NDMA-has-failed-to-achieve-objectives-task-force-says/articleshow/24119665.cms, accessed on November 10, 2017.

need to redesign the NDMA's structure, ensuring greater objectivity and transparency in selecting members,

NDMA should not remain merely a think tank without any link with ground realities. Its role and functions should cover policies, plans, guidelines and regulations relating to prevention, mitigation and preparedness…

The NEC, which has been assigned crucial, and multifarious, activities under the Act, has failed to deliver. There is a lack of functional integration between the NDMA and the NEC on the one hand, and the NDMA and the MHA on the other…

The NDMA needs to be empowered so as to enable it to discharge its responsibilities more effectively. At the same time, it should be held accountable for the satisfactory performance of the tasks assigned to it."

The aforementioned task force report noted that India's efforts were focused on rescue and relief operations, the NDRF being singled out for praise, rather than on disaster mitigation. Moreover, it noted the failure of states to effectively develop state-level disaster management authorities.[36] This lack of commensurate effort has been remedied in the cases of several states but it is still the case that at state and local level, disaster management and emergency response forces are underequipped and often severely undermanned. This delays reaction times with fatal results.

The Uttarakhand floods marked the nadir of the NDMA's reputation in many ways, with its functioning coming under scathing criticism for its bungled coordination of relief efforts despite the good performance of the NDRF and armed forces in rescuing trapped and stranded people. One press report derisively mocked its operations in the following terms:[37]

---

36. Ibid.
37. Abhishek Bhalla and Bhuvan Bagga, "The Uttarakhand Tragedy Casts Shame on India's Disaster Management. So Why DID the Committee meant to Plan for Flood Emergencies Fail to Meet for FOUR YEARS?," *Daily Mail India*, (June 24, 2013). http://www.dailymail.co.uk/indiahome/indianews/article-2347624/NDMA-The-Uttarakhand-tragedy-casts-shame-Indias-disaster-management-So-DID-committee-meant-plan-flood-emergencies-fail-meet-FOUR-YEARS.html, accessed on November 10, 2017.

It's headquartered in South Delhi's plush Safdarjung Enclave. It holds press conferences about human tragedies in luxurious five-star hotels. The Prime Minister is its ex officio chairman, and its vice-chairman equals a Cabinet minister in status. Other members, mostly retired bureaucrats and police officers, rub shoulders with ministers of state. Welcome to the National Disaster Management Authority (NDMA). With its performance—or more accurately, the abysmal lack of it—in the rain-ravaged Himalayan state exposing its defunct status, the NDMA stands exposed for the great man-made tragedy it is. Its National Executive Committee has not met at all between 2008 and 2012. Seven years after it came into being, the authority doesn't even have a working plan.

Moreover, besides being ineffective in Uttarakhand as a coordinating agency, the NDMA was chastised by India's audit agency—the Comptroller Auditor General (CAG) for not being able to compete any of the projects undertaken in a seven-year-period. A 2013 press report noted:[38]

The CAG report also highlighted several other loopholes in the functioning of NDMA. It said none of the major projects taken up by NDMA was complete even after seven years of its functioning. The projects were either abandoned midway or were being redesigned because of initial poor planning. The major projects include producing vulnerability atlases for floods, earthquakes and landslides, national landslide risk mitigation project, national flood risk mitigation project and national disaster management information system. As per the CAG report, NDMA has also not been performing several functions as prescribed in the Disaster Management Act. These include recommending provision of funds for the purpose of mitigation and recommending relief in repayment of loans or for grant of fresh loans. Besides, several critical posts in NDMA are vacant and consultants were used for day to day working.

---

38. Kumar Sambhav Shrivastava, "How Effective is India's Disaster Management Authority?," *Down to Earth,* (June 20, 2013). http://www.downtoearth.org.in/news/how-effective-is-india-s-disaster-management-authority--41415, accessed on November 10, 2017.

The NDMA's functioning was reviewed after disasters in 2014 and has been significantly streamlined with four expert members being appointed and older, political appointees removed—the board being reduced from nine to four members. All four members have extensive experience in disaster management and planning and should aid in the revitalisation of the NDMA. Furthermore, the rank equivalent of the members was downgraded to that of Secretary rather than the previously significantly higher rank of Minister of State. There has been a clear declaration of intent that the NDMA will no longer be a 'dumping ground' for politicians and bureaucrats with no experience, knowledge or expertise of any sphere related to disaster management.[39] It is to be noted that much of the practical experience of the NDMA has come from the handling of natural disasters. The agency has had no experience of handling mass casualty incidents caused by the hostile action or chemical or nuclear accidents or incidents. It has therefore drawn up plans based on best practices and simulations.

As the NDMA has the major coordination role in any disaster, communications assumed importance and the failure of the same was responsible in part for a subsequent lack of a coordinated response. In recognition of that, a new mechanism for an uninterrupted communication network is being developed. The Department of Telecommunications was tasked with the setup of a robust communications system with a greater capacity to withstand natural disasters.[40] Command and control for the NDMA and the broader Ministry of Home Affairs (MHA) is facilitated by the National Emergency Operations Centre, formerly known as the MHA Control Room, which the Indian draft national disaster management plan described as follows:[41]

An Emergency Operations Center (Control Room) exists in the nodal Ministry of Home Affairs, which functions round the clock, to assist the Central relief commissioner / designated officer in the discharge

---

39. "Government Approves Appointment of 3 Experts as NDMA Members," *Press Trust of India*, (December 21, 2014). http://www.dnaindia.com/india/report-government-approves-appointment-of-3-experts-as-ndma-members-2045959, accessed on November 10, 2017.

40. "Government to Restructure and Revamp NDMA," *GK Today*, (September 30, 2014). https://currentaffairs.gktoday.in/government-restructure-revamp-ndma-09201414966.html, accessed on November 10, 2017.

41. "National Disaster Management Plan Part-1: Draft," p. 61.

of his duties. The activities of the Control Room include collection and transmission of information concerning natural calamity and relief, keeping close contact with governments of the affected States, interaction with other Central Ministries/Departments/Organizations in connection with relief, maintaining records containing all relevant information relating to action points and contact points in Central Ministries etc., keeping up-to-date details of all concerned officers at the Central and State levels.

The NDRF

Perhaps the most successful element within the NDMA is the NDRF. It is a force of 12 battalions, organised on paramilitary lines, and manned by persons on deputation from the Central Armed Police Forces of India: three battalions from the Border Security Force, three from the Central Reserve Police Force, two from the Central Industrial Security Force, two from the Indo-Tibetan Border Police and two more from the Sashastra Seema Bal. The total strength of each battalion is approximately 1149.[42] Each battalion is capable of providing 18 self-contained specialist search and rescue teams of 45 personnel, each including engineers, technicians, electricians, dog squads and medical/paramedics.[43] NDRF, in addition to being able to respond to natural disasters, has four battalions capable of responding to radiological, nuclear, biological and chemical disasters with one platoon in each of the other eight battalions being so equipped for contingencies—a situation that is still somewhat unsatisfactory.

The NDRF battalions are located at 12 different locations throughout India based on a careful assessment of the vulnerability profile. This enables the force to cut down the response time for its deployment. Where early warning of a natural disaster is forthcoming, during this preparation period in an imminent or prospective disaster situation, the proactive deployment of these the NDRF will be carried out by the NDMA in consultation with state authorities or upon their request. At present, the 12 NDRF battalions are located as follows:[44]

42. NDRF, "About Us," http://ndrf.gov.in/ndrf, accessed on November 10, 2017.
43. Ibid.
44. Ibid and "Arunachal Government Assures Land to Set Up NDRF Unit Headquarter," *Economic Times*, (August 22, 2015). http://articles.economictimes.indiatimes.com/2015-

Table 6.1

S. No.	NDRF Unit	State	Central Police Forces (CPF)
4	01 Bn NDRF, Guwahati	Assam	Border Security Force(BSF)
3	02 Bn NDRF, Kolkata	West Bengal	BSF
5	03 Bn NDRF, Mundali	Odisha	Central Industrial Security Force (CISF)
6	04 Bn NDRF, Arakkonam	Tamil Nadu	CISF
7	05 Bn NDRF, Pune	Maharashtra	Central Reserve Police Force (CRPF)
8	06 Bn NDRF, Gandhinagar	Gujarat	CRPF
1	07 Bn NDRF, Ghaziabad	Uttar Pradesh	Indo-Tibetan Border Police (ITBP)
2	08 Bn NDRF, Bhatinda	Punjab	ITBP
9	09 Bn NDRF, Patna	Bihar	BSF
10	10 Bn NDRF, Vijayawada	Andhra Pradesh	CRPF
11	11 Bn NDRF, Varanasi	Uttar Pradesh	Sashastra Seema Bal (SSB)
12	12 Bn NDRF, Itanagar	Arunachal Pradesh	SSB

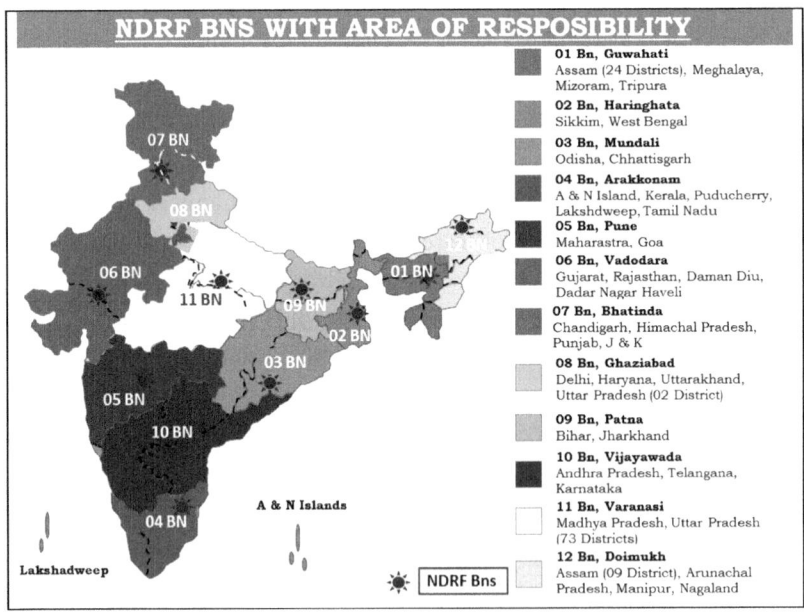

08-22/news/65739754_1_ndrf-unit-ndrf-personnel-state-capital, accessed on November 09, 2017.

Appreciating the need for specialised skills and the future requirement for the same, being the key to efficient disaster response, the NDRF has tried to ensure the effectiveness of its initial and refresher training programs. Specialist skills once taught need to be refreshed. With this in mind, a detailed 'Training Regime for Disaster Response' has been prepared by the NDMA for the NDRF to identify the specific disaster response training courses to be undertaken. Furthermore, unified, structured and uniform series course modules, as well as a syllabus for these training courses, have been prescribed. It is envisaged that this unified, structured, uniform series of course modules and syllabus will initially enable the training of all twelve NDRF battalions, with all personnel undertaking these courses successfully and thereafter, the State Disaster Response Forces (SDRF) and other stakeholders will be trained on the same lines. The NDRF appreciates the need for a uniformly structured series of course modules as once all the NDRF battalions and other 'first responders' undergo the same training programs, the coordination between different stakeholders would significantly improve, enabling effective planning and efficient use of resources in major disasters where different NDRF battalions, SDRF battalions and other stakeholders would be working and operating together in close coordination with each other.[45]

The NDRF has seen extensive service during rescue and relief operations during natural disasters where their specialist rescue skills and equipment have proved invaluable. However, they also have some considerable experience in dealing with collapsed structure search and rescue operations, some examples being a six storey building collapsed at Bellary (Karnataka) in January 2010 wherein, a meticulously planned, round-the-clock operation lasting seven days, the NDRF rescued 20 trapped live victims and retrieved 29 bodies. Subsequently, when a multistorey factory building collapsed in Jalandhar (Punjab) in April 2012, the NDRF successfully rescued 12 live victims trapped under a huge rubble of debris and also recovered 19 dead bodies. In 2015, during the Bilaspur tunnel accident in Himachal Pradesh where two workers were trapped for 9 days, the NDRF successfully rescued

45. NDRF Website, "NDRF Training Regime," http://ndrf.gov.in/Media/inapnacms/ TRAINING/taining%20regime.pdf, accessed on November 10, 2017.

the trapped workers.[46] The NDRF also has a modicum of CBRN experience during the recovery of Cobalt 60 from Mayapuri, Delhi during April/May 2010.[47] Further experience was garnered during NDRF operations to contain lethal ammonia leakage in Ludhiana in 2015 and Kanpur in 2017 where they were required to assist local first responders.[48]

The NDRF, therefore, forms an effective, highly skilled and reasonably well-equipped response force capable of tackling a nontraditional CBRN attack. However, with only four battalions so specialised, it is debatable if they could successfully cope with multiple such incidents. In addition, there is a question as to whether the transportation assets available to the NDRF are adequate. Concerns have emerged on their overreliance on vehicles from an affected area and their lack of integral air transport assets. While this is not likely to improve in the short term, it must be stated that in a CBRN emergency, it is exceedingly unlikely that the existing Fire and Emergency Services outside a few select areas would be able to cope with such a contingency. While the NDRF is geographically dispersed, it cannot supplant the role of a well-equipped first response unit.

Fire and Emergency Services

India's fire and emergency services are controlled by the Directorate General of Civil Defence, in the Ministry of Home Affairs. This acts as the nodal office responsible for providing Advisories to State Governments on Fire Prevention, Fire Protection, Fire Legislation and Training matters. The Fire Services in many of India's states are largely the responsibility of local bodies which are themselves seriously starved of resources.

This has meant that the Fire Services and Emergency Services in India are largely undermanned, badly organised and poorly equipped. While the lack of funds has been the main constraint in equipping the fire services and providing adequate fire safety cover to the population in

---

46. NDRF, n. 42.
47. "Disaster Response Force Base Comes Up In Delhi, To Respond To Bio, Nuclear Attacks," *Press Trust of India*, (June 11, 2017). https://www.ndtv.com/india-news/ndrf-base-comes-up-in-delhi-to-respond-to-bio-nuclear-attacks-1710679, accessed on November 10, 2017.
48. "Kanpur: Ammonia Gas Leak Causes Explosion in Cold Storage; Five Killed, Several Still Trapped," *First Post*, (May 15, 2017). http://www.firstpost.com/india/kanpur-ammonia-gas-leak-causes-explosion-in-cold-storage-five-killed-several-still-trapped-3335870.html, accessed on November 10, 2017.

a uniform manner, there is also a distinct lack of focus on these services with the consequent effect that outside major metropolitan centres, the fire and emergency services are in poor conditions. The existing framework for fire services in the country is completely heterogeneous and not conducive to effective protection against the increasing incidents of fires brought about by urbanisation, careless agricultural practices and industrialisation.[49]

There is an acute shortage of modern fire-fighting appliances. Outside some metropolitan centres, which have made an effort to modernise their fire and emergency services, most of the State Fire Services either completely lack or are short of their authorised complement of specialist fire-fighting appliances like turntable ladders, hydraulic platforms, crash tenders and foam tenders and rescue vehicles. Furthermore, these Fire Services lack either completely or in adequate quantities proper types of rescue equipment, high-pressure pumps, communication facilities and other specialist types of fire-fighting apparatus with an acute shortage of protective gear being evident. What is worse is that a large number of State Fire Services lack an adequate number of conventional fire-fighting appliances such as water tenders and bowsers, not to speak of portable pumps so as to provide fire-fighting cover in urban areas and to extend timely fire cover in an emergency to a remotely located area.[50] Even in New Delhi, there are only three HAZMAT vehicles available.

In metropolitan cities, high-rise buildings can constitute major fire hazards. In India, lax enforcement of fire codes mean that these buildings lack adequate in-built fire protection systems and the existing equipment is often not effective to fight fires externally on the highest floors. As such, these structures are potentially very vulnerable to any kind of disaster, fire or earthquakes being the most likely. The lack of appliances with extendable ladders is an acute problem.

The shortage of manpower, infrastructure and equipment is nothing short of catastrophic. The MHA Fire Cell notes:[51]

---

49. Civil Defence, "Fire Cell," http://ndrfandcd.gov.in/fire.aspx
50. Ibid.
51. Ibid.

As against 70,868 fire stations as per Standing Fire Advisory Council norms, there are only 1705 Fire Stations with 6026 Fire Tenders/Vehicles manned by total 49,769 fire professionals. Besides, there are 284 Fire Stations operating in industrial sectors with a fleet of 1064 appliances and vehicles of various specifications manned by 13,843 fire personnel. There is a shortage of 97.59% fire stations, 96.28% fireman and 80.04% Fire Tenders and Rescue vehicles. Urban fire services suffer a deficiency of 72.75% in fire stations, 78.79% in man power and 22.43% in fire fighting and rescue vehicles.

In 144 towns having population more than one lakh, there is huge deficiency of fire fighting infrastructure in these cities alone. Fire Service need 1257 fire stations, 2230 Water Tenders, 61 Rescue Tenders, 1633 Ambulances, 1633 Extra Heavy Water Tenders more to bring adequate fire fighting facilities as per norms fixed by Standing Fire Advisory Council (SFAC).

To say that there is an urgent need for the creation of an adequate number of well-staffed fire stations in each state to extend fire cover to all areas within a reasonable time is an understatement. The shortage of manpower and equipment is exacerbated by uneven training standards and a lack of training infrastructure and though multiple recommendations have been made by the NDMA, state governments have been slow to act with their efforts to date, producing limited results with deficiencies continuing to be the norm rather than the exception.[52]

A modicum of support exists in the form of the CISF Fire Wing. The CISF is the only Central Armed Police Force having a full-fledged Fire Service Wing which is adequately equipped and reasonably well trained in multi-scenario operations. The CISF Fire Service Wing claims it is the largest professional, best trained and best-equipped firefighting force in the country. It provides fire prevention and fire protection to a plethora of highly sensitive, vulnerable and hazardous units such as petro-chemical

---

52. "Fire Hazard and Risk Analysis in the Country for Revamping the Fire Services in the Country Final Report—Fire and Emergency Services Training Infrastructure in the Country November 2012," *Directorate General NDRF & Civil Defence (Fire) Ministry of Home Affairs*, http://ndrfandcd.gov.in/WriteReadData/userfiles/file/Pilot%20phase/Final_Report_Training_Requirement_in_FireService.pdf

complexes, refineries, steel plants, chemical and fertiliser plants, port trusts, the Space Research Organisation, power plants—including nuclear power plants, Defence Ministry installations and establishments under the Finance Ministry. In total, the CISF Fire Wing is providing fire safety coverage to over 100 different installations all over India. It should be noted that the CISF Fire Wing maintains its own procurement procedures and has independent training establishments given its mandate and the variety of installations it protects.

With a strength of 7099 fire professionals, the CISF is indeed the largest single fire and emergency service in India but its modest strength and limited deployment means that it can at best respond to a situation at a proximate location leaving the poorly equipped state units to cope until assistance can arrive from either other state units or the central government.[53] However, unlike these undermanned state fire and emergency units, the CISF Fire Wing periodically receives sanctions for increasing its strength to ensure adequate coverage of the facilities to which it is assigned. What is less clear is whether timely sanction for new equipment is given.[54]

Additionally, to bolster CBRN readiness, the Government of India has indicated it will establish four 'superspecialty' CBRN centres in four metropolitan cities and 21 smaller centres in places where nuclear power corporation facilities are located.[55] This reflects a desire on the part of the central government to prepare for contingencies arising out of CBRN incidents whether caused by accident or deliberate action. It is to be noted that the Ministry of Health and Family Welfare jointly with the Ministry of Defence would establish these CBRN centres. In support of these efforts, the Ministry of Defence has been running a CBRN training curriculum which is especially designed to assist the Armed Forces Medical Services (AFMS), an interservice organisation, to improve its emergency preparedness. As reported by the Standing Committee on Defence, the

53. CISF, "CISF Fire Wing," http://www.cisf.gov.in/fire-wing/
54. "Govt Sanctions 481 CISF Fire Wing Posts for Five PSU Units," *Press Trust of India*, (March 31, 2010). http://www.dnaindia.com/india/report-govt-sanctions-481-cisf-fire-wing-posts-for-five-psu-units-1365831, accessed on November 10, 2017.
55. R. Krishna Kumar, "CBRN Disaster-Handling Centres to be Set Up in Four Metros," *The Hindu*, (March 20, 2016). http://www.thehindu.com/news/national/karnataka/cbrn-disasterhandling-centres-to-be-set-up-in-four-metros/article8376879.ece, accessed on November 10, 2017.

AFMS is responsible for training medical officers and paramedics as part of capacity building for CBRN preparedness, stating that "There has been an increasing threat of a non-conventional war…in the future. A training module has been started and preparation is on."[56] This is intended to ensure the armed forces are in a position to support civilian agencies in the event of a CBRN incident.

The Civil Defence Organization

One outfit that gets completely neglected in discussing India's capability to respond or otherwise cope with the effects of either a traditional or nontraditional CBRN attack is the Civil Defence Organization which is a volunteer force intended for mobilisation in wartime to provide civil defence support. However, this organisation, despite its impressive paper plans and structural format, is largely defunct in peacetime and mobilisation of volunteers for exercises to prepare for disaster—either natural or as a result of human intervention—has produced less than satisfactory results.

After a brief flurry of activity during the Second Word War, the Civil Defence concept once again received some degree of priority in the period immediately after the Sino-Indian conflict of October 1962. The post of Director General Civil Defence (DGCD) was created and the first DGCD was appointed on November 14, 1962. The purpose of the Civil Defence Organization is to save life, minimising damage to the property and maintaining continuity of industrial production in the event of a hostile attack.[57] Industrial sites would require effective plans to protect them from attack.

The Civil Defence Policy of the Government of India, prior to the declaration of emergency in 1962, was confined to making the states and union territories conscious of the need of civil protection measures and to ask them to keep ready civil protection paper plans for major cities and towns under the then Emergency Relief Organisation scheme. Subsequently, the Sino-Indian war of 1962 and the India–Pakistan War of 1965 led to a re-

---

56. Nayanima Basu, "Armed Forces Undergoing Nuclear, Biological Warfare Training," *The Hindu Business Line*, (August 11, 2017). http://www.thehindubusinessline.com/news/national/armed-forces-undergoing-nuclear-biological-warfare-training/article9813830.ece, accessed on November 10, 2017.

57. "Civil Defence," http://ndrfandcd.gov.in/Civildefence.aspx

examination of India's Civil Defence Policy. As a result, the Civil Defence Policy as it still exists today was evolved and Civil Defence legislation was enacted in the Parliament in 1968. During the 1971 war, despite not being seriously tested, as no sustained attacks were made against civilian targets, it has been reported that the Civil Defence Organization acquitted itself adequately and enthusiastically.

It is to be noted that although the Civil Defence Act 1968 is applicable throughout the country, the organisation is only raised in such areas and zones that the Government of India considers tactically and strategically vulnerable from enemy attack point of views, plus around nuclear power stations. At present, Civil Defence activities are restricted to 225 categorised towns spread over 35 states/union territories, however, the category and number of these towns are revised periodically and the number has increased as more areas become vulnerable to hostile attack. Certain towns are classed as Category-1A due to their proximity to nuclear power plants. In these towns, some minimal awareness and training are given to the volunteers to assist in the event of either a nuclear or radiological emergency.

The Civil Defence Organization is primarily comprised of volunteers except for a small nucleus of paid staff and professionals—including some 500 specialists which are augmented during emergencies. There has been a chronic shortage of Civil Defence Volunteers with the sanctioned number being 1,308,000 of which only 569,000 have been trained.[58] These volunteers are trained in one of twelve services namely:

- Headquarters Service,
- Warden Service,
- Communication Service,
- Casualty Service,
- Fire Fighting Service,
- Rescue Service,
- Welfare Service,
- Salvage Service,
- Corpse Disposal Service,
- Depot and Transport Service,

---

58. Ibid.

- Training Service,
- Supply Service.

The Civil Defence Organization has made some provisions for early warning and its network of sirens is tied into the Indian Air Force's warning network. To cater to the early warning communication requirement against an enemy attack, a reliable and flexible network, both on telephone lines and radio/wireless, has been planned and established in most of the categorised Civil Defence towns. The Civil Defence Organization notes that against the target of 165, the Ministry has already provided a full complement of video home system sets. In addition, 288 latest generation state-of-art high-frequency radio sets have already been supplied. Communication facilities, on telephone lines and radio, have also been planned and established in most of the Civil Defence towns for the purpose of command and control, co-ordination and liaison and also for mutual aid and co-operation. For this, fax machines have already been authorised for all Civil Defence Control Centres in Categorised Towns in addition to normal line and radio. In addition, electronic solid state APP Equipment and also Wireless Controlled ARP (W-ARP) for Simultaneous Broadcast Facilities and Centres Control of Sirens has also been developed in collaboration with ITI, Bangalore which would reduce both reaction time and errors.[59]

Attempts to use the Civil Defence Organization's volunteers for activities including assistance to the administration in relief and rescue work during natural calamities such as flood, earthquake, cyclone and drought have been relatively successful with volunteers making a useful contribution to the rescue and relief efforts during natural calamities. This is despite the abysmal allowance of Rs 30 per day allocated to them, which invariably impacts on the morale. Uniforms for Civil Defence Volunteers are very basic and in peacetime, they are issued with a high visibility vest and a red helmet. Little else by way of protective gear is provided which shows continuing neglect.

Training for the Civil Defence Organization takes place at the local, state and national levels with state governments having civil defence training establishments. The quality of training is relatively basic with

---

59. Ibid.

limited training equipment and infrastructure being available. However, in contrast, the National Civil Defence College at Nagpur is a centre for excellence and conducts multiple, high-quality courses in a wide range of civil defence spheres and has specialised courses to cope with various contingencies arising from a CBRN attack or incident with suitable equipment available.[60]

In practical terms, the Indian Civil Defence framework relies heavily on existing entities. At the state level, local governments are responsible for fire fighting, maintenance of municipal roads, water supply and conservation. The Public Works Department is responsible for the provision of shelters, sandbags, trenches, salvage, repairs and demolition. The other state government branches—health, labour, railways for example—assist in their various fields, as in the case of the central government. The Commissioner, District Magistrate and Sub-Divisional Officer are the ultimate authority for Civil Defence in the Division, District and Subdivision respectively. The District Magistrate functions as the Controller of Civil Defence, but in certain cases, there may be a need for a separate and autonomous Civil Defence Controller to give additional assistance to the local authorities. The Civil Defence Controller nominates various departmental heads of the district as the commanders of the various Civil Defence services. For example, the Chief Medical Officer functions as the head of the casualty service and the Executive Engineer—Public Works Department (Building and Roads) as head of the Rescue and Demolition Service.[61]

Augmenting the Civil Defence Volunteers are the somewhat better trained (this being a relative term) and equipped (again a relative term) HGs. The role of the HGs is to serve as an auxiliary to the police in maintenance of internal security, and to help their respective community in any kind of emergency—in the event of an air raid, fire, cyclone, earthquake, or epidemic as examples—helping in maintenance of essential services, and performing Civil Defence duties. The total sanctioned strength of HGs in

---

60. National Civil Defence College Website, "Our Achievements," http://www.cddrm-ncdc. org/e39343/e41087/.

61. Sanjay Badri-Maharaj, "Civil Defence Capabilities of the Indian State," *Bharat Rakshak Monitor* vol. 4, no. 2, September-October 2001.

India is 573,793 against which the present raised strength is 486,401 HGs. The organisation is spread over in all states and union territories except in Kerala.[62] While a potentially useful source of manpower, the HGs are often relegated to being auxiliaries to the civil police in such tasks as traffic control. In the event of an emergency, they are assigned rescue and fire-fighting duties and for that, there is a modicum of equipment such as trailer pumps, limited quantities of breathing apparatus and basic rescue tools such as pickaxes, shovels and ropes.[63]

The net result is that in the case of both the HGs and Civil Defence Organization, a potentially vital asset to assist in the minimisation of panic and disruption in the event of a non-traditional CBRN attack has been largely neglected in terms of its equipment and training. This is unfortunate as these organisations provide a vital link to the public. Despite repeated attempts to deploy them during natural disasters, a systematic revamping and re-equipping program remains a theoretical plan with deleterious effects on the performance of both organisations.

Conclusion

India faces a very real threat from a non-traditional CBRN attack. The principal agency tasked with dealing with planning for and, thereafter, mitigating the consequences of such an attack, the NDMA has been severely wanting in performance in the past. With new and professional personnel and a revamped structure, there is the possibility that it will perform somewhat more effectively in the future. Its efforts at laying down guidelines and contingency plans for CBRN incidents are creditable but more sustained efforts are needed to ensure effective measures.

The core of any response to a CBRN incident is the 12 battalions of the NDRF. These units, of which four are specialised CBRN formations, are dispersed geographically and while their record has been very good thus far, they have not been seriously tested in a serious CBRN environment. Moreover, the decision to not equip all 12 battalions for

---

62. "Home Guards," http://dgcd.nic.in/home_guards.htm
63. In 2009, this photograph shows the array of basic rescue equipment available to the Home Guards http://www.delhi.gov.in/wps/wcm/connect/ad17a200457f502d82c2ba63dd2acccc/P+320.jpg?MOD=AJPERES&lmod=-357501517

CBRN as well as other disasters is seemingly irrational. While it might have been understandable in the early days of the NDRF, at present, there exists no reason for the force not to be fully trained and equipped for such contingencies. This step would enhance the flexibility of the NDRF substantially.

Unfortunately, the first responders to any CBRN incident will be India's beleaguered Fire and Emergency Services. These units are severely undermanned and under-equipped. This continuing neglect is incomprehensible given the multi-hazard environment that exists in India, to which the contingency of a CBRN threat must be added. Equally neglected but even more poorly trained and equipped are the HGs and Civil Defence Volunteers. These are potentially invaluable organisations that could be of great assistance in the event of a disaster or an attack. Their continued neglect is unfortunate and should be reversed on a priority basis.

Finally, while India has some considerable capacity to cope with one or more localised non-traditional CBRN attacks, a sustained and large-scale attack—EMP, CBRN or multiple acts of sabotage—would present a qualitatively and quantitatively greater challenge. In such circumstances, it is unclear if India's existing systems would be able to provide an adequate response. It may be necessary, therefore, for India to review, reorganise and expand its existing systems to cope with a threat on a larger scale in terms of prevention, amelioration and recovery.

Unlike more traditional CBRN attacks, deterrence will not work in respect of these non-traditional threats. The only way for India to deal with such attacks is through a combination of measures to prevent attacks through active and passive defensive measures, methods of minimising damage in the event of an attack and an aggressive and viable plan for postattack recovery. To date, India's efforts in this regard present a somewhat mixed picture with some good planning and guidelines being established with some emergency response assets being created to deal with limited situations. However, with continuing severe weaknesses in civil defence forces and fire and emergency services, India's ability to cope with a non-traditional CBRN attack is compromised. With respect to an EMP attack, however, India has not brought any discussion on this to the fore, with even its National Critical Information Infrastructure Protection Centre being geared up to deal mainly with cybersecurity threats rather than with the possibility of such infrastructure being disrupted by an EMP attack. India, therefore, has much work to do to create the necessary mechanisms, assets and capabilities needed to cope with these emerging threats.

7

The Indian Doctrine:
Credibility and Capability = Strategy

The Indian Nuclear Doctrine as detailed in a press release on January 04, 2003, is a starkly simplistic document. Indeed, the cabinet note from that meeting spoke of 'operationalising' the nuclear doctrine. The 2003 doctrine derives from a much more detailed draft doctrine of 1999.

On August 17, the then Indian National Security Advisor Brajesh Mishra released a draft report from the National Security Advisory Board on Indian Nuclear Doctrine. This report outlines in broad terms India's rationale and intentions regarding the development of its "minimum nuclear deterrent," was never formally approved by the 1999 government of then Prime Minister Vajpayee. However, given the brevity of the 2003 doctrine, the rationale outlined therein can serve as an important guide to the reasons for the approach India has taken to the doctrine. The two doctrines are now replicated in full.

Draft of Indian Nuclear Doctrine[1]

Preamble

The use of nuclear weapons in particular, as well as other weapons of mass destruction, constitutes the gravest threat to humanity and to peace and stability in the international system. Unlike the other two categories of weapons of mass destruction, biological and chemical weapons which have been outlawed by international treaties, nuclear weapons remain instruments for national and collective security, the possession of which on a selective

---

1. Arms Control, "India's Draft Nuclear Doctrine," https://www.armscontrol.org/act/1999_07-08/ffja99

basis has been sought to be legitimised through a permanent extension of the Nuclear Non-proliferation Treaty in May 1995. Nuclear weapon states have asserted that they will continue to rely on nuclear weapons with some of them adopting policies to use them even in a non-nuclear context. These developments amount to a virtual abandonment of nuclear disarmament. This is a serious setback to the struggle of the international community to abolish weapons of mass destruction.

India's primary objective is to achieve economic, political, social, scientific and technological development within a peaceful and democratic framework. This requires an environment of durable peace and insurance against potential risks to peace and stability. It will be India's endeavour to proceed towards this overall objective in cooperation with the global democratic trends and to play a constructive role in advancing the international system toward a just, peaceful and equitable order.

Autonomy of decision-making in the developmental process and in strategic matters is an inalienable democratic right of the Indian people. India will strenuously guard this right in a world where nuclear weapons for a select few are sought to be legitimised for an indefinite future, and where there is growing complexity and frequency in the use of force for political purposes.

India's security is an integral component of its development process. India continuously aims at promoting an ever-expanding area of peace and stability around it so that developmental priorities can be pursued without disruption.

However, the very existence of an offensive doctrine pertaining to the first-use of nuclear weapons and the insistence of some nuclear weapons states on the legitimacy of their use even against non-nuclear weapon countries constitute a threat to peace, stability and sovereignty of states.

This document outlines the broad principles for the development, deployment and employment of India's nuclear forces. Details of policy and strategy concerning force structures, deployment and employment of nuclear forces will flow from this framework and will be laid down separately and kept under constant review.

Objectives

In the absence of global nuclear disarmament, India's strategic interests require effective, credible nuclear deterrence and adequate retaliatory capability, should deterrence fail. This is consistent with the UN Charter, which sanctions the right of self-defence.

The requirements of deterrence should be carefully weighed in the design of Indian nuclear forces and in the strategy to provide for a level of capability consistent with maximum credibility, survivability, effectiveness, safety and security.

India shall pursue a doctrine of credible minimum nuclear deterrence. In this policy of 'retaliation only', the survivability of our arsenal is critical. This is a dynamic concept related to the strategic environment, technological imperatives and the needs of national security. The actual size components, deployment and employment of nuclear forces will be decided in the light of these factors. India's peacetime posture aims at convincing any potential aggressor that:

- any threat of use of nuclear weapons against India shall invoke measures to counter the threat and
- any nuclear attack on India and its forces shall result in punitive retaliation with nuclear weapons to inflict damage unacceptable to the aggressor.

The fundamental purpose of Indian nuclear weapons is to deter the use and threat of use of nuclear weapons by any state or entity against India and its forces. India will not be the first to initiate a nuclear strike, but will respond with punitive retaliation should deterrence fail.

India will not resort to the use or threat of use of nuclear weapons against States which do not possess nuclear weapons or are not aligned with nuclear weapon powers.

Deterrence requires that India maintain:

- sufficient, survivable and operationally prepared nuclear forces;
- a robust command and control system;
- effective intelligence and early warning capabilities
- comprehensive planning and training for operations in line with the strategy and
- the will to employ nuclear forces and weapons.

Highly effective conventional military capabilities shall be maintained to raise the threshold of outbreak both of conventional military conflict as well as that of threat or use of nuclear weapons.

Nuclear Forces

India's nuclear forces will be effective, enduring, diverse, flexible and responsive to the requirements in accordance with the concept of credible minimum deterrence. These forces will be based on a triad of aircraft, mobile land-based missiles and sea-based assets in keeping with the objectives outlined above. Survivability of the forces will be enhanced by a combination of multiple redundant systems, mobility, dispersion and deception.

The doctrine envisages assured capability to shift from peacetime deployment to fully employable forces in the shortest possible time and the ability to retaliate effectively even in a case of significant degradation by hostile strikes.

Credibility and Survivability

The following principles are central to India's nuclear deterrent:

Credibility

Any adversary must know that India can and will retaliate with sufficient nuclear weapons to inflict destruction and punishment that the aggressor will find unacceptable if nuclear weapons are used against India and its forces.

Effectiveness

The efficacy of India's nuclear deterrent can be maximised through synergy among all elements involving reliability, timeliness, accuracy and weight of the attack.

Survivability

India's nuclear forces and their command and control shall be organised for very high survivability against surprise attacks and for a rapid punitive response. They shall be designed and deployed to ensure survival against a first-strike and to endure repetitive attrition attempts with adequate retaliatory capabilities for a punishing strike which would be unacceptable to the aggressor.

- Procedures for the continuity of nuclear command and control shall ensure a continuing capability to effectively employ nuclear weapons.

Command and Control

Nuclear weapons shall be tightly controlled and released for use at the highest political level. The authority to release nuclear weapons for use resides with the Prime Minister of India or the designated successor(s).

An effective and survivable command and control system with requisite flexibility and responsiveness shall be in place. An integrated operational plan, or a series of sequential plans, predicated on strategic objectives and a targeting policy shall form part of the system.

For an effective employment, the unity of command and control of nuclear forces including dual capable delivery systems shall be ensured.

The survivability of the nuclear arsenal and effective command, control, communications, computing, intelligence and information systems shall be assured.

The Indian defence forces shall be in a position to execute operations in a nuclear, biological and chemical environment with minimal degradation.

Space-based and other assets shall be created to provide early warning, communications, and damage/detonation assessment.

Security and Safety

Security: Extraordinary precautions shall be taken to ensure that nuclear weapons, their manufacture, transportation and storage are fully guarded against possible theft, loss, sabotage, damage or unauthorised access or use.

Safety: Safety is an absolute requirement and tamper-proof procedures and systems shall be instituted to ensure that unauthorised or inadvertent activation/use of nuclear weapons does not take place and the risks of an accident are avoided.

Disaster control: India shall develop an appropriate disaster control system capable of handling the unique requirements of potential incidents involving nuclear weapons and materials.

Research and Development

India should step up efforts in research and development to keep up with technological advances in this field.

While India is committed to maintaining the deployment of a deterrent which is both minimum and credible, it will not accept any restraints on building its research and development capability.

Disarmament and Arms Control

Global, verifiable and non-discriminatory nuclear disarmament is a national security objective. India shall continue its efforts to achieve the goal of a nuclear-weapon-free world at an early date.

Since no-first-use (NFU) of nuclear weapons is India's basic commitment, every effort shall be made to persuade other States possessing nuclear weapons to join an international treaty banning first use.

Having provided unqualified negative security assurances, India shall work for internationally binding unconditional negative security assurances by nuclear weapon states to non-nuclear weapon states.

Nuclear arms control measures shall be sought as part of the national security policy to reduce potential threats and to protect our own capability and its effectiveness.

In view of the very high destructive potential of nuclear weapons, appropriate nuclear risk reduction and confidence-building measures shall be sought, negotiated and instituted.

Following this draft, a Press Information Bureau release of January 04, 2003, gave the first indication of which elements of the draft nuclear doctrine had been agreed upon and which ones had either been omitted or changed somewhat.

Cabinet Committee on Security Reviews Progress in Operationalising India's Nuclear Doctrine[2]

The Cabinet Committee on Security (CCS) met today to review the progress in operationalising of India's Nuclear Doctrine. The Committee

---

2. http://pib.nic.in/archieve/lreleng/lyr2003/rjan2003/04012003/r040120033.html

decided that the following information regarding the nuclear doctrine and operational arrangements governing India's nuclear assets should be shared with the public.

India's Nuclear Doctrine can be summarised as follows:

- building and maintaining a credible minimum deterrent;
- a posture of 'NFU' nuclear weapons will only be used in retaliation against a nuclear attack on Indian territory or on Indian forces anywhere;
- nuclear retaliation to a first strike will be massive and designed to inflict unacceptable damage;
- nuclear retaliatory attacks can only be authorised by the civilian political leadership through the Nuclear Command Authority;
- nonuse of nuclear weapons against non-nuclear weapon states;
- however, in the event of a major attack against India, or Indian forces anywhere, by biological or chemical weapons, India will retain the option of retaliating with nuclear weapons;
- a continuance of strict controls on the export of nuclear and missile-related materials and technologies, participation in the Fissile Material Cut-off Treaty negotiations and continued observance of the moratorium on nuclear tests;
- continued commitment to the goal of a nuclear-weapon-free world, through global, verifiable and non-discriminatory nuclear disarmament.

The Nuclear Command Authority comprises a Political Council and an Executive Council. The Political Council is chaired by the Prime Minister. It is the sole body which can authorise the use of nuclear weapons.

The Executive Council is chaired by the National Security Advisor. It provides inputs for decision-making by the Nuclear Command Authority and executes the directives given to it by the Political Council.

The CCS reviewed the existing command and control structures, the state of readiness, the targeting strategy for a retaliatory attack and operating procedures for various stages of alert and launch. The Committee expressed satisfaction with an overall preparedness. The CCS approved the appointment of a Commander-in-Chief, Strategic Forces Command (SFC), to manage and administer all Strategic Forces.

The CCS also reviewed and approved the arrangements for alternate chains of command for retaliatory nuclear strikes in all eventualities.

Differences between the Draft Doctrine and the Operationalised Doctrine

Writing for the Institute for Defence Studies and Analyses, Dr Ali Ahmed made the following telling observations:[3]

> The National Security Advisory Board came up with a Draft Nuclear Doctrine (Draft) positing 'massive retaliation' for consideration by the government in August 1999 after the Kargil conflict of that summer. In the Draft, the relevant portion has been articulated thus: "Any nuclear attack on India and its forces shall result in punitive retaliation with nuclear weapons to inflict damage unacceptable to the aggressor" {Para 2.3 (b)}.In the wake of Operation Parakram of 2001-02, the government, through a press release from the Cabinet Committee on Security on January 4, 2003, confirmed the adoption of the nuclear doctrine that was explicated in a press release. The appropriate portion is extracted below:
> "(ii) A posture of "No First Use": Nuclear weapons will only be used in retaliation against a nuclear attack on Indian territory or on Indian forces anywhere;
> (iii) Nuclear retaliation to a first strike will be massive and designed to inflict unacceptable damage."
> The doctrine is now one of 'assured retaliation' to nuclear use by an adversary with the proviso that this would be massive in the case of first strike. In other words, retaliation in face of sub 'first strike' levels or usage could be of a lower order. In effect, India's nuclear doctrine has moved away from one of assuredly inflicting 'unacceptable damage' posited in the Draft to one that potentially includes 'flexible' or 'graduated' response. This shift from 'assured destruction' to 'graduated deterrence' has not been adequately registered in strategic commentaries, with most commentators continuing to believe that India's nuclear doctrine continues to be one of retaliation of a massive order.

---

3. Ali Ahmed, "The Need for Clarity in India's Nuclear Doctrine," *Institute for Defence Studies and Analyses,* (November 11, 2008). https://idsa.in/idsastrategiccomments/ TheNeedForClarityInIndiaSNuclearDoctrine_AAhmed_111108, accessed on November 13, 2008.

In case the sub para (ii) of the press release (reproduced above) is being over-interpreted and meanings not meant to be derived are being arrived at here, then it points to the element of confusion induced by the press release—referred to in the introductory paragraph of this article. There is, therefore, a need to clarify to the strategic community, the interested public and indeed, more importantly, to potential adversaries, exactly what is intended. In case India's nuclear deterrence is in accord with the popularly subscribed view in the strategic community, then the words 'first strike' would require to be substituted by 'first use' in a review of the doctrine. In such a case, the official doctrine requires to reiterate the Draft's wordings that "India can and will retaliate with sufficient nuclear weapons to inflict destruction and punishment that the aggressor will find unacceptable" (Para 4.1) for any form of nuclear 'first use'.

These subtle shifts in terminology are not merely semantic, as they do have a significant meaning. In the chapter on tactical nuclear weapons (TNWs), it was noted that the Indian Nuclear Doctrine seems to have inherent flexibility build in with some scholars noting that a tactical strike on a military formation in enemy territory does not fall within the ambit of a 'first strike'. Dr Ahmed suggests that with this change of wording, India has moved away from the concept of "massive retaliation" towards one of a "flexible response" stating:[4]

It needs to be highlighted that the possibility of a shift away from 'assured destruction' through 'massive retaliation' was already thoughtfully worked into the Draft (Para 2.4) in the following manner:

"India's peace time (Italics added) posture aims at convincing any potential aggressor that:

(a) any threat of use of nuclear weapons against India shall invoke measures to counter the threat; and

(b) any nuclear attack on India and its forces shall result in punitive retaliation with nuclear weapons to inflict damage unacceptable to the aggressor."

Interestingly, the term 'massive' has not been used in the Draft but finds mention in the press release. That it has not been used in the Draft indicates

---

4. Ibid.

that retaliation need not have 'massive' connotations, so long as its quantum would make it 'unacceptable' to the aggressor. 'Punitive retaliation' to inflict 'unacceptable' damage does not necessarily require massive retaliation. Therefore, the quantum of retaliation was left as a matter of political and operational choice to be dictated by the circumstance. The decision maker is thus not constrained in the options available for nuclear retaliation, which could be massive while not being necessarily so.

The question that is unknown is whether India itself believes that it has adopted a 'flexible response' doctrine or is still thinking in terms of a 'massive' retaliation. The question as to what will India's retaliation be to sub-first-strike attacks is open to question. That 'massive' retaliation seems to be limited to a response to a 'first-strike' suggests that a response to a lower level attack could be 'flexible'. Dr Ali Ahmed is clear in his views on this:[5]

Such a critique is not mere hair-splitting for these terms have specific definitions and are not inter-changeable. For the distinction, a resort to noted nuclear pundit Lawrence Freedman's Evolution of Nuclear Strategy is in order. 'First strike' is the opening volley directed against largely counter-force targets with the intent of crippling the adversary's means of nuclear retaliation. This would amount to nuclear first use of a high order against which massive retaliation would be rational, politically acceptable and legitimate.

First strike is, however, not necessarily the only manner of nuclear first use. A sub-first strike level of nuclear first use is feasible and may even be rational and legally and politically sustainable in the circumstance of the conflict. Against such a form of nuclear first use, such as against military forces that threaten the nuclear threshold of a belligerent, 'assured retaliation', may not be the best response option and most certainly should not be the sole response option. On receipt of a nuclear first use by the enemy not amounting to 'first strike', several factors would impact nuclear decision making. These include the aspect of self-deterrence; the need for proportionality and discrimination in keeping with the laws of armed

---

5.   Ibid.

conflict; escalatory potential of response options; international pressures; economy of force considerations; need for equivalence between the crime and punishment; and the need to win subsequent peace. Therefore, 'flexible response' has much to recommend it. If this is the nuclear doctrine India has apparently moved to, it requires acknowledging this explicitly.

This is evident from the fact that the Draft does not mention the nature of the retaliation during war time, restricted as it is to the projection of the posture in peace time. For in-conflict deterrence posture to be different from a peace time posture is sensible and has been catered for in the Draft accordingly. Thus, the Draft has been a precursor for the officially adopted doctrine and there is an element of continuity between the two. The nature of the deterrent posture in war time not having been reflected on indicates that other options have not been ruled out. The Draft, in not overly restricting the government's nuclear options, had potentially ruled in 'flexible response', which the official nuclear doctrine has virtually accepted. In case this is an incorrect impression, then there is no reason for the word 'peace time' to have figured in the Draft. It has evidently been used advisedly and calls for an interpretation along the line contended here.

Yet one has to ask whether the change in wording has served the interests of clarity. It is suggested that the answer to this is in the negative. Clarity has to be not only in the minds of Indian decision-makers but also in the minds of potential adversaries. While a degree of ambiguity is sometimes useful, it is suggested that the wording of India's Nuclear Doctrine needs clarification so as to avoid unnecessary misunderstanding. This view finds concurrence with Dr Ali Ahmed who states:[6]

That it has, however, given rise to an interpretation at variance with the commonly held notion of Indian deterrence, there is a case for clarifying the issue. To this author, the official doctrine is indeed one positing 'flexible response' as evident from its use of 'first strike' as against 'first use' in the relevant sentence. That this fact has not been registered by the wider strategic community is why the point being raised here for wider debate.

---

6.   Ibid.

The only fallout from acknowledging the shift would be on India's position that nuclear weapons are only for deterring. This is not affected in a major way by the shift to 'flexible response' since having a menu of options does not degrade deterrence. Instead, an 'assured destruction' posture is not credible against enemy nuclear first use of a lower order, such as a counter force attack on invading forces on his own territory. Therefore, there is a case for the shift and acknowledging the shift openly. The strategic commentaries that have largely missed the shift should also reflect on its implications. In this manner the public—that has a right to know in a democratic system—and the enemy—that needs to know as per deterrence theory—would be in a better position to appreciate the nuclear doctrine in the correct perspective.

The question as to whether this requires a complete revisiting of the nuclear doctrine is less clear. Revisiting the doctrine may become necessary in the event that there is a significant development among potentially hostile nations that affects the viability of the doctrine which should not deter India from revising the same. However, it is suggested that mere clarification of terms could be done without the wholescale revisiting of the doctrine with the attendant risks therein.

Satish Chandra, a former Deputy to the National Security Advisor of the Government of India, wrote an extensive piece on the question of revisiting the nuclear doctrine and notes that many of the calls for revisiting the doctrine emanate from a position which questions the credibility of the deterrence and the doctrine against Pakistani nuclear weapons. As Dr Ali Ahmed has noted—and echoed in the earlier quoted piece by Dr G. Balachandran and K. Patil[7]—the Indian Nuclear Doctrine is not without flexibility and should not necessarily need revisiting or revising with respect to a response against Pakistani TNWs and their use. This finds resonance with former National Security Advisor, Shivshankar Menon, who asserts that India's nuclear doctrine is more flexible than it normally gets credit for.[8]

---

7. G. Balachandran and Kapil Patil, "Revisiting India's Nuclear Doctrine," *Institute for Defence Studies and Analyses*, (March 27, 2017). https://idsa.in/idsacomments/revisiting-india-nuclear-doctrine_gbala-kpatil_270317, accessed on November 13, 2017.

8. Dhruva Jaishankar, "Decoding India's Nuclear Status," *Brookings*, (April 03, 2017). https://www.brookings.edu/opinions/decoding-indias-nuclear-status/, accessed on March 18, 2018.

Satish Chandra notes that there are several factors which make a revision of the Indian Nuclear Doctrine somewhat less than desirable, stating:[9]

There are many factors which militate against revisiting our nuclear doctrine and sacrificing the restraint it encapsulates by for instance abandoning NFU some of which are enumerated below:

All the gains enjoyed by us in the international community by the restraint of our nuclear posture would be frittered away. These do not merely constitute intangibles but entailed the termination of sanctions, support for our entry into the multilateral nuclear export control regimes as well as our civil nuclear cooperation agreements.

It would enormously complicate and increase the expenditure incurred by us in regard to our command and control mechanisms which would have to be reconfigured to engage in calibrated nuclear war fighting.

It would weaken the possibility of our engaging in conventional warfare insulated from the nuclear overhang.

It would encourage the use of tactical nuclear weapons against us under the illusion of no massive response.

It would facilitate the painting of South Asia as a nuclear flashpoint and thereby encourage foreign meddling.

It is interesting, however, to note that Chandra sees a revision of doctrine largely in terms of changing the concept of NFU. This point about NFU has become one which has come to the fore on occasion and it is not entirely clear what benefit India could derive from the same.

India adopting the first-use doctrine against a larger nuclear power such as China would be impractical, not to mention unnecessarily provocative without any strategic benefit while adopting the first-use doctrine against Pakistan is unnecessary in any circumstance. Ambiguity over possible first use at this stage would be counter-productive as a change from the NFU would be seen as adopting a potential first-use doctrine. To this end, it is

---

9. Satish Chandra, "Revisiting India's Nuclear Doctrine: Is it Necessary?," *Institute for Defence Studies and Analyses,* (April 30, 2014). https://idsa.in/issuebrief/RevisitingIndiasNuclearDoctrine_schandra_300414, accessed on November 13, 2017.

suggested that the policy of NFU be retained and revisions, if any, to the Indian doctrine be confined to clarifying ambiguities.

Having said that, this imposes some requirements upon the Indian deterrent and the progress towards the same will determine whether the NFU doctrine is credible, viable and sustainable. These include issues of command and control, the numerical size and nature of the warheads, their readiness levels as well as, most importantly, the survivability of a large enough force to ensure a level of unacceptable destruction on any adversary. In this respect, Chandra has expounded on what the requirements are for a "credible minimum deterrent":[10]

> The concept of "credible minimum deterrence" is the cornerstone of India's nuclear doctrine. It, used in conjunction with the concepts of "No First Use" (NFU) and "Non Use" against nuclear weapon states, clearly indicates that India envisages its nuclear weapons as only a deterrent merely for defensive purposes and not as a means to threaten others, that it is not in the business of building up a huge arsenal and that it will not engage in arms racing.
>
> The concept, however, also recognizes that for deterrence to be effective it must be "credible".
>
> The prerequisites for the credibility of our deterrent in the context of our nuclear doctrine may be listed as follows:
>
> Sufficient and Survivable nuclear forces both in terms of warheads and means of delivery able to inflict unacceptable damage;
>
> Nuclear Forces must be operationally prepared at all times;
>
> Effective Intelligence and Early Warning Capabilities;
>
> A Robust Command and Control System;
>
> The Will to Employ Nuclear Forces;
>
> Communication of Deterrence Capability.
>
> The size and nature of India's nuclear arsenal would essentially have to be a function of its threat perceptions, its being able to absorb a first strike (on account of its no first use commitment) and thereafter retaining the capability of inflicting "unacceptable damage". India's current security environment is by no means rosy. Accordingly, a sizeable nuclear weapons

---

10. Ibid.

arsenal is essential as we need to factor in the possibility that the same would undergo a substantial degradation, despite all precautions, in a first strike, that some of our own attacks could be negated by defensive measures and above all what we have to inflict is "massive" and "unacceptable damage". The survivability of our nuclear forces would need to be ensured by a combination of multiple redundant systems, mobility, dispersion, and deception. This also requires that India's nuclear forces are based on a triad of aircraft, mobile land based missiles and sea based assets.

The need for operational preparedness at all times of the nuclear forces in order for our nuclear deterrent to be credible is self evident. It has been ensured by the creation of a C-in-C Strategic Forces Command to manage and administer our Strategic Forces. He functions under the overall control of the Chairman Chiefs of Staff Committee who is the channel of communication between him and the Government.

Effective Intelligence and Early Warning Capabilities always important in any conflict are critical in the context of a nuclear attack not merely as a means to counter it but also for purposes of retaliation. An apex techint organization notably the NTRO has been set up which would *inter alia* provide the required intelligence for this purpose.

Robust Command and Control System is essential for the credibility of deterrence. India has for this purpose established a Nuclear Command Authority comprising a Political Council chaired by the Prime Minister and an Executive Council chaired by the National Security Advisor. In keeping with the stipulation in our Nuclear Doctrine the Political Council is the sole body which can authorize the use of nuclear weapons. The role of the Executive Council is to provide inputs for decision making by the Nuclear Command Authority and to execute the directives given to it by the Political Council. The fact that the survivability of the command and control system has not been lost sight of is reflected in the press release of January 4th 2003 which indicated that the CCS "reviewed and approved the arrangements for alternate chains of command for retaliatory strikes in all eventualities".

The demands on India's Command and Control system as indeed on its Strategic Forces Command have been simplified due to the nature of its nuclear doctrine. Whereas most nuclear weapon states contemplate the possibility of escalatory nuclear war fighting scenarios the Indian doctrine essentially caters for massive Indian nuclear retaliation in the eventuality of a nuclear attack on it or on its forces. In essence, as per the Indian doctrine, if India or its forces are attacked with nuclear weapons it would more or less automatically unleash a devastating nuclear attack in retaliation. No prolonged nuclear war fighting scenarios are envisaged. This enormously eases the task of the Indian nuclear command, control and communications systems and greatly reduces the costs incurred thereon.

In the chapter on India's nuclear arsenal, it has been stated that India's missiles are all based on mobile launchers and secure mountain storage areas are housing the missiles and warheads not ready to use. A question which has not been addressed, however, is how would de-mated or a partially de-mated arsenal work in the event of a pre-emptive strike be aimed against either the warheads or delivery systems? To cater for such a contingency, it was suggested, in that chapter that India should aim to keep a proportion of its arsenal—particularly now with canisterised systems and submarine-launched ballistic missiles coming into the arsenal—in a fully-mated state. One can draw the distinction between a pre-emptive strike, launched without warning or provocation and one which is the final stage in an escalating conventional conflict. In the latter case, it would be presumed that measures would be taken to secure the arsenal from attack, deploy a proportion of it and signal that any attack would be met with retaliation.

The question as to how far India has come along the path to have a credible deterrent as well as a viable doctrine that merges into a coherent strategy in the event of a conflict is open to some debate. The reticence of Indian officials to comment on the state of the nuclear deterrent reflects the overarching and decidedly unhelpful air of secrecy in respect of all things 'nuclear'. Yet, it would not only be naïve to think that no progress has been made but it would also reflect ignoring certain key elements in the discourse on India's nuclear deterrent which could prove instructive. It is to be noted that all of India's weapons delivery systems have been designed to be survivable—rail or road mobile—and relatively difficult to detect. From

2003, the doctrine has spoken of a command authority and it makes explicit mention of alternate chains of command and measures to be taken to direct a retaliatory strike.

So in respect of the criteria that Chandra has outlined for the credibility of India's deterrent, what has India achieved to date? The closest that we have to an official statement in this respect comes from former National Security Advisor Shyam Saran who delivered a lecture in 2013 on the credibility of the Indian nuclear deterrent.

Command and Control

In respect of command and control, Saran made the following statement:[11]

The National Command Authority is in charge of India's nuclear deterrent. At its apex is the Political Council which is headed by the Prime Minister and includes all the ministerial members of the Cabinet Committee on Security such as the Ministers of Defence, Home and External Affairs. Below the Political Council is the Executive Council which is headed by the National Security Advisor and includes the Chiefs of the three armed forces, the C-in-C of India's Strategic Forces Command, a three star officer, among others. There is an alternate National Command Authority which would take up the functions of nuclear command in case of any contingency when the established hierarchy is rendered dysfunctional. The NCA has access to radiation hardened and fully secured communications systems where, too, redundancies have been put in place as back-up facilities.

This suggests that India has considered the command, control and communications difficulties that would cater to the possibilities of disruptions to the National Command Authority (NCA) in the event of an attack. Though he has not, in this part of his statement, indicated the survivability of the NCA, he made the following pertinent comments earlier on:[12]

---

11. Shyam Saran, "Is India's Deterrent Credible?," India Habitat Centre, (April 24, 2013). http://www.armscontrolwonk.com/files/2013/05/Final-Is-Indias-Nuclear-Deterrent-Credible-rev1-2-1-3.pdf, accessed on November 13, 2017.

12. Ibid.

India does have a credible theory of how its nuclear weapons may be used and that is spelt out in its nuclear doctrine. One may or may not agree with that doctrine but to claim that India does not have a credible theory about the use of nuclear weapons does not accord with facts. Since January 4, 2003, when India adopted its nuclear doctrine formally at a meeting of the Cabinet Committee on Security (CCS), it has moved to put in place, at a measured pace, a triad of land-based, air-delivered and submarine-based nuclear forces and delivery assets to conform to its declared doctrine of no-first use and retaliation only. It has had to create a command and control infrastructure that can survive a first strike and a fully secure communication system that is reliable and hardened against radiation or electronic interference. A number of redundancies have had to be created to strengthen survivability. India today has a long range ballistic missile capability and is on the road to a submarine—based missile capability. These capabilities will be further improved as time goes on and more resources become available. In all these respects, significant progress has been achieved. To expect that these should have emerged overnight after May1998 is a rather naïve expectation. The record since the May 1998 nuclear tests demonstrates quite clearly a sustained and systematic drive to operationalize the various components of the nuclear deterrent in a manner best suited to India's security environment. This is not the record of a state which considers nuclear weapons as "instrument of national pride and propaganda". (Emphasis mine)

Corroboration for these efforts at protecting the NCA has come from as far back as 2003 when the then government of Atal Bihari Vajpayee initiated the construction of two hardened shelters—reputedly capable of withstanding a direct hit from the equivalent of a B61 thermonuclear penetrating warhead—established in Delhi with an alternate within a 400-km radius of the capital, enabling easy movement of the NCA in the event of need.[13]

---

13. "India Building nuclear-proof bunkers for top leaders," *Silicon India*, September 23, 2003. http://www.siliconindia.com/shownews/India_building_nuclearproof_bunkers_for_top_leaders-nid-20887-cid-Top.html, accessed on November 13, 2017.

One might assume that suitable command and control arrangements extend to ensure that launch orders are received by various weapon crews as well as ensuring that the crews and their weapons are themselves protected in the event of an attack. A 2010 Pakistan Observer report suggested that India was working on a more extensive shelter plan for military installations and using the metro lines in Indian cities to house shelters.[14] This secure command and control network is an essential part of making India's deterrent credible. It should be also noted that neither the survivability of the Indian NCA nor the nature of the alternate NCA has been discussed openly.

Professor Bharat Karnad, writing in 2008, noted that the 2003 arrangements were somewhat makeshift and one contingency involved a plan to move the Prime Minister via underground metro rail and thereafter by helicopter to a safe and secure location. Since then, with a scheduled completion in 2010/11, a dedicated nuclear command centre with two alternate sites has been designed and approved. These centres are designed to withstand the shockwave produced by a thermonuclear explosion as well as the blast. This would ensure the survivability and sustainability of the NCA.[15] Shyam Saran's statements in respect of the survivability of the NCA and its alternate may be indicative of the completion of this project.

India has made it clear that its NCA rests in civilian, political hands. This has given rise to the somewhat unwarranted comment that the Indian military is kept 'out of the loop' in respect of India's nuclear arsenal. It is submitted that this is a serious exaggeration and misrepresents the situation. Civilian control does not mean military exclusion. With the establishment of the SFC, the military has custody of the arsenal while the control vests in political hands. Shyam Saran is particularly scathing in respect of this issue, saying:[16]

The thesis that India's nuclear deterrent is mostly symbolic is, for some, driven by the perception that India's armed forces are not fully part of

---

14. https://defence.pk/pdf/threads/india-starts-building-nuclear-shelters.83066/, accessed on November 13, 2017.
15. Karnad, India's Nuclear Policy, p. 102.
16. Chandra, n. 10.

the strategic decision-making process and that they play second fiddle to the civilian bureaucracy and the scientific establishment. Even if this perception was true, and in fact it is not, one cannot accept that the credibility of India's nuclear deterrence demands management by its military. The very nature of nuclear deterrence as practiced by a civilian democracy dictates that decisions relating to the nature and scope of the arsenal, its deployment and use, be anchored in the larger architecture of democratic governance.

It is the civilian political leadership that must make judgments about domestic political, social and economic priorities as well as the imperatives imposed by a changing regional and global geopolitical environment. The military must be enabled to provide its own perspectives and inputs, just as other segments of the state must do. Undoubtedly the military's inputs and its advice would have to carry weight, especially in operational matters. But to equate exclusive military management of strategic forces, albeit under the political leadership's overall command, as the sine qua non of deterrence credibility is neither necessary nor desirable. One should certainly encourage better civil-military relations and coordination. It may also be argued that the military's inputs into strategic planning and execution should be enhanced to make India's nuclear deterrent more effective. But one should not equate shortcomings in these respects with the absence of a credible nuclear deterrent.

In order to support the NCA, a Strategy Programme Staff has been created in the National Security Council Secretariat to carry out general staff work for the National Command Authority. This unit is charged with looking at the reliability and quality of our weapons and delivery systems, collate intelligence on other nuclear weapon states particularly those in the category of potential adversaries and work on a perspective plan for India's nuclear deterrent in accordance with a ten year cycle. The Strategy Programme Staff has representatives from the three services, from our Science and Technology establishment and other experts from related domains, including External Affairs. A Strategic Armament Safety Authority has been set up to review and to update storage and transfer procedures for nuclear armaments, including the submarine based component. It will be responsible for all matters relating to the safety and security of our nuclear and delivery assets at all locations. This will function under the direct authority of the NCA.

This indicates that the services are part of the nuclear custody and command loop and, through the Strategy Program Staff, have an important role in establishing a link between the political and military in respect of nuclear issues. While there is an argument that the entire defence decision-making process in India could benefit from more military input, it is manifestly not the case that the military is 'out' of the nuclear policy loop and its perspective is considered by the NCA in policy-making.

There are still questions regarding the manner of functioning of the NCA. How will control work? It has been stated by Saran among others that the NCA works on a two-person rule for access to armaments and delivery systems.[17] Does this include the use of permissive action links? How will it function aboard a nuclear submarine or in the field with road and rail-mobile systems? Would this require the deployment of the Department of Atomic Energy or Bhabha Atomic Research Centre personnel alongside the military? The answers to these questions have yet to be disclosed publicly.

Survivability and Credibility of the Arsenal

As discussed in detail in the relevant chapter, India's nuclear arsenal has taken the form of a nuclear triad with deployed road and rail-mobile systems, a nascent or active airborne deterrent and developing a submarine-based deterrent. In all these instances, the systems are designed to be mobile, hard to detect and as such survivable. As discussed in the aforementioned chapter, mountain tunnel complexes for the storage and protection of land-based missiles have been constructed, with more being planned.[18] It is yet unclear as to how many of these mountain complexes will be constructed, how secure they would be from satellite detection or how survivable they would be to a direct hit. Undoubtedly, they render the systems stored therein reasonably, even highly, survivable but there are always doubts in this regard.

The Indian submarine-based deterrent is as yet in its infancy with the INS Arihant still undergoing trials and its short-ranged K-15 missiles

17. Chandra, n. 10.
18. Op.cit. n. 14

being impractical for deterrent purposes. Not until submerged launch tests of the K-4 missile are completed successfully will India's deterrent be deemed to have a viable triad. Even then, the 3500 km range of the K-4 is not a particularly impressive missile in respect of range and represents but a step towards a truly effective SSBN/submarine-launched ballistic missile combination.

Shyam Saran's comments in respect of the Indian deterrent are neither particularly useful nor accurate, making a series of mistakes in respect of the designation of missiles and their ranges. However, it is nonetheless worth repeating for it represents the closest to an official comment that has been available to date:[19]

If we look at the current status of India's nuclear deterrent and its command and control system, it is clear that at least two legs of the triad referred to in our nuclear doctrine are already in place. These include a modest arsenal, nuclear capable aircraft and missiles both in fixed underground silos as well as those which are mounted on mobile rail and road-based platforms. These land-based missiles include both Agni-II (1500 km) as well as Agni-III (2500 km) missiles. The range and accuracy of further versions for example, Agni V (5000 km) which was tested successfully only recently, will improve with the acquisition of further technological capability and experience. The third leg of the triad which is submarine-based, is admittedly a work in progress. We need at least three Arihant class nuclear submarines so that at least one will always be at sea. Submarine-based missiles systems have been developed and tested in the form of the Sagarika but these are still relatively short in range. It is expected that a modest sea-based deterrence will be in place by 2015 or 2016. There is also a major R&D programme which has been in place since 2005, for the development of a new, longer range and more accurate generation of submarine-based missiles which are likely to ready for deployment around 2020.

Rather than the actual details of the missile, the points that should be taken from Saran's comments are that the Indian government is determined

---

19. Chandra, n. 10

to have a submarine-based deterrent in place, is committed to creating and maintaining a triad and is aware of the shortcomings in existing systems and is working to eliminate these deficiencies with new designs. This has been evident in the evolution of the Agni-II into the Agni-IV and the Agni-III into the Agni-V. This evolutionary process speaks to the basic maturity of the Indian nuclear deterrent policy and augurs well for the future development of the arsenal and the credibility of the deterrent. Saran also revealed that there are regular rehearsals for nuclear scenarios and escalatory situations, indicating that the Indian NCA and its supporting Strategy Program Staff are catering for all contingencies:[20]

Regular drills are conducted to examine possible escalatory scenarios, surprise attack scenarios and the efficiency of our response systems under the no first use limitation. Thanks to such repeated and regular drills, the level of confidence in our nuclear deterrent has been strengthened. Specialized units have also been trained and deployed for operation in a nuclearized environment.

The Indian SFC rarely publicises any of its activities. The only time that its operations come to the fore is when it conducts user launches of ballistic missiles either as part of user trials or as routine training. The reticence of the SFC to publicise its operations and activities is somewhat unfortunate and not entirely desirable. This ties into the one area where the credibility of the Indian deterrent suffers—visibility. By keeping virtually every aspect of the workings of the SFC, the NCA, the Strategy Program Staff and so forth a secret, the Indian public is left largely, if not completely unaware as to the capabilities and viability of the Indian deterrent. This is not satisfactory as in an age where misinformation and rumour can undermine credibility more easily that one would like, it is necessary for a change in this posture.

In this respect it is important to consider Satish Chandra's views in this regard:[21]

---

20. Ibid.
21. Jaishankar, n. 8.

It is not sufficient to have a deterrence capability but also be perceived to have it as well as the will to use nuclear weapons if required to do so. In other words one must communicate or project the same to all concerned. Regrettably, insufficient attention has been paid to this aspect of establishing the credibility of our nuclear deterrent.

While it is imperative that the Indian population be assured as to the viability and credibility of the Indian deterrent, it is much more important that India's potential adversaries be similarly convinced. Indeed, much of the debate over the need to revise the nuclear doctrine has come about as a result of the concern that India's stated doctrine is not credible against TNWs, the need for clear communications and an unequivocal declaration of intent becomes necessary. Chandra further notes:

Since an important element behind the call for revisiting our nuclear doctrine emanates from a lack of confidence in our deterrent and in our willingness to resort to the use of nuclear weapons in a massive second strike in response to an attack on us with tactical weapons the same needs to be addressed by much more effective signaling and a demonstration that the government will do what it says and will not shy from making a robust response when necessary. The following could be some moves in this direction:

Government must restore faith in itself by doing what it says and not shying from biting the bullet. Firmness must be shown in all its actions, for instance, on issues of law and order, terrorism and addressing difficult neighbours.

Periodic statements about the nurturing and upgradation of our nuclear arsenal and systems including alternate command structure.

An indication that our nuclear arsenal will be large enough to take care of all adversaries and will have to be in the mid triple digits.

Appointment of a Chief of Defence Staff and upgradation of the NTRO as a capable apex techint organization which would in a fool proof manner provide indicators of any attack on us and ensure swift and massive nuclear retaliation inflicting unacceptable damage.

An indication that we have in place multiple, well camouflaged and well secured vectors which are constantly being further refined in order to enable the country to inflict unacceptable damage even after absorbing a first strike by its adversaries

These recommendations are eminently sensible and would certainly do much to assuage the concerns that have arisen in respect of the Indian deterrent. What is fascinating is that India has actually taken steps to put some of these measures in place but the communication of these has been extremely poor— non-existent on occasion. Even Shyam Saran was moved to say:[22]

The secrecy which surrounds our nuclear programme, a legacy of the long years of developing and maintaining strategic capabilities, is now counter-productive. There is not enough data or information that flows from the guardians of our strategic assets to enable reasoned judgments and evaluations. There has been significant progress in the modernization and operationalisation of our strategic assets, but this is rarely and only anecdotally shared with the public. The result is an information vacuum which then gets occupied by either ill-informed or motivated speculation or assessments. To begin with, I would hope that the Government makes public its nuclear doctrine and releases data regularly on what steps have been taken and are being taken to put the requirements of the doctrine in place.

It is not necessary to share operational details but an overall survey such as an annual Strategic Posture Review, should be shared with the citizens of the country who, after all, pay for the security which the deterrent is supposed to provide to them. An informed and vigorous debate based on accurate and factual information should be welcomed, because only through such debate can concepts be refined, contingencies identified and the most effective responses formulated. In a democracy, this is critical to upholding a broad consensus on dealing with the complex and constantly evolving security challenges our country confronts.

---

22. Chandra, n. 10.

If we are to consider the third recommendation made by Chandra in respect of the size of the nuclear deterrent, we see that some steps have been taken. While the actual number of weapons is unclear, as has been shown in the relevant chapter, India has the capability to make several hundred nuclear weapons and has retained the ability to surge weapons-grade plutonium production by keeping eight of its power reactors out of International Atomic Energy Agency safeguards. It is another matter as to whether India has in fact taken any such step to increase the weapons-grade material production or to manufacture more weapons than its current inventory of delivery systems will permit. However, it is noteworthy—as indicated in the aforesaid chapter—that India has increased production of the Agni-I and Agni-II missiles and might be expected to do the same for the others in the Agni family. Whether production delivers the requisite number in time is always debatable.

Similarly, as far as the first recommendation is concerned, it can be argued that the surgical strikes into Pakistan and the operations against terrorists operating out of Myanmar are indicative of a renewed resolve on the part of the Indian government to support its words with actions. While it would be impossible to expect these events to be a regular occurrence, the publicising of these two strikes might be indicative of a stronger determination to follow through on promises to deal with terrorism and other national security challenges. It remains to be seen, however, if this becomes a part of India's institutional response or is restricted to isolated cases for publicity.

In respect to the other recommendations made by Chandra, none have been articulated and in the case of the appointment of a Chief of Defence Staff, despite several governments giving hope for the same, there has been no progress in that regard whatsoever. This does not mean that there has been no progress, quite the contrary. It is clear that on recommendations two, three and five, the Indian government has taken steps to review, revise, modernise and expand the arsenal and has kept its ability to produce more weapons open and flexible. Furthermore, all its weapons development efforts have been towards survivable assets with mobility being a feature.

What has not been done is any articulation of these plans or policies in any coherent or even comprehensible way by official sources. This is patently absurd in the information age and it would serve India well to devise a clear and comprehensive articulation of its nuclear position, its doctrine and its broad intent. To some extent, this was done through the draft nuclear doctrine which did expound a rationale, an intent as well as a doctrine that was to inform India's development, deployment and use of nuclear weapons, but as Dr Ali Ahmed pointed out:[23]

> Here it must be acknowledged that the Draft was not to be taken as the government's position, even though it was released for discussion by the then National Security Advisor and Principal Secretary to the Prime Minister, Shri B Mishra. That it was not the official position was clarified after its release by a senior minister in the NDA government, Shri Jaswant Singh. The Draft can, however, be taken as informing the doctrine officially adopted and explicated in the press release. There are elements of continuities and discontinuities between the two. However, the press release is the authoritative statement and is very clear.

This means that analysts and adversaries are left to try and infer India's nuclear policy through two completely separate and somewhat different documents. That there was no official acceptance of the draft nuclear doctrine and the release of a mere summary of what was called India's Nuclear Doctrine adds to the unnecessary ambiguity, games of semantics and confusion surrounding Indian nuclear policy. A certain degree of ambiguity is not only desirable but also necessary, but it is submitted that India's approach goes to the extreme and has resulted in an excessive level of confusion. This situation is neither desirable nor necessary and should end.

Is India Abandoning NFU? Probably Not

In March 2017, Professor Vipin Narang of the Department of Political Science at the Massachusetts Institute of Technology made the somewhat

---

23. Ahmed, n. 3.

startling claim that India was rethinking its NFU nuclear doctrine. In an address delivered to the Carnegie International Nuclear Policy Conference, Professor Narang made the following statement:[24]

> There is increasing evidence that India will not allow Pakistan to go first. And that India's opening salvo may not be conventional strikes trying to pick off just Nasr batteries in the theater, but a full 'comprehensive counterforce strike' that attempts to completely disarm Pakistan of its nuclear weapons so that India does not have to engage in iterative tit-for-tat exchanges and expose its own cities to nuclear destruction. This thinking surfaces not from fringe extreme voices such as Bharat Karnad or retired Indian Army officers frustrated by the lack of resolve they believe their government has shown in multiple provocations, but from no less than a former Strategic Forces Command C-in-C Lt Gen BS Nagal and, perhaps more importantly and authoritatively, from the highly respected and influential former National Security Advisor Shivshankar Menon in plain sight in his recent 2016 book Choices: Inside the Making of Indian Foreign Policy. In short, we may be witnessing what I call a 'decoupling' of Indian nuclear strategy between China and Pakistan. The force requirements India needs in order to credibly threaten assured retaliation against China may allow it to pursue more aggressive strategies—such as escalation dominance or a 'splendid first strike'—against Pakistan. We may be seeing the emergence of this decoupling, or at least serious mainstream thinking about it, with the intention being a disarming strike against Pakistan.

If this is true, it would indeed mark a substantial and complete shift in India's Nuclear Doctrine which had hitherto been assumed to be firmly entrenched in the NFU approach to nuclear weapons. Professor Narang derives his postulations, at least in part, from a paragraph in a book written

---

24. Vipin Narang, "Plenary: Beyond the Nuclear Threshold: Causes and Consequences of First Use," *Carnegie International Nuclear Policy Conference* Washington, DC, (March 20, 2017). https://fbfy83yid9j1dqsev3zq0w8n-wpengine.netdna-ssl.com/wp-content/uploads/2013/08/Vipin-Narang-Remarks-Carnegie-Nukefest-2017.pdf, accessed on March 18, 2018.

by former Indian National Security Advisor, Shivshankar Menon which states:[25]

> If Pakistan were to use tactical nuclear weapons against India, even against Indian forces in Pakistan, it would effectively be opening the door to a massive Indian first strike, having crossed India's declared red lines. There would be little incentive, once Pakistan had taken hostilities to the nuclear level, for India to limit its response, since that would only invite further escalation by Pakistan. India would hardly risk giving Pakistan the chance to carry out a massive nuclear strike after the Indian response to Pakistan using tactical nuclear weapons. In other words, Pakistani tactical nuclear weapons use would effectively free India to undertake a comprehensive first strike against Pakistan.

However, there is a significant caveat in accepting Professor Narang's conclusions from this paragraph. While the words "comprehensive first strike" are used, it is clear from the context of the paragraph that Menon does not mean this at all. Indeed, it suggests the exact opposite with Menon meaning "second-strike" or some equivalent. This latter interpretation would be in accord with the remainder of the chapter in which the offending paragraph is to be found where Menon embarks upon a rigorous defence of India's NFU approach.[26] Indeed, to date, extrapolating such a stark shift in India's NFU stance and a 'decoupling' of India's doctrine versus Pakistan as opposed to its doctrine versus China is perhaps too much of a stretch to be drawn from this single paragraph.

This is especially so since doctrines cannot be seen in isolation and must be set against the path India has taken in developing its force structure. With its emphasis on mobility and survivability, it is suggested that there is no evidence of a shift away from an NFU doctrine on the part of India. Furthermore, it is suggested that India has always practically decoupled its approach to Pakistan and China owing to the latter's NFU doctrine and the former's propensity to relish in its

---

25. Shivshankar Menon, *Choices: Inside the Making of India's Foreign Policy* (Penguin Random House India: Brookings, Washington DC: 2016), p. 117.
26. Ibid, pp. 105–123.

rejection of the same. It is thus submitted that Professor Narang may be exaggerating to an extent.

However, Professor Narang's interpretation would not be the first time that the issue of India's NFU approach has been called into question. In 2014, the highly respected Lt General Balraj Nagal, Commander-in-Chief of the SFC between 2008 and 2011 and thereafter, the first Chief of the Strategy Program Staff, and neither known to be rash in either statements nor to be particularly hawkish, suggested that India adopt a policy of "ambiguity" without spelling out whether it adheres to an NFU doctrine or not. Writing in the magazine *Force*, Lt General Nagal made the following observations about the NFU doctrine:[27]

> In deterrence doctrine, NFU is a defensive policy, by indicating a reactive response to threats or use of nuclear weapons, a state has declared that it does not plan to use its nuclear arsenal for offensive or coercive policies. The state believes that by rejecting a first use, it signals to its adversary that nuclear weapons do not constitute the primary means of deterrence for conventional and sub conventional warfare. The primary focus of the state is to possess a capability, to retaliate if forced to by the adversary, to defend its vital interests and core values. It is a last resort option to take care of anticipated strategic or weapons of mass destruction (WMD) threats.
>
> NFU policy reassures global powers that India is not aggressive. Primary deterrence by nuclear weapons runs the risk of pre-emption strategy during a crisis situation, and therefore, is destabilising, whereas NFU does not imply similar actions. The policy also indicates that nuclear weapons do not figure in the nation's calculus to address local or limited wars, indirectly it can be construed that the lower level of war spectrum is delinked from the higher level of the war spectrum.
>
> ...It is a reactive policy, which limits the choice strategic planners and political leadership have in the face of crisis escalation, conflict escalation and imminent threat of nuclear strikes. A constrained or limited policy option provides inadequate manoeuvre space, a fait accompli situation.

27. B. S. Nagal, "Guest Column | Nuclear No First Use Policy: A Time for Appraisal," *Force*, (December 2014). http://forceindia.net/guest-column/guest-column-b-s-nagal/nuclear-no-first-use-policy/, accessed on March 18, 2018.

Deterrence credibility of a NFU state becomes suspect or doubtful, a state under first strike may lose control over its retaliatory capability due to destruction of its command, control and communication system, it will be the aim of a first strike nation to paralyse the decision making ability of the attacked state. Credibility is also lowered in case of successful counterforce strikes by the adversary.

...NFU policy prevents conduct of a first strike on the adversary's counterforce targets, thus allowing the adversary full opportunity to first utilise full capability and simultaneously disperse and conceal the second strike force. In the current environment of mobile system on land and SSBNs at sea, the probability of destruction of the adversary strategic assets will be extremely difficult, this, therefore, limits own retaliatory nuclear strikes to counter value targets, once again a strategic operational dilemma.

Under the survivability factor, NFU policy requires a very extensive and elaborate missile defence system to protect the nation and vital retaliatory systems; however, a system of this magnitude will require resources and technology that may be counterproductive from the financial angle, thus, a realistic system will allow defence at select points, leaving the nation exposed to nuclear strikes. The situation is further complicated by China and Pakistan possessing a large arsenal of similar nuclear and conventional missiles which can be used to overwhelm any limited BMD, leaving the nation exposed.

These arguments, while cogent, are perhaps somewhat exaggerated in particular with respect to the need of an elaborate Ballistic Missile Defense (BMD) system. Neither the Pakistani nor the Chinese possess an infinite number of nuclear warheads though it is admitted that saturation of a limited BMD network might be feasible. Moreover, whether adopting an NFU doctrine or not, India would be required to develop a survivable command and control system with a viable second-strike capability as the first-strike doctrine would necessarily invite retaliation, thus requiring India's capabilities to be survivable. It is therefore submitted that at least some of Lt General Nagal's apprehensions are overstated.

However, if one were to accept the validity of Lt General's concerns, his alternative of a policy of ambiguity might be worth examining as he elucidated in an earlier issue of *Force*:[28]

> It is time to review our policy of NFU. The other choices are ambiguity or first use. Ambiguity has four sub-options of first use i.e. pre-emption, launch on warning (LoW), launch on launch (LoL) and NFU. Pre-emption gives the choice of time, targets and scale to the initiator and will pay the best dividends to safeguard the nation but it is also the most destabilising if announced to the adversary, but better than NFU.
>
> The options of LoW have most first use advantages except there is a small window of opportunity for its execution, it depends on fine political judgment, but ensures protection of the country, and causes damage to the adversary's leadership, arsenal and strategic targets. LoL is dependent on real time surveillance and intelligence, has an extremely small window of a few minutes for decision-making, with a very large number of nuclear weapons on hair trigger alert, and is destabilising. The change from NFU to ambiguity will require better surveillance and monitoring systems, real time intelligence, high alert state of nuclear forces during crisis/war, better and faster readiness state in peace.
>
> A change of policy to ambiguity is recommended, as it encompasses four options including NFU. The benefits that accrue include deterring first strike on India. It may be called destabilising, but four other nuclear weapon states follow this policy. It enhances and improves the psychological state of the nation. A shift to a proactive policy is reassuring to the public. It does not allow destruction of the nation and strategic forces at the outset; hence the arsenal is intact for use. It provides a better range of options to launch decapitating and/ or disarming strikes to deal with the adversary leadership/ arsenal, and allows a proactive CBM policy.

---

28. B. S. Nagal, "Guest Column | Checks and Balances: A Regular Review and Appraisal of the Nuclear Doctrine would Help to Fine Tune it As Per Strategic Requirements," *Force*, (June 2014). http://forceindia.net/guest-column/guest-column-b-s-nagal/checks-and-balances/, accessed on March 18, 2018.

On the other hand, it is suggested that this policy of ambiguity might actually embody the worst of all scenarios. With clarity neither on NFU nor on a first-strike approach, the possibility of a doctrine of ambiguity destabilising what strategic balance might exist would be a distinct possibility. Furthermore, a shift to a policy of ambiguity, after having published, adhering to one of NFU could negate whatever diplomatic credits might have accrued to India through its adoption of the NFU doctrine. In addition, any overt shift would create wholly understandable alarm in Beijing owing to China's own NFU doctrine. In such circumstances, it is difficult to discern what advantage, either operationally, strategically or diplomatically, might be obtained from a shift in India's consistent assertion of its NFU doctrine. However, a much greater concern for all observers of India's Nuclear Doctrine, as has been alluded to before, is whether there is a consistent approach to India's nuclear weapons doctrine both in word and in practice.

A more significant issue, as indicated earlier in this chapter, is whether those articulating NFU have a clear understanding of the nuances therein. In nuclear issues, phraseology is important. One particular paragraph in Menon's book could potentially imply that India has not ruled out a strike before an adversary actually *detonates* a nuclear weapon against an Indian target:[29]

> *There is a potential gray area as to when India would use nuclear weapons first against another NWS [nuclear weapons state]. Circumstances are conceivable in which India might find it useful to strike first, for instance, against an NWS that had declared it would certainly use its weapons, and if India were certain that [an] adversary's launch was imminent.*

On the face of it, a literal interpretation of India's Nuclear Doctrine would suggest that the above scenario was precluded by NFU. However, that Menon chose to raise such a case might suggest that there has been some consideration given to the matter. It must be stressed, however, that *certainty* of an adversary's launch would be an extremely difficult

---

29. Op.cit. n.25.

proposition for India to ensure. Even with an elaborate provision for launch detection and effective intelligence of an adversary's intention, the practical difficulties in guaranteeing that, for example, an enemy missile launch is carrying a nuclear warhead should preclude abrogating the NFU doctrine in such circumstances.

It does not, however, preclude the use of conventional weapons to destroy an adversary's delivery systems before launch. While India still lacks sufficient assets to ensure a completely effective conventional counterforce strike, it is not inconceivable that India could, without perhaps undue difficulty, target munitions stockpiles and individual mobile missile launchers as part of a broader military campaign with, in the case of the short-range Nasr, a fair chance of success.

India's Nuclear Strategy: Combining Doctrine and Capability

Chitrapu Uday Bhaskar, reviewing Dr Manpreet Sethi's excellent 2009 book entitled 'Nuclear Strategy: India's March towards Credible Deterrence', noted that the aforesaid author stated that:[30]

> ...nuclear strategy must strike a balance between maintaining secrecy for enhancing deterrence while simultaneously allowing transparency, also for enhancing deterrence. Deterrence itself is visualised as a 'three-legged stool'— the legs being: capability, resolve to use that capability, and the communication of both—the capability and the resolve—to the adversary

In this respect, India's nuclear strategy is trying to construct that balance between secrecy and transparency for enhancing deterrence while simultaneously building its capability as well as shoring up confidence in its resolve to use that capability in addition to trying to communicate the same to its prospective adversaries. While India has been successful in building its capabilities and its resolve is as yet something untested—just as in the case of all nuclear powers—the communication of its capability and resolve has been less than satisfactory. It has been somewhat successful

---

30. Chitrapu Uday Bhaskar, "India's Nuclear Deterrence Strategy," *The Hindu*, (March 30, 2010), http://www.thehindu.com/books/Indias-nuclear-deterrence-strategy/article16630532.ece, accessed on November 13, 2017.

in communicating the former, but less so the latter. That being said, from the understanding that we have of India's capability, putative resolve and move towards credible deterrence, which inferences can we draw to suggest a nuclear strategy for India combining the vision outlined in its doctrine matched to its capabilities? India's doctrine speaks of a "credible minimum deterrent". India has never quantified what it has seen as a 'minimum' number. Nor should it. While the deterrent established and sustained should be well into the triple digits, expecting a number to be spelled out is completely unrealistic. However, in principle, the concept of the credible minimum deterrent means that India needs to match the numbers of its adversaries.

The numbers necessary for achieving this would be calculated on the bases of what Manpreet Sethi calls, "retributive unacceptable punishment" for the adversary and the level of survivability that can be ensured for India's own arsenal after absorbing a nuclear first strike.[31] Sethi's calculations suggest that if a minimum of 40–50 weapons are needed to inflict unacceptable damage upon an adversary, then given a survivability rate of 25 percent after the first strike by a 'second-tier' nuclear power like China, perhaps a little higher in the case of Pakistan, then at least 200 weapons would be needed plus a contingency for weapon malfunctions to provide the credible minimum deterrence that India seeks.[32] The size of India's potential arsenal and the various permutations and combinations of the arsenal needed by India have been extensively covered in an earlier chapter but Sethi's calculations are broadly in accord with the lower to midrange estimates of the desirable arsenal and thus carry a degree of pragmatism combined with an appreciation of the reality of India's existing and, short-term feasible fissile material and delivery systems production.

A nuclear strategy against China does not require India to match China warhead for warhead but, as indicated in an earlier chapter and citing Brigadier Gurmeet Kanwal, who notes that soft area targets such as the population and industrial centres that are likely to be the primary targets of India's countervalue and to destroy 10 such countervalue

---

31. Manpreet Sethi, *Nuclear Strategy: India's march towards Credible Deterrence* (New Delhi: KW Publishers, 2009), p. 253.
32. Ibid, p. 252.

targets in China, India would need a total of 40 nuclear warheads (at four 200-kt-warheads per target or as many as ten −20 kt warheads per target) to cause unacceptable damage on those cities or other countervalue targets chosen.

India should formulate its strategy using a two-fold approach. It should seek to undertake conventional modernisation to raise the nuclear threshold while at the same time, it needs to enhance the credibility of its deterrent by increasing the survivability of its arsenal by a combination of dispersal, hardened storage and increasing the number of warheads and delivery systems in order to ensure that the largest number of warheads and delivery systems survive a determined first-strike from China.[33] This combination provides a practical approach to both conventional strategy and nuclear deterrence versus China but does require budgetary support.

Against Pakistan, a viable nuclear strategy is rather more complicated in devising, this being directly related to its development of TNWs and its apparent desire to use them as a putative shield against Indian conventional attack. It is suggested that in this regard, India should give consideration for intensifying the preparedness of its conventional forces to operate in a CBRN environment, harden its military facilities against such an attack and also prepare its civil defence assets to deal with the results of a limited nuclear strike close to a populated area. This should have the effect of raising the nuclear threshold.

Furthermore, India should signal these developments unapologetically and without equivocation. In respect to its nuclear arsenal, it is suggested that India should consider dedicating a portion of its delivery system towards deterring Pakistan—making it 'Pakistan-specific'—and indicate the same. To some extent, this has already happened with the development of the Agni-I missile and has been hinted at during the testing of the Nirbhay cruise missile and the Shaurya system. The development of a BMD system to protect key cities and military installations may also be a potential asset for Indian deterrence versus Pakistan.

---

33. Ibid. See also Gurmeet Kanwal, "India's Nuclear Force Structure," *Institute for Defence Studies and Analyses*, (September 2000), http://www.idsa-india.org/an-sept2-00.html

Conclusion

The Indian Nuclear Doctrine has given rise to much comment, speculation and analysis. Yet, it has remained officially unchanged since 2003. As has been discussed, the doctrine is significantly more flexible than the traditional discourse may indicate and may have moved India towards a 'flexible response approach'. Yet, the communication of this has been poor and a degree of clarity should be encouraged in this regard. Better yet, consideration could be given to rewording the doctrine with a view to clarifying its intent. This would require a shift in the hitherto somewhat stoic and consistent affirmations of the current doctrine with its existing wording.

India has, as noted, built up its nuclear capabilities and its command and control is now securely in place. All the building blocks for a credible nuclear deterrent are in place. This deterrent combined with the doctrine hints at the approach to nuclear strategy that India will take. It is suggested that against both China and Pakistan, India should adopt a dual approach of raising the nuclear threshold by a combination of enhanced conventional deterrence with passive and active CBRN preparedness while simultaneously enhancing the credibility, survivability and efficacy of its own deterrent to ensure that retaliation after a first-strike is devastatingly effective. To date, however, India's efforts in CBRN preparedness and in developing its arsenal in respect of the numbers needed to ensure both credibility and survivability are not entirely clear. It is an unfortunate product of a combination of excessive secrecy, deliberate ambiguity and general uninformed discourse on national security issues that no clarity has been forthcoming, except for spotty, and at times confusing press releases and sound-bites.

The debate over India's continued adherence to an NFU doctrine is somewhat exaggerated with Indian pronouncements being taken somewhat out of context and at times an alarmist interpretation. However, there is no doubt that calls for India to review its nuclear doctrine have been ongoing for at least the last 4 years and it is probable that periodic reviews have been given consideration. As to the suggestion that India should abandon the NFU doctrine in favour of a doctrine of 'ambiguity', it is submitted that while the reasons for doing so may appear reasonable at present, there are potential consequences of such a shift, none of which seem to offer any significant advantage to India and have the potential of adversely impacting security.

There is one aspect that needs attention—clarity of wording and meaning. While keeping an adversary guessing about what the wording of a doctrine means could be perceived as an advantage, the problem arises when Indian scholars and informed writers confuse the issue with a variety of interpretations, each of which could have unintended consequences. As has been noted above, the wording of paragraphs in books or articles has a considerable meaning with respect to the analysis of India's nuclear strategy and doctrine and in such circumstances, it behoves both official and quasi-official sources to be consistent in their approach. While this should in no way seek to limit debate, it should be noted that misunderstanding, exaggeration and confusion seem to be the hallmark of the discourse to date. Yet, India seems committed to its credible minimum deterrent and at least the principle of NFU has shown no official indication of a change in either position. Its nuclear strategy, therefore, has evolved accordingly.

8

The Path Ahead: Shaping India's Nuclear Strategy in the Years to Come

—※—

India is perhaps unique among the nuclear powers in that its doctrine, strategy and capability remain discussed under a veil of secrecy so dense that making informed assessments of Indian intentions, force levels, capabilities or even threat perception is somewhat difficult. Yet, India has moved towards a coherent doctrine that reflects a degree of strategic maturity but has been poorly articulated by successive governments of India. Furthermore, there is a degree of uncertainty regarding India's capabilities which, despite the attempts of successive governments and their scientific advisors to clarity, remains to date.

Yet, one must now look forward to a path ahead. How will India's nuclear strategy evolve? Will India opt for a review of its nuclear no-first-use (NFU) doctrine or will it choose to manifest its nuclear strategy with NFU as its central tenet? These are core questions that will find answers eventually but on the basis of the analysis that has been undertaken in the foregoing chapters, the following observations might be made in respect to the challenges India faces:

• India will find itself faced with a growing Pakistani arsenal which will include increasingly advanced intermediate-range ballistic missiles (IRBMs) and medium-range ballistic missiles (MRBMs)—possibly with multiple independently targetable reentry vehicles (MIRVs). Pakistan has made its nuclear arsenal a critical component of its military strategy and while arguments can be made as to whether its doctrine is credible or not, Pakistan has proceeded to integrate its nuclear weapons into its military thinking in a way that India has not thus far done. It has further apparently accorded very high priority to bolstering its production capacity for weapons-grade plutonium as well as its ability to manufacture delivery systems. It is also pertinent to note that Pakistan has moved towards building a nuclear triad, albeit a triad limited by its lack of ballistic missile nuclear submarine (SSBNs).

- Pakistan's development and deployment of tactical nuclear weapons (TNWs) has effectively lowered the nuclear threshold while simultaneously potentially limiting India's ability to deploy its conventional forces against Pakistan. Pakistan's deployment of the short-range Nasr missile with its purported nuclear warheads is clearly intended for use against battlefield targets and though the effectiveness of TNWs against armoured formations is highly questionable, the fact that Pakistan has placed such emphasis on these weapons is a potentially ominous portent of its intentions to use such weapons in the event of hostilities.

- China's nuclear doctrine and strategy are continuously evolving as that nation continues its military modernisation efforts. Unlike either India or Pakistan, China has a well-articulated, debated and developed nuclear doctrine which it seems to have consistently followed in letter as well as spirit. While China's deployment of more intercontinental ballistic missiles (ICBMs), MIRVs and SSBNs with submarine-launched ballistic missiles (SLBMs) with intercontinental range are primarily aimed at achieving a degree of strategic parity with the United States, India must be vigilant as China replaces older IRBMs and MRBMs with newer, more accurate and more mobile systems. Furthermore, China's large arsenal of conventionally armed MRBMs and short-range ballistic missiles (SRBMs) will pose significant challenges for Indian planners as the deployment of such systems has the potential to disrupt Indian air operations and target Indian logistics depots and troop concentrations.

- China is intent on demonstrating technological prowess approaching that of the United States with its antisatellite (ASAT) program, its ICBMs and its conventional military build-up. This extends to the sphere of ballistic missile defence (BMD). China's BMD efforts have been relatively low-key to date but there have been at least four exoatmospheric interception tests. This has serious implications for India as India's concept of credible minimum deterrence will have to inevitably be revised in terms of numbers to overcome any deployed defences.

To date, India's response to these challenges is a phased and evolutionary approach to the development of its delivery systems, an assertion of its stated nuclear doctrine and a guarded approach to revealing its levels of preparedness to deal with a nuclear strike. India has further consistently reiterated its self-imposed moratorium on nuclear testing and has tried to refute persistent attempts to question the quality of its nuclear deterrent and the size of its arsenal. Moreover, despite separating its civilian and nuclear programs, it has kept a number of nuclear reactors outside the ambit of International Atomic Energy Agency safeguards but has never admitted their use for weapons. From these broad parameters, we may draw the following conclusions about existing nuclear strategy:

- India's nuclear arsenal is evolving with the Agni-IV and Agni-V missiles destined to form the core of its land-based mobile IRBM/ ICBM force. Its efforts to develop a nuclear triad are at present in progress with the INS Arihant undergoing trails while her sister-ships are being prepared for launch. The Indian Air Force's role has been somewhat downgraded as its aircraft currently lack a stand-off long-range cruise missile capable of delivering nuclear warheads. The Strategic Forces Command (SFC) is the designated body tasked with the management of the Indian arsenal, though the delivery systems remain part of the armed service to which they were assigned. As one of only two operational tri-service commands in India—the other being the Andaman and Nicobar Fortress Command—the SFC has devised mechanisms to ensure the smooth operational deployment of the components of the Indian arsenal.
- While not overtly stating so, India's strategy against Pakistan has been largely-decoupled from its strategy against China. This is evident from the priorities accorded to weapons development—the Agni-I MRBM remains India's primary weapons delivery system against Pakistan, replacing the shorter-ranged Prithvi missiles and little priority has

been accorded to the Shaurya canister-launched MRBM that might have been a possible candidate to supplement and later supplant the Agni-I. In contrast, India has given priority to developing the Agni-II, Agni-III, Agni-IV and Agni-V systems, all of which are likely to be deployable against China as opposed to Pakistan. India has sought to enhance the readiness levels of its SFC through periodic tests of its ballistic missiles by the respective units operating the Prithvi and Agni families of missiles but has been very wary of revealing any details of the SFC, its functioning or its order of battle.

- The size of the Indian arsenal is clouded in mystery. Part of that is understandable ambiguity but much of the confusion stems from the status of the eight unsafeguarded Canada Deuterium Uranium-type power reactors that could be used for the production of weapons-grade plutonium. Estimates of the Indian arsenal appear only to consider production from the Dhruva reactor and the now decommissioned CIRUS research reactor. Moreover, Indian nuclear weapons design will have a direct impact on the size of a deployable arsenal. Uncertainty over India's thermonuclear weapons continues to persist with speculation that the large payload capacity of the Agni series of missiles is intended for fusion-boosted-fission weapons with yields of several hundred kilotons but heavier than comparable pure fusion weapons and significantly more profligate in the use of fissile material. Miniaturisation does not appear to be an issue.

- Similar confusion persists over the number of nuclear delivery systems currently deployed by India. There is some evidence to show the production of over 200 Prithvi SRBMs but little evidence to suggest that production on a similar scale has taken place for the Agni missiles. Circumstantial evidence suggests that one group is being created for each Agni variant with an establishment of 12 launchers and an anticipated two missiles per launcher. Evidence also points to some 48 Agni-V missiles being planned for production over a four-year period with orders for that number of trailers being placed in 2015. It is entirely unclear whether similar numbers are planned for the other Agni variants but the number of deployable missiles does place an upper limit on the number of nuclear weapons India has likely deployed or is likely to deploy in the short to medium term. Whether the nascent SSBN and SLBM forces are deployed as expected—with delays being inevitable—there will be additional force accretions to the missile and warhead stockpiles. Furthermore, as India moves to deploy canister-launched missiles—the Agni-V initially—the concept of having a de-mated arsenal for recessed deterrence is seemingly abandoned in favour of a more practical approach which will require additional safeguards.

- India has chosen not to actively encourage its armed forces to develop a nuclear warfighting doctrine but has taken steps to improve its chemical, biological, radiological and nuclear (CBRN) passive defences, especially in its army formations facing Pakistan. While some limited publicity has been accorded to CBRN-protected troops participating in exercises, there is as yet no indication of such passive defensive measures being extended to troops facing China, although it is unlikely that any provision of such equipment will be publicised. Little indication of either Indian Air Force or Indian navy CBRN defensive measures has been given to date. Much research work has been done on BMD systems but a deployable two-tier BMD network is some years away.

- Indian command, control and communications systems are reputed to be hardened to survive a nuclear attack and the effects thereof. This has been publicly stated and is applicable to the Nuclear Command Authority (NCA) and the secondary NCA as well. However, it is somewhat unclear as to how survivable the Indian arsenal is. India has emphasised mobile land-based missile systems, with submarine-launched missiles now being developed. These are somewhat more survivable than fixed silos but it has been noted that India has invested in survivable mountain storage sites for its missiles and warheads to safeguard them from an enemy first-strike while maintaining the ability to be rapidly deployable. As India moves towards a viable SSBN capability—especially when longer range SLBMs become available—the survivability quotient of the Indian arsenal will be significantly enhanced with no adversary assured of being able to launch an effective counterforce first strike on India.

- India has made some efforts to prepare itself for a nontraditional CBRN attack, with some resources being allocated for both preventative measures and amelioration of the effects of an attack. These include the creation of the National Disaster Response Force, the establishment of the National Disaster Management Authority and the creation of some hardened facilities to protect communications and information from an electromagnetic pulse (EMP) attack. However, these measures are inadequate and a more thorough review of India's preparedness to counter the impact of a nontraditional CBRN attack has to be undertaken, especially with regard to its level of protection or its ability to recover from an EMP strike, whether as a result of a nuclear explosion or generated through non-nuclear means. Moreover, India's fire and emergency and other civil defence services are wholly inadequate, lacking the manpower, equipment and resources to enable them to function effectively.

- India's Nuclear Doctrine is stated to be based on the principles of NFU and 'massive retaliation'. Despite calls for the doctrine to be reviewed and revised in light of Pakistan's deployment of TNWs, India has remained adamant that it will adhere to the NFU principle and continues to state that any nuclear first-strike would lead to massive retaliation. However, it is to be noted that there is considerable divergence of opinion as to whether the Indian doctrine is inflexible or whether it possesses a degree of nuance and flexibility that could perhaps indicate that India may choose to respond 'disproportionately' rather than 'massively' with the connotations that the latter policy entails for solely attacking countervalue targets. This debate continues and it is interesting to note that India has not chosen to officially clarify its position in respect of its doctrinal nuances.

In light of what is currently known about India's strategy, it is pertinent to note that, whether intentionally or not, India has effectively created a somewhat ambiguous nuclear strategy. This has some benefits as it keeps adversaries guessing about its intent. On the other hand, it also proves to be somewhat confusing as to India's intentions and its capabilities in the event of a nuclear or other CBRN attack from an adversary. This confusion, it is submitted, may not be in India's interest as Pakistan in particular, has shown itself to be remarkably incompetent at reading India's resolve to respond to provocations as evidenced in Kargil. Nonetheless, in concluding, the following suggestions are made with a view to improving India's existing strategy:

- India needs to accelerate its production of fissile material and delivery systems with a view to creating a large enough arsenal to be able to survive a Chinese first-strike as well as to overwhelm any BMD system the latter may develop. This is already well within India's means and could be achieved by accelerated and expanded Agni-V production and by diverting at least two power reactors to fissile material production. Moreover, the development of longer-range missiles, especially land-based ICBMs and SLBMs will have to be undertaken.

- While not advocating a resumption of nuclear testing, at least not yet, India must refine its weapons designs with the aim of producing reliable weapons, which have the confidence of the user, and which make efficient use of fissile material. India would need to increase its investment in simulation facilities, inertial confinement fusion facilities and subcritical and hydro-nuclear testing systems. The decision on a resumption of nuclear testing is a political one but, given the nuclear tests undertaken by the Democratic People's Republic of Korea (DPRK) and the somewhat reticent international response to the DPRK/Pakistan nuclear/missile cooperation effort, India may wish to consider a resumption of testing to validate its thermonuclear weapons and its warhead designs. While there will inevitably be repercussions for such resumption, the cost-benefit ratio could favour such a step in the near future and while the repercussions cannot be understated, the potential strategic benefits could be worth the risk.

- Defensive measures such as the hardening of military and key civilian systems and infrastructure from both the impact and the effects of a CBRN attack have to receive a higher level of priority. Protection against EMP effects as well as fallout has to be provided as a matter of urgency. In addition, preparation of India's armed forces to fight in a contaminated environment has to be stepped-up with passive and active CBRN defences being deployed in sufficient quantities to provide protection to all of India's combat and combat support assets. This again is well within India's capabilities as much of its protective equipment is domestically designed and produced and merely requires increased orders and production.

- Defensive measures also entail the deployment of BMD systems for the defence of key military and civilian targets with a large-scale deployment of theatre missile defence systems to guard against short- and medium-range conventional missile attacks on military targets. While a nationwide strategic BMD system is not practical, a limited BMD system protecting some cities as well as strategic assets is very much viable. However, this will take time and some imports will be necessary. In the process, India must enhance its space-based assets to create an effective missile warning network and should consider the development of ASAT systems to incapacitate an adversary's systems.

- India cannot separate conventional and nuclear strategies. This is particularly true for China where India, in order to achieve effective deterrence, must enhance its conventional capabilities alongside its nuclear assets. In doing so, India would effectively raise the nuclear threshold as well as reduce the risk of hostile military action on the part of China.

- Finally, India needs to develop the confidence to articulate its nuclear stance clearly. It has made a start in this direction but, as we have seen, there is much room for interpretation. With strong capabilities at its disposal, India should not shy away from engaging in a discussion on its doctrine and the nuances thereof. It should not be apologetic about having nuclear weapons or about its doctrine and move to dispel any confusion about either.

Bibliography

1. Lawrence Freedman, "Nuclear Strategy," *Britannica*, https://www.britannica.com/topic/nuclear-strategy

2. Gregory Kulacki. "The Chinese Military Updates China's Nuclear Strategy," *Union of Concerned Scientists,* March 2015.

3. Hans M. Kristensen and Robert S. Norris, "Chinese Nuclear Forces," *Bulletin of the Atomic Scientists* vol. 72, no. 4, 2016.

4. Philip A. Karber, "Strategic Implications of China's Underground Great Wall," *Georgetown University Asian Arms Control Project,* September 11, 2011

5. M. Taylor Fravel and Evan S. Medeiros, "China's Search for Assured Retaliation: The Evolution of Chinese Nuclear Strategy and Force Structure," "International Security vol. 35, no. 2.

6. The Federation of American Scientists, "The Science of Military Strategy 2013," https://fas.org/nuke/guide/china/sms-2013.pdf

7. Anthony H. Cordesman with Joseph Kendall and Steven Colley, "China's Nuclear Forces and Weapons of Mass Destruction," *CSIS,* Working Draft: July 20, 2016

8. Chinese State Council Information Office, "China's National Defense in 2008," http://www.china.org.cn/government/central_government/2009-01/20/content_17155577_9.html

9. "China's National Defense in 2010," People's Republic of China Information Office of the State Council, March 31, 2011.

10. People's Republic of China Information Office of the State Council, "China's Military Strategy," *Xinhu,* May 26, 2015, Strategic Guideline for Active Defense, http://eng.mod.gov.cn/DefenseNews/2015-05/26/content_4586748.htm

11. Hans M. Kristensen and Robert S. Norris, "Pakistani Nuclear Forces," *Bulletin of the Atomic Scientists* vol. 72, no. 6, 2016.

12. " Week view No. PR94/2011-ISPR," (April 19, 2011). .https://www.ispr.gov.pk/front/main.asp?o=t-press_release&date=2011/4/19

13. "Press release No. PR248/2014-ISPR," (November 13, 2014). https://www.ispr.gov.pk/front/main.asp?o=t-press_release&date=2014/11/13

14. National Air and Space Intelligence Center (NASIC), "Ballistic and Cruise Missile Threat," (2013). http://fas.org/programs/ssp/nukes/nuclearweapons/NASIC2013_050813.pdf

15. "Press release No. PR92/2014-ISPR," (April 15, 2015). https://www.ispr.gov.pk/front/main.asp?o=t-press_release&date=2015/4/15

16. "Press release No. PR61/2015-ISPR. Inter Services Public Relations," (March 9, 2015). https://www.ispr.gov.pk/front/main.asp?o=t-press_release&date=2015/3/9

17. "Press release No. PR16/2016-ISPR. Inter Services Public Relations," (January 19, 2016). https://www.ispr.gov.pk/front/main.asp?o=t-press_release&date=2016/1/19

18. "Press release PR122/2012-ISPR," (May 19, 2012). https://www.ispr.gov.pk/front/main.asp?o=t-press_release&date=2012/5/19

19. A Conversation With Gen. Khalid Kidwai. 2015. "Carnegie International Nuclear Policy Conference 2015." Carnegie Endowment for International Peace. Transcript, 4–5, March 23. http://carnegieendowment.org/files/03-230315carnegieKIDWAI.pdf

20. Sanjay Badri-Maharaj, The Importance of Passive and Active CBRN Defensive Measures," *Institute for Defence Studies and Analyses: IDSA Issue Brief,* (October 17, 2016). https://idsa.in/issuebrief/importance-of-passive-and-active-cbrn-defensive-measures_sbmaharaj_171016

21. "We Have Low-yield N-weapons to Ward Off India's War Threat: Pakistan," *India Today,* October 20, 2015. http://indiatoday.intoday.in/articlePrint.jsp?aid=503185

22. George Perkovich, *India's Nuclear Bomb: The Impact on Global Proliferation* (London: University of California Press, 1999).

23. Bharat Karnad, Nuclear Weapons and Indian Security (New Delhi: Macmillan India Ltd, 2002).

24. R Raj Chengappa, Weapons of Peace (New Delhi: Harper Collins Publishers India, 2000), p. 327.

25. Shiv Aroor, "10 Reasons Why the Indian Rafale is Evolution Itself," *Daily O, (*July 04, 2017). http://www.dailyo.in/variety/rafale-aircraft-brahmos-nuclear-defence/story/1/18157.html, accessed on September 4, 2017).

26. Mrigank Tiwari, "Unprecedented Security at Trishul Airbase," *Times of India,* (January 03, 2016). http://timesofindia.indiatimes.com/city/bareilly/Unprecedented-security-at-Trishul-airbase/articleshow/50430273.cms

27. "India Plans Next Generation Bombproof Shelter for 108 Fighter Jets," *Sputnik News,* (July 03, 2017). https://sputniknews.com/military/201707031055187413-india-shelter-jets/, accessed September 04, 2017.

28. Bharat Karnad, *India's Nuclear Policy* (Westport, Connecticut: Praeger Security International 2008).

29. Raj Chengappa, "The Missile Man," *India Today,* April 15, 1994, pp. 40–42.

30. Manvendra Singh, "Agni-II adds Firepower to N-Deterrence," *Indian Express,* April 12, 1999.

31. Y. Mallikarjun, "Agni-II Missile Test-Fired Successfully," *The Hindu,* (May 17, 2010). http://www.thehindu.com/news/national/Agni-II-missile-test-fired-successfully/article16302660.ece, accessed on September 05, 2017.

32. T. Subramaniam and Y. Mallikarjun, "Agni-II Soars in Success," *The Hindu,* (September 30, 2011). http://www.thehindu.com/news/national/agniii-soars-in-success/article2499781.ece.

33. "Odisha: Nuclear capable Agni-II missile successfully test fired," *IBN Live,* (April 07, 2013). https://archive.is/20130628175643/http://www.bharat-rakshak.com/NEWS/newsrf.php.

34. "India Successfully Test-Fires Nuclear Capable Agni-II Missile Off Odisha Coast," *News 18,* (November 09, 2014). http://www.news18.com/news/india/india-successfully-test-fires-nuclear-capable-agni-ii-missile-off-odisha-coast-724952.html.

35. "India Test Fires Medium Range Nuclear Capable Agni-II Missile**,**" *Economic Times,* (February 20, 2018) https://economictimes.indiatimes.com/news/defence/india-test-fires-agni-ii-missile-off-odisha-coast/articleshow/62993975.cms.

36. "DRDO told to Test Upgraded Agni in August," *Deccan Chronicle,* July 15, 1998.

37. "India Successfully Test-fires N-capable Agni-I Ballistic Missile," *News 18,* (November 22, 2016). http://www.news18.com/news/india/india-successfully-tests-nuclear-capable-agni-i-ballistic-missile-1314397.html

38. "India Successfully Test-Fires Nuclear Capable Agni-1," *Times of India,* (February 06, 2018). https://timesofindia.indiatimes.com/india/india-successfully-test-fires-nuclear-capable-agni-1/articleshow/62801316.cms

39. T. Subramanian and Y. Mallikarjun, "Agni-III test-fired successfully," *The Hindu*, (May 08, 2008). http://www.thehindu.com/todays-paper/Agni-III-test-fired-successfully/article15218480.ece

40. Y. Mallikarjun, "Agni-III Test-Fired Successfully," *The Hindu*, (September 21, 2012). http://www.thehindu.com/news/national/agniiii-testfired-successfully/article3922230.ece

41. "Agni-III Successfully Test Fired from Odisha Coast," *Economic Times*, (April 16, 2015). http://economictimes.indiatimes.com/news/defence/agni-iii-successfully-test-fired-from-odisha-coast/articleshow/46941664.cms

42. "India Test-Fires Nuclear-Capable Agni III Ballistic Missile," *Economic Times*, (April 27, 2017). http://economictimes.indiatimes.com/news/defence/india-test-fires-nuclear-capable-agni-iii-ballistic-missile/articleshow/58396268.cms

43. PTI "Agni III could have 5,000 km Range: Russian General," *The Hindu*, http://www.defencetalk.com/forums/missiles-wmds/indian-nuclear-missile-development-news-discussions-7241-11/

44. "India to Test Fire Agni-V by Year-End," *The Hindu*, (June 03, 2011). http://www.thehindu.com/sci-tech/science/India-to-test-fire-Agni-V-by-year-end/article13821309.ece

45. "Long Range Strategic Missile Agni-IV Test-Fired," *The Hindu*, (September 19, 2012). http://www.thehindu.com/sci-tech/science/long-range-strategic-missile-agniiv-testfired/article3914340.ece

46. T. Subramanian, "Agni-IV Missile Successfully Test Fired," *The Hindu*, (January 20, 2014). http://www.thehindu.com/news/national/agniiv-missile-successfully-test-fired/article5596563.ece

47. Y. Mallikarjun, AMP and T. Subramanian, "Agni-V Propels India into Elite ICBM Club," *The Hindu*, (April 19, 2012). http://www.thehindu.com/news/national/agniv-propels-india-into-elite-icbm-club/article3330921.ece?homepage=true

48. "India Test-Fires Agni V with Range as far as China," *Hindustan Times*, (September 16, 2013). http://www.hindustantimes.com/india/india-test-fires-agni-v-with-range-as-far-as-china/story-28IHgfrhxGgUt9XLNPRiwN.html

49. Y. Mallikarjun and T. Subramanian, "Agni-V's Maiden Canister Trial a Roaring Success," *The Hindu*, (January 31, 2015). http://www.thehindu.com/news/national/maiden-canister-trial-of-agniv-a-roaring-success/article6841942.ece

50. Rajat Pandit, "India test-fires nuclear-capable ICBM Agni-V," *Times of India*, (January 18, 2018). https://timesofindia.indiatimes.com/india/india-test-fires-nuclear-capable-icbm-agni-v/articleshow/62550347.cms.

51. Hemant Kumar Rout, "India successfully test fires Agni-V missile for a reduced range," *New Indian Express*, (December 26, 2016). http://www.newindianexpress.com/nation/2016/dec/26/india-successfully-test-fires-agni-v-missile-for-a-reduced-range-1553219.html

52. "Agni-V can reach targets 8,000 km away: Chinese expert," *The Hindu*, (April 21, 2012). http://www.thehindu.com/todays-paper/tp-in-school/agniv-can-reach-targets-8000-km-away-chinese-expert/article3337202.ece

53. Dinakar Peri, "Now, India has a nuclear triad," *The Hindu*, (October 18, 2016). http://www.thehindu.com/news/national/Now-India-has-a-nuclear-triad/article16074127.ece

54. Ananatha Krishna M., "K-15 SLBM is a Beast with Gen-Next Tech," *New Indian Express*, (January 30, 2013). http://www.newindianexpress.com/nation/2013/jan/30/k-15-slbm-is-a-beast-with-gen-next-tech-445756.html

55. Violet Pereira, "N-capable Arihant submarine successfully test-fires unarmed missile," *Magalorean*, (November 26, 2015). http://www.mangalorean.com/n-capable-arihant-submarine-successfully-test-fires-unarmed-missile/

56. Ankit Panda, "India Inches Closer to Credible Nuclear Triad With K-4 SLBM Test," *The Diplomat*, (May 13, 2014). http://thediplomat.com/2014/05/india-inches-closer-to-credible-nuclear-triad-with-k-4-slbm-test/

57. Franz-Stefan Gady, "India Successfully Tests New Ballistic Missile," *The Diplomat*, (March 22, 2016). http://thediplomat.com/2016/03/india-successfully-tests-new-ballistic-missile/

58. Hemant Kumar Rout, "EXPRESS EXCLUSIVE: Maiden Test of Undersea K-4 Missile From Arihant Submarine," http://www.newindianexpress.com/nation/2016/apr/09/EXPRESS-EXCLUSIVE-Maiden-Test-of-Undersea-K-4-Missile-From-Arihant-Submarine-921990.html

59. Manu Pubby, "Setback for Indian missile programme: Two failures in a week, submarine version stuck," *The Print*, (December 24, 2017). https://theprint.in/2017/12/24/setback-for-indian-missile-programme-two-failures-in-a-week-submarine-version-stuck/, accessed on January 10, 2018.

60. Sandeep Unnithan, "From India Today magazine: A Peek into India's Top Secret and Costliest Defence Project, Nuclear Submarines," *India Today*, (December 07, 2017). http://indiatoday.intoday.in/story/india-ballistic-missile-submarine-k-6-submarine-launched-drdo/1/1104982.html

61. Manu Pubby, "India's Only Nuclear-Armed Submarine is Back in the Water after Contamination Fears," *The Print*, (January 08, 2018). https://theprint.in/2018/01/08/indias-only-nuclear-armed-submarine-ins-arihant-is-back-in-the-water/

62. "Indian Navy successfully test fires Dhanush missile: All you need to know," *India Today*, (November 26, 2015). http://indiatoday.intoday.in/education/story/dhanush/1/531950.html

63. Shiv Aroor, "True' BrahMos Unleashed Today, Next 900-km Weapon," *Livefist Defence*. https://www.livefistdefence.com/2017/03/true-brahmos-unleashed-today-next-1000-km-weapon.html

64. T.S. Subramanian, "Nirbhay Likely to be Test-Fired in April," *The Hindu*, (March 07, 2012). http://www.thehindu.com/todays-paper/tp-national/nirbhay-likely-to-be-testfired-in-april/article2968219.ece

65. Y. Mallikarjun and T. Subramanian, "Nirbhay Strays from Flight Path, Aborted," *The Hindu*, (March 12, 2013). http://www.thehindu.com/news/national/nirbhay-strays-from-flight-path-aborted/article4500527.ece

66. "India Test-Fires Nuclear-Capable Nirbhay Cruise Missile," *Times of India*, (October 17, 2014). http://timesofindia.indiatimes.com/india/India-test-fires-nuclear-capable-Nirbhay-cruise- missile/articleshow/44845526.cms

67. "Nirbhay, India's Indigenous Cruise Missile, Fails Test Midway," *NDTV*, (October 16, 2015). http://www.ndtv.com/india-news/nirbhay-indias-indigenous-cruise-missile-fails-midway-1233086

68. T. S. Subramanian, "Nirbhay Missile Test 'an utter failure'," *The Hindu*, (December 21, 2016). http://www.thehindu.com/news/national/Nirbhay-missile-test-%E2%80%9Can-utter-failure%E2%80%9D/article16915750.ece

69. "DRDO Conducts Successful Flight Trial of 'NIRBHAY' Sub-Sonic Cruise Missile," *Press Information Bureau*, (November 07, 2017). http://pib.nic.in/newsite/PrintRelease.aspx?relid=173291

70. "India to Join ICBM Club Soon—Interview with Dr. S. Christopher," *NDTV*, (July 11, 2015). http://www.ndtv.com/video/news/news/india-to-join-icbm-club-soon-374683

71. Sandeep Unnithan, "India has all the building blocks for an anti-satellite capability," *India Today*, (April 27, 2012). http://indiatoday.intoday.in/story/agni-v-drdo-chief-dr-vijay-kumar-saraswat-interview/1/186248.html

72. "Ballistic and Cruise Missile Threat 2017," *Defense Intelligence Ballistic Missile Analysis Committee* http://www.nasic.af.mil/Portals/19/images/Fact%20Sheet%20 Images/2017%20Ballistic%20and%20Cruise%20Missile%20Threat_Final_small. pdf?ver=2017-07-21-083234-343

73. Bharat Karnad, *Why India is not a Great Power (Yet)* (New Delhi: Oxford University Press, 2015).

74. "Make In India—New Deal For Defence—Transport Solutions India, Episode 9, Segment 1," YouTube video, from 7:20 minutes onwards. https://www.youtube.com/ watch?v=LIaQ3nOGmEI&t=640s

75. Robert S. Norris and William M. Arkin, "Russian Nuclear Forces," *Bulletin of the Atomic Scientists*, vol. 56, no. 4, 2000. https://www.highbeam.com/doc/1G1-63794409.html

76. Rajat Pandit, "Agni-V with China in Range Tested; Next in Line is Agni-VI, with Multiple Warheads," *Times of India*, (December 27, 2016). http://timesofindia.indiatimes.com/ india/agni-v-with-china-in-range-tested-next-in-line-is-agni-vi-with-multiple-warheads/ articleshow/56191362.cms

77. Ajai Shukla, "New-Age Agni to boost Pak-Focused Nuclear Deterrent," *Business Standard*, (December 17, 2016). http://www.business-standard.com/article/economy-policy/new- age-agni-to-boost-pak-focused-nuclear-deterrent-116121601111_1.html

78. T. Subramanian and Y. Mallikarjun, "India successfully Test-Fires Shourya Missile," *The Hindu*, (September 24, 2011). http://www.thehindu.com/sci-tech/science/india- successfully-testfires-shourya-missile/article2482010.ece

79. "Prithvi Missiles to be Replaced by More-Capable Prahar: DRDO," *The Hindu Business Line*, (June 30, 2013). http://www.thehindubusinessline.com/news/prithvi-missiles-to-be- replaced-by-morecapable-prahar-drdo/article4866081.ece

80. "India capable of Building Nuke Deterrence upto 200 kilotons: Kakodkar," *Deccan Herald*, (September 24, 2009). http://www.deccanherald.com/content/27047/india-capable- building-nuke-, accessed on September 07, 2017.

81. Nuclear Weapon Archive, "Complete List of All U.S. Nuclear Weapons," ,http:// nuclearweaponarchive.org/Usa/Weapons/Allbombs.html

82. Nuclear Weapon Archive, "France's Nuclear Weapons: Development of the French Arsenal," http://nuclearweaponarchive.org/France/FranceArsenalDev.html

83. Nuclear Weapon Archive, "Britain's Nuclear Weapons: British Nuclear Testing," http:// nuclearweaponarchive.org/Uk/UKTesting.html

84. Visual Reverence, "Orange Herald," http://visualreverence.tumblr.com/post/85541430823/ orange-herald-was-a-fusion-boosted

85. Arun Prakash, "Strategic Policy Making and the Indian System," *Maritime Affairs* vol. 5, no.2, Winter 2009, pp. 22–31.

86. Ajai Shukla, "India Launches 5,000-km Range Agni-5 Missile Successfully," *Business Standard*, (April 20, 2012). http://www.business-standard.com/article/economy-policy/ india-launches-5-000-km-range-agni-5-missile-successfully-112042002020_1.html

87. Press Information Bureau, "Press Statement by Dr. Anil Kakodkar and Dr. R. Chidambaram on Pokhran-II tests," (September 24, 2009). http://pib.nic.in/newsite/PrintRelease. aspx?relid=52814, accessed on September 20, 2017.

88. Press Information Bureau, "Pokhran—II Tests were Fully Successful; Given India Capability to build Nuclear Deterrence: Dr. Kakodkar and Dr. Chidambaram,"(September 24, 2009 http://pib.nic.in/newsite/PrintRelease.aspx?relid=52813

89. "Use plural, India has thermonuclear bombs: Kakodkar," *CNN-IBN Interview Transcript*, December 13, 2009.

90. Frank Barnaby, "Trials provide data for range of weapon yields," *Jane's Defence Weekly,* May 27, 1998.

91. "MIRVs to Make India's 'Agni' ICBM More Potent," *Sputnik,* (December 27, 2016). https://sputniknews.com/asia/201612271049036303-india-ballistic-missile/

92. Nuclear Weapon Archive, "Britain's Nuclear Weapons: History of the British Nuclear Arsenal," http://nuclearweaponarchive.org/Uk/UKArsenalDev.html

93. Humphrey Hawksley, "India's Nuclear Muscle," *BBC World Service,* (January 11, 2003). http://news.bbc.co.uk/2/hi/south_asia/2646979.stm

94. Shyam Saran, "Is India's Nuclear Deterrent Credible?," *Speech delivered at India Habitat Centre, New Delhi,* April 24, 2013.

95. Hans M. Kristensen and Robert S. Norris, "Indian Nuclear Forces, 2017," *Bulletin of the Atomic Scientists* vol. 73, no. 4, 2017.

96. Gurmeet Kanwal, *Nuclear Defence: Shaping the Arsenal* (New Delhi: Knowledge World, 2001).

97. Gurmeet Kanwal, "India's Nuclear Force Structure 2025," *Carnegie Endowment for International Peace,* (June 30, 2016). http://carnegieendowment.org/2016/06/30/india-s-nuclear-force-structure-2025-pub-63988

98. K. Subrahmanyam, "Nuclear Force Design and Minimum Deterrence Strategy for India," in Bharat Karnad ed., Future Imperilled: India's Security in the 1990s and Beyond, (New Delhi: Viking Penguin India, 1994).

99. K. Subrahmanyam, "China and Nuclear Rationale," *Economic Times,* July 26, 1997.

100. Jasjit Singh, "A Nuclear Strategy for India," in Jasjit Singh, ed., *Nuclear India,* (New Delhi: Knowledge World, 1998).

101. Maharajkrishna Rasgotra, "Countering Nuclear Threats," in Brahma Chellaney, ed., *Securing India's Future in the New Millennium,* (New Delhi: Orient Longman, 1999).

102. Krishnaswamy Sundarji, "Imperatives of Indian Minimum Deterrence," *Agni,* May 1996, p. 21.

103. V. K. Nair, *Nuclear India* (New Delhi: Lancer International, 1992).

104. Raja Menon, "The Nuclear Doctrine: Yoking a Horse and Camel Together," *Times of India,* August 26, 1999.

105. Bharat Karnad, "Going Thermonuclear: Why, With What Forces, at What Cost," *United Service Institution Journal* vol. 17, no. 3, July-September 1998, p. 315.

106. Pran Pahwa, *Organisation and Employment of Strategic Rocket Forces* (New Delhi: United Service Institution of India, 1999), pp. 294–6.

107. Pran Pahwa, "Minimum Deterrent: Defining the Concept," *Tribune,* February 11, 1999.

108. Gurmeet Kanwal, "India's Nuclear Force Structure," *Institute for Defence Studies and Analyses,* (September 2000). http://www.idsa-india.org/an-sept2-00.html

109. Gurmeet Kanwal, "Does India Need Tactical Nuclear Weapons?," *IDSA May 2003,* http://www.idsa-india.org/an-may-03.html

110. Sharon Squassoni, "India's Nuclear Separation Plan: Issues and Views—CRS Report for Congress," *Congressional Research Service,* (December 22, 2006)

111. Kalman A. Robertson and John Carlson, "The Three Overlapping Streams of India's Nuclear Programs," *Harvard Kennedy School, Belfer Centre for Science and International Affairs,* (April 2016).

112. "India has Fissile Material for 2,000 Warheads: Pak Media," *Times of India,* (September 10, 2015) http://timesofindia.indiatimes.com/world/pakistan/India-has-fissile-material-for-2000-warheads-Pak-media/articleshow/48895568.cms

113. Elizabeth Whitfield, "Fuzzy Math on Indian Nuclear Weapons," *Bulletin of the Atomic Scientists,* (April 19, 2017), http://thebulletin.org/fuzzy-math-indian-nuclear-weapons9343114. "Third Pakistani Nuclear Reactor Operational: US magazine," *The Nation,* (July 07, 2014) http://nation.com.pk/islamabad/07-Jul-2014/third-pakistani-nuclear-reactor-operational-us-magazine

115. A. Zaidi and H. Ehtisham, "The Indian threat is real," *The Tribune.pk,* (May 11, 2017). https://tribune.com.pk/story/1406430/indian-threat-real/

116. Andre Gsponer and Jean-Pierre Hurni, "The Physical Principles of Thermonuclear Explosives, Inertial Confinement Fusion, and the Quest for Fourth Generation Nuclear Weapons," *Independent Scientific Research Institute Geneva-12, Switzerland,* (January 20, 2009)

117. Mansoor Ahmed, "India's Nuclear Exceptionalism Fissile Materials, Fuel Cycles, and Safeguards," (Harvard Kennedy School, Belfer Centre for Science and International Affairs: Discussion Paper May 2017)

118. Ashley Tellis, "Atoms for War? U.S.-Indian Civilian Nuclear Cooperation and India's Nuclear Arsenal," *Carnegie Endowment for International Peace,* 2006,119. Zia Mian, et. al, "Plutonium Production in India and The U.S.-India Nuclear Deal."

119. Sanjay Badri-Maharaj, The Armageddon Factor: Nuclear Weapons in the India-Pakistan Context (New Delhi: Lancer, 2000).

120. M. Thomas, "An Analysis of the Threat Perception and Strategy for India," *Indian Defence Review,* January 1990.

121. S. Bhaduri, "The Artillery Division—Part II," *Indian Defence Review,* April 1992.

122. P. Sawhney, "If Pakistan and India Go to War," *The Asian Age,* November 12–13, 1994.

123. IDR Research Team, "Operational Scenario Alpha," *Indian Defence Review,* July 1992.

124. Gurmeet Kanwal, "India's Cold Start Doctrine and Strategic Stability," *Institute for Defence Studies and Analyses,* (June 01, 2010). https://idsa.in/idsacomments/IndiasColdStartDoctrineandStrategicStability_gkanwal_010610

125. Praveen Swami, "War and Games," *Frontline,* (February 15, 2002). http://www.frontline.in/static/html/fl1903/19030040.htm, accessed on October 23, 2017.

126. Manu Pubby, "No 'Cold Start' doctrine, India tells US," *Indian Express,* (September 9, 2010). http://archive.indianexpress.com/news/no--cold-start--doctrine-india-tells-us/679273/

127. Gurmeet Kanwal, "Cold Start: India's Pro-active Offensive Operations Doctrine for War in the Plains," http://gurmeetkanwal.com/ArticleDetails.aspx?id=391

128. Walter C. Ladwig III, "A Cold Start for Hot Wars?," *International Security* vol. 32, no. 3, (Winter 2007/08), pp. 158.http://www.mitpressjournals.org/doi/pdf/10.1162/isec.2008.32.3.158

129. Suman Sharma, "Army Mobilization Time: 48hrs," *DNA India,* (May 16, 2011). http://www.dnaindia.com/india/report-army-mobilisation-time-48-hours-1543679

130. Subhash Kapila, "Indian Army Exercise Sudershan Shakti-Revalidation Of Cold Start War Doctrine," *South Asia Analysis Group,* (December 10, 2011) https://web.archive.org/web/20120104045741/http://southasiaanalysis.org/papers49/paper4809.html

131. Sanjay Badri-Maharaj, "The Indian Air Force's Declining Squadron Strength—Options and Challenges," *Institute for Defence Studies and Analyses—Issue Brief,* (November 03, 2017). https://idsa.in/issuebrief/the-indian-air-force-declining-squadron-strength_sbmaharaj_031117

132. "IAF to reach full squadron strength by 2032: Air chief," *Indo-Asian News Service,* (October 05, 2017). http://economictimes.indiatimes.com/articleshow/60958636.cms?utm_source=contentofinterest&utm_medium=text&utm_campaign=cppst

133. "India will continue to operate the MiG-21 fighters until 2025," *Itar-Tass*, (October 09, 2013). https://www.rbth.com/economics/2013/10/09/india_will_continue_to_operate_the_mig-21_fighters_until_2025_30019

134. Sanjay Badri-Maharaj, "The IAF Fleet Needs Rejuvenating, And Needs It Now," *Swarajya*, (January 09, 2017). https://swarajyamag.com/defence/the-iaf-fleet-needs-rejuvenating-and-needs-it-now

135. "Nuclear Black Markets: Pakistan, A.Q. Khan and the rise of proliferation networks—A net assessment," *International Institute for Strategic Studies: Nuclear policy*, (May 02, 2007) https://www.iiss.org/publications/strategic%20dossiers/issues/nuclear-black-markets--pakistan--a-q--khan-and-the-rise-of-proliferation-networks---a-net-assessmen-23e1, accessed on October 23, 2017.

136. Sardar F. S. Lodhi, Pakistan's Nuclear Doctrine," *Defence Journal April 1999* http://www.defencejournal.com/apr99/pak-nuclear-doctrine.htmG. Balachandran and K. Patil, "Revisiting India's Nuclear Doctrine," *Institute for Defence Studies and Analyses* (March 27, 2017). https://idsa.in/idsacomments/revisiting-india-nuclear-doctrine_gbala-kpatil_270317

137. Pillalmarri Subramanyam, "Pakistan's Tactical Nuclear Weapons and India's Response," *Indian Defence Review Net Edition*, (October 30, 2016). http://www.indiandefencereview.com/news/pakistans-tactical-nuclear-weapons-and-indias-response/0/

138. C. Christine Fair, "Pakistan's army is building an arsenal of "tiny" nuclear weapons—and it's going to backfire," *Quartz India*, (December 21, 2015). https://qz.com/579334/pakistans-army-is-building-an-arsenal-of-tiny-nuclear-weapons-and-its-going-to-backfire/

139. Sanjay Badri-Maharaj, "The Importance of Passive and Active CBRN Defensive Measures," *Institute for Defence Studies and Analyses: Issue Brief*, (October 17, 2016), https://idsa.in/issuebrief/importance-of-passive-and-active-cbrn-defensive-measures_sbmaharaj_171016

140. Shahid K. Abbas, "Brahmos anti-ship missile to be produced in 2003," *Rediff.com*, (June 01, 2002). http://www.rediff.com/news/2002/jun/01war11.htm

141. "Indian Army May Soon get Bio-Chem Suits," *Rediff.com*, (May 11, 2011). http://www.rediff.com/news/report/indian-army-may-soon-get-bio-chem-suits/20110511.htm

142. Arkadev Ghoshal, "India to Procure Anti-Chemical, Anti-Nuclear Suits from US for Rs 480 crore," *IB Times*, (May 12, 2017). http://www.ibtimes.co.in/india-procure-anti-chemical-anti-nuclear-suits-us-rs-480-crore-726410, accessed on October 23, 2017.

143. Gurmeet Kanwal, "Does India Need Tactical Nuclear Weapons?," *Institute for Defence Studies and Analyses*, (May 2003). https://www.idsa-india.org/an-may-03.html

144. "National Security", Fundamentals, Doctrine and Concepts—Indian Army (Shimla: HQ ARTRAC, 1999), pp. 11–12.

145. General Krishnaswamy Sundarji, "Nuclear Deterrence Doctrine for India," *Trishul* vol. 5, no. 2, December 1992.

146. Brahma Chellaney, "Nuclear Deterrent Posture," in Brahma Chellaney, ed., Securing India's Future in the New Millennium, (New Delhi: Orient Longman Limited, 1999), pp. 209–214.

147. Pravin Sawhney, "How Inevitable is an Asian Missile Race?," *Jane's Intelligence Review*, January 2000, pp. 32.

148. Shyam Saran, "Is India's Nuclear Deterrent Credible?," Speech given at the India Habitat Centre, New Delhi, April 24, 2013.

149. Ali Ahmed, "Tit for Tat: A Nuclear Retaliation Alternative," *Institute for Defence Studies and Analyses*, (October 03, 2011). https://idsa.in/idsacomments/TitforTatANuclearRetaliationAlternative031011

150. Jasjit Singh, "A Nuclear Strategy for India," in Jasjit Singh, ed., *Nuclear India*, (New Delhi:

Knowledge World in association with Institute for Defence Studies and Analyses, 1998).

151. Swaran Singh, "China's Nuclear Weapons and Doctrine."Vivek Raghuvanshi, "Indian Excludes Foreign Vendors From Its Air-Defense Upgrade," *Defense News,* (June 13, 2016). https://www.defensenews.com/global/asia-pacific/2016/06/13/indian-excludes-foreign-vendors-from-its-air-defense-upgrade/

152. Chethan Kumar, "Six new Akash squadrons to give IAF missile muscle," *Times of India,* (February 17, 2015). https://timesofindia.indiatimes.com/india/Six-new-Akash-squadrons-to-give-IAF-missile-muscle/articleshow/46269673.cms

153. Ajai Shukla, "Army Orders Surface to Air Missile, Making it the First Tri-Service Weapon," *Business Standard,* (September 26, 2017). http://www.business-standard.com/article/economy-policy/army-orders-surface-to-air-missile-making-it-the-first-tri-service-weapon-117092500988_1.html

154. Jayant Baranwal, *SP's Military Yearbook 1992-93* (New Delhi: Guide Publications, 1993).

155. Prasun Sengupta, "Arudhra MPR Is EL/M-2084 MMR: Seeing Is Believing," *Trishul-Trident,* (June 04, 2011). http://trishul-trident.blogspot.com/2011/06/arudhra-mpr-is-elm-2084-mmr-seeing-is.html

156. Vimal Bhatia, "IAF to Deploy New Radar near Border Areas," *Times of India,* (October 02, 2011). https://timesofindia.indiatimes.com/city/jaipur/IAF-to-deploy-new-radar-near-border-areas/articleshow/10204373.cms

157. Prasun Sengupta, "IAF's Multi-Phase IACCCS Being Enhanced," *Trishul-Trident,* (January 22, 2012). http://trishul-trident.blogspot.com/2012/01/iafs-multi-phase-iacccs-being-enhanced.html

158. "Electronic Weapons: Instant Radar," *Strategy Page,* (February 21, 2009), https://www.strategypage.com/htmw/htecm/articles/20090221.aspx

159. Prasun Sengupta, "Poised for A Hattrick," *Force India October 2017.* http://forceindia.net/cover-story/poised-for-a-hattrick/

160. "India acquires Green Pine radars from Israel," *Press Trust of India,* (June 28, 2002), https://timesofindia.indiatimes.com/india/India-acquires-Green-Pine-radars-from-Israel/articleshow/14351441.cms

161. Pravin Sawhney, "Decks Cleared For the Contract Signing of S-400 ADMS in December," *Force Inda,* (October 17, 2017). http://forceindia.net/decks-cleared-contract-signing-s-400-adms-december/

162. "Missile defence shield to be ready in three years: India," *Dawn,* (December 13, 2007), https://www.dawn.com/news/280120

163. Saurav Jha, "Hit-to-Kill Successfully Demonstrated By DRDO's PDV Interceptor," *Delhi Defence Review,* (February 25, 2017). http://www.delhidefencereview.com/2017/02/25/hit-kill-successfully-demonstrated-drdos-pdv-interceptor/

164. T. S. Subramanian, "Smashing Hit," *Frontline,* (December 22, 2007–January 04, 2008). http://www.frontline.in/static/html/fl2425/stories/20080104242512300.htm

165. "Interceptor Missile Scores 'Direct Hit'," *The Hindu,* (December 07, 2007). http://www.hindu.com/2007/12/07/stories/2007120761241800.htm

166. "Interceptor Missile Test Fired Successfully," *NDTV.com,* March 06, 2011."India Successfully Test-Fires AAD Missile Interceptor," November 23, 2012.

167. Y. Mallikarjun, "Interceptor Missile Test Off Odisha Coast Fails," *The Hindu,* (April 06, 2015). http://www.thehindu.com/news/national/intercepter-missile-test-odisha-coast-wheeler-island drdo/article7073662.ece?ref=sliderNews, accessed on November 08, 2017.

168. Y. Mallikarjun, "Upgraded Interceptor Missile Successfully Hits Virtual Target," *The Hindu,* (November 22, 2015). http://www.thehindu.com/news/cities/Hyderabad/

upgraded-interceptor-missile-successfully-engages-electronically-simulated-target-missile/article7905298.ece

169. "India Successfully Test-Fires Supersonic Interceptor Missile," *Tribune India,* (May 15, 2016). http://www.tribuneindia.com/news/nation/india-successfully-test-fires-supersonic-interceptor-missile/237107.html, accessed on November 08, 2017.

170. T. S. Subramanian, "Interceptor Missile Mission a 'Failure'," *The Hindu,* (May 23, 2016), http://www.thehindu.com/news/national/Interceptor-missile-mission-a-%E2%80%98 failure%E2%80%99/article14333898.ece

171. DDR Staff, "DRDO's AAD Ballistic Missile Defence Interceptor Heads Toward Induction With Latest Test," *Delhi Defence Review,* (December 29, 2017). http://www. delhidefencereview.com/2017/12/29/drdos-aad-ballistic-missile-defence-interceptor-heads-toward-induction-with-latest-test/

172. Saurav Jha, "DRDO's AAD Endo-atmospheric Ballistic Missile Interceptor Hits Bullseye," *Delhi Defence Review,* (March 01, 2017). http://www.delhidefencereview.com/2017/03/01/ drdos-aad-endo-atmospheric-ballistic-missile-interceptor-hits-bullseye/

173. *Trishul-Trident Blogspot,* (January 01, 2018). http://trishul-trident.blogspot.in/2018/01/ aad-endo-atmospheric-interceptor-headed.html

174. Air Marshal Narayan Menon, "Ballistic Missile Defence System for India," *Indian Defence Review,* Vol 27, July-September 3, 2012. http://www.indiandefencereview.com/spotlights/ ballistic-missile-defence-system-for-india/

175. "India Successfully Test-Fires New Interceptor Missile," *Outlook India,* (April 27, 2014). https://web.archive.org/web/20140428163936/http://news.outlookindia.com/items. aspx?artid=838755

176. M. Somasekhar, "India's 'Interceptor' May Make Ballistic Missile Shield Real," *The Hindu Business line,* (February 12, 2017). http://www.thehindubusinessline.com/news/indias-interceptor-may-make-ballistic-missile-shield-real/article9537665.ece

177. "Defence Acquisition Council okays purchase of Russian air defence missile systems," *Press Trust of India,* (December 17, 2015). http://www.dnaindia.com/india/report-defence-acquisition-council-okays-purchase-of-russian-air-defence-missile-systems-2156916

178. Andrei Kislyakov, "Russia to roll out new hypersonic missiles," *Russia Beyond,* (December 18, 2012). https://www.rbth.com/articles/2012/12/18/russia_to_roll_out_new_hypersonic_ missiles_21107

179. Jeffrey Lin and P. W. Singer, "China Shot Down Another Missile in Space," *Popular Science,* (February 13, 2018). https://www.popsci.com/china-space-missile-test

180. Wang Ting, "Agni V and China/India Ballistic Missile Defense," (presentation, Carnegie Endowment for International Peace, n.d.), http://carnegieendowment.org/files/Wang_ Ting%20Presentation.pdf. The presentation took place during the week of October 2, 2012.

181. Sarah Weiner, "Recap: 'China-India Nuclear Crossroads'," *Center for Strategic and International Studies,* (October 9, 2012). http://csis.org/blog/event-recap-china-india-nuclear-crossroads

182. Minnie Chan, "China Plans Sea-Based Anti-Missile Shields 'for Asia-Pacific and Indian Ocean'," *South China Morning Post,* (February 08, 2018). https://www.cnbc.com/2018/02/08/ china-plans-sea-based-anti-missile-shields-for-asia-pacific-and-indian-ocean.html

183. Franz-Stefan Gady, "China, Russia Kick Off Anti-Ballistic Missile Defense Exercise," *The Diplomat,* (December 12, 2017). https://thediplomat.com/2017/12/china-russia-kick-off-anti-ballistic-missile-defense-exercise/

184. Brad Roberts, "China and Ballistic Missile Defense: 1955 to 2002 and Beyond," *IDA Paper P-3826,* September 2003, p. 21, n. 80, http://www.dtic.mil/cgi-bin/

GetTRDoc?AD=ADA418710 (citing Wan Yung-Kui, "Can the Chinese Armed Forces Successfully Protect the Three-Gorges Dam?," *Hong Kong Tangai*, No. 31 [October 15, 1993]

185. Bruce W. MacDonald and Charles D. Ferguson, "Chinese Strategic Missile Defense: Will It Happen, and What Would It Mean?," *Arms Control Today*, (November 2015), https://www.armscontrol.org/ACT/2015_11/Features/Chinese-Strategic-Missile-Defense-Will-It-Happen-and-What-Would-It-Mean?utm_source=Arms+Control+Association+E-Updates&utm_campaign=114a736ce4-The_November_2015_ACT_Issue_Features&utm_medium=email&utm_term=0_0bf155a1a2-114a736ce4-79430281#notes

186. Doug Tsuroka, "China Pursuing Missile Defenses; Indian Nukes are Main Worry," *Asia Times*, (January 19, 2018). http://www.atimes.com/article/china-pursuing-missile-defenses-indian-nukes-main-worry/

187. David Willman, "$40-Billion Missile Defense System Proves Unreliable," *La Times*, (June 15, 2014), http://www.latimes.com/nation/la-na-missile-defense-20140615-story.html

188. Sebastein Roblin, "America's Missile Defenses Against North Korea Have a Big Problem (They Only Work Half the Time)," *National Interest*, (May 27, 2017). http://nationalinterest.org/blog/the-buzz/americas-missile-defenses-against-north-korea-have-big-20872?page=show

189. Boris Toucas, "Ballistic Missile Defense: Proceed With Caution," *ArmsControl.org*, (November 2017). https://www.armscontrol.org/act/2017-11/features/ballistic-missile-defense-proceed-caution

190. Kyle Mizokami, "Moscow's Defender: Russia Tests Modernized Ballistic Missile," *Popular Mechanics*, (February 21, 2018). https://www.popularmechanics.com/military/weapons/a18567468/moscows-defender-russia-tests-modernized-ballistic-missile/

191. Laura Zhou, "China and Russia Criticise THAAD Missile Defence System as Destabilising Region," *South China Morning Post*, (July 09, 2016). http://www.scmp.com/news/china/diplomacy-defence/article/1987103/china-and-russia-criticise-thaad-missile-defence-system

192. "India Has the World's 7th Largest Satellite Fleet," *Times of India*, (September 09, 2016) https://timesofindia.indiatimes.com/india/India-has-the-worlds-7th-largest-satellite-fleet/articleshow/54222923.cms, accessed on March 03, 2018.

193. "Network Centric Warfare Department of Defense Report to Congress," (July 27, 2001). *Department of Defence*, http://www.dodccrp.org/files/ncw_report/report/ncw_main.pdf

194. Rui C. Barbosa, "China continues Build Up of Yaogan-30 constellation," *Nasa Spaceflight*, (December 26, 2017). https://www.nasaspaceflight.com/2017/12/china-continues-yaogan-30-build-up/

195. William Graham, "Atlas V Launches with SBIRS GEO-4," *Nasa Spaceflight*, (January 19, 2018). https://www.nasaspaceflight.com/2018/01/atlas-v-sbirs-geo-4-launch-cape-canaveral/

196. Curt Godwin, "Soyuz Rocket Successfully Delivers Eks-2 Early-Warning Satellite To Rare Orbit," *Spaceflight insider*, (May 25, 2017). http://www.spaceflightinsider.com/organizations/roscosmos/soyuz-rocket-successfully-delivers-eks-2-early-warning-satellite-rare-orbit/

197. "India sets up Integrated Space Cell," *NDTV*, (June 10, 2008). https://web.archive.org/web/20080614000739/http://www.ndtv.com/convergence/ndtv/story.aspx?id=NEWEN20080052615

198. Air Marshal Anil Chopra, "India's Military Space Program," *South Asia Defence and Strategic Review* http://www.defstrat.com/india%E2%80%99s-military-space-program

199. "Cartosat-2f," *Spaceflight 101*, http://spaceflight101.com/pslv-c40/cartosat-2f/

200. Surendra Singh, "Military using 13 Satellites to Keep Eye on Foes," *Times of India,* (June 26, 2017). https://timesofindia.indiatimes.com/india/military-using-13-satellites-to-keep-eye-on-foes/articleshow/59314610.cms

201. Rajat Pandit, "After Agni-V Launch, DRDO's New Target is Anti-Satellite Weapons," *Times of India,* (April 21, 2012). https://timesofindia.indiatimes.com/india/After-Agni-V-launch-DRDOs-new-target-is-anti-satellite-weapons/articleshow/12763074.cms

202. Harsh Vasani, "India's Anti-Satellite Weapons," *The Diplomat,* (June 14, 2016). https://thediplomat.com/2016/06/indias-anti-satellite-weapons/

203. Atul Pant, "EMP Weapons and the New Equation of War," *Institute for Defence Studies and Analyses,* (October 13, 2017). https://idsa.in/idsacomments/emp-weapons-new-equation-of-war_apant_131017

204. Scott Stewart, "Gauging the Threat of an Electromagnetic Pulse (EMP) Attack," *Stratfor Worldview,* (September 9, 2010). https://worldview.stratfor.com/article/gauging-threat-electromagnetic-pu...

205. Edward E. Conrad et al., "Collateral Damage to Satellites from an EMP Attack," *Defence Threat Reduction Agency,* (August 2010). http://www.dtic.mil/dtic/tr/fulltext/u2/a531197.pdf

206. Jatinder Kaur Tur, "India Developing E-bomb to Paralyze Networks," *Times of India,* (August 29, 2013). https://timesofindia.indiatimes.com/india/India-developing-E-bomb-to-paralyze-networks/articleshow/22127411.cms

207. "Is India's Nuclear Deterrent Credible?," Speech by Shyam Saran at the India Habitat Centre, New Delhi, April 24, 2013.

208. "Developing Threats: Electro-Magnetic Pulses (EMP)," *Tenth Report of Session 2010–12,* United Kingdom House of Commons, (February 08, 2012), https://publications.parliament.uk/pa/cm201012/cmselect/cmdfence/1552/1552.pdf.

209. "New Delhi Prepares for War, Plans Underground Bunkers Against WMD Attacks *Sputnik,* (October 17, 2016). https://sputniknews.com/asia/201610171046419397-india-war-bunker/

210. Amy E. Smithson and Leslie-Anne Levy, "Chapter 3—Rethinking the Lessons of Tokyo," *Ataxia: The Chemical and Biological Terrorism Threat and the US Response* (Report). Henry L. Stimson Centre. pp. 91, 95, 100. Report No. 35.

211. "Amerithrax or Anthrax Investigation, U.S.," *Federal Bureau of Investigation,* https://www.fbi.gov/history/famous-cases/amerithrax-or-anthrax-investigation

212. Simon Shuster, "Inside the Uranium Underworld: Dark Secrets, Dirty Bombs," *Time,* (April 10, 2017). http://time.com/4728293/uranium-underworld-dark-secrets-dirty-bombs/

213. Tom Allard and Agustinus Beo Da Costa, "Exclusive: Indonesian militants planned 'dirty bomb' attack—sources," *Reuters,* (August 25, 2017). https://www.reuters.com/article/us-indonesia-security/exclusive-indonesian-militants-planned-dirty-bomb-attack-sources-idUSKCN1B51FW

214. "Does India Face A 'Dirty Bomb' Threat? Top Nuclear Scientist Explains," *Press Trust of India,* (May 10, 2016). https://www.ndtv.com/india-news/does-india-face-a-dirty-bomb-threat-top-nuclear-scientist-explains-1404739

215. Sruthjith K. K., "Delhi Gradually Ushering in CWG Juggernaut," *Economic Times,* (September 27, 2010). https://economictimes.indiatimes.com/delhi-gradually-ushering-in-cwg-juggernaut/articleshow/6632785.cmsRoli Varma and Daya R. Varma, "The Bhopal Disaster of 1984," *Bulletin of Science, Technology and Society* vol. 25, no. 1, 2005.

216. "Madhya Pradesh Government: Bhopal Gas Tragedy Relief and Rehabilitation Department, Bhopal," Mp.gov.in. Archived from the original, (May 18, 2012). https://web.archive.org/web/20120518020821/http://www.mp.gov.in/bgtrrdmp/relief.htm

217. A. K. Dubey, "Bhopal Gas Tragedy: 92% Injuries Termed 'Minor'," *First14 News*, (June 26, 2010). https://www.webcitation.org/5qmWBEWcb?url=http://www.first14.com/bhopal-gas-tragedy-92-injuries-termed-minor-822.htmlNational Disaster Management Plan, May 2016,

218. Guidelines on Management of Nuclear and Radiological Emergencies as listed in Annexure-I of the NDMA National Disaster Management Plan 2016

219. *National Disaster Management Plan May 2016*, (New Delhi: NDMA, 2016), pp. 26–27.

220. Rahul Wadke, "Nuclear Plant to Have Eye in the Sky," *Hindu Business Line*, (April 02, 2017). http://www.thehindubusinessline.com/news/science/nuclear-plant-to-have-eye-in-the-sky/article9612475.ece

221. "DAE, CISF Review Security of Nuclear Power Plants," *Times of India*, (April 30, 2011). https://timesofindia.indiatimes.com/india/DAE-CISF-review-security-of-nuclear-power-plants/articleshow/8122343.cms, accessed on November 09, 2017.

222. Rajeswari Pillai Rajagopalan, "India's Nuclear Security: Strengths and Gaps," *Observer Research Foundation*, (June 14, 2017). http://www.orfonline.org/research/india-nuclear-security-strengths-gaps/

223. National Disaster Management, "NDMA Vision," http://www.ndma.gov.in/en/about-ndma/vision.html

224. National Disaster Management, "Evolution of NDMA,"http://www.ndma.gov.in/en/about-ndma/evolution-of-ndma.html

225. National Disaster Management Authority, "Functions and Responsibilities," http://www.ndma.gov.in/en/about-ndma/roles-responsibilities.html

226. Disaster Management Act, [December 23, 2005.] no. 53 .

227. "Capacity Building and is bhavin Training," National Disaster Management Authority.

228. National Disaster Management Authority, "Fire Services," http://www.ndma.gov.in/en/fire-services.html

229. National Disaster Management Authority, "Trauma Care," http://www.ndma.gov.in/en/capacity-building/trauma-care.html

230. National Disaster Management Authority, "NDMA Roles and Responsibilities," http://www.ndma.gov.in/en/about-ndma/roles-responsibilities.html

231. Deeptiman Tiwary, "NDMA has failed to achieve objectives, task force says," https://timesofindia.indiatimes.com/india/NDMA-has-failed-to-achieve-objectives-task-force-says/articleshow/24119665.cms

232. Abhishek Bhalla and Bhuvan Bagga, "The Uttarakhand Tragedy Casts Shame on India's Disaster Management. So Why DID the Committee meant to Plan for Flood Emergencies Fail to Meet for FOUR YEARS?," *Daily Mail India*, (June 24, 2013). http://www.dailymail.co.uk/indiahome/indianews/article-2347624/NDMA-The-Uttarakhand-tragedy-casts-shame-Indias-disaster-management-So-DID-committee-meant-plan-flood-emergencies-fail-meet-FOUR-YEARS.html

233. Kumar Sambhav Shrivastava, "How Effective is India's Disaster Management Authority?," *Down to Earth*, (June 20, 2013). http://www.downtoearth.org.in/news/how-effective-is-india-s-disaster-management-authority--41415

234. "Government Approves Appointment of 3 Experts as NDMA Members," *Press Trust of India*, (December 21, 2014). http://www.dnaindia.com/india/report-government-approves-appointment-of-3-experts-as-ndma-members-2045959

235. "Government to Restructure and Revamp NDMA," *GK Today*, (September 30, 2014). https://currentaffairs.gktoday.in/government-restructure-revamp-ndma-09201414966.html

236. "National Disaster Management Plan Part-1: Draft," p. 61.

237. NDRF, "About Us," http://ndrf.gov.in/ndrf

238. Arunachal Government Assures Land to Set Up NDRF Unit Headquarter," *Economic Times*, (August 22, 2015). http://articles.economictimes.indiatimes.com/2015-08-22/news/65739754_1_ndrf-unit-ndrf-personnel-state-capital

239. NDRF Website, "NDRF Training Regime," http://ndrf.gov.in/Media/inapnacms/TRAINING/taining%20regime.pdf

240. "Disaster Response Force Base Comes Up In Delhi, To Respond To Bio, Nuclear Attacks," *Press Trust of India*, (June 11, 2017). https://www.ndtv.com/india-news/ndrf-base-comes-up-in-delhi-to-respond-to-bio-nuclear-attacks-1710679

241. "Kanpur: Ammonia Gas Leak Causes Explosion in Cold Storage; Five Killed, Several Still Trapped," *First Post*, (May 15, 2017). http://www.firstpost.com/india/kanpur-ammonia-gas-leak-causes-explosion-in-cold-storage-five-killed-several-still-trapped-3335870.html

242. Civil Defence, "Fire Cell," http://ndrfandcd.gov.in/fire.aspx

243. "Fire Hazard and Risk Analysis in the Country for Revamping the Fire Services in the Country Final Report—Fire and Emergency Services Training Infrastructure in the Country November 2012," *Directorate General NDRF & Civil Defence (Fire) Ministry of Home Affairs*, http://ndrfandcd.gov.in/WriteReadData/userfiles/file/Pilot%20phase/Final_Report_Training_Requirement_in_FireService.pdf

244. CISF, "CISF Fire Wing," http://www.cisf.gov.in/fire-wing/

245. "Govt Sanctions 481 CISF Fire Wing Posts for Five PSU Units," *Press Trust of India*, (March 31, 2010). http://www.dnaindia.com/india/report-govt-sanctions-481-cisf-fire-wing-posts-for-five-psu-units-1365831

246. R. Krishna Kumar, "CBRN Disaster-Handling Centres to be Set Up in Four Metros," *The Hindu*, (March 20, 2016). http://www.thehindu.com/news/national/karnataka/cbrn-disasterhandling-centres-to-be-set-up-in-four-metros/article8376879.ece

247. Nayanima Basu, "Armed Forces Undergoing Nuclear, Biological Warfare Training," *The Hindu Business Line*, (August 11, 2017). http://www.thehindubusinessline.com/news/national/armed-forces-undergoing-nuclear-biological-warfare training/article9813830.ece

248. "Civil Defence," http://ndrfandcd.gov.in/Civildefence.aspx

249. National Civil Defence College Website, "Our Achievements," http://www.cddrm-ncdc.org/e39343/e41087/

250. Sanjay Badri-Maharaj, "Civil Defence Capabilities of the Indian State," *Bharat Rakshak Monitor* vol. 4, no. 2, September-October 2001.

251. "Home Guards," http://dgcd.nic.in/home_guards.htm

252. In 2009 this photograph shows the array of basic rescue equipment available to the Home Guards http://www.delhi.gov.in/wps/wcm/connect/ad17a200457f502d82c2ba63dd2acccc/P+320.jpg?MOD=AJPERES&lmod=-357501517

253. Arms Control, "India's Draft Nuclear Doctrine," https://www.armscontrol.org/act/1999_07-08/ffja99

254. http://pib.nic.in/archieve/lreleng/lyr2003/rjan2003/04012003/r040120033.html

255. Ali Ahmed, "The Need for Clarity in India's Nuclear Doctrine," *Institute for Defence Studies and Analyses*, (November 11, 2008). https://idsa.in/idsastrategiccomments/TheNeedForClarityInIndiaSNuclearDoctrine_AAhmed_111108, accessed on November 13, 2008.

256. G. Balachandran and Kapil Patil, "Revisiting India's Nuclear Doctrine," *Institute for Defence Studies and Analyses*, (March 27, 2017). https://idsa.in/idsacomments/revisiting-india-nuclear-doctrine_gbala-kpatil_270317

257. Dhruva Jaishankar, "Decoding India's Nuclear Status," *Brookings,* (April 03, 2017). https://www.brookings.edu/opinions/decoding-indias-nuclear-status/

258. Satish Chandra, "Revisiting India's Nuclear Doctrine: Is it Necessary?," *Institute for Defence Studies and Analyses,* (April 30, 2014). https://idsa.in/issuebrief/RevisitingIndiasNuclearDoctrine_schandra_300414

259. Shyam Saran, "Is India's Deterrent Credible?," India Habitat Centre, (April 24, 2013). http://www.armscontrolwonk.com/files/2013/05/Final-Is-Indias-Nuclear-Deterrent-Credible-rev1-2-1-3.pdf

260. "India Building nuclear-proof bunkers for top leaders," *Silicon India,* September 23, 2003. http://www.siliconindia.com/shownews/India_building_nuclearproof_bunkers_for_top_leaders-nid-20887-cid-Top.html

261. https://defence.pk/pdf/threads/india-starts-building-nuclear-shelters.83066/

262. Vipin Narang, "Plenary: Beyond the Nuclear Threshold: Causes and Consequences of First Use," *Carnegie International Nuclear Policy Conference* Washington DC, (March 20, 2017). https://fbfy83yid9j1dqsev3zq0w8n-wpengine.netdna-ssl.com/wp-content/uploads/2013/08/Vipin-Narang-Remarks-Carnegie-Nukefest-2017.pdf

263. Shivshankar Menon, *Choices: Inside the Making of India's Foreign Policy* (Penguin Random House India: Brookings, Washington D.C: 2016)

264. B. S. Nagal, "Guest Column | Nuclear No First Use Policy: A Time for Appraisal," *Force,* (December 2014). http://forceindia.net/guest-column/guest-column-b-s-nagal/nuclear-no-first-use-policy/

265. B. S. Nagal, "Guest Column | Checks and Balances: A Regular Review and Appraisal of the Nuclear Doctrine would Help to Fine Tune it As Per Strategic Requirements," *Force,* (June 2014). http://forceindia.net/guest-column/guest-column-b-s-nagal/checks-and-balances/

266. Chitrapu Uday Bhaskar, "India's Nuclear Deterrence Strategy," *The Hindu,* (March 30, 2010), http://www.thehindu.com/books/Indias-nuclear-deterrence-strategy/article16630532.ece

267. Manpreet Sethi, *Nuclear Strategy: India's march towards Credible Deterrence* (New Delhi: KW Publishers, 2009).

268. Gurmeet Kanwal, "India's Nuclear Force Structure," *Institute for Defence Studies and Analyses,* (September 2000), http://www.idsa-india.org/an-sept2-00.html

Index

AAD, 171–175, 176, 179–182, 183, 184, 187, 196

ADGES, 156–157, 158, 159–160

Agni, 37–45, 46, 51–55, 58–59, 61, 62, 63, 64, 65, 67–68, 70, 95, 96, 195, 205, 262, 263, 266, 276, 281–283, 285

Air Defence, 105, 120, 128, 131–133, 144, 152, 155, 156 –157, 158, 159, 160, 161, 162, 163, 164, 165, 166, 167, 171–183, 185, 191, 195, 211

Aircraft , 3, 4, 5, 9, 19, 21–23, 27, 31, 32–36, 56, 65, 66, 67, 70, 71, 77, 119, 121, 132, 133, 149, 152, 156, 158–159, 160, 163, 165, 167

Akash, 132, 133, 157–158, 168, 169

Arighat, 47

Arihant, 31, 45–47, 64, 65, 69, 84, 261, 262, 281

Arsenal, 1–99, 127, 149, 151, 152, 156, 189, 192, 193, 194, 195, 196, 243, 245, 254, 256, 259–264, 266, 270, 271, 272, 275, 276, 277, 279–283

Artillery, 5, 6, 15, 77, 101,102, 104, 105, 106, 109, 115, 118, 119, 128, 129, 131, 136, 151, 160, 181

ASAT, 187, 188, 189, 202, 205, 208, 280, 286

Babur, 20, 23, 26, 27, 28, 166

BADZ, 156, 157, 160,

Ballistic Missile Defence (BMD), 155–196

Biological, 77, 101, 144, 209, 227, 241, 245, 247, 283

BMD. *See* Ballistic Missile Defence

Bomb, 4, 19, 21, 33–34, 35, 56, 57, 60–61, 66, 71, 74, 209, 211–212, 213–214, 220

Boosted–Fission, 32–33, 43, 56, 57–58, 59, 61–63, 69, 74, 77, 94, 95, 97, 282

BrahMos, 31, 48–49, 77, 96

CARTOSAT, 203–204, 205, 206

CBRN, 101, 118, 122, 127, 128–134, 144–145, 147, 149, 151, 152, 153, 209–240, 276, 277, 283–285

Chemical, 77, 101, 129, 144, 209, 210, 213, 215–219, 220, 226, 227, 233, 241, 245, 247, 283

China, 1–17, 26, 30, 35, 43, 70, 71, 72, 73, 74, 75, 76, 94–96, 99, 108, 110, 115, 140, 149–152, 156, 184, 185–190, 192, 193, 194, 195, 198, 200, 201, 207, 208, 211, 253, 268, 269, 271, 273, 275–276, 277, 280, 281–282, 283, 286

CISF, 219, 228, 232–233

Civil Defence, 209,210, 219–221, 230, 234–238, 239, 276, 284

Command and Control, 6, 15, 16, 31, 35, 64–66, 77–78, 135, 141, 148, 162, 164, 180, 183, 211, 226, 236, 243, 244–245, 247, 253–261, 262, 271, 277

Defence, 6, 12, 15, 35, 47, 70, 101–106, 108, 110, 120, 126, 128, 130, 131–136, 140, 143, 144, 149, 151, 152, 155–197, 199, 202, 203, 206, 208 –211, 219–221, 230, 233– 239, 243, 245, 248, 252, 253, 257, 259, 261, 264, 266, 269, 271, 276, 281, 283–286

Deterrence, 2, 11–13, 15, 17, 27–30, 37, 39, 56, 58, 60, 61, 65, 68–71, 75, 76, 105, 135, 138, 140, 146, 210, 239, 242–244, 248–252, 254, 255, 260, 262, 264, 270, 271, 274–277, 281, 283, 286

Deterrent, 2, 3, 8, 9, 12–13, 20, 23, 26, 28–29, 31–97, 127, 140, 141, 145, 146, 151, 156, 185–186, 189–190, 195, 200, 211, 241, 244, 246, 247, 251, 254–266, 275, 276, 277, 278, 281

Dhanush, 37, 47, 48, 67, 176

Doctrine, 2, 3, 11–13, 17, 28, 29, 30, 65, 68, 73, 78, 97, 100, 101, 103–107, 113–119, 122–126, 128, 134, 137, 138, 141–148, 150, 152, 153, 168, 193, 199, 241–258, 262, 264, 265, 267–275,

EMP, 8, 9, 14, 28–30, 34, 209–212, 239, 284, 285

F–16, 19, 21–23, 27, 121

Fissile Material, 3, 18, 19, 62, 63, 68, 76, 78, 84, –86, 88, 89, 92–94, 97, 148, 247, 275, 282, 285

Fission, 32, 33, 36, 43, 56, 63, 69, 70, 74, 77, 85, 87, 94, 95, 97, 282

Flexibility, 22, 28, 36, 40, 43, 55, 62, 64, 78, 134, 239, 245, 249, 252, 284

GSAT, 204, 205, 207

Hatf, 19–20, 23, 24, 25, 26, 146

Highly Enriched Uranium, 18, 56, 85–89

Home Guards, 220, 237–238, 239

IACCCS, 163–168, 195

ICBM, 5–7, 32, 37, 45, 54, 55, 71, 74, 95, 96, 149, 186, 188, 192, 194, 195, 200, 201, 280, 281, 285

Indian Air Force, 32, 33–34, 35, 37, 102, 108, 112, 117, 119–122, 129, 131, 132–133, 157–158, 160–167, 176, 181–183, 195 206, 281, 283

Indian Army, 37, 100, 103–105, 107–108, 109, 111, 113, 114–118, 127, 128, 129, 131, 132, 133, 137, 138, 151, 162, 166, 205, 268

Indian Navy, 163, 204, 205

Infantry, 101, 104, 105, 109, 110, 111, 118–119, 125, 126, 128–130, 131, 143, 145

INSAT, 204

IRBM, 25, 32, 38–42, 45, 55, 56, 68, 73–74, 96, 97, 149, 181, 182, 184, 188, 190, 192, 195, 208, 279, 280, 281

IRNSS, 204, 207

IRS, 199, 203, 205, 206

Jaguar, 32, 33, 66, 67, 119, 120, 121

K–15, 45–46, 47, 51, 55, 67, 69, 261–262

K–4, 31, 45–46, 47, 51, 67, 69, 262

Mirage, 19, 21–22, 27, 32, 33–34, 36, 66, 119, 120, 121, 157, 158

MRBM, 17, 25, 37, 40, 55, 72, 96, 97, 179, 182, 184, 188, 190, 195, 208, 279, 280, 281–282

MRSAM, 132

Nasr, 20, 23, 24, 26, 132, 133, 268, 274, 280

NBC, 144

NCA, 257–261, 263, 283

NDMA, 216, 217–227, 229, 232, 238

NDRF, 218, 219, 220, 224, 227–230, 238–239

Nirbhay, 31, 48–51, 77, 96, 276

No First Use, 248, 254

Nuclear, 1–153, 201–202, 215–219, 241–255, 267–268, 273, 274–276, 283, 284

PDV, 170, 176, 178–184, 185, 196, 205

Plutonium, 90, 92

Prithvi, 25, 36–38, 40, 47, 54, 55, 67, 70, 77, 88, 96, 152, 170–172, 175–177, 179, 281, 282

Ra'ad, 20, 22, 26, 27, 166

Radars, 118, 157, 159–177, 179, 181, 182, 187, 195, 197, 200, 203, 208

Reactors, 18, 76, 78–84, 87–91, 93, 94, 97, 216–217, 218, 266, 281, 282, 285

Respirators, 129, 130

RISAT, 203, 205, 206

S–400, 169, 176, 181–183, 193, 195

Satellite, 18, 52, 96, 159, 164, 169, 170, 181, 185, 188, 189, 197–207, 210, 211, 219, 261

Sensor, 156, 158, 161, 164, 169, 174, 179, 181, 183, 200

Shaheen, 19, 20, 23, 24–26

Shaurya, 55, 96, 276, 282

Space, 197–208, 245

SRBM, 7–8, 17, 23, 72, 96, 184, 280, 282

Strategic Forces Command, 25, 28, 31, 208, 247, 255, 257, 268, 281

Strategy, 241–286

Submarine, 3–5, 8, 10, 17, 20, 26, 28, 31, 32, 45–47, 64, 65, 89, 96, 141, 256, 258, 260–263, 280, 283

Sukhoi, 32, 34, 35, 119, 120, 121, 158

Survivability, 5, 9, 10, 16, 31, 35, 36, 40, 52, 63–65, 72, 75, 95, 119, 188, 243–245, 254–259, 261, 269, 271, 275–277, 283,

Tactical Nuclear Weapons, 24, 77, 78, 99, 101, 103, 105, 107, 109, 111, 113 , 115, 117, 119, 121, 123, 125, 126, 129, 131, 133, 134, 137, 139, 141, 143, 145, 146, 147, 149–151, 153, 249, 253, 269, 280

Tanks, 20, 21, 67, 129

Thermonuclear, 58–63, 69, 70, 73, 74, 83, 85, 86, 87, 94, 97, 258, 259, 282, 285

Threshold, 29, 100, 101, 103, 122–126, 137, 138, 145, 146, 150, 244, 250, 268, 276, 277, 280, 286

Yield, 4, 19, 29, 32, 33, 35, 43, 56–63, 66, 67, 69, 70, 73, 74, 77, 85–87, 94, 95, 97, 122, 124, 126, 136, 142, 143, 146, 148, 151–153, 209, 282